Professor Cl

NOTARY BEST PRACTICES

Expert's Guide to Notarization of Documents

Michael Closen

Published by:

National Notary Association
9350 De Soto Avenue
Chatsworth, CA 91311-4926
Telephone: (818) 739-4000
Fax: (818) 700-0920
Website: NationalNotary.org
Email: nna@NationalNotary.org

First Edition ©2018

ISBN: 978-1-59767-251-1

"Michael Closen has established himself as the premier expert on the law and best practices for notaries public in the country. His newest book on the subject is a phenomenal resource. It is the definitive text for document notarization procedures and a must-have for every notary. I highly recommend it."
— *Grant Dixon, Attorney and Illinois Notary*

"This is truly the book I have been hoping for! Professor Closen's book should be required reading for every commissioned notary public and for every person applying to be a notary. This is the first book to describe the true role of the notary — its importance, complexities, responsibilities, and liabilities. Even those who have been a notary for years, I'm confident, will find things here they were not aware of. As a corporate notary program director and supervisor, who has for many years managed and trained hundreds of notaries, I am sure using this book will 'raise the bar' for the accuracy and quality of notarizations. I predict this book will become the standard and necessary reference source for notary practice."
— *Kelcia Cannon, Minnesota Notary, Notary Expert and Corporate Notary Supervisor*

"I am a big fan of Professor Closen. Professor Closen's book is presented in a clear, concise, easy-to-understand manner. The topics are not only relevant to what notaries encounter daily but also are thought-provoking and interesting. Any individual who is serious about fulfilling the duties of a notary should read this book. It is fantastic!"
— *Marcy Tiberio, New York Notary and President, Professional Notary Services, Inc.*

"This book represents a watershed event not only for notaries, but also for attorneys and other business professionals. Drawing upon his vast notarial law knowledge and experience, Professor Closen presents the complexities of today's notary office and practice in an understandable manner unlike any other notary expert has done. And, as a law professor who has published on a wide variety of notary subjects for almost three decades, Closen has now sealed his place as a prophet of the notary's renewed vital importance to commerce and the legal system in the 21st century."
— *Tim Reiniger, Attorney, Information/Cyber Law and Notary Expert*

"Notaries across America finally have it — the definitive notary manual covering the most relevant and important subjects, authored by one of America's leading notary experts. Professor Closen has delivered a remarkably authoritative and useful tool for both notaries and their employers.

"Rarely are notaries given a true gift, but Professor Closen has wrapped and delivered the most relevant and useful reference manual for nationwide use. Both succinct and comprehensive, this no-fluff volume will surely guide notaries and their employers to sound and compliant practices."
— *Richard Burton, Utah Notary, Notary Instructor, Co-Owner, Notary Law Institute*

"Among the greatest challenges notaries face are a lack of training, and gaps in the law that leave notaries in the dark. Michael Closen takes on these challenges with ease, providing step-by-step tips and best practices that will not only protect and embolden the notary public but also will lend greater integrity to our profession. This book made me excited to perform my next notarization!"
— *Mike Phillips, Esq., California Notary, Notary Instructor, and Attorney*

"This book is a profoundly important contribution to our library of works on notarial law and ethics. Professor Closen — America's dean of notary law and best practices — has crafted a deeply insightful and comprehensive reference work. It expertly addresses a multitude of circumstances that notaries public regularly face, without statutory or regulatory provisions to inform them. The scope and relevance of this authoritative work cannot be overstated, nor can Professor Closen's passion for the office of notary public and every individual who holds that title. He has produced for all notaries public a work for the ages."
— *Kathleen Butler, Executive Director, American Society of Notaries, Florida Notary*

Table of Contents

How to Use This Book

This book is divided by topics and organized into 30 chapters. In order to find a topic or subtopic, the reader can consult either the detailed outline appearing early in the book or the index at the end of the book. At the end of each chapter is a "Relevant Model Notary Law" section relating to the topic of the respective chapter. If the reader wishes to undertake further reading or research, the bibliography near the end of the book provides the most extensive list of written notary reference materials ever published.

Many chapters contain case illustrations, notes, practice tips, and scope notes that are designated by the icons below.

Case Illustration: Contains events, details, and testimonies from actual court cases that support the topic of the chapter.

Note: Calls attention to additional comments from the author concerning specific details of the chapter topic.

Practice Tip: Contains recommendations from the author to assist while performing duties as notaries public.

Scope Note: Alerts the reader to certain content that will be omitted in the chapter.

Foreword

The world around U.S. notaries public is constantly changing. Demand for notarial services has reached record highs as the global economy expands and consumers become more vulnerable to sophisticated fraud schemes. And the evolution of industry business practices — particularly in real estate finance — has notaries performing their official acts under strict regulatory guidelines and, increasingly, in electronic environments. Amid this economic and cultural change, one thing has stayed the same for the nation's 4.4 million notaries: their basic role as a trusted impartial witness in ensuring that acts of attestation vital to commerce and law are executed legally, securely, and ethically.

There are few experts able to address and command the subject of notarial responsibility with more expertise than Michael Closen. He is respectfully referred to as the "dean of notary experts," and for good reason. Over his 40 years in the legal profession, he has developed a deep and abiding passion for the study of notary law and procedure, and he remains highly sought after as a notarial scholar, consultant, author, and legal expert.

I have known Michael for more than 25 years and he has deservedly earned his place in history as a leader and champion of the American notary office. While the general public often views notarization as a simple "stamp and sign" procedure with minimal understanding of its protections, Closen has dedicated much of his career to improving the performance and reliability of its practitioners as they serve the public. That's why his partnership with the National Notary Association has been so important. His research and expertise, coupled with the NNA's unmatched programs of service, support, advocacy, and communications have benefitted notaries and other stakeholders in business and government for several decades. Working together with the NNA, he helped blaze the trail for notary professionalism and engender a growing respect for the notary office through perfection of standards of care for notarial acts.

Always a riveting speaker at our annual conference, Closen has authored countless pieces in NNA publications, focusing on everything from proper notary journal procedures to what you should do when the law is silent about how a particular notarial practice should be executed. But his involvement with the NNA runs much deeper than that. He lent his leadership and expertise to the NNA as an active member of the drafting committee for the NNA's *Model Notary Act* of 2002, the *Model Notary Act* of 2010 and the *Model Electronic Notarization Act* of 2017. These landmark statutory models have served as indispensable blueprints for notary laws adopted by numerous states and jurisdictions throughout the country.

He also served on the drafting committee of the NNA's *Notary Public Code of Professional Responsibility*, first published in 1998. "The Code," as we refer to it, has become the nation's definitive guide on professional and ethical standards for notaries public, and is particularly useful when state statutes or rules fall short in being explicit about a notarial practice. Increasingly, you'll find The Code on just about every dedicated notary's bookshelf or saved in their browser bookmarks or mobile devices.

Closen's contributions to notaries and those who regulate or employ them earned him two prestigious awards from the NNA: The March Fong Eu Achievement Award in 1998 and the Lifetime Achievement Award in 2010.

As you read *Professor Closen's Notary Best Practices*, remember that you are receiving both practical guidance and invaluable insights from an industry "evangelist" whose work has inspired millions of notaries, and assisted thousands of government officials, business leaders, and regulators in this nation and abroad in the development of their notarial programs. This book is highly detailed and comprehensive, and every notary will benefit from its wisdom.

I am proud to say that Michael Closen is a true friend of mine, the NNA, and, more importantly, notaries everywhere.

Milt Valera
Chairman, National Notary Association
December 2017

Detailed Outline of Chapters and Best Practice Standards

7.3 The notary should not sign, or affix an official seal impression on, a notarial certificate prior to a document notarization ceremony.

7.4 The notary should complete the notarial certificate after creating the notary journal entry for the notarization.

7.5 The notary should complete a notarial certificate to facilitate the cross-border recognition of the notarization in other states, territories, and countries, especially including an official notary seal impression.

7.6 The notary should complete a thorough notarial certificate, including the venue, date, type of notarization, document signer's name and method of identification, notary's signature and seal, and other data.

7.7 The notary should be careful to satisfy the law's requirement to at least substantially comply with recording of the prescribed elements of the notarial certificate.

7.8 The notary should, when possible, have the document signer's signature appear on the transactional instrument on the same page with the notarial certificate.

7.9 The notary should securely affix the notarial certificate to the notarized instrument in such a manner as to prevent or reveal its removal or the substitution of an unauthorized certificate.

7.10 The notary should proofread the notarial certificate, and make any needed additions or corrections to it prior to the completion of the notarial ceremony.

7.11 The notary should, if an error is later discovered in a completed notarial certificate, not attempt to alter the certificate.

7.12 The notary should, if an error is later discovered in a completed notarial certificate and if requested by the document signer, perform a new and correct notarization.

8.1 The notary should obtain an official notary seal containing the notary's commission information, regardless of whether required by law.

8.2 The notary should not knowingly allow the seal impression to be used in a testimonial, promotion, or publicity effort of any kind.

8.3 The notary should affix a notary seal impression to each notarial certificate for every document notarization, regardless of whether required by law.

8.4 The notary should affix the notary seal impression on the notarial certificate clearly and legibly near the notary's signature.

8.5 The notary should, prior to completion of the notarial ceremony, proofread the affixed seal impression and cure any defects therein by striking the faulty impression and affixing a new seal impression.

8.6 The notary should not give, loan, sell, or otherwise relinquish possession of the notary seal to any party other than to a governmentally authorized individual.

8.7 The notary should, when the notary seal is not in use, secure the seal by lock and key under the notary's exclusive control, regardless of whether required by law.

8.8 The notary should acquire and possess one or possibly two notary seals but not have more than two active seals at a time.

8.9 The notary should, if the notary seal is damaged, lost, or stolen, promptly report such to the commissioning official or notary oversight agency and to law enforcement in the case of theft of the seal.

8.10 The notary should, when the notary commission is terminated or expires, deface or disable the notary seal and then destroy it, regardless of whether required by law.

CHAPTER 9. PERSONAL PRESENCE REQUIREMENT FOR DOCUMENT SIGNERS AT NOTARIZATIONS 125

9.1 The notary should understand the importance of the personal presence of document signers at notarizations.

9.2 The notary should require the document signer to be in the personal, physical presence of the notary for every notarization.

9.3 The notary should keep the document signer within the notary's line of sight throughout the notarization ceremony.

9.4 The notary should record the signer's personal presence at the notarization in the notarial certificate.

9.5 The notary should create a notary journal entry, including a present signature of the document signer, to verify the signer's presence at the notarization.

9.6 The notary should, unless prohibited by state or territorial law, request the document signer to place the signer's thumbprint in the journal entry to verify the signer's presence at the notarization.

9.7 The notary should be aware of the changing definition of personal presence in some jurisdictions regarding remote or webcam notarizations.

10.1 The notary should understand the importance of the proper identification of document signers.

10.2 The notary should be aware that under law the notary does not guarantee the accuracy of the identification of document signers.

10.3 The notary should be aware that the law requires the notary to exercise reasonable care to accurately identify document signers.

10.4 The notary should require each instrument signer to show one or more reliable ID documents and should closely examine those ID documents to ascertain their trustworthiness.

10.5 The notary should obtain and observe at least one present signature, and compare at least three signatures, of the document signer for each notarization.

10.6 The notary should note the method used to identify the document signer in the notarial certificate.

10.7 The notary should, if not prohibited by applicable law, request the document signer to affix a thumbprint in the notary journal entry.

10.8 The notary should record the ID document(s), and the month and year of expiration, relied upon to identify the instrument signer in the notary journal entry.

10.9 The notary should, prior to the completion of each notarization, proofread the signer identification sections of the notarial certificate and journal entry and make necessary additions and corrections.

15.4 The notary should understand the oath or affirmation requires the signer to pledge that the contents of the transactional document are correct and true.

15.5 The notary should formulate appropriate language for administration of the oral oath or affirmation to the document signer and consistently use that language for each jurat.

15.6 The notary should conduct the oral oath or affirmation in an appropriately solemn manner, in part by consistently incorporating corporal elements for each jurat.

15.7 The notary should note the administration of the oral oath or affirmation in the jurat certificate.

15.8 The notary should note the administration of the oral oath or affirmation in the journal entry.

15.9 The notary should, prior to completion of the notarial ceremony, proofread the portions of the notarial certificate and journal entry relating to the oath or affirmation and make any necessary corrections.

CHAPTER 16. SIGNING BY MARK AND PHYSICAL DISABILITIES AFFECTING SIGNING 219

16.1 The notary should, as a public official and public servant, treat all persons with dignity and respect.

16.2 The notary should be aware that every mentally competent individual possesses the legal right to execute a signature in some fashion which is entitled to be notarized.

16.3 The notary should take reasonable steps to accommodate document signers who wish to sign by mark.

16.4 The notary should take reasonable steps to accommodate document signers who are physically unable to execute their own signatures.

16.5 The notary should note in the notary certificate and the journal entry any accommodation used to assist a document signer in the execution of a signature.

16.6 The notary should, prior to completion of the notarization, proofread the portions of the notary certificate and journal entry noting accommodation of the document signer and make any necessary corrections.

least 10 years after the date of the last entry, unless directed otherwise by law.

17.15 The notary should understand that the notary journal is an official public record that is accessible by other parties under limited circumstances.

17.16 The notary should understand the confidential and private nature of certain contents of a journal entry and limit access accordingly.

17.17 The notary should record each request for access to journal information and its disposition in a separate journal entry.

CHAPTER 18. DOCUMENT SIGNER CONFIDENTIALITY AND PRIVACY 277

18.1 The notary should understand the confidential and private nature of document notarizations.

18.2 The notary should not reveal any information that would identify the notarized document or the document signer to unauthorized parties.

18.3 The notary should understand the confidential and private nature of certain personal information about the document signer acquired during a document notarization.

18.4 The notary should maintain the confidentiality and privacy of the personal information about the document signer acquired during a document notarization.

18.5 The notary should not make or retain copies of notarial certificates, transactional documents, or signer IDs prepared or reviewed during document notarizations.

18.6 The notary should, unless required by law to do otherwise, not record or retain serial numbers of signer IDs reviewed during document notarizations.

CHAPTER 19. NOTARY ETHICS AND AVOIDING CONFLICTS OF INTEREST 287

19.1 The notary should, as a commissioned public officer, understand that during the performance of official functions, the notary is governed by ethical standards.

19.2 The notary should be familiar with the published notary ethics standards.

19.3 The notary should abide by the ethical duty to become, and to remain, informed about notary law and best practices.

19.4 The notary should abide by the ethical duty to follow notary law and best practices in the performance of each document notarization.

19.5 The notary should abide by the ethical duty to act with reasonable care and prudence in the performance of each document notarization.

19.6 The notary should abide by the ethical duty to act with impartiality and honesty in the performance of each document notarization.

19.7 The notary should abide by the ethical duty to refrain from participating in an endorsement, promotion, testimonial, or campaign of any kind.

19.8 The notary should abide by the ethical duty to assess the document signer's mental competence and willingness.

19.9 The notary should abide by the ethical duty to avoid an actual or apparent conflict of interest in the performance of each document notarization.

19.10 The notary should abide by the ethical duty to refrain from notarizing the signature of the notary or notarizing a document in which the notary is named as a party in interest.

19.11 The notary should abide by the ethical duty to refrain from notarizing for any known member of the notary's family in any degree of relationship by blood, marriage, or adoption.

19.12 The notary should abide by the ethical duty to avoid profit or gain from a document notarization, other than the fee assessed for the notarization.

19.13 The notary should abide by the ethical duty to refuse any gift or gratuity in connection with past, present, or future service as a notary.

19.14 The notary should abide by the ethical duty to protect the integrity and corroborate the validity of each document notarization by preparing a notary journal entry for the notarization.

19.15 The notary should abide by the ethical duty to protect the confidentiality and privacy of information about the document signer and the notarized document.

19.16 The notary should abide by the ethical duty to provide sufficient personal assets, bond coverage, and/or liability insurance to adequately protect against notary mistakes and wrongdoing.

CHAPTER 20. THE SAVVY NOTARY AND AVOIDING LIABILITY 305

20.1 The notary should be savvy, understand more than just the rules of notary law and best practices, and consider the relevant surrounding circumstances.

20.2 The notary should recognize conditions which may increase the risk of making mistakes in the performance of a document notarization.

20.3 The notary should recognize factors which may increase the risk of heightened financial liability for wrongdoing committed in the performance of a document notarization.

20.4 The notary should understand the values of notarial knowledge, absolute impartiality, reasonable care, and thorough record-keeping in protecting against liability.

20.5 The notary should understand the potential for administrative liability for wrongdoing in the performance of a document notarization.

20.6 The notary should understand the potential for criminal liability for wrongdoing in the performance of a document notarization.

20.7 The notary should understand the potential for civil liability for wrongdoing in the performance of a document notarization.

20.8 The notary should provide sufficient financial resources to cover the costs relating to defense of claims of misconduct and to resulting liabilities.

CHAPTER 21. WHEN NOTARY STATUTES AND REGULATIONS ARE SILENT 321

21.1 The notary should understand that many matters relating to document notarizations remain unaddressed or unsettled by notary statutes or regulations.

21.2 The notary should understand how to deal with matters relating to document notarizations that remain unaddressed or unsettled by notary statutes or regulations.

21.3 The notary should, in the absence of statutory or regulatory treatment, understand that a document notarization will be upheld if the notary substantially complies with its legal requirements.

21.4 The notary should, in the absence of statutory or regulatory treatment, prepare a thorough notarial certificate for each document notarization.

21.5 The notary should, in the absence of statutory or regulatory treatment, not attempt to alter or correct a notarial certificate after the notarial ceremony has been completed.

21.6 The notary should, in the absence of statutory or regulatory treatment, understand that the standard of reasonable care applies to the official performance of the notary.

21.7 The notary should, in the absence of statutory or regulatory treatment, acquire a notary seal and affix a seal impression to each notarial certificate.

21.8 The notary should, in the absence of statutory or regulatory treatment, understand and implement procedures to secure and protect the notary seal.

21.9 The notary should, in the absence of statutory or regulatory treatment, understand how to correct an illegible or partial seal impression on a notarial certificate.

21.10 The notary should, in the absence of statutory or regulatory treatment, understand the name and signature requirements for signers for document notarizations.

21.11 The notary should, in the absence of statutory or regulatory treatment, understand the duty to identify the document signer with reasonable certainty, not to guarantee the signer's true identity.

21.12 The notary should, in the absence of statutory or regulatory treatment, identify document signers by reviewing one or more reliable signer IDs.

21.13 The notary should, in the absence of statutory or regulatory treatment, understand the duty to assess the document signer's mental competence and utilize a procedure reasonably calculated to do so.

21.14 The notary should, in the absence of statutory or regulatory treatment, understand the duty to assess the document signer's willingness and utilize a procedure reasonably calculated to do so.

21.15 The notary should, in the absence of statutory or regulatory treatment, understand whether to perform a document notarization for a minor.

21.16 The notary should, in the absence of statutory or regulatory treatment, not perform a document notarization for any known family member of any degree of relationship by blood, marriage, or adoption.

21.17 The notary should, in the absence of statutory or regulatory treatment, not serve as a lay witness and notary for the same document.

21.18 The notary should, in the absence of statutory or regulatory treatment, not serve in the dual roles as drafter, preparer, and/or reviewer of a client's document and as notary for the document notarization.

21.19 The notary should, in the absence of statutory or regulatory treatment, acquire a notary journal and prepare and preserve a detailed journal entry for each document notarization.

21.20 The notary should, in the absence of statutory or regulatory treatment, request the document signer to provide a thumbprint for each notary journal entry.

21.21 The notary should, in the absence of statutory or regulatory treatment, understand the procedure for allowing access to information in the notary journal.

21.22 The notary should, in the absence of statutory or regulatory treatment, not redact information from a journal entry disclosed due to a request for access, except for a signer's thumbprint.

21.23 The notary should, in the absence of statutory or regulatory treatment, understand and implement procedures to preserve and safeguard the notary journal.

21.24 The notary should, in the absence of statutory or regulatory treatment, understand the de facto notary doctrine and its possible effect after the notary commission has expired.

21.25 The notary should, in the absence of statutory or regulatory treatment, understand whether the notary's employer may impose restrictions when the notary is on duty for the employer.

21.26 The notary should, in the absence of statutory or regulatory treatment, understand the notary's employer may have vicarious liability for notary mistakes and wrongdoing.

21.27 The notary should, in the absence of statutory or regulatory treatment, understand the notary cannot avoid liability for wrongdoing because the notary employer ordered the faulty performance.

21.28 The notary should, in the absence of statutory or regulatory treatment, assure financial responsibility for financial injuries caused by notary mistakes and wrongdoing.

21.29 The notary should, in the absence of statutory or regulatory treatment, understand appropriate procedures to be utilized if the notary desires to charge fees for notarial services.

21.30 The notary should, in the absence of statutory or regulatory treatment, not share notarial fees with the notary's employer when the notary is on duty for the employer.

CHAPTER 22. NOTARY DISCIPLINE AND COMMISSION EXPIRATION AND RENEWAL 351

22.1 The notary should understand the disciplinary authority and process of the state or territorial notary oversight agency.

22.2 The notary should understand the disciplinary sanctions which may be imposed for notarial misconduct and their consequences.

22.3 The notary should self-report material mistakes and misconduct to the commissioning official or notary oversight agency and temporarily cease notarial functions until approved.

22.4 The notary should report the material mistakes and misconduct of other notaries to the commissioning official or notary oversight agency.

22.5 The notary should report any material change in status to the commissioning official or notary oversight agency and temporarily cease notarial functions until approved.

22.6 The notary should be aware of the commission expiration date and record the commission expiration date on each notarial certificate.

22.7 The notary should, after the expiration of the notary commission, not perform notarizations or other notarial functions, except in connection with the maintenance and accessing of the notary journal.

22.8 The notary should, if intending to renew the notary commission, timely apply for renewal in order to avoid a lapse in the notary commission.

22.9 The notary should, prior to completion of each notarial ceremony, proofread the notary commission expiration date in the notarial certificate.

CHAPTER 23. NOTARY BONDS AND LIABILITY INSURANCE 361

23.1 The notary should understand the advantages and disadvantages of notary bonds.

23.2 The notary should acquire a bond, if required by law, and maintain the bond in good standing during the term of the notary commission.

23.3 The notary should understand the advantages and disadvantages of notary liability insurance.

23.4 The notary should acquire notary liability insurance in an amount sufficient to protect against negligent notarial performance.

23.5 The notary should promptly report notary mistakes or misconduct to notary bond and insurance companies.

23.6 The notary should cooperate with any investigation of alleged notarial mistakes or misconduct undertaken by bond and insurance companies.

CHAPTER 24. PROPER ROLES OF NOTARY-EMPLOYEES AND THEIR EMPLOYERS 375

24.1 The notary-employee should, when necessary, assist the employer to understand and accept its proper role in their unique relationship.

24.2 The notary-employee should understand the limited role which the employer has in the supervision and control of the notary-employee in the performance of official notarial functions.

24.3 The notary-employee should not allow the employer to direct or influence the notary-employee to violate notary law or notary best practices in the performance of official notarial functions.

24.4 The notary-employee should not allow the employer to possess, use, alter, discard, or destroy the notary-employee's official notary seal, journal, or other records under any circumstances.

24.5 The notary-employee should restrict access to the notary journal and should require the employer to access the notary journal in the same manner as any other party.

24.6 The notary-employee should, unless the law provides otherwise, not permit the employer to determine whether the notary-employee will charge notarial fees, the amount of the fees, or whether to share fees with the employer.

24.7 The notary-employee should understand that the employer may have vicarious liability for the misconduct of the notary-employee in the performance of official notarial functions.

24.8 The notary-employee should request the employer to pay for a notary bond for the notary-employee and liability insurance for the notary-employee and the employer.

24.9 The notary-employee should request the employer to provide notary education and to purchase a membership in at least one notary association for the notary-employee.

CHAPTER 25. ATTORNEYS, NOTARY-ATTORNEYS AND CONFLICTS OF INTEREST 393

25.1 The notary who is not an attorney and who is employed or supervised by an attorney should assist the attorney to understand the significance of proper notarial functioning and notary best practices.

25.2 The notary-attorney and the attorney who employs or supervises a notary should understand the significance of proper performance of notarizations.

25.3 The notary-attorney and the attorney who employs or supervises a notary should understand the substantial legal and ethical risks associated with violations of notary law and sound notarial practice.

25.4 The notary-attorney and the attorney who employs or supervises a notary should insist upon strict compliance with notary law and sound notarial practice.

25.5 The notary-attorney and the attorney who employs or supervises a notary should not direct or influence a notary to violate notary law or sound notarial practice.

25.6 The notary-attorney should not serve in the dual role as attorney and notary for a document drafted, prepared, or reviewed on behalf of a legal client.

25.7 The notary-attorney and the attorney who employs or supervises a notary should complete, or direct the completion of, a notary journal entry for each document notarization.

25.8 The notary-attorney and the attorney who employs or supervises a notary should self-report notarial misconduct committed by the attorney and by a notary employed or supervised by the attorney.

25.9 The notary-attorney and the attorney who employs or supervises a notary should report notarial misconduct committed by other attorneys and notaries.

25.10 The notary-attorney and the attorney who employs or supervises a notary should assure that an adequate notary bond and insurance are acquired.

CHAPTER 26. AVOIDING THE NOTARY'S UNAUTHORIZED PRACTICE OF LAW 407

26.1 The notary who is not an attorney should understand that the unauthorized practice of law constitutes a serious violation of law.

26.2 The notary who is not an attorney should not claim to be an attorney nor create the appearance that she or he is an attorney.

26.3 The notary who is not an attorney should not use the designation *"notario"* or *"notario publico,"* or any non-English translation of "notary" or "notary public."

26.4 The notary who is not an attorney should not advise, counsel, or represent a notary client in such a way as to engage in the unauthorized practice of law.

26.5 The notary who is neither an attorney nor a professional in a law-related field should not draft or prepare the instrument to be notarized.

26.6 The notary who is neither an attorney nor a professional in a law-related field should not advise or consult the signer about the document to be notarized.

26.7 The notary who is neither an attorney nor a professional in a law-related field should not read or review the document to be notarized.

26.8 The notary who is not an attorney, but who is a professional in a law-related field, should be especially careful to avoid engaging in the unauthorized practice of law.

26.9 The notary who is not an attorney should be authorized to advise the notary client in the selection of the type of document notarization to be performed.

CHAPTER 27. INTERSTATE AND INTERNATIONAL RECOGNITION OF NOTARIAL ACTS 421

27.1 The notary should understand that notarized documents may cross borders and need to be recognized in other U.S. and foreign jurisdictions.

27.2 The notary should understand that U.S. states and territories have adopted statutes which expressly recognize lawful notarizations performed in sister states and territories.

27.3 The notary should understand that a lawful U.S. notarization must be recognized in a sister state or territory under the U.S. Constitution's "Full Faith and Credit Clause."

27.4 The notary should understand that the law of the place of notarization will govern whether the notarization is lawful and entitled to recognition in another U.S. jurisdiction.

27.5 The notary should understand that whether a U.S. notarization will be recognized in a foreign country is a matter of discretionary judgment exercised by the recipient country.

27.6 The notary should be especially careful in completing the notarial certificate, including affixing the notary seal impression, to foster possible cross-border recognition of a notarized document.

27.7 The notary should be especially careful in completing an official notary journal entry to foster possible cross-border recognition of a notarized document.

CHAPTER 28. NOTARY FEES AND TRAVEL COSTS..... 433

28.1 The notary should understand the notary's unique role as the only public official permitted to bill for official services and to personally retain the fees collected.

28.2 The notary should understand that there is no obligation to charge fees to notarial clients.

28.3 The notary should, if fees are to be charged and unless provided otherwise by law, not share those fees with notary employers.

28.4 The notary should charge no more than the statutory maximum or reasonable levels and should charge such fees uniformly to clients.

28.5 The notary should, if fees are to be charged, create a written fee schedule and conspicuously post or publish that schedule to inform prospective clients prior to the rendition of services.

28.6 The notary should, if fees are to be charged, orally inform prospective clients of the fees prior to the rendition of services and obtain agreement from clients to pay such fees.

28.7 The notary should, if compensation for travel costs is to be assessed, inform prospective clients prior to the rendition of services and obtain agreement to pay such costs.

28.8 The notary should, if paid for fees and travel costs, provide an itemized receipt to each client and retain a copy for the notary's purposes.

28.9 The notary should note in the journal entry that no fee was assessed or note the amount of any payment for fees and travel costs.

28.10 The notary should, prior to the completion of the notarial ceremony, proofread the itemized receipt and the journal entry notation of fees and costs and make any necessary corrections.

29.1 The notary should understand the substantial benefits provided by notary membership, education, and advocacy organizations.

29.2 The notary should join, and actively participate in, one or more notary membership, education, and advocacy organizations.

30.1 The notary should understand that, with the passage of time, there will be changes affecting the notary's duties.

30.2 The notary should undertake continuing education on a regular basis, at least annually.

30.3 The notary should, at the time of commission renewal, engage in continuing education, regardless of whether required by law. ■

About the Author

Michael Closen has been called "the dean of notary experts." He is widely regarded as one of the leading authorities on notary ethics, law, and practice in the United States. He is the author or co-author of 20 books, he possesses a background of more than 40 years of experience in the legal profession, and he has served over 25 years as a commissioned notary public and specialist on notarial issues. In 2011, the National Notary Association wrote: "Michael Closen is one of the foremost experts on notary law. He is a leading instructor on notary law and procedures. He has taught notary education programs in numerous states and is a respected consultant on model notary statutes."

Closen earned BS and MA degrees from Bradley University, and a JD degree in law from the University of Illinois. He began his career as an instructor, teaching university-level communications and law. He went on to serve as Judicial Clerk for the Illinois Appellate Court. He then began a long career as a Professor of Law at the John Marshall Law School in Chicago in 1976, lasting until his retirement from that school in 2003. Along the way he taught as a Visiting or Adjunct Professor at the University of Arkansas in Fayetteville, Northern Illinois University, Loyola University of Chicago, and St. Thomas University in Florida. He is now a Professor Emeritus from John Marshall Law School.

While teaching law, Closen served briefly as a prosecutor in Chicago. He also engaged in the private practice of law for 25 years, handling numerous civil and criminal trial and appellate cases in both the state and federal courts, arguing three cases in the Illinois Supreme Court, and handling numerous pro bono matters. He taught continuing education for Illinois judges as a Professor-Reporter under the auspices of the Illinois Judicial Conference for more than 20 years. He served as a frequent arbitrator of commercial and construction disputes for the American Arbitration Association for more than 25 years, and as an arbitrator for the Circuit Courts of both Cook and Will counties in Illinois for more than a decade. For some 20 years, Closen taught education courses for Illinois lawyers as an author-lecturer for the Illinois Institute for Continuing Legal Education. He also taught the professional bar review program for BAR-BRI for more than 25 years. He authored or co-authored 10 law textbooks, several chapters in various law treatises, 34 law review articles, and many other periodical and law journal articles. He was voted a "Professor of the Year" seven times by his law students, and he has lectured widely on legal topics in 10 countries and more than 25 states.

In the notary public field, Michael Closen has served as a commissioned notary for more than 25 years — first in Illinois from 1990 to 2003 and in Florida since 2004. He has written extensively on notary subjects for the periodical publications of the American Society of Notaries, the Notary Law Institute, and the National Notary Association. He remains associated with those three leading notary organizations., and he is a life member of both the American Society of Notaries and the National Notary Association. He has published 10 law review articles on notary topics, as well as numerous notary articles in various state and national law journals. He has lectured widely on notary topics in some 17 states and the District of Columbia, including numerous presentations at the annual conferences of the American Society of Notaries and the National Notary Association, and many notary continuing education lectures for paralegals, lawyers, and other business professionals. He also taught a number of semester-long law school courses on notary ethics, law, and practice.

Closen co-authored, and served as editor for, the textbook *Notary Law & Practice*, published by the National Notary Association in 1997. He served on the drafting committees for the *Notary Public Code of Professional Responsibility* of 1998, for the *Model Notary Act* of 2002, the *Model Notary Act* of 2010, and the *Model Electronic Notarization Act* of 2017. In 1998, he was honored with the Annual Achievement Award from the National Notary Association, and in 2010 with its Lifetime Achievement Award (which has been awarded only three times in the NNA's more than 50 year history). He has been retained as an expert consultant on several lawsuits around the country, and he testified as an expert witness on notary issues in court cases in California and Illinois. In 2001, the Notary Law Institute wrote: "Professor Closen is highly esteemed nationally for his expertise and contributions to the subject of notary law and practice." Also in 2001, the American Society of Notaries noted: "Professor Closen is known nationally as an authority on notary issues and an expert in the field of notary law." In 1998, the National Notary Association concluded: "This respected law professor has become the nation's leading legal scholar on notarization, having written or inspired numerous penetrating articles on the role of the notary public." ■

Introduction

This book is about the increasingly important subject of proper notarization of documents. Although notaries in some jurisdictions perform a variety of other incidental functions (such as certifying copies of documents, inventorying abandoned bank lock boxes, performing wedding ceremonies, certifying automobile odometer readings, and so on), this book does not address those activities. The book focuses on the most frequent and most important notarial responsibility, which is to notarize traditional documents (so the book also will not cover e-documents, e-notarizations, or notary e-journals).

Historically, the notary ideal has universally pictured a public official of absolute impartiality and unwavering integrity. Add to that ideal the habits of diligence and prudence, and we have the public servant envisioned by this book if those notaries abide by its suggested best practices. The goal of this book is to inspire and foster today's notary to always perform thorough and sound document notarizations as explained in the coming chapters. That is why more than 230 best practice standards are included here. Those notary best practice standards have been drawn from notary statutes and regulations, from common law court opinions, from model laws proposed by private organizations, from publications of experts in the notary field, and from my own experiences as an attorney and law professor, notary public, and notary educator and consultant. To qualify as a best practice, a standard must be one that is generally accepted as proper by the great majority of expert practitioners and thoughtful regulators in the notary field, that has stood the test of time, and that represents the most reasonable and prudent approach to a notarial issue. Yet, in the end, I am the final arbiter of what that means, and I take full responsibility for the contents of this book. The book does not necessarily represent the position of the National Notary Association or any other individual or organization.

This book's detailed statement of best practice standards for notaries is made necessary because the notary statutes and regulations of the states and territories have often failed to do so, because notaries need help in performing their duties, and because of the dramatic increase in identity theft and document fraud. Unfortunately, many notaries have not taken their responsibilities seriously enough. For instance, over the years this author has been consulted on lawsuits involving seven notarizations of multimillion dollar transactions; all of those seven notarizations were faulty in one or more ways, and not one of them was recorded in a notary journal entry. The notary statutes and regulations are not clear enough, current enough, or comprehensive enough to do the three critical things this book does. That is, (1) to tell notaries what to do, (2) to tell notaries how to do it, and (3) to tell notaries why to do it. When people understand what, how, and why to do a thing, they usually get the message. They remember and act accordingly because they understand, rather than because they have tried to memorize a procedure or because they have simply been ordered to take action.

Notary statutes began to be enacted in America in the original English colonies when there were only a handful of notaries, and later in the U.S. states and territories. Almost all of those early statutes were brief, ambiguous, and inadequate, but most of them survived for generations, and many are still out-of-date. For instance in those early days, there was no such thing as an ID document like a driver's license or passport. Back then, there was little or no identity theft and document fraud with which today's notaries must contend, and few notary statutes have done enough to help protect against these modern threats. Furthermore, as time went on the number of notaries exploded, and at present we have more than 4,450,000 notaries public serving in the U.S. states and territories. Such a large population of notaries portends difficulties among them in their caliber, their integrity, their knowledge, and their notarial skills.

Importantly, in terms of the most fundamental features, notaries everywhere in the U.S. (with the exception of the notaries of Louisiana and Puerto Rico) are quite similar in their statutorily mandated qualifications, their disinterested witnessing purpose, and their document notarization functions. And, the basic types of document notarizations — acknowledgments, jurats (verifications on oaths or affirmations) and signature witnessings — are virtually identical in nature throughout the U.S. Nevertheless, there are some differences in substance in notary law from place to place. Therefore, a note of caution is in order, that will be repeated regularly. Every U.S. notary should refer specifically to her or his jurisdiction's notary law in regard to the issues treated in this book and the recommendations suggested by this author to ensure that my advice satisfies and squares with the individual nuances of each jurisdiction's statutes and regulations.

Practice Tip: *Reference Tools of the Trade.* Every notary should have a personal copy of her or his jurisdiction's notary statutes and regulations readily available for reference at the time of every notarization — and for comparison while reviewing this book. Additionally, every jurisdiction publishes a notary public handbook, guide, or manual in hard copy and/or online format or otherwise provides helpful information for their notaries. Each notary should obtain that handbook, guide, manual, or other official information, and study it and have it readily available at notarizations — and for comparison to this book, too.

No statute is ever 100% complete. It simply is not possible for the law to consider every possible nuance associated with document notarizations, nor to anticipate every conceivable occurrence and variation that may arise and affect or be affected by those laws. In the field of notarization, these problems have been especially acute, because as already noted many notary laws have historically remained incomplete and because the steps to proper notarization procedure are numerous and have not been well described or explained in the laws. Yet, document notarization around the U.S. is uniform enough to be treated by this book of nationwide standards. Therefore, describing notary public best practices for the country should help to fill the numerous statutory and regulatory gaps and shortcomings and to improve the performance of document notarizations. Best practice standards are regularly adopted by government agencies and courts to become part of the administrative rules and common law court decisions that fill gaps in notary statutes.

Case Illustration. Believe it or not, very few notary statutes declare what standard of care is required by notaries in order for them to avoid being liable for negligence or notary malpractice. So, when faced with the issue, several courts around the country have decided to apply the well-known reasonable care standard. That is, if a notary has performed his or her notarial duties with reasonable care and, nevertheless, makes a mistake causing financial injury to a document signer or some third party affected by the faulty notarization, the notary will not be liable. No notary law in the state of Illinois had established the standard of care for notaries prior to 2008, when this author testified as an expert witness in a notary trial and concluded that the reasonable care standard applied to Illinois notaries. The trial court agreed with me, and on appeal of

> the case in 2010, the Illinois Supreme Court also agreed and cited my testimony as authority for the position that Illinois notaries are bound by the obligation to perform with reasonable care or else face financial liability for negligence. My opinion prevailed, because the notary statute said nothing about the issue and because the Illinois Supreme Court declared the reasonable care standard for notaries to be part of the common law of Illinois. See *Vancura v Katris,* 238 Ill.2d 352 (2010).

Additionally, there are other ways to help fill the gaps in notary laws and to help educate notaries about proper document notarization procedure. In the U.S., we are fortunate to have numerous organizations providing a variety of notary-related membership, education, and advocacy services. The author is proud to have been associated with three of the leading national organizations — the American Society of Notaries, the Notary Law Institute, and the National Notary Association. And, I am currently a life member of, and closely associated with, the National Notary Association, the world's largest and most active notary organization. Every notary should become a member of one or more notary organizations and take advantage of their programs.

Indeed, in this author's opinion, the most significant contributions in U.S. history to the advancement of notary legislation, to the establishment of ethical standards to guide notaries, and thus to the identification of notary best practices have been the series of model laws developed and published through the financial support and involvement of expert consultants provided by the American Society of Notaries and most significantly by the National Notary Association. This series of model notary laws and ethics codes has influenced legislators, notary regulators, judges, business people, and, of course, notaries beginning in the 1980s. The American Society of Notaries published a one-page, 12-point ethics code for notaries called the *Responsibility Code of Ethics* in 1980. More recently, the National Notary Association developed and published a number of substantial documents including the *Model Notary Act* of 1984, the *Notary Public Code of Professional Responsibility* of 1998, the *Model Notary Act* of 2002, the *Model Notary Act* of 2010, and the *Model Electronic Notarization Act* of 2017 (and this author has been honored to serve on the drafting committees for those latter four NNA projects). In addition, in 2010, the highly regarded national legal organization known as the Uniform Law Commission adopted its detailed model law, called the *Revised Uniform Law on Notarial Acts.*

At the end of each chapter, I will refer repeatedly to relevant provisions of these various model notary laws, for they almost always embody the generally accepted best practices to which notaries should adhere. In only a few instances will I suggest doing other than is set out in those model notary laws, and when I do so, I will always present the position of the model laws and explain why I recommend a different course of action. Again, notaries should abide by the requirements of their own commissioning jurisdictions.

The bibliography of notary publications at the end of this book includes more than 250 listings of books, articles, reports, and other writings. That number of listings makes this part of my book the most extensive notary bibliography ever published, and I am pleased to have the great majority of those publications in my personal library of notary materials. The bibliography should prove helpful for anyone wishing to read or research more fully any of the many subjects covered by the best practice standards set out here.

Finally, I want to extend my appreciation and thanks to the several notary experts from whom I have learned so much over the years, including Kathleen Butler, Kelcia Cannon, Lori Hamm, John Henderson, Malcolm Morris, Mike Phillips, Timothy Reiniger, Ozie Stallworth, and Peter Van Alstyne. Also, I am sincerely grateful for the continuing association with, and support of, the staff of the National Notary Association, and especially for the nurturing of several of its longtime and highly capable officers — Milton Valera, Thomas Heymann, Bill Anderson, Steven Bastian, Phillip Browne, Charles Faerber, and Deborah Thaw. The major writing process culminating in publication of this volume could not have been achieved without some 25 years of active involvement in the programs and publications of the NNA, including countless in-depth exchanges from which I have benefited profoundly. ■

1938, black and white, press photograph of Oregon notary public Mrs. M.T. Edwards administering the oath of office to newly appointed U.S. Senator A. Evan Reames of Oregon in his law office in Medford, Oregon, prior to his departure for Washington. Oregon Governor Charles Martin had appointed Reames when one of the state's sitting senators resigned, and Governor Martin assigned notary Edwards to administer the oath of office to Reames.

Chapter

1

Notary Qualifications

STANDARDS SUMMARY

1.1 The notary applicant should understand the qualifications required to become a commissioned notary public.

1.2 The notary applicant should strive to exceed the minimum qualifications required to become a notary public.

1.3 The notary applicant, and then the notary, should read and study the state or territorial notary statute and the official state or territorial notary handbook or manual, if any.

1.4 The notary should keep abreast of developments in notary ethics, law, and practice and incorporate advancements in notary ethics, law, and practice into the notary's official service.

STANDARDS EXPLANATIONS

The notaries of the world have enjoyed a mostly proud heritage and history of public service and attendant public respect. Notaries public in the U.S., although not as esteemed as civil law notaries and English notaries, are expected to be honorable, diligent, impartial, and prudent public servants. Those aspirational qualities begin with the notary applicant who is well-qualified to serve and hopefully will continue to grow and improve as the notary gains experience in notarial practice.

1.1 The notary applicant should understand the qualifications required to become a commissioned notary public.

The qualifications to become a notary are clearly set out in the various state and territorial notary statutes and vary considerably from place to place. However, the qualifications for notaries generally include a minimum age requirement of 18 years in the vast majority of jurisdictions and 19 years in the few others, a U.S. citizenship or permanent legal resident requirement, a state or territorial residency or place of business requirement, a requirement of an absence of civil or criminal evidence of dishonesty or moral corruption, and a requirement of literacy in the English language. The requirements in Puerto Rico are significantly different, for its notaries are civil law notaries whose qualifications and functions are significantly different from those of notaries elsewhere in the U.S.

Note: *Electronic Notaries.* There are different and additional requirements for individuals who wish to become electronic notaries. Individuals interested in serving as electronic notaries should be familiar with and have access to the necessary technology and should consult the statutes and regulations of their commissioning jurisdictions regarding required qualifications.

Of course, the notary applicant must file an application, pay the application fee, and in more than 30 jurisdictions obtain a notary bond. In conjunction with the filing of the application, and with the possible acquisition of a notary bond, the notary applicant must ordinarily swear or affirm that the substance of the application is correct, that the applicant will act with honesty and fidelity as a notary, and possibly that the notary applicant will be loyal to the federal, and state or territorial, constitutions and laws (an oath of office). In a few jurisdictions, there is also a requirement for the notary applicant to participate in a course of study in notary law and practice, and some places require the notary applicant to take and pass an examination on notary law and practice.

Note: *Literacy and Interpreters.* Notary statutes and regulations seldom address the subjects of the required literacy of the notary, use of interpreters, and the language to be used in notarized documents and oral oaths and affirmations — other than to sometimes specify that the notary must be literate in English. This author advises that the notary should be fully literate in the written language of the notarial certificate and the oral language of the document signer in order to serve in the official role effectively, to follow the required notarial procedures, and to perform the assessments of the signer's identity and mental competence and willingness to execute the document to be notarized. That is, the notary should be able to converse orally with the document signer in order to assess the signer's identity, mental competence, and willingness, and the notary should not rely upon the translation of an interpreter of the signer's oral statements or identification documents. To make the identity, mental competence, and willingness assessments, only the notary should consider the words, tone, emphasis, and other nuances of oral language of the signer in conjunction with the signer's accompanying body language and demeanor (which can only be properly interpreted if one understands the oral language). Obviously, if an oath or affirmation needs to be administered, both the notary and the document signer would need to be literate in the oral language of the pledge. Further, the notary should be literate in the written language of the notarial certificate because the certificate constitutes the notary's certification of the steps taken in the performance of the document notarization. The notary cannot certify in a language which the notary cannot read, and the notary should not trust an interpreter when it comes to the legal responsibility to certify the proper notarial procedure. In other words, the notary should not need and should not use the services of an interpreter in the performance of a document notarization. However, the notary would not need to be familiar with the language of the instrument to be notarized, as the content of that document is beyond the purview of the notary's authority — provided that the notary is able to determine the type and nature of the document for purposes of assessing signer mental capacity and of noting the type of document in the notary journal entry for the notarization. Of course, document signers do not have to be able to read and/or write in order to obtain notarizations. Individuals who are illiterate and cannot sign their names in the usual manner are permitted to sign by mark (as will be discussed in Chapter 16). Finally, the notary journal entry should note any special information about the uses of language other than English in the transactional instrument, the notarial certificate, and the oral communications between the notary and document signer.

The statutorily required qualifications to become a notary public tend to be quite minimal, with no minimum level of formal school education required (except for an elementary school education requirement in one state). Thus, if one is old enough, has not been convicted of too serious an offense involving dishonesty or moral turpitude, obtains the nominal bond mandated in some jurisdictions, files the necessary application, and pays the application fee, she or he is likely to be approved to become a notary public. In fact, as already noted, there are more than 4,450,000 U.S. notaries — far more than the total of all of the world's civil law notaries and English notaries combined. So, the qualifications and application procedure for one to become a notary cannot be too substantial or difficult.

Note: *Notary Place of Residence and Place of Business.* Just about every jurisdiction will have enacted in their notary statutes or regulations an eligibility provision declaring that a notary must reside, work, or be employed in the state or territory which will issue the notary commission, or in some statutes that the notary must reside in an adjoining state. Individuals should consult the laws of their home states and any others where they wish to obtain notary commissions.

1.2 The notary applicant should strive to exceed the minimum qualifications required to become a notary public.

The states and territories do not require notaries to be well-educated, do not require notaries to be very mature by age, and do not require notaries to be genuinely financially accountable for their mistakes and wrongdoing. Indeed, even an elementary school dropout of little financial means can become a notary and can perform notarizations involving multimillion dollar transactions, with no notary bond required in many states and territories or with a required notary bond of $25,000 or less in the other states and territories. Although a couple of states allow liability insurance as an alternative to a notary bond, no state or territory requires its notaries to carry errors and omissions liability insurance, let alone to carry such insurance in an amount satisfactory to protect the interests of notary clients and notaries themselves.

With more than 4.45 million notaries in the U.S., there is no scarcity of them. This author's opinion is that everyone who desires to become a notary public should rise above the lowest common denominator of qualifications. Every notary aspirant can delay application until such time as she or he is well-qualified to serve.

What are the things every notary aspirant should accomplish before seeking a notary commission? First and foremost, a notary should have achieved a sufficient amount of formal general education to be capable enough to thoughtfully read and genuinely understand notary statutes, agency regulations (if any), and published notary ethics codes. Notarial service is serious business, affecting significant personal and financial interests of the document signers who seek notarizations, affecting the interests of parties who rely upon notarized instruments, and affecting the public interest as well.

The states and territories unfortunately impose no minimum general education requirement on notary applicants, except for Wisconsin, which requires notaries to have merely grade school educations. This author urges that no one should ever become a notary with less than a high school education, and preferably no one should become a notary with less than a two- or four-year college education. Notarization is not child's play, so a child's education is woefully insufficient for today's notaries. The document notarization procedure is increasingly complex and monetarily significant, and notaries must increasingly be educated and experienced enough to perform the heightened duties incumbent on notary professionals.

Certainly, notaries should also be well-informed, specifically about notarial practice, ethics, and law, even if the jurisdiction of commissioning does not require notary education or testing. Notaries in some states and territories will need to undertake self-education on those subjects. The agency which oversees notaries in each jurisdiction can provide resources for self-study, including notary statutes and regulations and official notary manuals or handbooks. Notary membership and education organizations can also provide helpful resources. This critical topic will be addressed more fully in the next section. See also the discussion of notary organizations in Chapter 29 and of notary continuing education in Chapter 30.

In conjunction with my suggestion that individuals should not seek to become notaries before attaining a two- or four-year college education, this author would urge notary applicants to be at least 21 years of age. In order to earn a two- or four-year college degree, one would usually have to be about that old anyway. These few years in age difference will move the youngest notaries from their teenage years to their early twenties, and at that very youthful time, three years is far more significant proportionately than three years will be in later life. Interestingly, various laws deemed to be particularly important require individuals to be at least 21 years old, including some laws on alcohol, tobacco, and marijuana purchase and consumption and on gun purchase and possession. As I have said before, notarization is not child's play, and I would prefer to err on the side of caution. Remember, since we already have millions of U.S. notaries, there is no urgency in rushing teenagers to apply.

Another substantial part of the qualifications to participate as a professional in every field of endeavor (in banking, legal practice, accounting, medical care, engineering, and the like) is to provide financial backing in the event errors or omissions, or intentional wrongdoing, result and cause injury to individuals or entities that deserve to be compensated for such mistakes and misconduct. It is generally called financial responsibility. As will be discussed at greater length elsewhere in this book, notaries have full personal legal liability for financial injuries caused by mistakes and misconduct. Thus, notaries should have good jobs with salaries or income sufficient to purchase substantial notary bonds and/or substantial notary malpractice insurance. Or, notary employers should acquire such bonds and insurance for their notary-employees. It is simply unfair to the public to allow public officials such as notaries to serve when those public officials lack the financial responsibility to pay for the monetary injuries that occasionally, but inevitably, will result from notarial mistakes and misconduct.

Finally, a notary should possess a genuine spirit for public service. That spirit includes the responsibilities to deal fairly with all people, to perform the notarial duties with prudence and diligence, and to serve for modest compensation. The position of notary is a public-servant post to be taken only with the most serious conviction to do good for one's fellow citizens.

1.3 The notary applicant, and then the notary, should read and study the state or territorial notary statute and the official state or territorial notary handbook or manual, if any.

Some jurisdictions require some extent of notary training, and a small number require notary testing, as a prerequisite to commissioning. However, most of these steps are modest requirements. Thus, notary self-education is something every notary should willingly and diligently pursue. No one can be too well-informed about a service which carries with it the obligation to protect the interests of the general public and which carries with it full legal liability on notaries for financial injuries caused by their mistakes and misconduct. See also the discussion about avoiding notary wrongdoing in Chapter 20 and about notary bonds and insurance in Chapter 23.

The most fundamental and important source of knowledge of notary best practices is the notary law of the state or territory where the notary is commissioned, and that law is embodied in the notary statutes and administrative regulations (if any) of the state or territory. These statutes and regulations are readily available as part of the notary application materials or in the published notary handbook or manual either produced in hard copy format or appearing online through the auspices of the agency which appoints notaries and oversees their performance (usually the office of the secretary of state).

Every notary should obtain a personal copy of the notary statutes and regulations, fully read and reread them, study them, and keep them present and available as resource material for each notarization. In addition, notaries should periodically review their jurisdictions' notary laws, because almost none of us have photographic memories that will serve us in perpetuity to recall the details of these laws. We need to revisit material as complex as notary statutes and regulations in order to maintain mastery of them. Furthermore, notary laws and regulations occasionally change, and notaries should become aware of such changes. See also the discussions of notary membership and education organizations in Chapter 29 and of continuing education in Chapter 30.

1.4 The notary should keep abreast of developments in notary ethics, law, and practice and incorporate advancements in notary ethics, law, and practice into the notary's official service.

Inherent in the position of every government officer and every professional business person is the obligation of continuing self-education and betterment. It is simply the right thing for such individuals to do. Notaries are included in this group and are bound by this basic tenet. It is a basic qualification for the post of notary to remain current about notarial ethics, law, and practice.

The good news is that notary ethics principles, legal requirements, and best practices do not tend to change frequently or dramatically. But, they do sometimes change, so notaries should remain vigilant in keeping informed about such developments in the notary field. Importantly, advancing technology often affects notarial practice and prompts relevant changes in notary statutes and regulations. Notaries can follow the updates on official governmental notary websites, join notary membership and education organizations and follow their publications and online sources, and enroll in notary education classes in which the latest changes and developments in the notary arena will be addressed.

Of course, it is not enough to simply become aware of developments in notary ethics, law, practice, and technology. As the old saying goes "knowledge is power." But, knowledge without applying it is not power; it is a lost opportunity. Notaries should incorporate improvements in notarial ethics, law, practice, and technology into their performance of document notarizations. See also the discussion of notary continuing education in Chapter 30. ■

***RELEVANT MODEL NOTARY LAW**

Each notary should read, study, and abide by the notary statute and regulations, if any, of his or her commissioning state or territory.

"To uphold the trust placed in me by the public I serve;

To maintain a professional manner suitable to the office I hold; ...

To keep informed of the law regarding the duties and powers of the office of Notary Public in my jurisdiction and not compromise that law; ...

To always conduct myself and perform my duties in a manner which will bring credit to myself, my office and the [American] Society [of Notaries]." *Responsibility Code of Ethics* (1980).

"The Notary shall, as a government officer and public servant, serve all of the public in an honest, fair and unbiased manner." *Notary Public Code of Professional Responsibility,* Guiding Principle I (1998).

"The Notary shall give precedence to the rules of law over the dictates or expectations of any person or entity." *Notary Public Code of Professional Responsibility*, Guiding Principle V (1998).

"The Notary shall seek instruction on notarization, and keep current on the laws, practices and requirements of the notarial office." *Notary Public Code of Professional Responsibility*, Guiding Principle X (1998).

"Purposes. This [Act] shall be construed and applied to advance its underlying purposes, which are: (1) to promote, serve, and protect the public interest; ... (3) to foster ethical conduct among notaries; ..." *Model Notary Act*, Section 1-2 (2010).

"Qualifications. (a) Except as provided in Subsection (c), the [commissioning official] shall issue a notary commission to any qualified person who submits an application in accordance with this Article.

(b) A person qualified for a notary commission shall: (1) be at least 18 years of age; (2) reside or have a regular place of work or business in the [State]. as defined in Section 2-18; (3) reside legally in the United States; (4) read and write English; (5) pass a course of instruction requiring a written examination under Section 4-3; and (6) submit fingerprints to allow a criminal background check.

(c) The [commissioning official] may deny an application based on: (1) submission of an official application containing material misstatement or omission of fact; (2) the applicant's conviction or plea of admission or nolo contendere for a felony or any crime involving dishonesty or moral turpitude, but in no case may a commission be issued to the applicant within 5 years after such conviction or plea; (3) a finding or admission of liability against the applicant in a civil lawsuit based on the applicant's deceit; (4) revocation, suspension, restriction, or denial of a notarial commission or professional license by this or any other state or nation, but in no case may a commission be issued to the applicant within 5 years after such disciplinary action; and (5) an official finding that the applicant had engaged in official misconduct as defined in Section 2-12, whether or not disciplinary action resulted. ..." *Model Notary Act,* Section 3-1 (2010).

"Course And Examination. (a) Every applicant for a notary commission shall take, within the 3 months preceding application, a course of instruction of at least 4 hours approved by the [commissioning official], and pass a written examination of this course.

(b) The content of the course and the basis for the written examination shall be notarial laws, procedures, and ethics." *Model Notary Act*, Section 4-3 (2010).

"Application Fee. Every applicant for a notary commission shall pay to this [State] a non-refundable application fee of [dollars]." *Model Notary Act*, Section 4-5 (2010).

"Liability of Notary, Surety, and Employer. (a) A notary is liable to any person for all damages proximately caused that person by the notary's negligence, intentional violation of law, or official misconduct in relation to a notarization.

(b) A surety for a notary's bond is liable to any person for damages proximately caused that person by the notary's negligence, intentional violation of law, or official misconduct in relation to a notarization during the bond term, but this liability may not exceed the dollar amount of the bond or of any remaining bond funds that have not been disbursed to other claimants. Regardless of the number of claimants against the bond or the number of notarial acts cited in the claims, a surety's aggregate liability shall not exceed the dollar amount of the bond. ..." *Model Notary Act*, Section 13-1 (2010).

"Commission As Notary Public; Qualifications ... (b) An applicant for a commission as a notary public must: (1) be at least 18 years of age; (2) be a citizen or permanent legal resident of the United States; (3) be a resident of or have a place of employment or practice in this state; (4) be able to read and write [English]; and (5) not be disqualified to receive a commission under Section 23 [; and (6) have passed the examination required under Section 22(a)].

(c) Before issuance of a commission as a notary public, an applicant for the commission shall execute an oath of office and submit it to the [commissioning officer or agency]. ..." *Revised Uniform Law on Notarial Acts*, Section 21 (2010).

Notarial Certificate. H. Anstice & Co., Stationers, 23 Nassau St., N. Y.

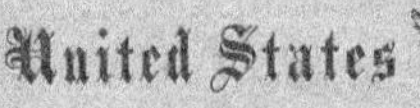

United States of America.

STATE OF NEW-YORK, ss.

By this Public Instrument be it known to all to whom the same doth or may in anywise concern, that I, James Gerard a Public Notary, in and for the State of New-York, by Letters Patent, under the Great Seal of the said State duly commissioned and sworn, dwelling in the City of New-burgh,

Do hereby Certify, That on this day of March A.D. 1872. I did personally deposit in the Post Office in the city of Newburgh, N.Y. in time for the mail, one package, sealed with five seals, containing five bonds of the Danville, Urbana, Bloomington and Pekin Railroad Company of the State of Illinois, First Mortgage 1909, numbered 394-395-396-444-294 of the denomination of One thousand dollars each, signed by C. N. Griggs, President of said railroad, also by R. G. Rolston, President of the Farmer's Loan and trust Company, having the seal of the Company on the left hand corner, having each seventy four coupons attached of the denomination of thirty five dollars each, payable on the first day of April and October in each & every year, addressed: Mr Henry Simson, No 13 Beechaven Terrace, Glasgow, Scotland, between the hours of 2 & 3 o'clock P.M.

In Testimony whereof, I have subscribed my name, and caused my Notarial Seal of Office to be hereunto affixed, the Eleventh day of March in the year of our Lord one thousand eight hundred and seventy-two.

James Gerard
Notary Public
Orange Co.

1872, one-page notarial certificate bearing a red notary seal of New York public notary James Gerard, confirming his dispatch by mail of five enumerated and described bonds of the Danville, Urbana, Bloomington, and Pekin Railroad Company.

Chapter

2

Notary Jurisdiction and Venue

STANDARDS SUMMARY

2.1 The notary should understand the jurisdiction or geographic boundaries within which the notary has authority to perform document notarizations.

2.2 The notary should perform document notarizations only within the jurisdiction or geographic boundaries where the notary is authorized to act.

2.3 The notary should record the venue or place where the notarization is performed in the notarial certificate for each document notarization.

2.4 The notary should record the venue or place where the notarization is performed in the notary journal entry for each document notarization.

2.5 The notary should proofread the venue section of the notarial certificate and journal entry and make any needed corrections prior to completion of the notarial ceremony.

STANDARDS EXPLANATIONS

Jurisdiction and venue are two separate, but related, features critical to every document notarization. Jurisdiction refers to the statewide or territory-wide area within which a notary is authorized to act. Venue refers to the narrower place of the specific county within the notary's jurisdiction where a particular notarization is performed. For example, an Illinois notary's jurisdiction is the state of Illinois, and the venue where a notarization might be performed could be in Cook County, in Peoria County, in Sangamon County, or in any of the other counties in Illinois.

All public officials have limits imposed by law upon their authority to act, such as the geographic boundaries within which officers possess the jurisdiction to serve. City officials have jurisdiction within their cities, county officials have jurisdiction within their counties, and state or territorial officials have jurisdiction within their states or territories. Thus, to assure jurisdictional validity for official acts, the venue must be designated to establish the proper authority of the government official.

This chapter is about jurisdiction, the geographic area in which notaries are authorized to perform official duties. And, it is about venue, the area noted on a notarial certificate as the place where the document notarization is performed. It is not about the place of residence or place of business of the notary, for that subject is about the eligibility of someone to become a notary. See also the discussion of notary qualifications in Chapter 1.

2.1 The notary should understand the jurisdiction or geographic boundaries within which the notary has authority to perform document notarizations.

Generally, notaries public, as state or territorial officials, enjoy the authority to perform document notarizations only within the states and territories where they are commissioned. The formal term is "jurisdiction," which refers to the legal authority to act as a government official.

Incidentally, although generally a U.S. notary can act only within the state or territory where she or he is commissioned, in a few small western states where the neighboring states have mutually agreed to allow reciprocity of notarial authority, a notary can act in more then one state (i.e., in a state where the notary is not commissioned). That is, notaries commissioned in an adjacent state have authority to act in the neighboring state, but only in the few states that have enacted laws expressly authorizing this practice.

Although it is not often an issue, notaries could encounter difficulties about their jurisdiction to act when they perform notarizations near borders in unfamiliar areas or when they perform notarizations on airplanes, boats, trains, or other vehicles near state or territorial boundaries. After all, many U.S. borders are bounded by metropolitan areas on each side of the boundary — with little distinction from one state or territory to the next state or territory. Nevertheless, the law on the matter of jurisdiction is absolute. That is, if a notary performs a notarization in a location where he or she is not empowered to act as a notary, the notarization in question is null and void.

2.2 The notary should perform document notarizations only within the jurisdiction or geographic boundaries where the notary is authorized to act.

For U.S. notaries performing traditional paper document notarizations, they have authority to act anywhere and everywhere within the borders of the states and territories in which they are commissioned, but not beyond those boundaries. This rule is absolute, with only the small exception for the notaries of a few neighboring states noted in the preceding section. It is worth repeating that the general rule is firm — if a notary performs a notarization beyond the borders of the state or territory where the notary is commissioned or otherwise empowered to act, the attempted notarization is absolutely invalid.

Unfortunately, many notaries are asked to perform notarizations in violation of notary statutes. Friends, family members, employers, or notary customers will sometimes urge notaries to perform notarizations for them while the notaries are outside their lawful jurisdictions. These other people often do not appreciate the fundamental importance of lawful jurisdiction to the integrity of the notarial process. But, notaries cannot allow themselves to be tempted to falsely notarize in places where they are not authorized. To do otherwise is not only improper and dishonest, but also may constitute criminal conduct, such as official misconduct and/or impersonation of a notary — since the "notary" is not a notary in a state or territory where she or he is not commissioned.

Note: *Electronic Notarizations and Remote Electronic Notarizations.* Technology is changing the way notarizations are being performed and the way we think about some of the fundamental concepts of notarization. For instance, jurisdiction and venue are affected. Should it matter where an electronic notarization is performed? In the case of a remote electronic notarization, in which the electronic notary and document signer are not face-to-face in the same room, the electronic notary might be situated in one jurisdiction, and the document signer could be located in another jurisdiction. Some statutes are authorizing electronic notaries to perform electronic notarizations beyond the borders of their states and territories of commissioning. Individuals who become electronic notaries should consult the electronic notarization laws of their commissioning jurisdictions regarding issues of jurisdiction and venue.

2.3 The notary should record the venue or place where the notarization is performed in the notarial certificate for each document notarization.

The discussion above about the essential nature of proper jurisdiction to a lawful notarization should emphasize to every notary why the "'venue" section of every notary certificate is critically important. The venue section is where the notary identifies the county (or parish in Louisiana) and state or territory in which the notarization is performed. The venue section establishes and documents the notary's jurisdictional authority to perform the notarization.

The properly completed venue section of the notary certificate serves as prima facie evidence (or legally presumptive evidence) of jurisdiction of the notary to perform the notarization. Although the completed venue section of the certificate creates a presumption of proper jurisdiction, it is a rebuttable presumption that can be disproven by evidence if the notary was actually outside his or her jurisdiction at the time and place of the notarization ceremony.

To put the matter differently, if a notary certificate either contained no venue section at all, or if the venue section were not filled in with the county or parish and state or territory where the notarization was conducted, then a challenge to the validity of the notarization could be asserted on the basis of the failure of the notary to have proper jurisdiction. Thus, the venue section is terribly important, and the omission of the venue, or an error in identifying the proper venue, could be fatal to a notarization. See also the discussion of the certificate of notarization in Chapter 7.

2.4 The notary should record the venue or place where the notarization is performed in the notary journal entry for each document notarization.

Because proper jurisdiction is an essential element of a lawful notarization, not only should the venue be recorded in the notarial certificate, it also should be noted in the notary journal entry for the notarization. In fact, in the event of the failure to complete the venue section of the notary certificate, or of a mistake in correctly stating the venue in the notarial certificate, or of the loss or destruction of the notarial certificate, the notation of the correct venue in the notary journal may cure the venue defect. In other words, the information recorded in the journal entry can supplement or correct the contents of the certificate of notarization. After all, the notary journal entry is an official record of a public officer — the notary — and should be given great evidentiary weight.

Furthermore, one of the main reasons for notaries to maintain notary journals is to protect their notarizations by further documenting them and, thus, by shielding their notarizations against challenges to their validity. That is why it is so important to properly record the venue in journal entries. If the format of a particular notary journal does not have a section or column for the venue or the place of the notarization, the notary should write the county and state or territory of the notarization into the area for additional or other information, or simply write onto the next line or area of the journal in order to record the venue. It is far more important to record full information than it is to abide by the lines or spaces in a professionally printed notary journal. See also the discussion of the notary journal in Chapter 17.

Practice Tip: Sometimes the exact place where a challenged notarization has been performed will be relevant information in the process of deciding the contest about the validity of the notarization. For example, in a few of the cases in which this author has served as an expert consultant and expert witness, the precise place of the notarization became important. In one instance, it was alleged that the notarization by a bank notary took place in an automobile in the bank parking lot so that the 99-year-old signer who was severely ill did not have to be assisted into the bank, and for the unscrupulous motive to prevent him from realizing his signature was being notarized. In two other separate cases, doubt was cast upon the legitimacy of the questioned notarizations because one was allegedly performed at the notary's workplace on a Saturday evening although the notary was off duty, and because the other notarization was allegedly performed in the afternoon on Thanksgiving Day at the home of the signer (taking the notary away from her home and family around dinnertime on that important holiday). So, in addition to noting the county and state or territory for venue purposes in the notary journal entry, the notary should also note the time of day and the address or premises location where the notarial ceremony is conducted.

2.5 The notary should proofread the venue section of the notarial certificate and journal entry and make any needed corrections prior to completion of the notarization ceremony.

Always proofread! I will repeatedly advise proofreading of the various components of the notarial certificate and the journal entry in order to emphasize this basic best practice procedure — although it is obvious that I will have ended up advising to proofread the entire certificate and the entire journal entry. Proofreading should help notaries to avoid simple, absentminded, technical mistakes which, if uncorrected, become fatal substantive omissions or errors in notarial certificates and journals.

Corrections of notarial certificates and journal entries must be made before the conclusion of the notarization ceremony because the notary's official authority as to each notarization ends when the ceremony ends. Certificates and journals cannot be corrected later. Do not lose this opportunity to get it right — PROOF-READ! ■

***RELEVANT MODEL NOTARY LAW**

Each notary should read, study, and abide by the notary statute and regulations, if any, of her or his commissioning state or territory.

"To keep informed of the law regarding the duties and powers of the office of Notary Public in my jurisdiction and not compromise that law." *Responsibility Code of Ethics* (1980).

"The Notary shall, as a government officer and public servant, serve all of the public in an honest, fair and unbiased manner." *Notary Public Code of Professional Responsibility*, Guiding Principle I (1998).

"The Notary shall give precedence to the rules of law over the dictates or expectations of any person or entity." *Notary Public Code of Professional Responsibility*, Guiding Principle V (1998).

"The Notary shall record every notarial act in a bound journal or other secure recording device and safeguard it as an important public record." *Notary Public Code of Professional Responsibility*, Guiding Principle VIII (1998).

"Purposes. This [Act] shall be construed and applied to advance its underlying purposes, which are: (1) to promote, serve, and protect the public interest; ..." *Model Notary Act*, Section 1-2 (2010).

"Jurisdiction And Term. A person commissioned as a notary public may perform notarial acts in any part of this [State] for a term of [4] years, unless the commission is earlier revoked under Section 13-3 or resigned under Section 12-2." *Model Notary Act*, Section 3-2 (2010).

"Journal Entries. (a) For every notarial act, the notary shall record in the journal at the time of notarization at least the following: ... [(9)] the address where the notarization was performed, if not the notary's business address ..." *Model Notary Act*, Section 7-2 (2010).

"Notarial Certificate. (a) For every notarial act involving a document, a notary public of this [State] shall properly complete a notarial certificate that contains or states: ... (3) the venue of the notarial act, including the name of the [State] and of the pertinent [county] [parish] [district] ..." *Model Notary Act*, Section 9-1 (2010).

"Impersonation. Any person not a notary who knowingly acts as or otherwise impersonates a notary is guilty of a [class of offense], punishable upon conviction by a fine not exceeding [dollars] or imprisonment for not more than [term of imprisonment], or both." *Model Notary Act*, Section 14-1 (2010).

Vintage 1950s–60s, plastic-covered cardboard sign promoting the services of a bonded notary public.

Chapter

3

Notary Advertising

STANDARDS SUMMARY

3.1 The notary should, if advertising the availability of notarial services, do so in a dignified and professional manner befitting a government official.

3.2 The notary should not advertise in a manner, or knowingly perform a notarization, which will be published or used to endorse or promote a candidate, cause, entity, product, or service.

3.3 The notary should not use the term *"notario," "notario publico,"* or any other non-English translation of "notary" or "notary public" in advertising or signage or in any other manner.

3.4 The notary should, if fees for notarial services are to be charged, prominently display a printed statement detailing those fees to inform prospective customers before notarial services are rendered.

STANDARDS EXPLANATIONS

The notarization of transactional instruments and the provision of notary services are important features of commercial and governmental life in the U.S. Notaries may wish to advertise their services, whether those notaries intend to charge fees for their services or not. Some individuals become notaries entirely of their own accord in order to provide the public with notarial services and without any desire to be compensated for those services. Other individuals become notaries at the urging of their employers or to provide notarial services as part of their business activities, and those businesses may wish to advertise the provision of notarial services. Of course, notaries and businesses that employ notaries are not required to advertise notarial services.

Some jurisdictions have adopted statutes and/or administrative regulations about specific details regarding advertising and signage for notaries and notary services, and those laws and rules should be consulted and followed.

3.1 The notary should, if advertising the availability of notarial services, do so in a dignified and professional manner befitting a government official.

Notaries may choose to advertise in one or more of numerous ways, such as through business cards, letterheads, signs, phone listings, newspaper and magazine ads, billboards, websites, and other methods. Notaries have even placed their promotional information on matchbook covers, ballpoint pens, and drink mugs. If a notary decides to advertise, such advertising should be conducted in a respectful and professional manner that is appropriate for a commissioned public official, whose responsibility is to provide a valuable public service and to act in a disinterested and honorable fashion.

Certainly, notaries do not have to make themselves available to the public at all hours of the day and night. Hence, notaries who desire to limit the time periods when they will provide notarization services should include the days and hours of their availability, or times of their unavailability, in their advertising materials. Some notaries have placed advertising or signage on their vehicles, so they may even find themselves being approached when stopped at gas stations, car washes, parking lots, and anywhere else their vehicles are visible.

3.2 The notary should not advertise in a manner, or knowingly perform a notarization, which will be published or used to endorse or support a candidate, cause, entity, product, or service.

The cardinal rule for the conduct of notaries is for them to serve as disinterested and unbiased official governmental witnesses to document notarizations. Thus, the knowing endorsement or promotion of candidates, causes, entities, products, or services is absolutely forbidden for notaries — at least, while serving in their official capacities. Of course, when not acting as notaries, individuals are free to engage in those other activities (without reference to their status as notaries public).

Similarly, notaries should not knowingly allow their positions as notaries to be appropriated and used by others for commercial or political gain or promotions, or in connection with the endorsement or promotion of public causes. There may be situations when notaries will be taken advantage of by promoters who do not tell the notaries that their notarizations or images of their notarizations or notary seals will be publicized or published in campaigns, causes, or endorsements. And, such rare circumstances cannot be fully avoided. But, if a notary is forewarned that her or his picture, notarization, or notary seal will be utilized in any kind of publicity or promotion, the notary should decline to perform the notarization in question. And, of course, the notary should note the refusal to notarize and the circumstances in a notary journal entry for the date when the refusal occurred.

3.3 The notary should not use the term *"notario," "notario publico,"* or any other non-English translation of "notary" or "notary public" in advertising or signage or in any other manner.

Notary advertising cannot be misleading. That is why in the U.S. (except for Puerto Rico) notaries should not use any term other than "notary" or "notary public" to describe themselves, because other labels such as *"notario"* or *"notario publico"* are likely to mislead individuals who are familiar with the notary systems of the Hispanic or civil law countries. In those Hispanic and civil law countries, the civil law notary (often called *"notario"* or *"notario publico"*) is typically an attorney at law who provides services far more substantial than the document notarizations performed by U.S. notaries. Additionally, because of the heightened level of services performed by the *"notario"* or *"notario publico,"* those officials are entitled to charge significantly higher fees for their more substantial services. Notaries who are not licensed attorneys should avoid engaging in the unauthorized practice of law and should avoid appearing to be licensed as lawyers. See the discussion of avoiding the unauthorized practice of law in Chapter 26.

The area where perhaps the greatest risk of confusion and misrepresentation is likely to occur is in the field of immigration law and practice. Immigrants who are familiar with the Hispanic or civil law notary systems and who seek qualified assistance with immigration matters may be duped by an individual claiming to be a *"notario"* or *"'notario publico."* There may be some misunderstanding about the qualifications of the service provider, about the substantive services to be rendered, and about the appropriate level of fees to be charged. If one is qualified to assist with immigration matters, she or he will be a lawyer or an immigration specialist and will be authorized to advertise as such — but not solely as a notary, *notario*, notary public, or *notario publico*.

3.4 The notary should, if fees for notarial services are to be charged, prominently display a printed statement detailing those fees to inform prospective customers before notarial services are rendered.

Although notaries, as public servants, are not required to charge fees for notarial services, they are entitled to charge and collect fees. Some jurisdictions have adopted statutes or regulations which set the maximum fees that may be charged for particular notarial services. Notaries in those jurisdictions may charge less than the maximum or no fees at all. If a jurisdiction has no such mandatory maximum fee schedule, the notary may charge either no fees or may charge fees that are not unreasonable or excessive. A more thorough discussion of notary fees and disclosure and documentation of fees is included in Chapter 28.

Basic fairness and transparency demand that all businesses and governmental agencies should disclose their fees to prospective clients and customers in advance of sales and services. Notaries are included within the coverage of this proposition because notaries are public officials and, thus, are fiduciaries or trusted agents of the public whom they serve.

The most effective way to provide advance notice to prospective notarization customers is to disclose the notary's fee schedule by (1) displaying one or more signs large enough to draw one's attention and written in large enough dark print to be easily read and (2) providing each prospective document signer a copy of the material published on the sign — prior to the commencement of the notarization ceremony. The provisions of the model notary laws set out immediately below provide further guidance about how to achieve full and fair disclosure regarding notary fees. If the notary's jurisdiction has enacted a maximum fee schedule for various notarial services, the notary should use that schedule as a guide in creating the notary's posted and published fees.

To corroborate and document fees charged and paid for notarial services, notaries should provide written receipts for such payments to their customers and should record the notarial fees as part of the notary journal entries for all document notarizations. See the discussion about the notary journal in Chapter 17 and the discussion of notary fees in Chapter 28. ■

*RELEVANT MODEL NOTARY LAW

Each notary should read, study, and abide by the notary statute and regulations, if any, of his or her commissioning state or territory.

"To uphold the trust placed in me by the public I serve;

To maintain a professional manner suitable to the office I hold;

To treat each individual fairly and equally, with kindness and respect; ...

To keep informed of the law regarding the duties and powers of the office of Notary Public in my jurisdiction and not compromise that law;

To not use the office of Notary Public as a means of financial gain, for myself or others, in any other business or profession; ...

To always conduct myself and perform my duties in a manner which will bring credit to myself, my office and the [American] Society [of Notaries]." *Responsibility Code of Ethics* (1980).

"The Notary shall, as a government officer and public servant, serve all of the public in an honest, fair and unbiased manner." *Notary Public Code of Professional Responsibility*, Guiding Principle I (1998).

"The Notary shall act as a ministerial officer and not provide unauthorized advice or services." *Notary Public Code of Professional Responsibility*, Guiding Principle VI (1998).

"The Notary shall affix a seal on every notarized document and not allow this universally recognized symbol of office to be used by another or in an endorsement or promotion." *Notary Public Code of Professional Responsibility*, Guiding Principle VII (1998).

"The Notary shall record every notarial act in a bound journal or other secure recording device and safeguard it as an important public record." *Notary Public Code of Professional Responsibility*, Guiding Principle VIII (1998).

"Purposes. This [Act] shall be construed and applied to advance its underlying purposes, which are: (1) to promote, serve, and protect the public interest; ... (3) to foster ethical conduct among notaries; ..." *Model Notary Act,* Section 1-2 (2010).

"Testimonials. A notary shall not use the official notary title or seal to endorse, promote, denounce, or oppose any product, service, contest, candidate, or other offering." *Model Notary Act,* Section 5-11 (2010).

"Unauthorized Practice of Law. A non-attorney notary shall not assist another person in drafting, completing, selecting, or understanding a document or transaction requiring a notarial act." *Model Notary Act,* Section 5-12(a) (2010).

"Misrepresentation and Improper Advertising. (a) A notary shall not claim to have powers, qualifications, rights, or privileges that the office of notary does not provide, including the power to counsel on immigration issues.

(b) A non-attorney notary who advertises notarial services in a language other than English shall include in the advertisement, notice, letterhead, or sign the following, prominently displayed in the same language: (1) the statement: 'I am not an attorney and have no authority to give advice on immigration or other legal matters'; and (2) the fees for notarial acts specified in Section 6-2(a).

(c) A notary may not use the term 'notario publico' or any equivalent non-English term in any business card, advertisement, notice, or sign." *Model Notary Act,* Section 5-14 (2010).

"Notice of Fees. Notaries who charge for their notarial services shall conspicuously display in their places of business, or present to each principal [document signer] outside their places of business, an English-language schedule of fees for notarial acts, as specified in Section 6-2(a). No part of any notarial fee schedule shall be printed in smaller than 10-point type." *Model Notary Act,* Section 6-5 (2010).

"Prohibited Acts. ... (b) A notary public may not engage in false or deceptive advertising.

(c) A notary public, other than an attorney licensed to practice law in this state, may not use the term 'notario' or 'notario publico' ..." *Revised Uniform Law on Notarial Acts,* Section 25 (2010).

Early black and white reproduction of an 1890s–1900s photograph of the famous old West business premises for "Judge Roy Bean, Notary Public, Justice of the Peace, Law West of the Pecos." Since the very beginnings of this country, notaries have been needed in every corner of America.

Chapter

4

Acknowledgment Notarizations

STANDARDS SUMMARY

4.1 The notary should understand the purpose and importance of the acknowledgment form of document notarization.

4.2 The notary should understand the differences between an acknowledgment, a jurat, and a signature witnessing.

4.3 The notary should comply with the elements required for an acknowledgment, especially the proper identification of the document signer.

4.4 The notary should create a journal entry that correctly identifies and thoroughly records the acknowledgment notarization, especially that includes the signer's present signature.

STANDARDS EXPLANATIONS

The focus of this book is upon standard paper document notarizations, including the three common forms of document notarizations: (1) acknowledgements, (2) jurats or verifications on oath or affirmation, and (3) signature witnessings. These types of notarizations will be addressed in this and the following two chapters.

In other chapters of this book, numerous features common to all types of documents notarizations will be addressed at length. For instance, all document signers should be personally present at notarizations and should be satisfactorily identified. Notaries should assess whether all signers are mentally competent and acting voluntarily. All notarizations should be evidenced by properly completed notarial certificates and should be further recorded by properly completed notary journal entries. And so on.

As is the case with each type of notarization, the kind of notarization can be discerned from the notarial certificate, which basically describes the steps that have been taken in the performance of the notarization. It should be noted, however, that certificates of notarization do not typically label themselves as an "acknowledgment," or "jurat," or "signature witnessing." Interestingly, though, in the case of an acknowledgment, the notary certificate will almost certainly refer to some form of the term "acknowledge," because there is hardly any other way to describe what transpires in the performance of such a notarization.

The most common type of notarization is the acknowledgment, simply because of its historical origin with real estate transactions and because of its continuing widespread use in both real estate matters and routine kinds of commercial and governmental instruments. It is a basic form of notarization in which no oath or affirmation is needed or administered. And, an acknowledgment can be signed like other notarizations at the time of the notarial ceremony, or curiously, it can be signed ahead of time and merely acknowledged by the signer at the later notarial ceremony. See a sample acknowledgment notarial certificate at the end of this chapter under the heading "Relevant Model Notary Law."

4.1 The notary should understand the purpose and importance of the acknowledgment form of document notarization.

The fact that acknowledgment notarizations are far and away the most frequently sought form of notarization is important simply because notaries will have to perform them most often. Millions upon millions of acknowledgment notarizations are performed in this country every year. Historically, it was the standard method by which buyers and sellers could deal with one another at a distance in olden times when the parties could not necessarily come together in person to finalize their transactions. Then and now, the acknowledgment substantiates both the identity of the document signer and the validity of the signature on the instrument, which can then be sent or delivered to the other party to a transaction.

It should also be pointed out that because of its ancient origin, many acknowledgment certificate forms have been saddled with old-fashioned language reminiscent of the era when form seemed more important than substance.

Still today, most acknowledgment certificates contain language about the acknowledgment having been "voluntarily" signed "for its intended purpose." But alas, every notarization should be voluntarily undertaken by the document signers and every signing should be undertaken for the intended purpose of the transactional document. Yet, if that magic language is missing, some receiving agencies may reject an acknowledgment. So, the superfluous acknowledgment language tends to linger on, and on. There is a ray of hope for a more streamlined form of acknowledgment certificate. See the contrasting sample forms from the *Model Notary Act*, Section 9-4 (2010) and the *Revised Uniform Law on Notarial Acts*, Section 16(1) (2010) at the end of this chapter.

Note: *A Not-Too-Serious Suggestion.* This author believes the acknowledgment type of notarization should be eliminated and replaced by the signature-witnessing notarization. I believe there has never been much of a legitimate reason to create a notarization in which the signer can sign the transactional instrument prior to the notarial ceremony if the signer is going to be required to appear at the notarial ceremony anyway. Why not simply require the signer to execute the document in the presence of the notary at that ceremony, as the other forms of notarization are handled? However, to do as I suggest would effectively convert an "acknowledgment" into the equivalent of a "signature witnessing" (which is discussed in Chapter 6). Hence, because over hundreds of years the acknowledgment has become so well-entrenched in real estate transactions, in notarial practice, and in the law, I cannot image that it will ever be eliminated or changed in its core features.

4.2 The notary should understand the differences between an acknowledgment, a jurat, and a signature witnessing.

For an acknowledgment, a document signer "acknowledges" that the signature appearing on the document is hers or his. This can be done in one of two ways. In the great majority of instances, this result is accomplished by document signers presently signing acknowledgments in the physical presence of notaries at the times of the notarizations. That is, by presently signing, document signers certainly acknowledge those signatures to be theirs.

However, there is another way for signers to acknowledge the authenticity of their signatures — and this process makes the "acknowledgment" type of notarization unique. An "acknowledgment" may have been signed prior to the time of the notarization and outside the presence of the notary — perhaps because a document was time-sensitive and needed to be signed prior to the time of the notarization. Or perhaps, the signer may have wished to sign the document when other parties were available to observe the signing or when some special occasion or celebration was occurring. This procedure is permissible, if at the time of the notarization the signer attends and indicates to the notary that the signature appearing on the document is his or hers — such as by pointing to the signature and orally stating it belongs to him or her.

Note: *A Criticism of Pre-Signed Acknowledgments.* This author cannot resist commenting about the reasons just noted for the execution of a document prior to the notarial ceremony, for those reasons seem flimsy and inconsequential to me. If the document is signed at an earlier time than the occasion of the notarial ceremony, then such signature is unverified by an impartial public officer. Moreover, if the reason is to meet a time deadline, why not utilize a notarial ceremony which takes only a matter of minutes to complete? If a signer wishes other parties to attend the earlier signing, there is no reason that a notary could not be among them to perform a notarization as well. There seems to be no significant reason to allow a signer to execute a document before the notarial ceremony, especially when such a procedure diminishes the security and integrity of a notarized instrument.

No specific procedure is required for the manner of acknowledging a previously executed signature. The key is the signer should clearly demonstrate the intention, and communicate to the notary by words and conduct, that she or he is adopting or authenticating the previously executed signature as hers or his. Probably, the notary will need to ask the signer if the signature is hers or his, and the notary should also ask the signer to point to the signature and to read it aloud for the notary. Importantly, the notary public should maintain a notary journal, and as explained in section 4.4, the savvy notary should obtain a present signature of the document signer as part of the journal entry for the notarization, regardless of when the transactional document to be acknowledged was actually signed.

Unlike acknowledgments, both jurat and signature witnessing notarizations require present signatures for every notarization. Unlike jurats, acknowledgments do not include oaths or affirmations. The notary certificate language will help guide the notary through an acknowledgment, for it will make reference to some form of the word "acknowledge," and it will not make reference to the signer being sworn or to any form of the words "oath" or "affirmation."

4.3 The notary should comply with the elements required for an acknowledgment notarization, especially the proper identification of the document signer.

There are some standard notarial practices which must be satisfied in order to have a proper notarization in the case of each type of document notarization (acknowledgments, jurats, and signature witnessings). For instance, the document signer must be present at all three kinds of notarizations. The signer must be known to the notary, or the signer's identity must be established by satisfactory evidence. The notary should assess the willingness and mental competence of the signer and should perform the notarization only if the signer is competent and acts of her or his free will. No oath or affirmation is administered as part of an acknowledgment.

One of the most serious and most common faults and statutory violations with notarizations is the failure of the notary to require the personal presence of the signer at the notarial ceremony. That failure dramatically heightens the danger of imposters and other parties obtaining falsified notarizations. Regarding acknowledgments, the key matters for the notary to understand are that the acknowledgment is the most frequently used form of notarization and that an acknowledgment is the one and only type of notarization in which the document signer may have executed the instrument prior to the notarization ceremony. This unique feature causes the acknowledgment, if the signer's signature is executed prior to the notarial ceremony, to be the type of notarization most at risk for forgery by an imposter. Nevertheless, that risk can be minimized if the notary follows the best practice habits of properly identifying the document signer and keeping a contemporaneous and detailed notary journal, including a present signature of the document signer in the journal (as will be more fully discussed in Chapter 17 about notary journals). Those two steps can only be legitimately accomplished if the signer is present at the notarization.

Note: *Real-Life Language Controversy.* Acknowledgment notarizations are sometimes challenged and rejected because of the lack of specific wording. There is an ongoing controversy in regard to the language necessary to describe an acknowledgment in the notary certificate. As noted above, historically, acknowledgment certificates virtually always utilized language to the effect that the signer had "executed the document voluntarily for the purposes stated therein." Some statutes, including the *Model Notary Act* quoted below, continue to require that comparable language about "voluntary signing for the purposes stated in the document," or substantially similar language, is mandatory for an acknowledgment notarization. This author was recently consulted about just such a legal case in which the certificate did not contain that old-fashioned language, but instead recited merely "the signature was lawfully acknowledged." The view that specific words are required elevates form over substance and should not continue to guide the notary community. Because the statutes usually allow for "substantially similar" language, as did the law in this case, I opined that the acknowledgment was valid. After all, every signed document, whether a commercial contract or a notarized instrument, should be voluntarily signed for the purposes of the document. Yet, no one argues for these same special words to be included in the language of notary certificates for jurats or signature witnessings. Thankfully, the acknowledgment certificate form found in the *Revised Uniform Law on Notarial Acts,* Section 16(1) (2010), as set out below, adopts a progressive, streamlined, and appropriate approach consistent with this author's view.

4.4 The notary should create a journal entry that correctly identifies and thoroughly records the acknowledgment notarization, especially that includes the signer's present signature.

The notary should journalize every document notarization and correctly identify the type of notarial act performed — in this instance, an acknowledgment. In a way, each notarization performed by a notary should be treated like a test of the notary's knowledge and skills. And, it's a written test in two parts — the notary journal entry and the notarial certificate. Those two instruments should be detailed and correct, and the information in them should match each other.

As noted previously, the acknowledgment is the one and only kind of document notarization in which the signer may have signed the transactional instrument before the notarial ceremony. If that unusual circumstance were ever to happen, the notary should be certain to make note of it in the journal entry. Every thoroughly prepared journal format includes a column or category for "other information" or "additional information," which is where this circumstance can be noted. If need be, the notary could simply use an additional row or column in the journal to describe this peculiar circumstance, for it is far more important to have a thorough journal entry than it is for the notary to write neatly within the lines, columns, and rows. See also the discussion of notary journals in Chapter 17.

Many experts agree that the most important element of a notary journal entry is the present signature of the document signer. The signer's present signature verifies that the signer actually attended the notarial ceremony. The signer's signature also provides a key factor in the thorough identification of the document signer, for the present signature in the journal can be compared with the signature on the transactional document and on the signer's ID document. Moreover, the notary should observe the actual making of the present signature in the journal to discern whether it is a fluid and natural signing, as opposed to a halting and unnatural signing as would be executed by an imposter attempting to replicate another person's signature. In most notarial ceremonies, the diligent notary observes and obtains two present signatures of the signer — one on the transactional document to be notarized and the other in the notary journal entry.

However, the signer's present signature in the journal would be particularly important for an acknowledgment in which the signature had been affixed to the transactional document prior to the notarial ceremony and merely acknowledged at the ceremony. The reason is that the signature in the journal would be the one and only present signature obtained in such a ceremony. ■

***RELEVANT MODEL NOTARY LAW**

Each notary should read, study, and abide by the notary statute and regulations, if any, of her or his commissioning state or territory.

§ 9-4 General Acknowledgment Certificate.
A notary shall use a certificate in substantially the following form in notarizing the signature or mark of any person acknowledging on his or her own behalf or as a partner, corporate officer, attorney in fact, or in any other representative capacity:

[State] of ___________
[County] of _________
On this _______ day of ___________,20___, before me, the undersigned notary, personally appeared ________________________ (name of document signer),
(personally known to me)
(proved to me through identification documents, which were ____________________,)
(proved to me on the oath or affirmation of ____________, who is personally known to me and stated to me that (he)(she) personally knows the document signer and is unaffected by the document,)
(proved to me on the oath or affirmation of ____________ and ____________, whose identities have been proven to me through identification documents and who have stated to me that they personally know the document signer and are unaffected by the document,)
to be the person whose name is signed on the preceding or attached document, and acknowledged to me that (he)(she) signed it voluntarily for its stated purpose(.)
(as partner for ______________, a partnership.)
(as ___________ for ___________, a corporation.)
(as attorney in fact for ___________, the principal.)
(as ___________ for ___________, (a)(the) ______________.)

____
(official signature and seal of notary)

Model Notary Act, Section 9-4 (2010).

(1) For an acknowledgment in an individual capacity:

State of ______________________________

[County] of ______________________________

This record was acknowledged before me on ________ by ____________________
Date Name(s) of individual(s)

____
Signature of notarial officer

Stamp

[______________________________]
Title of office

[My commission expires: ________]

Revised Uniform Law on Notarial Acts, Section 16(1) (2010).

"To always be satisfied that the individual appearing before me understands the contents of the document to be executed or oath to be administered before proceeding;

To always satisfy myself as to the identity of the individual appearing before me in my capacity as Notary Public; ...

To keep informed of the law regarding the duties and powers of the office of Notary Public in my jurisdiction and not compromise that law ..." *Responsibility Code of Ethics* (1980).

"The Notary shall require the presence of each signer and oath-taker in order to carefully screen each for identity and willingness, and to observe that each appears aware of the significance of the transaction requiring a notarial act." *Notary Public Code of Professional Responsibility,* Guiding Principle III (1998).

"The Notary shall not execute a false or incomplete certificate, nor be involved with any document or transaction that the Notary believes is false, deceptive or fraudulent." *Notary Public Code of Professional Responsibility,* Guiding Principle IV (1998).

"The Notary shall give precedence to the rules of law over the dictates or expectations of any person or entity." *Notary Public Code of Professional Responsibility,* Guiding Principle V (1998).

"The Notary shall affix a notary seal on every notarized document and not allow this universally recognized symbol of office to be used by another or in an endorsement or promotion." *Notary Public Code of Professional Responsibility,* Guiding Principle VII (1998).

"The Notary shall record every notarial act in a bound journal or other secure recording device and safeguard it as an important public record." *Notary Public Code of Professional Responsibility*, Guiding Principle VIII (1998).

"Powers of Notary. A notary is empowered to perform the following notarial acts: (1) acknowledgments; (2) oaths and affirmations; (3) jurats; (4) signature witnessings ..." *Model Notary Act,* Section 5-1 (2010).

"Acknowledgment. 'Acknowledgment' means a notarial act in which an individual at a single time and place: (1) appears in person before the notary and presents a document; (2) is personally known to the notary or identified by the notary through satisfactory evidence; and (3) indicates to the notary that the signature on the document was voluntarily affixed by the individual for the purposes stated within the document and, if applicable, that the individual had the authority to sign in a particular representative capacity." *Model Notary Act,* Section 2-1 (2010).

"Requirements for Notarial Acts. A notary shall perform a notarial act only if the principal [document signer]: (1) is in the presence of the notary at the time of notarization; (2) is personally known to the notary or identified by the notary through satisfactory evidence; (3) appears to understand the nature of the transaction requiring a notarial act; (4) appears to be acting of his or her own free will; (5) signs using letters or characters of a language that is understood by the notary; and (6) communicates directly with the notary in a language both understand." *Model Notary Act,* Section 5-2 (2010).

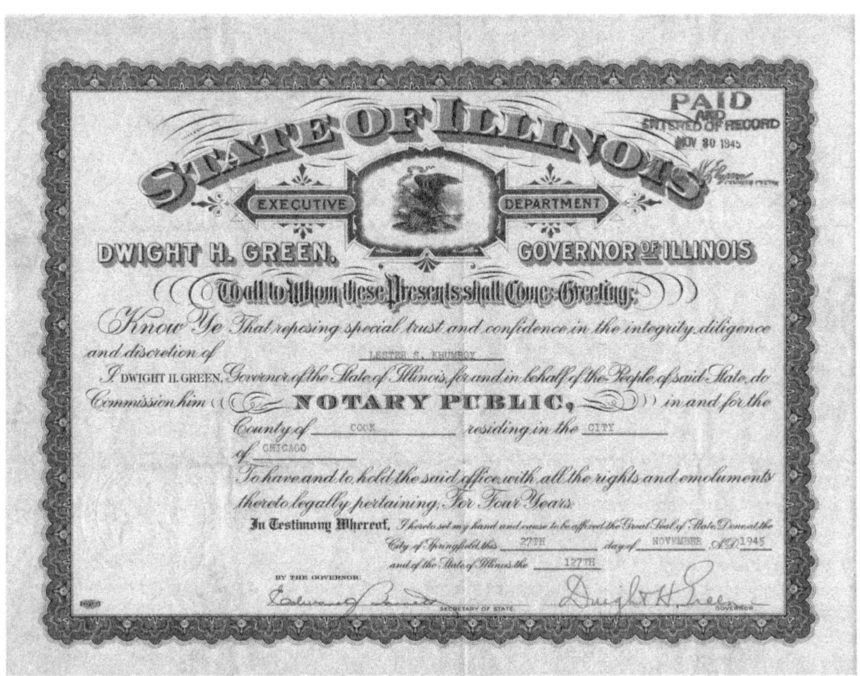

PAID AND ENTERED OF RECORD NOV 30 1945

STATE OF ILLINOIS

EXECUTIVE DEPARTMENT

DWIGHT H. GREEN, GOVERNOR OF ILLINOIS

To all to Whom these Presents shall Come, Greeting:

Know Ye That reposing special trust and confidence in the integrity, diligence and discretion of LESTER S. KRUMROY

I, DWIGHT H. GREEN, Governor of the State of Illinois, for and in behalf of the People of said State, do Commission him NOTARY PUBLIC, in and for the County of COOK residing in the CITY of CHICAGO

To have and to hold the said office with all the rights and emoluments thereto legally pertaining, For Four Years.

In Testimony Whereof, I hereto set my hand and cause to be affixed the Great Seal of State. Done at the City of Springfield this 27TH day of NOVEMBER A.D. 1945 and of the State of Illinois the 127TH

BY THE GOVERNOR:

SECRETARY OF STATE

GOVERNOR

1945, official State of Illinois notary public commission for Lester Krumroy from Governor Dwight Green. Importantly, this commission noted that the Governor reposed "special trust and confidence in the integrity, diligence and discretion" of the new notary. The reference to "discretion" was highly unusual, as notaries, particularly at that time in history, were not thought to be authorized to exercise discretionary judgment.

Chapter

5

Jurat (Verification on Oath or Affirmation) Notarizations

STANDARDS SUMMARY

5.1 The notary should understand the purpose and importance of the jurat form of document notarization.

5.2 The notary should understand the differences between a jurat, an acknowledgment, and a signature witnessing.

5.3 The notary should comply with the elements required for a jurat notarization, especially the requirement to administer an oral oath or affirmation to the document signer.

5.4 The notary should create a journal entry that correctly identifies and thoroughly records the jurat notarization, especially that includes administration of an oral oath or affirmation.

STANDARDS EXPLANATIONS

The jurat form of document notarization suffers from its Latin name which intimidates and confuses many people. But, the jurat should not be scary at all because it is not complex or difficult. If the name bothers some people, they should just call it by its longer synonym — a "verification on oath or affirmation." There is no difference in substance or procedure between the two. The jurat is also a popular type of notarization and is the type of notarization usually employed whenever an affidavit is involved. See a sample jurat notarial certificate at the end of this chapter under the heading "Relevant Model Notary Law."

5.1 The notary should understand the purpose and importance of the jurat form of document notarization.

Throughout history there has been a need for some important documents to be more trustworthy than other ordinary instruments, and the way to achieve the heightened reliability of special documents has been to have them verified upon oath or affirmation. In other words, the signers of documents will pledge by oral oath or affirmation that the contents of the documents are true and correct, with the major legal consequence that if the signers knowingly include falsehoods in the notarized documents, the signers can be charged with the crime of perjury and punished accordingly. A classic example of such a document is the affidavit, which is used to support statements filed in courts, administrative agencies, arbitrations, and in numerous other settings.

The term jurat is from a Latin word meaning "to swear." So, a jurat is the certification by the notary that the document has been sworn to, or affirmed by, the document signer. This outcome is accomplished when the document signer presently signs the document in the presence of the notary and during the same ceremony takes an oral oath or affirmation administered by the notary attesting to the truth of the material recited in the document.

It is the administration of the oath or affirmation by a public official, in this case the notary, that subjects the document signer to the law of perjury — such that a knowing falsehood contained in a document bearing a jurat notarization would subject the dishonest signer to possible criminal prosecution for perjury. On the contrary, if no oath or affirmation is administered by the notary, there can be no crime of perjury committed by a document signer who includes false statements in the instrument.

Thus, the great value of the jurat notarization is that it heightens the security of documents in three substantial ways. It gives assurance about the identity of the signer, it establishes that the signer executed a present signature at the time of the notarization, and it provides a degree of credibility to the substantive contents of the notarized document (or, at least the expectation that the threat of a perjury prosecution will have deterred the signer from swearing falsely to information in the document).

5.2 The notary should understand the differences between a jurat, an acknowledgment, and a signature witnessing.

The jurat type of document notarization is particularly important because it is the only form of notarization in which the document signer pledges, subject to the law of perjury, that the information contained in the instrument is true and correct. Only a jurat type of document notarization includes an oral oath or affirmation administered by the notary, which is why this form of notarization is also called a "verification on oath or affirmation." Neither an acknowledgment nor a signature witnessing involves the signer taking an oral oath or affirmation.

The jurat also requires a present signature of the document signer because the notarization can only occur with the document signer being present and doing two things during the notarial ceremony: (1) signing the document and (2) swearing to or affirming the document's truthfulness. Thus, a jurat is unlike an acknowledgment, which may involve a signature executed prior to the time of the notarization (an existing signature that is simply acknowledged at the notarial ceremony).

5.3 The notary should comply with the elements required for a jurat notarization, especially the requirement to administer an oral oath or affirmation to the document signer.

Importantly, as with the other kinds of notarizations of documents, the certificate of notarization (which is usually preprinted or typed onto the end of the transactional document) should reveal the type of notarial act that is to be performed. In the case of the jurat, there will be a reference in the certificate to the document signer "swearing or affirming on oath" or that the document has been "subscribed and sworn to." Incidentally, the certificate will not contain the actual language of the oral oath or affirmation, but it will always reference the administration of an oath or affirmation. Interestingly, the notarial certificate will almost never include a reference to the term "jurat," although when an affidavit is prepared, it will usually be labeled "affidavit."

The law does not specify which element is to be performed first — the administration of the oral oath or affirmation to the document signer, or the present signature of the document signer. This author suggests that the oral oath or affirmation should be administered first, followed by the signing of the document signer. This sequence makes sense because the signing then confirms that the oath or affirmation was in fact administered.

It should be emphasized that the notary is required to actually administer an oral oath or affirmation. Unfortunately, the failure of notaries to really administer oaths and affirmations during jurat notarization ceremonies is probably the most common fault of U.S. notaries, and this serious fault leaves many jurat notarizations subject to possible challenge and invalidation. Alarmingly, various notary authorities, including this author, have estimated that notaries fail to actually administer an oral oath or affirmation in the great majority of jurats — perhaps in 80% or more of all jurat notarizations. It is a very serious fault because it involves the misrepresentation and dishonesty by notaries in falsely completing their jurat certificates, which recite the administration of oaths or affirmations. Each is a certification of a lie. This problem is the reason why this section emphasizes the need for notaries to actually administer the oaths or affirmations orally. Of course, as with each type of notarization, the notary should meticulously perform each required step and fully complete both the notarial certificate and the journal entry.

Suggested language for an oath or affirmation appears in Chapter 15, which addresses issues relating to oaths and affirmations.

Since the notarial certificate records the official steps the notary has taken in the course of the notarization, the jurat certificate should note both the administration of the oath or affirmation and should note the execution of the signer's signature in the presence of the notary. Additionally, both of those steps should be confirmed by the notary in a journal entry for the jurat notarization (as described in the section immediately below). See also the discussion of oaths and affirmations in Chapter 15 and the discussion of notarial certificates in Chapter 7.

5.4 The notary should create a journal entry that correctly identifies and thoroughly records the jurat notarization, especially that includes the administration of an oral oath or affirmation.

Because each of the three types of document notarizations is different from the other two, it is most important for the notary to correctly identify the kind of notarial act performed in the notary journal entry. The correct identification provides evidence that the notary knew the requirements for the type of notarization identified and complied with those required steps.

By completing the journal entry before filling in the notarial certificate, the notary can then use the journal entry as a road map of sorts to help guide the notary correctly through the notarization and the filling in of the certificate.

Most current notary journals include a column or space referencing the administration of an oath or affirmation. If you are a notary and your notary journal does not have such a category, then you should change journals. The notary should perform all the required steps of the notarization and complete both the notarial certificate and journal entry, especially the confirmation of the administration of the oral oath or affirmation because it is the unique feature of a jurat and is so often neglected. Without the oral oath or affirmation, the central purpose of a jurat is lost. See also the discussion of oaths and affirmation in Chapter 15 and of notary journals in Chapter 17. ■

***RELEVANT MODEL NOTARY LAW**

Each notary should read, study, and abide by the notary statute and regulations, if any, of his or her commissioning state or territory.

(3) For a verification on oath or affirmation:

State of ______________________________

[County] of ____________________________

Signed and sworn to (or affirmed) before me on ________ by ____________________
Date — Name(s) of individual(s) making statement

____
Signature of notarial officer

Stamp

[______________________________]
Title of office

[My commission expires: ________]

Revised Uniform Law on Notarial Acts, Section 16(3) (2010).

"To always be satisfied that the individual appearing before me understands the contents of the document to be executed or oath to be administered before proceeding;

To always satisfy myself as to the identity of the individual appearing before me in my capacity as Notary Public; ...

To keep informed of the law regarding the duties and powers of the office of Notary Public in my jurisdiction and not compromise that law ..." *Responsibility Code of Ethics* (1980).

"The Notary shall require the presence of each signer and oath-taker in order to carefully screen each for identity and willingness, and to observe that each appears aware of the significance of the transaction requiring a notarial act." *Notary Public Code of Professional Responsibility*, Guiding Principle III (1998).

"The Notary shall not execute a false or incomplete certificate, nor be involved with any document or transaction that the Notary believes is false, deceptive or fraudulent." *Notary Public Code of Professional Responsibility*, Guiding Principle IV (1998).

"The Notary shall give precedence to the rules of law over the dictates or expectations of any person or entity." *Notary Public Code of Professional Responsibility*, Guiding Principle V (1998).

"The Notary shall record every notarial act in a bound journal or other secure recording device and safeguard it as an important public record." *Notary Public Code of Professional Responsibility*, Guiding Principle VIII (1998).

"Powers of Notary. A notary is empowered to perform the following notarial acts: (1) acknowledgments; (2) oaths and affirmations; (3) jurats; (4) signature witnessings ..." *Model Notary Act*, Section 5-1 (2010).

"Requirements for Notarial Acts. A notary shall perform a notarial act only if the principal [document signer]: (1) is in the presence of the notary at the time of notarization; (2) is personally known to the notary or identified by the notary through satisfactory evidence; (3) appears to understand the nature of the transaction requiring a notarial act; (4) appears to be acting of his or her own free will; (5) signs using letters or characters of a language that is understood by the notary; and (6) communicates directly with the notary in a language both understand." *Model Notary Act*, Section 5-2 (2010).

"Jurat. 'Jurat' means a notarial act in which an individual at a single time and place: (1) appears in person before the notary and presents a document; (2) is personally known to the notary or identified by the notary through satisfactory evidence; (3) signs the document in the presence of the notary; and (4) takes an oath or affirmation from the notary vouching for the truthfulness or accuracy of the signed document." *Model Notary Act*, Section 2-7 (2010).

1997, cover of the 630-page *Notary Law & Practice: Cases & Materials* by Michael Closen, Glen-Peter Ahlers, Robert Jarvis, Malcolm Morris and Nancy Spyke. It was published by the National Notary Association.

Chapter

6

Signature-Witnessing Notarizations

STANDARDS SUMMARY

6.1 The notary should understand the purpose and importance of the signature-witnessing form of document notarization.

6.2 The notary should understand the differences between a signature witnessing, an acknowledgment, and a jurat (verification on oath or affirmation).

6.3 The notary should comply with the elements required for a signature-witnessing notarization, especially the requirement of a present signature of the document signer.

6.4 The notary should create a journal entry that correctly identifies and thoroughly records the signature-witnessing notarization, especially that includes the signer's present signature.

STANDARDS EXPLANATIONS

Many, although not all, U.S. jurisdictions authorize their notaries to perform the kind of document notarization called a "signature witnessing." It is the newest of the three kinds of document notarizations, and it is the simplest and most basic form of document notarization. See a sample form for a signature-witnessing notarial certificate at the end of this chapter under the heading "Relevant Model Notary Law."

6.1 The notary should understand the purpose and importance of the signature-witnessing form of document notarization.

Because the signature witnessing is the simplest form of document notarization, it is a valuable type of notarization which should grow in usefulness as time progresses. When a simple present signature of the document signer on an instrument is all that is needed, the signature-witnessing form of notarization fills the bill. This is because it should be remembered all document notarizations must satisfy the same fundamental requirements — namely, that all signers must appear at the time of the notarizations, that all signers must be identified with reasonable certainty, that all notarized instruments must be voluntarily entered into by the signers, and that all signers must be mentally competent to execute lawful signatures.

6.2 The notary should understand the differences between a signature witnessing, an acknowledgment, and a jurat (verification on oath or affirmation).

Every notary should know the differences, not by rote, but by truly understanding what each of the notarizations is all about. For a signature witnessing, the document signer merely executes a present signature on the transactional document. The signer cannot have signed the document prior to the notarization ceremony (that is allowed only for an acknowledgment). The signer is not placed under oath or affirmation (that is done only for a jurat).

6.3 The notary should comply with the elements required for a signature-witnessing notarization, especially the requirement of a present signature of the document signer.

Simplification can be advantageous. As already noted, for a signature witnessing, a present signature of the document signer executed in the physical presence of the notary at the time of the notarization is required. There can be no signing prior to the notarization ceremony, and no oath or affirmation is required.

This simplified notarization still requires the usual steps to be taken with the other types of document notarizations, including especially the need for the physical presence of the signer at the notarization. It has been pointed out that the most serious and very frequent violation committed by notaries is their failure to insist upon the physical presence of signers at notarial ceremonies.

The signature witnessing notarization should also be recorded by the notary in a contemporaneous journal entry. Thus, although a signature witnessing is simplified in substance, it should be just as secure and well-recorded as other notarial formats. See also the discussion of notary journal entries in Chapter 17.

6.4 The notary should create a journal entry that correctly identifies and thoroughly records the signature-witnessing notarization, especially that includes the signer's present signature.

Every proper notary journal form includes a space in its format where the notary is asked to identify the type of notarization performed. That space elicits the most basic information but is quite important. The notary should correctly identify the type of notarization, in this instance a "signature witnessing." This space is so important because, if the notary can correctly identify the type of notarization, then presumably the notary is familiar with the procedure for conducting such a notarization. But, if the wrong kind of notarization is listed, the opposite conclusion is suggested.

Case Illustration. Several years ago, this author was retained to consult as an expert to testify in a lawsuit against a notary who had performed more than 1,000 notarizations, which had been recorded in her notary journals. On review of those journals, I discovered that every one of the more than 1,000 entries had identified the type of notarization performed as an "acknowledgment." There was never a "jurat" and never a "signature witnessing." It became quickly and abundantly clear as I considered the type of document also identified in the journal entries and as I examined several notarial certificates for some of those notarizations that the notary had incorrectly identified the type of notarial act performed for many of the notarizations. The large number of notarial acts misidentified in the notary's journal revealed the notary's misunderstanding of basic notarial knowledge. These numerous errors undoubtedly created a negative image of the notary in the minds of the jurors.

A notary should meticulously complete the journal entry. There is a space in the journal format to obtain the present signature of the document signer, showing that the signer was actually present for the ceremony and avoiding an all-too-common and serious fault committed by notaries. See also the discussions of notary journals in Chapter 17. ■

***RELEVANT MODEL NOTARY LAW**

Each notary should read, study, and abide by the notary statute and regulations, if any, of her or his commissioning state or territory.

(4) For witnessing or attesting a signature:

State of ______________________

[County] of ______________________

Signed [or attested] before me on ________ by ______________________
Date Name(s) of individual(s)

____
Signature of notarial officer

Stamp

[______________________]
Title of office

[My commission expires: ________]

Revised Uniform Law on Notarial Acts, Section 16(4) (2010).

"To always be satisfied that the individual appearing before me understands the contents of the document to be executed or oath to be administered before proceeding;

To always satisfy myself as to the identity of the individual appearing before me in my capacity as Notary Public; ...

To keep informed of the law regarding the duties and powers of the office of Notary Public in my jurisdiction and not compromise that law ..." *Responsibility Code of Ethics* (1980).

"The Notary shall require the presence of each signer and oath-taker in order to carefully screen each for identity and willingness, and to observe that each appears aware of the significance of the transaction requiring a notarial act." *Notary Public Code of Professional Responsibility*, Guiding Principle III (1998).

"The Notary shall not execute a false or incomplete certificate, nor be involved with any document or transaction that the Notary believes is false, deceptive or fraudulent." *Notary Public Code of Professional Responsibility*, Guiding Principle IV (1998).

"The Notary shall give precedence to the rules of law over the dictates or expectations of any person or entity." *Notary Public Code of Professional Responsibility*, Guiding Principle V (1998).

"The Notary shall affix a notary seal on every notarized document and not allow this universally recognized symbol of office to be used by another or in an endorsement or promotion." *Notary Public Code of Professional Responsibility*, Guiding Principle VII (1998).

"The Notary shall record every notarial act in a bound journal or other secure recording device and safeguard it as an important public record." *Notary Public Code of Professional Responsibility*, Guiding Principle VIII (1998).

"Powers of Notary. A notary is empowered to perform the following notarial acts: (1) acknowledgments; (2) oaths and affirmations; (3) jurats; (4) signature witnessings ..." *Model Notary Act*, Section 5-1 (2010).

"Requirements for Notarial Acts. A notary shall perform a notarial act only if the principal [document signer]: (1) is in the presence of the notary at the time of notarization; (2) is personally known to the notary or identified by the notary through satisfactory evidence; (3) appears to understand the nature of the transaction requiring a notarial act; (4) appears to be acting of his or her own free will; (5) signs using letters or characters of a language that is understood by the notary; and (6) communicates directly with the notary in a language both understand." *Model Notary Act*, Section 5-2 (2010).

“Signature Witnessing. ‘Signature witnessing’ means a notarial act in which an individual at a single time and place: (1) appears in person before the notary and presents a document; (2) is personally known to the notary or identified by the notary through satisfactory evidence; and (3) signs the document in the presence of the notary.” *Model Notary Act*, Section 2-21 (2010).

2015, cover of the 126-page *Florida Notary Handbook*, published by the American Society of Notaries.

Chapter

7

Notary's Certificate of Notarization

STANDARDS SUMMARY

7.1 The notary should understand the purpose of the notarial certificate is to record and certify the steps that have been taken in performing the notarization.

7.2 The notary should complete a certificate of notarization for each document notarization to create a written record of the notarization and to provide a symbol of officiality.

7.3 The notary should not sign, or affix an official seal impression on, a notarial certificate prior to a document notarization ceremony.

7.4 The notary should complete the notarial certificate after creating the notary journal entry for the notarization.

7.5 The notary should complete a notarial certificate to facilitate the cross-border recognition of the notarization in other states, territories, and countries, especially including an official notary seal impression.

7.6 The notary should complete a thorough notarial certificate, including the venue, date, type of notarization, document signer's name and method of identification, notary's signature and seal, and other data.

7.7 The notary should be careful to satisfy the law's requirement to at least substantially comply with recording of the prescribed elements of the notarial certificate.

7.8 The notary should, when possible, have the document signer's signature appear on the transactional instrument on the same page with the notarial certificate.

7.9 The notary should securely affix the notarial certificate to the notarized instrument in such a manner as to prevent or reveal its removal or the substitution of an unauthorized certificate.

7.10 The notary should proofread the notarial certificate and make any needed additions or corrections to it prior to the completion of the notarial ceremony.

7.11 The notary should, if an error is later discovered in a completed notarial certificate, not attempt to alter the certificate.

7.12 The notary should, if an error is later discovered in a completed notarial certificate and if requested by the document signer, perform a new and correct notarization.

STANDARDS EXPLANATIONS

If a document is going to be notarized, there has to be a place where the facts of notarization are recorded and certified. Since the act of notarization has legal significance and is the act of a public officer, the area where the notarization is set out is called the "certificate of notarization," or the "notarial certificate," or the "notary certificate." Those phrases emphasize the fact that the certificate is the exclusive province of the notary, acting in the capacity of a commissioned public official.

Additionally, it should be emphasized that the notarial certificate is a separate document unto itself — that simply happens usually to appear on the same page as part of the transactional instrument which is being notarized by the certificate. In some jurisdictions, such as California, a separate "loose" notarial certificate is expressly recognized or required, which "loose" certificate is to be attached at the end of the transactional instrument. Typically the notarial certificate appears as the last portion of the combination of the transactional document and notarial certificate. The certificate commonly appears immediately after the signature area of the document that is to be notarized.

Even though the notarial certificate is the notary's certificate, it most often has been typed or preprinted by someone else after the end of the instrument to be notarized (although the notary could actually handwrite or type the certificate). It is written, typed, or pre-printed with blank spaces to be filled in by the notary during the notarial ceremony. That is, someone else has usually composed and prepared the certificate, which the notary then adopts. If the notary wishes to make changes to the certificate, the notary may do so, because it is the notary's certificate. Therefore, regardless of how the notarial certificate is composed and attached to the document to be notarized, the ultimate responsibility for its format and substance resides completely with the notary.

Practice Tip: *Certificate's Significance.* Because of the great importance of the notarial certificate, this chapter is one of the most important chapters in the book. Notaries should pay special attention here, as this material is about the notary's document — the certificate of notarization.

7.1 The notary should understand the purpose of the notarial certificate is to record and certify the steps that have been taken in performing the notarization.

As the name suggests, the notary certificate or certificate of notarization is the place where the notary certifies or states in detail the steps the notary has taken in performing the notarization. It is absolutely crucial to the performance of a proper notarization. It is the familiar official-looking segment usually appearing after the signature(s) at the end of a transactional instrument that should always contain an official notary seal impression. It looks official because it is an official governmental record of what transpired at the notarization.

Effectively, the certificate memorializes that a proper and lawful notarization was performed. Thus, the notary is the party solely responsible for the contents of the certificate, even if someone else has written or typed the form of the certificate. No one other than the notary should fill in the blank spaces in a notarial certificate because, as already noted, the certificate is itself a distinct document and is the exclusive province of the notary. Because the certificate is the official certification of a public officer, it is the equivalent of an oath or affirmation that its contents are true and correct. A false material statement knowingly made by the notary in the certificate constitutes a crime, usually called "official misconduct." Such an intentional material falsehood could be regarded as false swearing or perjury by the notary. And depending on the circumstances, it might constitute tampering with evidence or obstruction of justice. Thus, notaries should never falsify any of the information in a certificate. The notary should not record the wrong location of the notarization, or the wrong date of the notarial ceremony. The notary should not state that the signer was present for the notarization if the signer was absent. The notary should not state that the signer was sworn if no oral oath or affirmation was administered. Everything of consequence in the certificate must be truthful, or it's a crime.

Practice Tip: *How to Visualize the Certificate.* Think of it this way. The certificate is the exclusive domain of the notary. Only the notary writes on the preprinted or pretyped certificate. No one else writes anything there. The document signer does not sign the notarial certificate; the signer signs the transactional instrument (the document to be notarized). On the other hand, the notary should not write anything at all on the instrument to be notarized. The document signer will sign that transactional instrument, and perhaps the signer will date it and initial and number the pages. Perhaps, a witness will sign the transactional instrument, or a lawyer will date and number the pages. But, the notary should not write anything on the transactional document. So, notaries must be strictly territorial — they write on the certificate, and they do not allow anyone else to do so.

Incidentally, a total of three distinct documents should result from each documentary notarization — (1) the transactional document that is notarized, (2) the notary's certificate of notarization, and (3) the notary journal entry for the notarization. See the discussion of the notary journal in Chapter 17.

7.2 The notary should complete a certificate of notarization for each document notarization to create a written record of the notarization and to provide a symbol of officiality.

The notary bears the duty to perform a lawful notarization of a document that will be upheld in the face of a legal challenge and that will assist the document and its notarization to be recognized far and wide. In this regard, the notary's certificate serves both symbolic and substantive purposes. The appearance of the notary's certificate is significant in both domestic and international commerce and governmental affairs.

Although two states permit document notarizations without notarial certificates, the other U.S. states and territories require certificates of notarization. Those two states do not prohibit the use of notarial certificates, although notaries there should not take it upon themselves to add certificates. Instead, document signers in those states should select and add the appropriate certificate forms to their documents.

Business people and government agents expect to see a certificate with an official seal on notarized instruments, and when a notarial certificate appears on a document, that certificate causes the document to be treated with greater respect and deference. The presence of a notarial certificate, which is complete and lawful on its face, raises the presumption of the validity of the notarization and of the authenticity of the transactional document and makes the transactional document with its certificate presumptively admissible in evidence. The notarial certificate gives the notarized instrument an air of officiality. These consequences are significant because they mean the presence of the certificate verifies and validates the notarization, unless a party comes forward to challenge a notarization with evidence to establish it contains material faults or is fraudulent.

Most importantly, the notary certificate is the symbol of the notarization. Without the required notarial certificate having been completed, there can be no notarization. Thus, a notary should never simply sign, or sign and seal, a document without certificate wording — even if the law of a particular state or territory might unwisely allow such a practice. The notary certificate converts an ordinary document into a special document with legal significance, for it has then been witnessed and certified by an independent and impartial public official. See the discussion of domestic and international recognition of notarial acts in Chapter 27. The notarial certificate is an official public record that should be corroborated by another official record, namely a notary journal entry for the notarization in question. See the discussion of the notary journal in Chapter 17.

Practice Tip: *Always Certify.* This tip addresses a real concern because signers sometimes bring to notaries only the documents they wish to have notarized, with no certificates attached. Some notaries might then be tempted to simply sign, date, and seal the documents without notarial certificate language. Notaries should not do so. The absence of a certificate will cause the purported "notarization" to be invalid everywhere in the U.S., except in two states. Notaries faced with documents lacking attached notarial certificates should request document signers to provide or select the form of certificate to be attached. Notaries could provide sample certificate forms from which signers could choose and attach to their documents.

7.3 The notary should not sign, or affix an official seal impression on, a notarial certificate prior to a document notarization ceremony.

Notary statutes, regulations, and ethics standards make clear that a notarial certificate should only be prepared at the time of the notarial ceremony. Besides, it seems obvious that signing by the notary should be the last step in the process of completing the notarial certificate, as the notary's signature there certifies the previous steps in the notarization procedure.

Notaries may sometimes be tempted to sign and affix seal impressions on uncompleted notarial certificates in advance of notarial ceremonies to expedite future notarizations. Such temptation is particularly attractive to notaries who perform large quantities of notarizations. However, this practice is dangerous and improper. Furthermore, it may be a start down the slippery slope toward intentional misconduct by the notaries who begin partially completing certificates in advance.

Notarial certificates and notarizations can be falsified and misused. One of the easiest ways for a non-notary to falsify a notarization is to obtain a partially completed notarial certificate already bearing a notary's signature and/or official seal impression. A wrongdoer could then simply fill in the blank spaces of the certificate to fit a document and circumstances that fulfill the wrongdoer's fraudulent scheme.

The other problem with signing and sealing certificates in advance is the temptation for the notary who does so to engage in further misconduct. Since partial completion of certificates in advance is unlawful, the next step is to allow other parties to use the partially completed certificates to fill in the remaining information, thereby involving impersonation of the notary and falsification of the notarizations.

7.4 The notary should complete the notarial certificate after creating the notary journal entry for the notarization.

Even though the notarial certificate is effectively the most important writing reflecting that a notarization has been performed, there is a major pragmatic problem regarding the certificate. That is, the certificate is affixed to the underlying instrument, and when the notarization ceremony is complete, the document signer usually takes away the transactional instrument with the certificate attached to it. The notary is left without a copy of the completed notarial certificate. This result is the main reason for the notary to keep and maintain a notary journal of all official acts.

It should be emphasized for reasons to be addressed later in this book that the notary must not make or retain copies of notarized instruments, of notarial certificates, or of ID documents associated with notarizations — as the notary journal entry will suffice as the method for adequate notary record-keeping. Moreover, maintaining copies of the highly confidential information contained in transactional documents and ID documents risks breaches of security and privacy. See the discussion of confidentiality and privacy issues in Chapter 18.

The notary journal entry for the notarization should be started first, prior to the completion of the notarial certificate. Almost all of the information appearing in a notarial certificate will have been entered into the notary journal entry, for the journal and the certificate go hand in hand and complement one another. When completed first, the journal entry will serve to guide the notary through the completion of the certificate, and that sequence should enhance the likelihood of accuracy in the performance of the notarization as reflected in the notary certificate. Additionally, an advantage of preparing the journal entry first is that the required elements of the notarization will have to be performed and entered into the journal's fields one element at a time — such as obtaining a present signature of the signer in the journal, proper identification of the signer, assessment of the signer's willingness, and assessment of the signer's mental competence. If for any reason the notarization must be refused by the notary, the basic information needed to record the refusal in the journal will already have been obtained and recorded. So, the signer cannot simply walk away from a refused notarization before the notary has had time to collect the basic information needed to record the refusal. See also the discussion of journal entries in Chapter 17.

7.5 The notary should complete a notarial certificate to facilitate the cross-border recognition of the notarization in other states, territories, and countries, especially including an official notary seal impression.

Tradition matters. Appearance matters. Importantly, both of those factors matter in regard to the cross-border recognition of document notarizations.

In this era of the frequent mobility of documents and transactions between the states and territories of the U.S., the presence of a complete notarial certificate attached to a transactional document will assist its acceptance and recognition by private and public agents of business and government entities across U.S. borders. All U.S. states and territories have enacted laws authorizing and governing the notarization of instruments, all have enacted laws for the interstate and interterritorial recognition of notarizations, and the jurisdictions are therefore well-acquainted with the presence of notarial certificates on documents. The appearance of a notary seal on a notarial certificate is a longstanding tradition throughout the U.S., although several states do not require their notaries to possess and use such seals. No state or territory prohibits its notaries from affixing seals on notarized instruments, and because notaries will not know where their notarizations will travel, all notaries are well-advised to affix seal impressions to their certificates.

Even more so in the international arena, notarial certificates on instruments are expected and valuable for cross-border recognition. After all, the notaries of the rest of the world (the civil law notaries and the English notaries) have been in existence for centuries longer than U.S. notaries, and their notarizations have been traveling across international borders since long before the birth of the U.S. In this era of the global village, the frequency of the international use and exchange of instruments can only be expected to increase. Authorities in most other countries of the world expect and require notarized instruments to be accompanied by certificates, especially bearing official notarial seals. Tradition and appearance matter in regard to the presence of notary seals. See the discussion of notary seals in Chapter 8 and of domestic and transnational notarization recognition in Chapter 27.

7.6 The notary should complete a thorough notarial certificate, including the venue, date, type of notarization, document signer's name and method of identification, notary's signature and seal, and other data.

The presence and proper completion of the notarial certificate establishes that a valid and lawful document notarization has been accomplished — and, in turn, that an authentic transactional instrument is attached to it. Furthermore, the detailed notarial certificate makes the misuse, alteration, or forgery of a document much more difficult. A proper notary certificate includes a special format and formal language reciting the name of the document signer(s), the details about the notarization, its venue, the present date, the signature of the notary, and an impression of the official notary seal (which is uniquely manufactured to identify the particular notary). If a notarized document is to be misused, altered, or forged by someone planning mischief, the detailed elements of the completed notary certificate will pose obstacles to such wrongdoing. These same detailed features will assist in securing interstate and international recognition of notarized instruments.

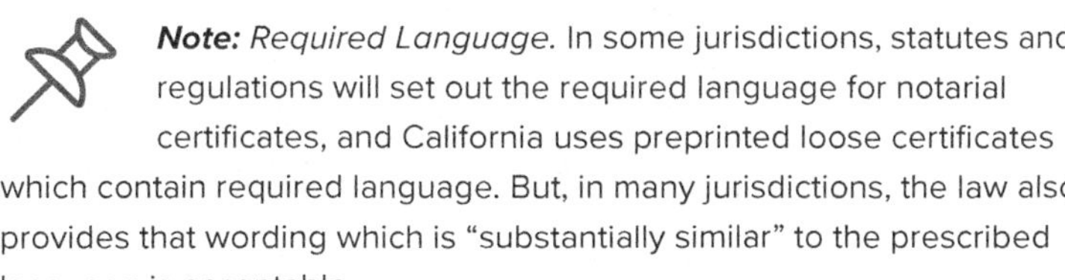

Note: *Required Language.* In some jurisdictions, statutes and regulations will set out the required language for notarial certificates, and California uses preprinted loose certificates which contain required language. But, in many jurisdictions, the law also provides that wording which is "substantially similar" to the prescribed language is acceptable.

Let us consider each of the elements of a thorough certificate of notarization. There should be at least eight such features. (1) the venue, (2) the present date, (3) the name of the document signer(s), (4) the method of identifying the signer(s), (5) a notation that the notary assessed the signer's mental competence and willingness to execute the document to be notarized, (6) the description of the notarial act, (7) the official notary seal impression, including or along with the notary commission expiration date, and (8) the notary's signature. Admittedly, many notarial certificates do not contain all of these elements, but they should. We should be moving in the direction of conforming the certificate to the current responsibilities of notaries to correctly identify document signers and to assess the mental competence and willingness of those signers.

1. The Venue. Most commonly, the very first portion of the certificate of notarization is designated as the venue section, in which the state or territory and the county or parish where the notarization was performed are identified. In the U.S., notaries have statewide or territory-wide authority to carry out their official duties. The information in the venue section is critical because it establishes that the notarization was performed within the area of the notary's jurisdiction. The county identified in the venue section should be the county where the notarial ceremony occurred, rather than the county where the notary was commissioned, resides, or has an office or place of business.

2. The Present Date. The date of a notarization is a critical piece of information to be recorded in the certificate, because the notary has jurisdiction or authority to perform notarizations only during the term of the notary's commission, i.e., from the start date to the end date of the commission. Hence, the date of a particular notarization must fall within those dates. The absolute rule is that the date appearing in the certificate of notarization is to be the present date — no exceptions. Regardless of what date appears on the transactional instrument, or on what date the instrument was signed, the present date must always appear on the notarial certificate. Thus, it is possible that the transactional instrument will bear one date, that it will have been signed by the document signer on a second date (in the case of an acknowledgment), and that the notarization will be performed on a third date — the present date. Notaries are not allowed to predate or postdate notarial certificates. The present date should also be recorded in the notary journal entry for the notarization, and if the instrument bears a different earlier date, or if the document signer had signed on an earlier date, those dates should be noted in the journal entry. See also the discussion of notary journal entries in Chapter 17.

3. The Name of the Document Signer(s). It is possible for a notary to notarize for more than one signer on the same transactional instrument, so long as the notary conducts a full notarial procedure for each signer. The purpose of this piece of information is to assure that a legible record of the signer's name is obtained. Further, the name of the signer and the signer's signatures on the other documents (the transactional instrument and ID[s]) should match the name in the notarial certificate. Ideally, the document signer will sign the transactional instrument at the time of the notarization (or possibly earlier for an acknowledgment), usually near the end of the instrument and immediately preceding the section for the certificate of notarization. The document signer should not sign within the certificate of notarization, for the certificate is the exclusive province of the notary. In the notarial certificate, only the name (not the signature) of the document signer should be typed, printed, or written in a legible manner — since many hand-scrawled signatures are not really legible. Incidentally, in a highly prepared instrument, the name of the document signer may be preprinted or pretyped not only in the instrument itself but also in the notarial certificate — and such practice is permissible. If by chance the document signer were to mistakenly sign in the certificate section itself, and if the signature is not readable, the notary can simply print or write the name of the signer in close proximity to the signature. Additionally, the notary should record the legible name of the signer in the journal entry for the notarization. See also the discussion of names and signatures in Chapter 11 and the discussion of notary journal entries in Chapter 17.

4. The Method of Identifying the Document Signer(s). Proper, reliable identification of document signers is one of the most important responsibilities of notaries. That is why the method of identifying the document signer(s) for each notarization should be noted by the notary in the notarial certificate — although many certificates are not currently formatted to include such a reference. The notary should indicate what ID document or documents were viewed and examined to establish the identity of the instrument signer(s). This same information will be recorded in the notary journal entry for the notarization. Incidentally, for the protection of the confidentiality and privacy of the signer, the notary should not record the serial number for the ID document, but instead, should record the type of document and its month and year of expiration (in both the certificate and the journal entry). For the record, almost every state and territory currently allows notaries to rely upon personal knowledge of the document signer to be the method of identification. However, it is this author's opinion that, even if the document signer is personally known to the notary, the notary should require every signer to produce one or more ID documents, in order to establish reasonable care exercised by the notary and to provide heightened reliability of the identification. See also the discussion of identification of document signers in Chapter 10 and the discussion of the notary journal in Chapter 17.

5. The Assessments of Signer Mental Competence and Willingness. Many notarial certificates are not presently formatted with language for the notary to confirm the assessment of the document signer's mental competence and willingness to execute the instrument to be notarized. This author believes this omission should be corrected to allow for a full certification by the notary of the steps taken in the process of the notarial ceremony. Perhaps, the format could include boxes to be checked or blank spaces to be marked by the notary to confirm the two assessments. Even if the notary certificate does not include a typed or printed reference to these two assessments, the notary should write a notation about the conduct of the two assessments to confirm they were done. Parenthetically, the assessments of mental competence and voluntariness should be corroborated in the notary journal entry for the notarization. See also the discussion of signer mental competence in Chapter 13, of signer willingness in Chapter 14, and of the notary journal in Chapter 17.

6. The Description of the Notarial Act. The notarial certificate is the written portion of the notarization in which the notary certifies what steps he or she has performed. This statement will identify and describe the kind of document notarization that has been conducted — whether an acknowledgment, a jurat, or a signature witnessing, although rarely do the certificates ever use those labels. Yet, it would be permissible and helpful to use those terms to identify the kind of document notarization involved. The notary certificate for an acknowledgment will typically reference the signer having acknowledged her or his signature. The notary certificate for a jurat will usually refer to the signer having been sworn. For a signature witnessing, the certificate will commonly refer simply to signing in the presence of the notary. See also the discussion of acknowledgments in Chapter 4, of jurats in Chapter 5, and of signature witnessings in Chapter 6. Sample notarial certificates are included in each of those chapters.

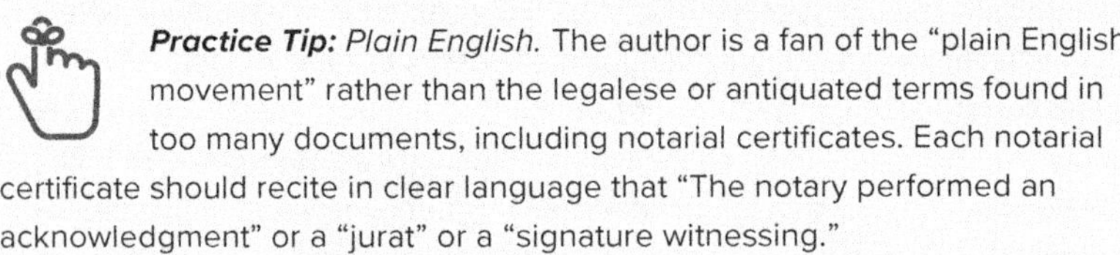

Practice Tip: *Plain English.* The author is a fan of the "plain English movement" rather than the legalese or antiquated terms found in too many documents, including notarial certificates. Each notarial certificate should recite in clear language that "The notary performed an acknowledgment" or a "jurat" or a "signature witnessing."

7. The Official Notary Seal Impression. The notary's seal impression should appear on the notarial certificate, regardless of whether required by state or territorial law. The inclusion of a seal impression is a highly valuable feature of a notarization, and no state or territory prohibits its notaries from possessing and affixing seals on notarial certificates. The notary should affix a clear and legible seal impression near the notary's signature. In addition to other information, the seal impression should include the state of commissioning and the date of the notary commission expiration, for the state and expiration date should confirm that the notary's commission is current and that the notary is authorized to perform the notarization within the identified state or territory. If the seal impression does not include the commission expiration date, the notary should write that information on the certificate near the notary's signature and seal impression. See also the discussion of notary seals in Chapter 8.

8. The Notary's Signature. The notary's signature constitutes an essential element of a notarial certificate, perhaps more important than the notary seal impression and perhaps the most important feature authenticating a notarization. After all, the notary is the commissioned public official who performs notarizations, so the notary's signature confirms the notary's identity. The notary should presently sign the certificate using blue or black ink. Some jurisdictions prescribe the use of black ink. The notary should sign the notary's name just as it appears on the notary commission and on the notary seal. A notary should never sign blank notarization forms in advance of notarizations, for such practice is forbidden and invites falsification of notarizations. See also the discussion of signatures in Chapter 11.

Practice Tip: *Blue Ink?* If the state or territorial law does not prescribe the use of black ink for the notary's signature on a notarial certificate, this author recommends the use of blue ink. The reason is that, if black ink is used for the notary's signature, it can be nearly impossible to tell whether the certificate is original or a photocopy. But, if the notary signs with blue ink, the original certificate will be readily identifiable because a standard photocopy will reproduce the image in black ink. Even a color photocopy will not ordinarily reproduce a blue signature of sufficient quality to look original.

Practice Tip: *Multiple Original Notarial Certificates.* Sometimes, parties will wish to have multiple original records of notarizations of the same instrument signed by the same signer. In litigation practice under the law of evidence, there is the "best evidence rule," which insists that original documents be produced because they represent the best evidence on a matter. Creating multiple original notarial certificates is permissible and can be satisfied by the notary, if the notary performs multiple notarizations. The notary should perform one notarial ceremony, record each notarization in a separate notarial certificate, and complete one journal entry (noting the number of identical document notarizations performed).

7.7 The notary should be careful to satisfy the law's requirement to at least substantially comply with recording of the prescribed elements of the notarial certificate.

What happens if the notary makes a mistake in completing one or more elements of the certificate? The question could be posed whether notaries public are required by law to perform their duties perfectly. Or, in other words, if a notary does not perform perfectly, will the resulting imperfect notarization be invalid? Since notaries are human and therefore susceptible to making occasional errors and omissions, a legal requirement of perfect notarial performance would be unrealistic. It would also result in the harsh result for document signers or parties relying upon documents that the imperfect notarizations would be invalid even if only minor errors or omissions were committed by notaries. Not surprisingly, the law does not require notaries to act perfectly in order to comply with legal requirements.

Since the government can act only through its public officials, who are human and susceptible to committing errors and omissions, the law does not require government agents to perform perfectly. It requires public officers to substantially comply with legal requirements. If public officials have made errors and/or omissions in their performance but have, nevertheless, substantially complied with statutory and regulatory requirements, their official acts are held to be valid.

The common law has correctly held that a notarization will be valid provided the notary has substantially complied with the legal requirements for the notarization, which effectively means that the notarial certificate will be the focus of attention. The notarial certificate certifies what the notary did in the course of the notarization. Thus, a notarization may suffer from one or more faults, but the fault or faults will only be fatal to the notarization if, under all of the circumstances, the notarial certificate does not substantially comply with legal requirements. Importantly, this legal test means that each case of a challenge to a faulty notarization will be unique. Each case will have to be decided on its own peculiar facts.

The analysis of the full circumstances will include the significance of the error or omission, who is challenging the validity of the notarization (the document signer or a third party who has relied upon the notarized document), whether a journal entry was prepared for the notarization, whether the error or omission was known or should have been known to the document signer or to a third party who has relied upon the notarized document, the recollections of the parties (the notary, document signer, any witnesses, and the third party who relied upon the notarization), and other relevant considerations.

Most important is the question whether the error or omission can be cured or corrected by referring to the transactional instrument and/or the notary journal entry for the notarization. Often, the content of the notarized document or the journal entry will refer to a subject about which the error or omission occurred in the notarial certificate. If so, and if the subject was correctly included in the notarized document and/or the journal entry, a court would likely conclude the notary had substantially complied with the legal requirements and would approve the notarization.

Certainly, some notarial defects are far more serious than others. The failure of the notary to sign the certificate or to affix the notary seal are significant. Whereas, the omission of the present date from the certificate, or an incorrect date in the certificate, may be less serious, especially if the correct date appears in the notarized document and/or the journal entry. The same could be said of the failure to include the name of the document signer in the certificate, or placing an incorrect name of the signer in the certificate, if that mistake is a technical glitch. This technical glitch would be shown by the correct signature appearing on the transactional document and by the correct name and signature appearing in the journal entry. Again, each case will be unique. The test is whether the notarial certificate is in substantial compliance with its legal requirements under all of the circumstances (including the circumstance of correct information being found elsewhere in the documents involved in a notarization). See also the discussion of the notary journal in Chapter 17.

7.8 The notary should, when possible, have the document signer's signature appear on the transactional instrument on the same page with the notarial certificate.

Most of the time, notaries have no control over the format of the instruments they notarize. Yet, poor formatting of instruments may result in heightened opportunities for wrongdoers to alter or tamper with instruments once notarizations have been completed. Indeed, notaries should not be acting as the notaries on documents they have prepared, as there would be a conflict of interest in such situations. See the discussion of notary ethics and conflicts of interest in Chapter 19.

The obvious reason to have both the signer's signature and the notary certificate appear on the same page is to deter forgery and fraud. The best practice for the formatting of a document to be notarized is to have part of the text of the document, the document signer's signature, and the notarial certificate appear on the same page. It will make the falsification of the certificate more difficult. If the notarial certificate is placed on a separate page, that page could be removed and replaced with a forged certificate. However, in order to falsify a page containing text, the signer's signature, and the notarial certificate, all three elements would have to be reproduced and forged and would have to fit together — a very substantial task. In order to falsify a page containing just the signer's signature and the notarial certificate, a wrongdoer would have to forge both the signer's signature and the notary certificate — a less substantial, but worthy, challenge.

It will often not be possible for the notary to control whether the notarial certificate appears on the same page as the signer's signature. Yet, when notaries are asked in advance about the format, they should have the signer's signature and the notarial certificate appear on the same page.

The notary should use the journal entry as the place to note any concern about the format of the document, such as the location of the certificate on a separate page. If the certificate does appear on a separate page, all of the pages should be numbered, including the page for the certificate. The total number of pages should be noted in the journal entry. See also the discussion of the notary journal in Chapter 17.

7.9 The notary should securely affix the notarial certificate to the notarized instrument in such a manner as to prevent or reveal its removal or the substitution of an unauthorized certificate.

The various pages of multipage instruments that are notarized should not be allowed to remain loose, be placed next to one another in file folders or envelopes, or be held together merely by paper clips. Such loose or nominally attached pages are tempting targets for forgery, tampering, and document fraud.

Practice Tip: *Self-Protection.* The notary should remember that document security is about protection not only for the signer and parties relying on the notarized document but also for the notary. If an imposter or other wrongdoer commits document fraud, and if someone is injured financially, the notary's performance will be examined to determine whether the notary contributed to the successful fraud and financial injury. The notary could face claims of misconduct and liability. Hence, it is in the notary's self-interest to be savvy and diligent about document security.

A conscientious and diligent notary should take steps to protect document security by attaching the notarial certificate to the transactional instrument in such a way that its removal and/or substitution will be evident. The pages of the instrument and its certificate should be stapled together, although it is even possible that staples can be removed and the pages carefully restapled through the same staple holes. But, stapling does help security to some extent.

If the pages are not already numbered, the notary should request the document signer to number and initial all of the pages of the instrument to be notarized, including the page containing the notarial certificate. The notary should ask that the last two pages be notated to refer to one another (or what is called incorporation by reference). Notaries have no authority to write upon transactional documents outside the areas of the notarial certificates, and notaries cannot require signers to number and initial pages, nor to notate pages to refer to one another. Yet, if document signers are unwilling to cooperate in taking these modest, sensible, and reasonable security measures, notaries could refuse to notarize or at least could and should note these security issues in the journal entry.

Practice Tip: *Use of an Embosser Seal to Link Pages.* Another security procedure that will help attach or link pages together is for the notary, in addition to using an ink-stamp notary seal on the notarial certificate, to utilize an embosser notary seal to press through the last two or three pages of the notarized instrument and certificate. When the embosser seal is pressed through the pages at the same time, the pages and the embosser impressions will line up exactly. It would be almost impossible to remove and substitute the last page, because the substituted page would not match the embosser seal or its location. See also the discussion of notary seals in Chapter 8.

Further, the notary should use the notary journal entry as the place to record anything important about the format of the transactional instrument. For instance, if the notary takes steps to have the pages of the instrument numbered and initialed, those steps should be noted in the journal entry. The total number of pages should be noted in the journal, as well as the tactic of having the last two pages incorporate one another by reference or the tactic of using an embosser seal on the final pages. See also the discussion of the notary journal in Chapter 17.

7.10 The notary should proofread the notarial certificate and make any needed additions or corrections to it prior to the completion of the notarial ceremony.

Proofreading is a step that should become habit with everyone on every piece of writing of consequence, especially on an instrument which will be seen by more than just its writer. I proofread every email, letter, and check that I send. I proofread every checkbook entry and income tax record entry that I make. Everyone makes simple, stupid mistakes at times — mistakes which should be detected and corrected upon proofreading. Proofreading is simply a daily practice of diligent and prudent individuals. The same should especially be true for all notaries, for all of the certificates they prepare.

The notary's certificate must be proofread before the notarization ceremony is completed. The reason is that corrections can be made to a notary's certificate if errors or omissions are discovered before the notarization is completed. Once the notarization is finished, it is too late to make any changes or corrections (see the next section concerning a difference of view on this point). If a serious and uncorrected mistake has been made to a notarization, the notarization may be challenged and may be invalidated, and a new notarization may be the only way to effectively correct the fault. However, in the case of a time-sensitive notarized instrument or transaction, it may be too late even to execute a new notarization.

The most common error that is likely to be found at the proofreading stage is an omission. An omission can easily be cured by simply filling in the necessary information. The proofreading should be performed after both the notary journal entry and the notary's certificate have initially been completed, and both the journal entry and the notary's certificate should be proofread — in that order and at about the same time. See also the discussion of notary journals in Chapter 17.

7.11 The notary should, if an error is later discovered in a completed notarial certificate, not attempt to alter the certificate.

After a notarization has been completed, it cannot be cancelled or undone. After a notarial ceremony is completed, a notarial certificate should not be amended, altered, or corrected.

The focus of this section is about material errors or omissions or major substantive mistakes having the potential to cause the notarization to be rejected or invalidated. Minor, trivial, or technical mistakes are not important enough to warrant correction. For example, the minor misspelling of the name of a month, parish or county, or state or territory should be inconsequential.

A number of reasons support the view that after a notarial ceremony is concluded, it is too late to alter or correct a notarial certificate. First, if a notary is considered to have continuing authority to amend a notarial certificate, how long does it last — a month, a year, five years, in perpetuity? There needs to be finality at some identifiable and standardized point, and for certificates of notarization that finality comes at the point of completion of the notarial ceremony.

Second, if a completed notarization is rejected by an agency, invalidated by a court, or challenged by a lawsuit, could a notary then intervene, correct the questioned notarial certificate, and thereby rehabilitate the notarization? There is a legal presumption in favor of the official work of notaries, which is a presumption of the regularity and propriety of the official acts of notaries. This is a presumption that favors the innocent document signer who, when he or she seeks out a notary to perform a notarization, desires to have a valid notarization which will withstand any challenge to it. This presumption in the law should be sufficient to protect the finished notarization, without the need to continue to shield an erroneous notarial certificate in perpetuity or for some unspecified lesser period of time.

Third, might well-intentioned efforts to correct completed notarizations actually cause more complications and problems in many circumstances? Not all errors in notarial certificates are the same. Some are minor and technical such that the notarizations would be valid even in the face of the faults, while others are major and possibly fatal to the validity of the notarizations. We should not want notaries to be forced to make all manner of corrections. Moreover, who should have the standing to seek a correction — only the document signer, a party to a transaction about which there is a notarized instrument, a party who receives or is relies on a notarized document, or anyone at all? If a notary were to correct a notarial certificate, the correction may not become known to all parties who have an interest in knowing about the correction. Moreover, efforts to correct certificates and/or to inform individuals about the corrections might actually plant the idea to contest the notarization in individuals who otherwise would not have been aware of the fault or would not have been inclined to challenge notarizations or the underlying transactions. In other words, this procedure might unnecessarily stir up a hornet's nest, especially if a nonmaterial or nonfatal error were involved.

Note: *The Controversy About This Issue.* There are at least two points of view about whether, in regard to a notarization that has been completed, an error in a notarial certificate may be corrected or whether it is too late to do so. Some people favor the view that notaries should have authority to make corrections to completed certificates. Supporters do so with good intentions. They have a most fundamental and idealistic motive in their favor — namely, the desire for accuracy and correctness. The authoritative and influential National Notary Association has proposed Section 9-3 of the *Model Notary Act* of 2010, adopting the position to allow notaries to correct notarial certificates. It's a brand new provision, set out below under the heading "Relevant Model Notary Law." *Model Notary Act*, Section 9-3 provides the authority for notaries to correct erroneous notarial certificates, but this authority does not appear in any prior laws and is untested. In this author's opinion, the new provision is incomplete and is likely to be misunderstood by notaries who may well undertake to make alterations in notarial certificates that did not involve mistakes of fact but rather that involved mistakes of judgment by document signers at the times of the notarizations. Buyer's and seller's remorse sometimes happens. Errors of judgment that document signers simply wish to change with the help of hindsight should not be reversed by notaries. Additionally, the section does not place any time limit on the opportunity of notaries to make such corrections. Further, Section 9-3 may permit a notary to attempt to cover up his or her own wrongdoing by "correcting" a certificate. The section also allows the notary to replace a faulty certificate, but such a procedure may allow the destruction of evidence of the error or omission which triggered the need for a correction. Instead, the section should require the preservation of the faulty original certificate. If the basic idea of Section 9.3, correcting certificates of notarization, is to be promoted, the procedure should receive more attention and refinement.

7.12 The notary should, if an error is later discovered in a completed notarial certificate and if requested by the document signer, perform a new and correct notarization.

This practice standard is included because, as noted in section 7.11, a notary should not attempt to amend, alter, or correct a completed notarial certificate. After a notarial ceremony is completed, the only way to right an error or omission in a notarization is to inform the document signer of the mistake and possibly to schedule an appointment to perform a new notarization. A completed notarization cannot be cancelled and should not be altered.

Unquestionably, the notary should take appropriate steps to mitigate the circumstances if the notary learns of an error or omission in one of his or her completed notarial certificates. The document signer should be informed of the error or omission to allow the signer to consider its significance and what to do. If the document signer is the one who initially brings the error or omission to the attention of the notary, this step will have been satisfied. In either case, the notary should be sure there is a paper trail about the matter by sending the signer a notice about the mistake or a confirmation of the signer's notification of a mistake. Also, the notary should inform the state or territorial notary commissioning official or oversight agency about the error or omission. Self-reporting is an important ethical obligation of a notary. See also the discussion of notary ethics in Chapter 19.

The notary should place a new entry into the notary journal bearing the date when the error was learned or discovered by the notary. This new entry should reference the original notarization, explain the nature of the error, and explain what steps were taken by the notary to advise the document signer and the notary commissioning official or oversight agency about the error. Importantly, the notary should not make any changes to the original journal entry for the erroneous notarization — other than to reference the new entry and its date so that it can be found in the journal.

If the signer decides that the error or omission is important enough to warrant further action, if other informal methods to mitigate the situation are unavailable or unsuccessful, and if it is not too late for a new and correct notarization of the same instrument to be worthwhile to the signer, the signer could request the original notary or a different notary to perform a new and correct notarization. Obviously, the signer's preference in this regard will depend upon the amount of time which has elapsed before the error or omission is discovered and disclosed and whether the notarized instrument or its transaction is time-sensitive or already completed. The new notarization should be performed like any other notarization. If the original notary is asked to perform the new and correct notarization, the journal entry for the new notarization should cross-reference the original notarization, and a short note should be added to the original journal entry merely to cross-reference the date of the new notarization. See also the discussion of the notary journal in Chapter 17.

Of course, an error or omission in a notarization may raise concerns for the notary about legal liability if financial injury results because of the error or omission. See also the discussion of notary liability in Chapter 20 and of notary bonds and insurance in Chapter 23. ■

***RELEVANT MODEL NOTARY LAW**

Each notary should read, study, and abide by the notary statute and regulations, if any, of his or her commissioning state or territory.

JURAT WITH AFFIANT STATEMENT

State of California
County of Los Angeles } ss.

☒ See Attached Document (Notary to cross out lines 1–7 below)
☐ See Statement Below (Lines 1–7 to be completed only by document signer[s], not Notary)

1 ______
2 ______
3 ______
4 ______
5 ______
6 ______
7 ______

Signature of Document Signer No. 1

Signature of Document Signer No. 2 (if any)

Subscribed and sworn to (or affirmed) before me

this 12th (Date) day of January (Month), 2017 (Year), by

Michael T. Smith
Name of Signer No. 1

Name of Signer No. 2 (if any)

Pat R. Jones
Signature of Notary Public

Place Notary Seal/Stamp Above

Any Other Required Information (Residence, Expiration Date, etc.)

OPTIONAL

This section is required for notarizations performed in Arizona but is optional in other states. Completing this information can deter alteration of the document or fraudulent reattachment of this form to an unintended document.

Description of Attached Document

Title or Type of Document: Affidvait of Loss

Document Date: 1-2-2017 Number of Pages: One

Signer(s) Other Than Named Above: No other signers

Sample jurat with affiant statement notary certificate

INDIVIDUAL ACKNOWLEDGMENT

State/Commonwealth of Wyoming }
County of Laramie } ss.

On this the 18th (Day) day of July (Month), 2017 (Year), before me, Pat R. Jones (Name of Notary Public), the undersigned Notary Public, personally appeared Mary T. Richards (Name(s) of Signer(s)),

☒ personally known to me – **OR** –

☐ proved to me on the basis of satisfactory evidence

to be the person(s) whose name(s) is/are subscribed to the within instrument, and acknowledged to me that he/she/they executed the same for the purposes therein stated.

WITNESS my hand and official seal.

PAT R. JONES
Notary Public – Wyoming
Laramie County
My Commission Expires Jan 30, 2020

Place Notary Seal/Stamp Above

Pat R. Jones
Signature of Notary Public

Pat R. Jones
Any Other Required Information (Printed Name of Notary, Expiration Date, etc.)

OPTIONAL

This section is required for notarizations performed in Arizona but is optional in other states. Completing this information can deter alteration of the document or fraudulent reattachment of this form to an unintended document.

Description of Attached Document

Title or Type of Document: Grant Deed

Document Date: 7/14/17 Number of Pages: 4

Signer(s) Other Than Named Above: No Other Signer

Sample individual acknowledgment notary certificate

WITNESSING OR ATTESTING A SIGNATURE

State of Arizona
County of Maricopa } ss.

Signed (or attested) before me on May 20, 2017 (Date) by Mary T. Richards (Name(s) of Individual(s)).

Pat R. Jones
Signature of Notarial Officer

PAT R. JONES
Notary Public – Arizona
Maricopa County
My Comm. Expires Jan 30, 2020

Place Notary Seal/Stamp Above

Notary Public
Title of Office

My commission expires: January 30, 2020

OPTIONAL

This section is required for notarizations performed in Arizona but is optional in other states. Completing this information can deter alteration of the document or fraudulent reattachment of this form to an unintended document.

Description of Attached Document

Title or Type of Document: Informed Consent Declaration

Document Date: 1/14/17 Number of Pages: 1

Signer(s) Other Than Named Above: No Other Signers

Sample witnessing or attesting a signature notary certificate

"Notarial Certificate And Certificate. 'Notarial certificate' and 'certificate' mean the part of, or attachment to, a notarized document that, in the performance of the notarization, is completed by the notary, bears the notary's official signature and seal, and states the date, venue, and facts attested by the notary in the particular notarial act." *Model Notary Act*, Section 2-9 (2010).

"To always be satisfied that the individual appearing before me understands the contents of the document to be executed or oath to be administered before proceeding;

To always satisfy myself as to the identity of the individual appearing before me in my capacity as Notary Public; ...

To keep informed of the law regarding the duties and powers of the office of Notary Public in my jurisdiction and not compromise that law ..." *Responsibility Code of Ethics* (1980).

"The Notary shall require the presence of each signer and oath-taker in order to carefully screen each for identity and willingness, and to observe that each appears aware of the significance of the transaction requiring a notarial act." *Notary Public Code of Professional Responsibility,* Guiding Principle III (1998).

"The Notary shall not execute a false or incomplete certificate, nor be involved with any document or transaction that the Notary believes is false, deceptive or fraudulent." *Notary Public Code of Professional Responsibility,* Guiding Principle IV (1998).

"The Notary shall give precedence to the rules of law over the dictates or expectations of any person or entity." *Notary Public Code of Professional Responsibility*, Guiding Principle V (1998).

"The Notary shall affix a seal on every notarized document ..." *Notary Public Code of Professional Responsibility,* Guiding Principle VII (1998).

"The Notary shall record every notarial act in a bound journal or other secure recording device and safeguard it as an important public record." *Notary Public Code of Professional Responsibility*, Guiding Principle VIII (1998).

"Purposes. This [Act] shall be construed and applied to advance its underlying purposes, which are: (1) to promote, serve, and protect the public interest; ... (4) to enhance cross-border recognition of notarial acts; ..." *Model Notary Act,* Section 1-2 (2010).

"Notarial Certificate. (a) For every notarial act involving a document, a notary public of this [State] shall properly complete a notarial certificate that contains or states: (1) the official signature of the notary, in accordance with Section 8-1; (2) an impression of the official seal of the notary, in accordance with Section 8-2; (3) the venue of the notarial act, including the name of this [State] and of the pertinent [county] [parish] [district]; (4) the date of the notarial act; and (5) the facts and particulars attested by the notary in performing the respective notarial act, as defined in Chapter 2.

(b) A notarial certificate shall be sufficient for a particular notarial act only if it meets the requirements of Subsection 9-1(a) and is in a form that: (1) is set forth for that act in this Chapter; (2) is otherwise prescribed for that act by the law of this [State]; (3) is prescribed for that act by a law, regulation, or custom of another jurisdiction, provided it does not require actions by the notary that are unauthorized by this [State]; or (4) describes the actions of the notary in such a manner as to meet the requirements of the particular notarial act, as defined in Chapter 2.

(c) A notarial certificate shall be worded and completed using only letters, characters, and a language that are read, written, and understood by the notary public." *Model Notary Act,* Section 9-1 (2010).

"Attaching Notarial Certificate. A paper notarial certificate that is attached to a document during the notarization of the signature of a principal [[document signer]] shall: (1) be attached by stapling or other method that leaves evidence of any subsequent detachment; (2) be attached, signed, and sealed only by the notary and only at the time of notarization and in the presence of the principal [document signer]; (3) be attached immediately following the signature page if the certificate is the same size as that page, or to the front of the signature page if the certificate is smaller; and (4) contain all of the elements described in Section 9-1 on the same sheet of paper." *Model Notary Act,* Section 9-2 (2010).

"Correcting Notarial Certificate. A notary public may correct an error or omission made by that notary in a notarial certificate if: (1) the original certificate and document are returned to the notary; (2) the notary verifies the error by reference to the pertinent journal entry, the document itself, or to other determinative written evidence; (3) the notary legibly corrects the certificate and initials and dates the correction in ink, or replaces the original certificate with a correct certificate; and (4) the notary appends to the pertinent journal entry a notation regarding the nature and date of the correction." *Model Notary Act,* Section 9-3 (2010).

"Improper Certificate. (a) A notary shall not execute a notarial certificate containing information known or believed by the notary to be false.

(b) A notary shall not affix an official signature or seal on a notarial certificate that is incomplete.

(c) A notary shall not affix an official signature or seal on a notarial certificate other than at the time of notarization and in the presence of the principal [document signer].

(d) A notary shall not provide or send a signed or sealed notarial certificate to another person with the understanding that it will be completed or attached to a document outside of the notary's presence." *Model Notary Act,* Section 5-8 (2010).

"Certificate Of Notarial Act. (a) A notarial act must be evidenced by a certificate. The certificate must: (1) be executed contemporaneously with the performance of the notarial act; (2) be signed and dated by the notarial officer and, if the notarial officer is a notary public, be signed in the same manner as on file with the [commissioning officer or agency]; (3) identify the jurisdiction in which the notarial act is performed; (4) contain the title of office of the notarial officer; and (5) if the notarial officer is a notary public, indicate the date of expiration, if any, of the officer's commission.

(b) If a notarial act regarding a tangible record is performed by a notary public, an official stamp must be affixed to or embossed on the certificate. ...

(c) A certificate of a notarial act is sufficient if it meets the requirements of subsections (a) and (b) and: (1) is in a short form set forth in Section 16; (2) is in a form otherwise permitted by the law of this state; (3) is in a form permitted by the law applicable in the jurisdiction in which the notarial act was performed; or (4) sets forth the actions of the notarial officer and the actions are sufficient to meet the requirements of the notarial act as provided in Sections 5, 6, and 7 or law of this state other than this [act].

(d) By executing a certificate of a notarial act, a notarial officer certifies that the officer has complied with the requirements and made the determinations specified in Sections, 4, 5, and 6.

(e) A notarial officer may not affix the officer's official signature to, or logically associate it with, a certificate until the notarial act has been performed.

(f) If a notarial act is performed regarding a tangible record, a certificate must be part of, or securely attached to, the record. ..." *Revised Uniform Law on Notarial Acts,* Section 15 (2010).

STATE OF GEORGIA

OFFICE OF STATE LIBRARIAN

To the Honorable C. S. Swain, *Greeting:*

WHEREAS, in conformity with the provisions of the Act of the General Assembly, approved August 21, 1916, you were on the 29th *day of* March *Nineteen Hundred and* Twenty-six *appointed*

A Notary Public for the State at Large

NOW, THEREFORE, By virtue of the authority vested in me by the law, and in pursuance of your appointment, I do hereby issue this Certificate of Appointment, commissioning you, the said C. S. Swain *A NOTARY PUBLIC FOR THE STATE AT LARGE.*

THIS COMMISSION shall continue in force from the 29th *day of* March *19*26, *to the* 29th *day of* March *19*30, *unless the same shall be sooner vacated or annulled in the manner authorized by law.*

Given under my hand and seal at the Capitol, in the City of Atlanta, the 2nd day of April 1926.

Ella May Thornton State Librarian.

1926, State of Georgia commission by which the state librarian appointed C.S. Swain as a notary public.

Chapter

8

Notary's Official Seal

STANDARDS SUMMARY

8.1 The notary should obtain an official notary seal containing the notary's commission information, regardless of whether required by law.

8.2 The notary should not knowingly allow the seal impression to be used in a testimonial, promotion, or publicity effort of any kind.

8.3 The notary should affix a notary seal impression to each notarial certificate for every document notarization, regardless of whether required by law.

8.4 The notary should affix the notary seal impression on the notarial certificate clearly and legibly near the notary's signature.

8.5 The notary should, prior to completion of the notarial ceremony, proofread the affixed seal impression and cure any defects therein by striking the faulty impression and affixing a new seal impression.

8.6 The notary should not give, loan, sell, or otherwise relinquish possession of the notary seal to any party other than to a governmentally authorized individual.

8.7 The notary should, when the notary seal is not in use, secure the seal by lock and key under the notary's exclusive control, regardless of whether required by law.

8.8 The notary should acquire and possess one or possibly two notary seals but not have more than two active seals at a time.

8.9 The notary should, if the notary seal is damaged, lost, or stolen, promptly report such to the commissioning official or the notary oversight agency and to law enforcement in the case of theft of the seal.

8.10 The notary should, when the notary commission is terminated or expires, deface or disable the notary seal and then destroy it, regardless of whether required by law.

STANDARDS EXPLANATIONS

Tradition can be important. The use of a seal on important written instruments dates to ancient times. Sealed governmental and commercial documents have always been treated as special. The tradition of affixing a seal impression of some kind has been continued in the notarization of instruments to the present time because there are several benefits to be derived from the seal procedure. Importantly, sealed instruments more readily identify them as having been notarized in both domestic and international settings, and sealed instruments are more secure. Sealed instruments are also more difficult to forge.

Today, in connection with paper documents, there are two basic types of notary seals in use: (a) the embosser seal, which is a two-sided metal device into which a page or pages can be slipped and which device can be pressed together to emboss raised words, letters, numbers, and designs into the paper and (b) the ink-stamp seal, or self-inking seal, which is usually a wood or plastic device with an ink source that allows for a stamp impression to be inked onto a page, preferably in black ink.

Ink-stamp notary seals have virtually replaced entirely the embosser seals because the ink-stamp seals allow for photocopy reproduction of the seal impressions, whereas it is difficult to obtain a satisfactory photocopy of embosser seal impressions. Thus, almost all states that require the use of notary seals now require them to be ink-stamp seals (usually with black ink). However, there is typically no prohibition against a notary using two seals — both an ink-stamp seal and an embosser seal — in performing a notarization (the explanation for which will be provided below).

Many states and territories have adopted statutes or regulations which specify the size, shape, border, design, and content of their notary seals, and notaries should consult the law of their own states or territories to ensure their seals comply with the official requirements. Additionally, some states and territories limit and restrict the manufacture and sale of new notary seals in order to minimize the opportunity of wrongdoers to order and acquire false notary seals from seal vendors and manufacturers — although such restrictions are not universal and can be circumvented by diligent wrongdoers who deal with vendors or manufacturers in states or territories in which there are no such restrictions.

8.1 The notary should obtain an official notary seal containing the notary's commission information, regardless of whether required by law.

While the great majority of jurisdictions require their notaries to obtain and use official seals to notarize documents, several jurisdictions do not. However, no jurisdiction prohibits its notaries from acquiring notary seals and affixing seal impressions as part of the notarization procedure. Because of the significant benefits to the use of notary seals, every notary should obtain an official seal.

The contents of the notary seal provide significant features of a sound and lawful notarization. The contents should commonly include the notary's name, the commission or serial number, the jurisdiction (the county or parish and state or territory of commissioning), the words "Notary Public," and the commission expiration date. Many states and territories prescribe the exact size and design for the notary seal and the exact information to be included in the seal, and those requirements should be strictly followed by notaries.

A seal impression with the listed information included will cloak the notarization with officiality and will be recognized everywhere as an official notary seal. A seal containing the listed information will be more difficult to forge or falsify and will provide evidence of the authority of the notary to act as such. That is, the name of the state or territory of commissioning will verify the jurisdiction in which the notary is authorized to act, and the commission expiration date will verify that the notary's commission is in effect at the time of the notarization. If any question does arise about the validity of the notarization, the notary's name and commission or serial number will allow individuals and commissioning and regulating officials to identify the notary, contact the notary, and proceed to investigate the notarization in question.

Practice Tip: *Sample Seal Impression in Journal.* The notary should place a current seal impression somewhere on the inside of the active notary journal and repeat this practice with each new seal and each new journal. Then, if for any reason the notary were to need an exemplar of either an expired or current seal, one would always be available. This unlikely situation could arise if a current seal were lost or stolen and the notary wished to report the occurrence to police or to the notary oversight agency and to provide a copy of the seal impression. Or, if there were a concern about alleged forgery of a notarization from years earlier, the original notary seal would have been disabled and destroyed — so an exemplar impression would be helpful to investigators and attorneys.

8.2 The notary should not knowingly allow the seal impression to be used in a testimonial, promotion, or publicity effort of any kind.

Just as other public officers should not generally participate or engage in a private or commercial endorsement, promotion, testimonial, or campaign in their official capacities, notaries should not do so either. This prohibition applies as well to political campaigns, as notaries are to serve as disinterested and impartial witnesses and should not become involved in partisan politics while in their official capacities. As part of that admonition to avoid taking direct part in an endorsement, promotion, testimonial, or campaign, the notary should not knowingly allow the notarial title or the notarial seal impression to be used in any of those activities. If the notary learns or even suspects that a document signer plans to use a document notarization as part of an endorsement, promotion, or campaign, the notary should decline to notarize or should inquire about the document signer's intention to use the seal impression and decline the notarization if an improper use of the notary seal impression is planned.

8.3 The notary should affix a notary seal impression to each notarial certificate for every document notarization, regardless of whether required by law.

The notary seal has been compared to the badge of a police officer or the stethoscope of a doctor, for each of these objects is a key tool of the trade of its owner and identifies the owner's business as well. Members of the public simply expect that a notary will possess and use a seal. In fact, the seal, when properly manufactured, and the seal impression, when affixed to a notary's certificate, bring significant value to the act of notarization. As noted above, no jurisdiction prohibits its notaries from obtaining and using notary seals. So, all notaries can and should possess and utilize seals as a central feature of document notarization for the following reasons.

First and foremost, the seal adds a level of protection against forgery of a document. When a notarization includes a seal impression, in order for a wrongdoer to forge an instrument, the notary seal impression must be forged as well. This step would require the forger to steal or create a seal, and that extra step may prevent some forgeries, either by discouraging some would-be forgers or by exposing faults in attempted forgeries of seal impressions. Moreover, when older-style embosser notary seals are used along with ink-stamp seals, such seal practice provides a significant protection against document forgery (as will be described below).

Second, the seal brings an air of formality and officiality to the notarization ceremony. After all, notarization is an official governmental act, performed by a government officer — the notary public. It is important that document signers appreciate that when their signatures on documents are notarized, such occasions represent special circumstances with legal ramifications. For centuries, in the U.S. and around the world, notarizations have been performed with notary seals included as part of the ceremony, and their presence is part of the notarial tradition.

Third, the presence of a notary seal on documents helps to identify such instruments and to satisfy the requirements for recording or recognizing them. When documents are carried from state to state or from country to country, the presence of notary seals assists the receiving jurisdictions in their willingness to recognize the validity of the instruments. It is simply a commonly expected part of notarization practice.

8.4 The notary should affix the notary seal impression on the notarial certificate clearly and legibly near the notary's signature.

The proper affixing of the notary seal to the notary certificate, along with the notary's signature, are the most important symbolic features of a notarization. To most fully serve the symbolic and fraud-prevention purposes of the seal, the seal impression must be done soundly in a number of respects. First of all, the seal impression needs to be legible. It should not be smeared or smudged. The seal impression should be made with black ink, and the seal should not be placed on top of any print or writing on the certificate. Nor should anything be written or printed on top of the seal impression. The seal impression should appear in close proximity to the signature of the notary, for in actuality the seal is a symbol of the authority of the notary just as is the notary's signature. The two elements go hand in hand. One without the other does not fully identify the notary. See also the discussion of the notary certificate in Chapter 7.

Note: *Multiple Originals.* An important pragmatic reason for achieving a clear, nonobscured, and legible seal impression is the frequent need to reproduce or duplicate the image of notarized documents. While most often a photocopy of a notarized document will suffice for interested parties, there are times when the parties each prefer to have an original document. Many people mistakenly believe that there can be only one original, but that is a layperson's myth. It is entirely permissible to produce multiple original notarized documents — by simply executing as many original notarizations of a document as the interested parties request (as long as each notarization is treated as an original notarization with original signatures, original seal impressions, and separate notary journal entries).

8.5 The notary should, prior to completion of the notarial ceremony, proofread the affixed seal impression and cure any defects therein by striking the faulty impression and affixing a new seal impression.

Occasionally, notary seal impressions will be faulty. They may be smeared or smudged, they may be misplaced over existing print or partially off the page, or they may be rendered incomplete by imperfections in paper or by irregular surfaces underneath them that prevent full seal impressions from being achieved. If anything happens to spoil the seal impression, that fault must be corrected immediately — prior to the completion of the notarization ceremony.

The way to identify a defect in a notary seal impression is simply to proofread the notarial certificate area containing the seal impression. If it is possible to promptly and efficiently print another copy of the page containing the blank notarial certificate form and to re-execute that page, the problem of a faulty seal impression will be solved. By the way, the page containing the faulty impression should then be shredded or torn up. The other way to cure a defect in a notary seal impression is to strike it out (with a line or an "X" through it, as well as with the notary's initials and date to verify the change), and to place a second seal impression on the notary certificate. Such second seal impression should be clear, nonobscured, and legible. The new seal impression should be placed as close as possible to the notary's signature. The notary should not attempt to correct a faulty seal impression by making a handwritten correction or modification of the existing faulty image.

Of course, the other step that should then be taken when a fault with the seal impression arises is to record that fact in the notary journal entry, along with the steps taken to cure the defective seal impression.

Note: *Clarification About Minor Deviations.* This author does not want to suggest that every imperfection of the seal impression is so serious as to invalidate the notarization. Indeed, recall that some jurisdictions do not even require their notaries to use seals. A court, for example, might conclude that a challenged seal impression is not material, that the seal impression substantially complies with legal requirements, and that, therefore, the notarization is valid. The point behind this best practice statement is to avoid a possible challenge to a notarization altogether by correcting even a minor defect in a seal impression immediately during the notarization procedure. See also the discussion of the substantial compliance doctrine in connection with notary certificates in Chapter 7.

Case Illustration. A few years ago, this author was consulted about a lawsuit resulting from a missing notary seal. A bank notary had notarized seven documents for the owner of a construction company who, as document signer, was going to include those documents in a sealed bid for a government project. The notary performed six of the notarizations perfectly but forgot to affix the official notary seal on the seventh document. Consequently, the government agency refused to consider the faulty bid, which would have been the lowest bid and, thus, the successful bid. The company therefore lost more than $100,000. The company sued the notary and the notary's employer, the bank. If the notary had proofread the notary seal section of the notarial certificate, the omission would have been discovered and cured, the loss of more than $100,000 would have been avoided, and the lawsuit would not have been pursued. The lesson: Proofread, proofread, proofread!

8.6 The notary should not give, loan, sell, or otherwise relinquish possession of the notary seal to any party other than to a governmentally authorized individual.

Did you know that you can find actual official notary seals, both expired and occasionally unexpired, for sale at flea markets, yard sales, antiques malls, estate sales, thrift stores, and online sites? This practice is one more unfortunate example of how unimportant many people consider notaries and notarizations to be.

Resold or carelessly discarded official notary seals (both current and expired) can be used to commit document fraud, much like stolen ID documents can be used to commit identity theft. Forgers would love to have possession of current, or even expired, notary seals in order to make the forgery of documents one step easier. A forger may well want to falsify a document bearing an earlier date because a forged document may appear more authentic due to its vintage age. Even better is to forge both the document and a notarization of it. An expired notary seal could be quite helpful. Hence, like fine wine, the older the notary seal, the better it may be — to wrongdoers.

Thus, notaries should not give, loan, or sell their current or expired notary seals to anyone, including their employers or former employers. Even if the notary employer paid for the notary-employee's official seal, the seal bears the name of the notary, not of the employer. Nor should the notary carelessly discard a current or expired, working, operable notary seal that might be retrieved and misused. The seal belongs to the notary whose name it bears, regardless of who purchased the seal. If the seal is misused to falsify a notarization, and if a third party is injured financially as a result, the notary could be liable for the injury if the notary was negligent in allowing a wrongdoer to obtain and misuse the seal.

The only exception to the directive just explained is that the notary should allow a governmentally authorized party to take possession of the notary seal, presumably for a lawful purpose. Perhaps, the police or a prosecutor will obtain a subpoena for the seal to allow for examination of it in the course of a criminal investigation or to serve as evidence in a trial. Or, perhaps the governmental notary oversight agency will request possession of the seal for purposes of an investigation into alleged document fraud or impersonation of a notary.

If the notary were asked to deliver possession of the seal to a governmentally authorized party, the notary should be certain to obtain and preserve a written request for the seal, showing to whom the seal is to be provided and the party approving the request. If neither the party approving the request nor the party to whom the seal is to be delivered is an official of the notary oversight agency, then the notary should inform the notary oversight agency of the disposition of the seal. Additionally, the notary should make an entry regarding the request and the delivery in the notary journal, as these matters are certainly official notary business that should be recorded and preserved.

8.7 The notary should, when the notary seal is not in use, secure the seal by lock and key under the notary's exclusive control, regardless of whether required by law.

In general, too many notary statutes are incomplete and lacking in concern about security issues in particular. Security of notary seals (and journals) is an area too often neglected by notary laws. Custody of the notary seal is the responsibility of the notary at all times.

Many notaries have the unfortunate habit of allowing their notary seals, when not being used, to remain lying openly out and about their workspaces. Consequently, there have been numerous reported instances in which a forger or other wrongdoer has surreptitiously borrowed or stolen a notary seal and then misused it to perform one or more fraudulent notarizations. Often, the culprit has been an employer or supervisor of the notary or a fellow employee, each of whom has had access to the work area where the notary's unprotected seal was located.

Since the affixing of the notary's seal impression to a notary's certificate is one of the most significant symbolic features of the notarization, protecting the seal against theft and unauthorized use is quite important. If a wrongdoer intent upon falsifying a document were to obtain a real notary seal, the borrowed or stolen seal would make the forgery of a signature or of a document much easier than it would otherwise be. In fact, carelessness about the security of the notary seal can and should cause serious liability concerns for a notary. Thus, if a notary negligently or intentionally allows someone else to use her or his seal in performing a false notarization, the notary can face administrative and criminal sanctions, and if a third party suffers financial injury due to the fraudulent notarization, the notary may face civil liability for the financial losses (perhaps including punitive damages).

How should the notary protect the security of the official seal? The notary should keep the seal (along with the notary journal) under lock and key when the seal is not in use, and the notary must be the only party to have access to the key. It is not enough, for instance, for the notary to have the seal in a locked office at work if the employer or co-workers have keys to the office. So, the seal might be kept in a locked desk drawer, closet, safe, or box, with the key in the exclusive control of the notary. The notary is the one and only public official entitled to use the seal and must be the only one with access to the key. The seal belongs exclusively to the notary, not the notary's employer — even if the employer required the employee to become a notary and even if the employer purchased or paid for the seal.

8.8 The notary should acquire and possess one or possibly two notary seals but not have more than two active seals at a time.

State and territorial notary statutes almost never prohibit a notary from possessing more than one current, active notary seal (although as a practical matter, it may be difficult in some places to acquire more than one such seal because in some jurisdictions a notary cannot obtain a seal unless he or she presents a document from the government agency that commissions notaries authorizing the manufacture of a notary seal to a seal company). And, most notaries apparently never even consider the possibility of purchasing more than one seal. But, could they, and should they, think about possessing two seals?

The reason to address this practice point is that almost all notaries who are employed somewhere must commute from their homes to their places of work and back again, each and every workday. Many of those notaries perform notarizations both at the workplace and at home. In order to do so, those notaries must necessarily transport their notary seals (and journals) back and forth from home to work and back again, each and every day. While commuting, there is an increased risk of loss, theft, or damage occurring to the notary seal. Thus, many notaries may prefer to keep one official seal at home and another duplicate official seal at the workplace.

For many years, this author maintained two official notary seals at the same time. When I lived in the Chicago suburbs, I drove from home to a commuter railroad station where I would board a train for an hour-long ride to my office in Chicago each business day. And, of course, at the end of the day, I reversed the procedure. I did not wish to expose myself to the heightened risk of carrying my notary seal back and forth to and from work each day — not to mention the commonly undertaken incidental deviations to go to gas stations, grocery stores, shopping malls, and the like while on my way to work or on my way home after work.

Therefore, if not prohibited by the applicable notary statute, the practice of having two notary seals should be allowed, rather than to be discouraged. We should want notaries to be diligent and to be public-spirited enough to be willing to perform notarizations at work and at home. And, we should want those notaries to be genuinely concerned about the security of their official seals. If notaries with two active seals secure both of them when not in use under lock and key, subject to the exclusive control of the respective notaries, there should be no cause for alarm. Moreover, society will have the benefit of access to more notarial services.

Incidentally, the same concern also arises with regard to the commuting notary and his or her notary journal. In my personal example cited above, when I had two notary seals, I also had two active notary journals — one at home and one at work. See the discussion of notary journals in Chapter 17.

***Note:** A Difference of Opinion.* To be clear, not everyone agrees with the position this author has taken to permit notaries to acquire two active official seals. And, a few states and territories may have statutes or regulations to the contrary. So, notaries should check the law of their state or territory or contact their notary oversight agency to inquire before obtaining a second notary seal.

***Practice Tip:** Using Both Embosser and Ink-Stamp Seals.* Because both the old-fashioned embosser seal and the currently preferred ink-stamp seal have their own advantages, some very conscientious notaries have chosen to use both on each notarization — especially regarding important transactions. The "official" seal is typically the government-mandated ink-stamp seal because it can be easily photocopied to allow for reproduction, and it is affixed on the notary certificate near the notary's signature. Then, the embosser is used as well, so that two notary seal impressions appear on the same page. On multipage instruments, placing the last two or three pages of the instrument between the two metal sides of the embosser and pressing the embosser together results in a raised seal image in the identical location on each of those pages. It would then be nearly impossible for a forger to exchange the signature page with its attached notary certificate, because to do so would require the forger to get the embosser impressions on the final two or three pages to line up perfectly. If a very diligent notary uses these tactics, the notary should be sure to note the procedure in the notary journal entry for any such dual-sealed notarization.

8.9 The notary should, if the notary seal is damaged, lost, or stolen, promptly report such to the commissioning official or notary oversight agency and to law enforcement in the case of theft of the seal.

If the security precautions recommended above and below for the protection of notary seals are followed, there should be little risk of damage, loss, or theft of notary seals. Nevertheless, if a notary seal is damaged (and unusable), lost, or stolen, as soon as the notary discovers the mishap, the notary should immediately inform the commissioning official or notary oversight agency.

There are a couple of very valuable reasons to take this notification step, especially in the case of a lost or stolen seal. First, it will tend to show reasonable care on the part of the notary — that the notary was diligent enough to quickly discover the loss or theft and was concerned enough to advise the commissioning official or oversight agency in the hope that the seal would be found and returned. The prudence of the notary is important and should help the notary's image if perchance the lost or stolen seal ends up in the hands of a forger who falsely notarizes an instrument, causing financial injury to someone who in turn sues the notary for negligence in allowing the culprit to acquire the seal. The notary should not have liability if the notary acted with reasonable care. Second, without a seal the notary cannot perform document notarizations, so the notary should advise the commissioning official or oversight agency of the damage, loss, or theft and inquire about the proper procedure to replace the damaged or missing seal.

If the notary seal is stolen, that theft is a crime and should be reported to the appropriate law enforcement agency. Again, a major part of the reason for the notary to report the theft is to demonstrate prudence and reasonable care in the event that the stolen seal is misused and the notary is sued for damages in connection with a falsified notarization.

Practice Tip: *Creating a Paper Trail.* In the case of damage, loss, or theft of a notary seal and reporting by the notary to the commissioning official or notary oversight agency and possibly to law enforcement, the notary should be certain to create a paper trail to document the notary's reporting. Firstly, the notary should create an entry in the notary journal to record as much detail as possible about the damage, loss, or theft, including the reporting to official authorities. Also, the notary should add a note to the entry about a replacement seal, if one is obtained, and the date it is received. Secondly, the notary should make the report to government authorities in writing and, of course, should retain a copy of the written report.

8.10 The notary should, when the notary commission is terminated or expires, deface or disable the notary seal and then destroy it, regardless of whether required by law.

Unfortunately, too few notary statutes are thorough enough to treat the subject of what to do with a notary seal when the notary commission expires or is revoked or terminated. If a jurisdiction does have a statute establishing a procedure for the handling of a seal under those circumstances, that law should be followed. But, if there is no law governing the subject, the following procedure is reasonable and prudent.

Promptly upon the expiration of the notary's commission (whether the notary renews the commission or not), or upon the termination of the notary's commission for any reason such as death of the notary or revocation of the commission, the notary or the notary's guardian, representative, or surviving family, in the case of the incompetency or death of the notary, should disable and destroy the notary seal. The seal should not simply be discarded, for someone else may find it and misuse it if it is not disabled. The seal should be destroyed (smashed, burned, or broken), and then disposed of in a secure way.

Upon termination or expiration of the notary's commission, the notary should not turn the notary seal over to the notary's employer, even if the notary's employer had required the employee to become a notary and/or had paid for the seal at the beginning of the notary's commission term. Remember, the notary is the public official, and the seal belongs to the notary — not to the notary's employer. Even if the notary employer also happens to be a notary, that person will have a personal notary seal and is not entitled to possess another notary's seal.

The notary's contemporary notary seal that is current or expired should never be given away or sold. Such a notary seal could readily be misused by a villain to forge notarizations. Yet, recently expired notary seals are regularly available for purchase at yard sales, flea markets, and online sites. Notaries risk liability for falsified notarizations created with the use of their current or expired notary seals if the notaries fail to act with reasonable care to secure and safeguard their seals.

Of course, a written record reflecting the method of disabling and disposing of the defunct notary seal should be created and preserved by the notary. The notary (or more accurately, the former notary) should prepare a notary journal entry which describes the steps taken to disable and discard the seal. And, the notary should even send a note to the same effect to the notary oversight agency, retaining a copy for the notary's files. Finally, the notary should even take a photograph of the disabled seal and attach a copy of the photo to both the relevant notary journal entry and to the note addressed to the oversight agency. ■

***RELEVANT MODEL NOTARY LAW**

Each notary should read, study, and abide by the notary statute and regulations, if any, of her or his commissioning state or territory.

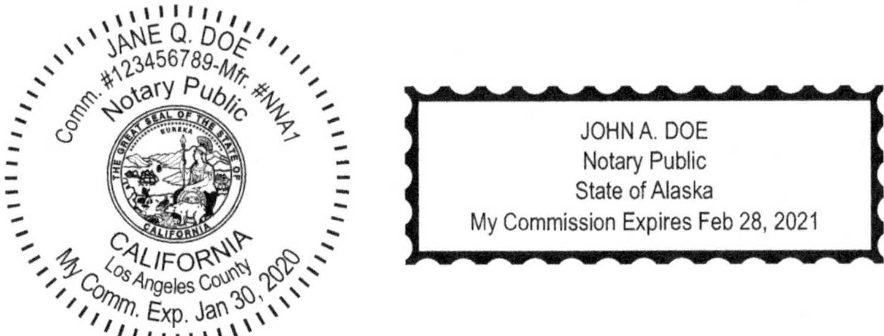

"Official Seal. 'Official seal' means: (1) a device authorized by the [commissioning official] for affixing on a paper notarial certificate an image containing a notary's name, title, jurisdiction, commission expiration date, and other information related to the notary's commission; or (2) the affixed image itself." *Model Notary Act*, Section 2-13 (2010).

"The Notary shall affix a seal on every notarized document and not allow this universally recognized symbol of office to be used by another or in an endorsement or promotion." *Notary Public Code of Professional Responsibility*, Guiding Principle VII (1998).

"To exercise extreme care to insure that the notarial seal, stamp and records are kept in a safe place and are not used by any other person ..." *Responsibility Code of Ethics* (1980).

"Purposes. This [Act] shall be construed and applied to advance its underlying purposes, which are: (1) to promote, serve, and protect the public interest; ... (4) to enhance cross-border recognition of notarial acts; ..." *Model Notary Act*, Section 1-2 (2010).

"Testimonials. A notary shall not use the official notary title or seal to endorse, promote, denounce, or oppose any product, service, contest, candidate, or other offering." *Model Notary Act*, Section 5-1 (2010).

"Official Seal. (a) In notarizing a paper document, a notary public shall affix an official seal on the notarial certificate at the time the notarial act is performed.

(b) The official seal of a notary public shall not be used for any purpose other than performing lawful notarizations.

(c) The official seal shall: (1) be the exclusive property of the notary; (2) not be affixed by any other person; (3) be kept secure and accessible only to the notary; and (4) not be surrendered to an employer upon termination of employment. ...

(e) Within 10 days after the official seal of a notary is discovered to be stolen, lost, damaged, or otherwise rendered incapable of affixing a legible image, the notary, after informing the appropriate law enforcement agency in the case of theft or vandalism, shall notify the [commissioning official] by any means providing a tangible receipt, including certified mail and electronic transmission, and also provide a copy or number of any police report. Upon receipt of such notice, the [commissioning official] shall issue to the notary a new Certificate of Authorization to Purchase a Notary Seal, which shall be presented to a seal vendor in accordance with Section 8-4.

(f) As soon as reasonably practicable after resignation, revocation, or expiration of a notary commission, or death of the notary, the seal shall be destroyed or defaced so that it may not be misused." *Model Notary Act,* Section 8-2 (2010).

"Image of Official Seal. (a) Near the notary's official signature on each paper notarial certificate, the notary shall affix a sharp, legible, permanent, and photographically reproducible image of the official seal that shall include the following elements: (1) The notary's name as stated in the commission; (2) the identification number of the notary's commission; (3) the words 'Notary Public" and '[State] of [name of jurisdiction]' and 'My commission expires (commission expiration date)'; (4) the notary's business address; and (5) a border in a [rectangular] shape no larger than [dimensions], surrounding the required words.

(b) Illegible information within a seal impression may be typed or printed legibly by the notary adjacent to but not within the impression, or another impression may be legibly affixed nearby.

(c) An embossed seal impression that is not photographically reproducible may be used in addition to but not in place of the official seal described in Subsection (a).

(d) A seal as described in Subsection (a) shall not be affixed over printed or written matter." *Model Notary Act,* Section 8-3 (2010).

"Obtaining and Providing Official Seal. (a) In order to sell or manufacture notary seals, a vendor or manufacturer shall apply for a permit from the [commissioning official], who shall charge a fee of [dollars] for issuance of this permit and maintain a controlled-access telephone number or Internet site to allow vendors and manufacturers to confirm the business mailing address and current standing of any notary in the [State].

(b) A vendor or manufacturer shall not provide a notary seal to a purchaser claiming to be a notary, unless the purchaser presents a Certificate of Authorization to Purchase a Notary Seal from the [commissioning official] and a photocopy of the respective notary commission, and unless: (1) in the case of a purchaser appearing in person, the vendor or manufacturer identifies this individual as the person named in the commission and the Certificate of Authorization, through either personal knowledge or satisfactory evidence of identity; or (2) in the case of a purchaser ordering a seal by mail or delivery service, the vendor or manufacturer confirms the business mailing address and current standing through the controlled-access telephone number or Internet site.

(c) A vendor or manufacturer shall mail or ship a notary seal only to a mailing address confirmed through the controlled-access telephone number or Internet site.

(d) For each Certificate of Authorization to Purchase a Notary Seal, a vendor or manufacturer shall make or sell one and only one seal, plus, if requested by the person presenting the Certificate, one and only one embossing seal.

(e) After manufacturing or providing a notary seal or seals, the vendor shall affix an image of all seals on the Certificate of Authorization to Purchase a Notary Seal and send the completed Certificate to the [commissioning official], retaining a copy of the Certificate and the Commission for [period of time].

(f) A notary obtaining a seal or seals as a result of a name or business address change shall present a copy of the Confirmation of Notary's Name or Address Change from the [commissioning official] in accordance with Section 12-1 and 12-2.

(g) A vendor or manufacturer who fails to comply with this section shall be guilty of a [class of offense], punishable upon conviction by a fine not exceeding [dollars]. For multiple violations, a vendor's permission to sell or manufacture notary seals shall be withdrawn by the [commissioning official]. Such conviction shall not preclude the civil liability of the vendor to parties injured by the vendor's failure to comply with this section." *Model Notary Act,* Section 8-4 (2010).

"Certificate Of Notarial Act. ... (b) If a notarial act regarding a tangible record is performed by a notary public, an official stamp must be affixed to or embossed on the certificate. ..." *Revised Uniform Law on Notarial Acts,* Section 15 (2010).

"Official Stamp. The official stamp of a notary public must: (1) include the notary public's name, jurisdiction, [commission expiration date,] and other information required by the [commissioning officer or agency]; and (2) be capable of being copied together with the record to which it is affixed or attached or with which it is logically associated." *Revised Uniform Law on Notarial Acts,* Section 17 (2010).

"Stamping Device. (a) A notary public is responsible for the security of the notary public's stamping device and may not allow another individual to use the device to perform a notarial act. [On resignation from, or the revocation or expiration of, the notary public's commission, or on the expiration of the date set forth in the stamping device, if any, the notary public shall disable the stamping device by destroying, defacing, damaging, erasing, or securing it against use in a manner that renders it unusable. On the death or adjudication of incompetency of a notary public, the notary public's personal representative or guardian or any other person knowingly in possession of the stamping device shall render it unusable by destroying, defacing, damaging, erasing, or securing it against use in a manner that renders it unusable.]

(b) If a notary public's stamping device is lost or stolen, the notary public or the notary public's personal representative or guardian shall notify promptly the commissioning officer or agency on discovering that the device is lost or stolen." *Revised Uniform Law on Notarial Acts,* Section 18 (2010).

1966, cover of the 168-page *Customs and Practices of Notaries Public and Digest of Notary Laws in the United States* by National Notary Association founder Raymond C. Rothman. It was published by the National Notary Association.

Chapter

9

Personal Presence Requirement for Document Signers at Notarizations

STANDARDS SUMMARY

9.1 The notary should understand the importance of the personal presence of document signers at notarizations.

9.2 The notary should require the document signer to be in the personal, physical presence of the notary for every notarization.

9.3 The notary should keep the document signer within the notary's line of sight throughout the notarization ceremony.

9.4 The notary should record the signer's personal presence at the notarization in the notarial certificate.

9.5 The notary should create a notary journal entry, including a present signature of the document signer, to verify the signer's presence at the notarization.

9.6 The notary should, unless prohibited by state or territorial law, request the document signer to place the signer's thumbprint in the journal entry to verify the signer's presence at the notarization.

9.7 The notary should be aware of the changing definition of personal presence in some jurisdictions regarding remote or webcam notarizations.

STANDARDS EXPLANATIONS

Historically, notarial procedure has required the document signer to appear in person in the face-to-face physical presence of the notary at the time of the notarization ceremony. In early times before any modern technology when people did not travel great distances, physical presence of the signer was the only realistic way to conduct document notarizations. But today, in the age of improved communications technology, increasing interest has arisen in alternative methods for "personal appearance" of document signers. However, the old standard requiring face-to-face physical presence of the notary and signer together in the same location still applies — except in a few states which have approved so-called "remote" or "webcam" notarizations.

Unfortunately, one of the most frequent and most serious of all notarial faults is the failure of notaries to insist on the physical presence of signers at notarizations. Some notaries who do not understand or do not care about their responsibilities will permit third parties (their employers, friends, family members, or other third parties, including complete strangers) to obtain notarizations of documents without the signers of those documents being present at the notarization ceremonies. Of course, this absence of the signer is perpetrated by the third party presenting and the notary accepting a pre-signed document for notarization.

In previous decades, occasional proposals to allow paper notarizations when document signers would connect with notaries by telephone or by video were roundly refused. But, the times, communications technologies, and attitudes are changing. The key reasons for the requirement of personal appearance by the document signer are to assure the signer's identity can be reasonably ascertained and confirmed, allow the notary and signer to communicate in real time, permit the contemporaneous signing of a document by the signer and of a notarial certificate by the notary, allow the notary to adequately assess the mental competence and willingness of the signer, and provide a secure record as evidence of the notarization.

Note: *Reminder Regarding Electronic Notarizations.* As noted earlier, this book does not address issues of electronic notarizations, including the developing interest in remote or webcam notarizations. Also, this book does not cover the modified definitions of "personal appearance" by signers who are viewed in real time online while at remote sites. This author expects far greater acceptance of remote electronic notarizations will have been achieved by the time of the next edition of this book.

9.1 The notary should understand the importance of the personal presence of document signers at notarizations.

The most important requirement for the notary and the document signer in a notarization of a traditional paper document is the absolute obligation that the signer be physically present at the notarization ceremony. Only if the signer is personally present can several essential features about the signer be established or confirmed by the notary.

(1) Only with the notary and the signer present together can the notary positively identify the signer — or at least exercise reasonable diligence in attempting to identify the signer — by observing and questioning the signer and examining an ID document(s). See also the discussion of identification of document signers in Chapter 10.

(2) Only with the notary and signer present together can the notary witness the making of the signer's present signature on the instrument to be notarized, or in the case of an acknowledgment notarization, can the notary take the signer's acknowledgment that she or he had previously executed the signature on the instrument to be notarized. See also the discussion of name and signature requirements in Chapter 11.

(3) Only with the notary and signer present together can the notary take the steps necessary to diligently assess the mental competence of the signer to execute the instrument to be notarized. See also the discussion of assessment of signer mental competence in Chapter 13.

(4) Only with the notary and signer present together can the notary take the steps necessary to diligently assess the willingness of the signer to execute the document to be notarized. See also the discussion of assessment of signer willingness in Chapter 14.

(5) In the case of a jurat (verification on oath or affirmation) notarization, only with the notary and document signer present together can the notary reliably administer an oral oath or affirmation to the signer. See also the discussion of jurat notarizations in Chapter 5 and of oaths and affirmations in Chapter 15.

(6) Only with the notary and signer present together can the notary complete the notary journal entry to record the notarization, which includes a present signature of the document signer and possibly the affixation by the signer of her or his thumbprint. See also the discussion of the notary journal in Chapter 17.

9.2 The notary should require the document signer to be in the personal, physical presence of the notary for every notarization.

Notary statutes everywhere in the U.S. expressly or impliedly require document signers to personally appear at traditional, paper document notarization ceremonies. Many court decisions from around the country have confirmed this vital requirement. This mandate includes the requirement of the notary and the signer to appear in the physical presence of one another — as opposed to their simply being in the same building or rooms at an address without being personally together.

Yet, in addition to the legal duty, the highly valuable reasons for the document signer's personal appearance, set out immediately above, warrant the notary's demanding the presence of each document signer at each notarization. Moreover, the notary and the signer should remain together for the full duration of the notarial ceremony. This procedure can be important because there have been cases reported in which signers have been accompanied by family, caregivers, or friends to notarization ceremonies, in which the signers have promptly executed their signatures on transactional documents, and in which the signers were then quickly escorted away from the immediate vicinity of the notary while the remainder of the notarization ceremonies were completed. In other words, the signers apparently were unaware that their signatures were going to be notarized. Instead, the notary should be careful at each notarial ceremony to make abundantly clear to every signer that an official notarization bearing legal significance will be performed, and the notary and signer should remain together throughout the entire ceremony.

9.3 The notary should keep the document signer within the notary's line of sight throughout the notarization ceremony.

There are numerous reports of rather casual conduct of notarization ceremonies in which notaries and signers may be in the same general location but separated in different rooms or hidden from one another by walls, furnishings, or people, such that the notaries could not observe the signers for substantial segments of the ceremonies and could not witness the actual document signings. The notary should be sure to personally witness the actual signing of the transactional document, or in the case of an acknowledgment notarization, the acknowledging of the prior signing of the signature.

If signings occur outside the view of notaries, the notarization ceremonies could be corrupted by skillful wrongdoers who might forge signatures when signers are separated from the notaries, or switch signature pages or entire documents when the notaries cannot see the actual signings. Forgers and wrongdoers can be quite unscrupulous in planning their mischief, so notaries should be careful to observe the actual signing or acknowledging of the document. Notaries should not allow documents to be removed from their view or the view of document signers during notarial ceremonies to prevent switching of documents.

Case Illustration. Real cases often seem stranger than fiction. This author was consulted on a case in which a notary had been called to the home of a husband and wife to notarize a transfer of funds from the husband to the wife. The husband was terminally ill and bedridden at home in one of its bedrooms at the back of the house. Upon arrival of the notary and while in the living room, the wife had presented the husband's driver's license to the notary as his identification. The wife took the notary back to meet the husband, and the notary observed that it was the husband in bed and that he was conscious and alert. But then, the wife and notary returned to the living room where the wife showed the notary the document that was going to be signed by the husband and notarized by the notary. The wife then left the notary in the living room, taking the document to the back area of the home for signing by the husband out of the view of the notary. The wife returned with the signed document, and the notary completed the certificate of notarization. The state notary statute did not require the notary to maintain a notary journal, and this notary did not keep a journal. The husband soon died, and the husband's children from a previous marriage challenged the notarization, claiming the wife's lover was hiding in one of the other bedrooms and, when the wife brought the document to the lover, he forged the husband's signature that was then notarized by the notary. I expressed the opinion that the procedure followed in this case was improper, for the notary did not observe the signer throughout the notarial ceremony and did not even witness the actual signing of the document to be notarized. Proper observation by the notary should have prevented a possible forgery of the kind claimed in this case. Parenthetically, if the notary had kept a journal, the notary should have obtained a present signature of the husband in the journal while they were face-to-face in the presence of one another — thereby also preventing possible forgery by an imposter hiding in another room.

Furthermore, notarial ceremonies are typically brief, and yet notaries are expected to make assessments of signers' willingness and mental competence in those short time spans. Notaries should be making those assessments throughout the notarial ceremonies and should not forgo part of the limited opportunity to evaluate willingness and competence of signers by letting them out of view. Who knows what might be going on outside the view of notaries. Signers could be drinking alcohol, taking medications, or using illegal drugs. Third parties could be threatening signers. Signers could be saying or doing things relevant to their willingness or competence to sign.

Practice Tip: *Journalize.* The many values of the notary journal will be touted repeatedly throughout this book, and this author hopes the reader will bear with me and hear me out to help understand the various ways the journal can serve the notary. Importantly, as noted in the case example on the previous page, the notary should create a journal entry for each document notarization, including the execution of a present signature by the document signer. Notaries should never allow the removal of their notary journals from their immediate personal possession. Thus, the signing of the journal entry must be accomplished by the signer while in the immediate presence and line of sight of the notary. No exceptions. Similarly, if the applicable state or territorial law does not prohibit the practice, the notary should request that the signer place a thumbprint in the notary journal entry. That thumbprinting procedure must be done in full view of the notary. No exceptions. The journal should deter some wrongdoers from attempting misconduct and should prevent the switching of documents and signers. See also the discussion of notary journals in Chapter 17.

9.4 The notary should record the signer's personal presence at the notarization in the notarial certificate.

Earlier in this chapter, this author observed that one of the most serious and common faults committed by notaries is the performance of notarizations without the document signer being personally present. Absence of the signer from the notarial ceremony renders the notarization invalid, null, and void, and constitutes potentially criminal conduct by the notary — often called "official misconduct." Under such circumstances, it should be impressed upon every notary that there is an absolute obligation for the signer to personally appear for the notarial ceremony. Thus, every notarial certificate should recite, what most certificates already do, that the signer personally appeared before the notary for the notarial ceremony. If this requirement is stated in plain and clear language, and if the notary recognizes that she or he thereby certifies such appearance by the signer, under penalty of law for falsification, perhaps the frequent faults of the past will not continue to occur.

The law of notarization in every U.S. jurisdiction requires the document signer to personally appear for the notarial ceremony. Thus, even if the certificate of notarization were not to mention that the signer personally appeared, the signer would have been required to be personally present, the notary would have been required to have the signer personally present in order to perform the notarization, and the notary would have violated notary law and possibly criminal law if a notarization had been performed in the absence of the signer.

9.5 The notary should create a notary journal entry, including a present signature of the document signer, to verify the signer's presence at the notarization.

On the face of a certificate of notarization, it seems that the document signer must have appeared at the notarial ceremony. But, in reality that is not necessarily so. Negligent notaries too often allow pre-signed documents to be presented and notarized without the signers appearing. Usually, there is no other written evidence of the parties in attendance at notarizations. However, the notary journal can reliably provide corroboration that the signer was in fact present at the notarial ceremony. If a notary adheres to the practice of creating a journal entry for every official act, this routine will prevent the notary from notarizing for an absent signer because the signer must be present in order to sign the journal entry.

One of the significant values of the notary journal is that a proper journal is tamper-evident. It is a contemporaneous and chronological record, in a bound book so that the pages and entries cannot be removed or added without detection. Thus, if the notary journal includes a signature of the document signer, that signature must have been executed at the time of the notarization — unless the notary has colluded with other parties to falsify the notarization. And thankfully, notaries rarely engage in such dishonesty and fraud.

On the other hand, document signers sometimes get signer's remorse, change their minds about the desirability of their transactions, and falsely contend they did not attend the notarizations, asserting their signatures are forgeries. The journal entry with a present signature and other information included will help deter such fraud by a signer. The signature in the journal will show that someone attended the notarization and signed the transactional document and the journal entry, and the two signatures should match one another almost exactly. A forger would be less able to execute two nearly identical signatures while simultaneously attempting to replicate someone else's signature. Moreover, some of the other information in the journal should help to confirm it was the signer who really attended, as should be proven by the ID document expiration date and the thumbprint (which will be covered in the next section of this chapter).

9.6 The notary should, unless prohibited by state or territorial law, request the document signer to place the signer's thumbprint in the journal entry to verify the signer's presence at the notarization.

A serious problem with standard notarizations that do not include notary journal entries and thumbprints is that such notarizations are documented solely by their notarial certificates. If the certificates are clear and complete on their faces, those notarizations will enjoy a legal presumption of regularity and validity. Yet, it is possible (and unfortunately it happens with frequency) that the document signer will not really have appeared in the presence of the notary at the time of the notarization. Unfortunately, uninformed or dishonest notaries often allow this faulty practice. Yet the certificate will look valid, although it will contain the false representation by the notary that the signer was present. The certificate will look valid although either the transactional instrument was signed previously by the document signer, or the signer's signature was forged by someone else.

Some jurisdictions have enacted statutes generally prohibiting the collection of biometric data. And, some jurisdictions specifically prohibit notaries from obtaining the thumbprints or fingerprints of document signers, including prohibitions against notaries placing thumbprints in notary journals. If the applicable state or territorial law does not forbid notaries to do so, one method to better assure the reliability of the certificate's statement that the document signer personally appeared is to affix the thumbprint of the signer in the notary journal entry to virtually guarantee that the signer actually appeared at the time of the notarization. Because the journal remains in the notary's possession, there is almost no possibility the thumbprint can be falsified. Of course, the thumbprint is also highly valuable for identifying the signer, as will be addressed later. See also the discussion of notary journal entries in Chapter 17.

The thumbprint topic will also be addressed in the next chapter about identifying document signers because the thumbprint serves that purpose as well. See Chapter 10.

Practice Tip: *Protecting the Journal Thumbprint.* Notary journals containing signer thumbprints must be protected from theft or other unauthorized access. Such journals should be kept under lock and key in the exclusive possession of the notary. The notary whose journal includes signer thumbprints should redact such prints if copies are made of journal entries and released to private parties upon appropriate requests for access. See the more extensive discussion of journal and thumbprint security in Chapter 17.

9.7 The notary should be aware of the changing definition of personal presence in some jurisdictions regarding remote or webcam notarizations.

As noted previously, the times and the technology have changed in recent years, so a number of states have enacted statutes which approve of so-called "remote" or "webcam" notarizations. Such notarizations are conducted with the notary and document signer in different locations separated by some distance, but connected by an online audio and video link, with a secure digital recording of the notarial ceremony created and preserved. The topic is so important that this author felt it needed to be emphasized by allotting it a separate practice statement here.

Although the original and traditional definition of personal presence or personal appearance would not permit such notarizations, the definition has been modified to allow for remote or webcam notarial ceremonies because the general conclusion has become that the resulting notarizations are sufficiently rigorous and secure to be worthy of approval. Moreover, valuable commercial advantages are driving the technology, its security measures, and its notarial applications. Thus, for instance, the creation and maintenance of a digital record of each remote or webcam notarization constitutes a key element in the adoption of a modified view of personal presence or personal appearance in those jurisdictions which have to date endorsed remote or webcam notarizations.

Incidentally, remote or webcam notarizations lawfully performed in a U.S. state or territory should be legally recognized in other U.S. states and territories, even if those other jurisdictions have not yet enacted remote or webcam notarization laws. This author believes remote and webcam notarizations are part of the technological wave of the near future, and I expect that every U.S. jurisdiction will in due course adopt its own law authorizing such practices. ■

***RELEVANT MODEL NOTARY LAW**

Each notary should read, study, and abide by the notary statute and regulations, if any, of his or her commissioning jurisdiction.

"Personal Appearance. 'Personal appearance before the notary' and 'appears in person before the notary' mean that the notary is physically close enough to see, hear, communicate with, and receive identification documents from a principal [document signer] and any required witness." *Model Notary Act,* Section 2-15 (2010).

"The Notary shall require the presence of each document signer and oath-taker in order to carefully screen each for identity and willingness, and to observe that each appears aware of the significance of the transaction requiring a notarial act." *Notary Public Code of Professional Responsibility,* Guiding Principle III (1998).

"Requirements For Notarial Acts. A notary shall perform a notarial act only if the principal [document signer]: (1) is in the presence of the notary at the time of notarization ..." *Model Notary Act,* Section 5-2(1) (2010).

"Personal Appearance Required. If a notarial act relates to a statement made in or a signature executed on a record, the individual making the statement or executing the signature shall appear personally before the notarial officer." *Revised Uniform Law on Notarial Acts,* Section 6 (2010).

SHERIFF'S DEED. Foreclosure by Advertisement. Sec. 7479, '03 Code. THE TRANSCRIPT, New Rockford, N. D.

This Indenture, Made the 10th day of April, in the year of our Lord one thousand nine hundred and nineteen between M. C. Stenaby as Sheriff of the County of Eddy, in the State of North Dakota, party of the first part, and Gilbert Christenson of the County of Eddy and State of North Dakota party of the second part,

WITNESSETH: WHEREAS, default having been made by a certain Mortgage Deed bearing date the 2nd day of January, A. D. 1913, for the purpose of securing the payment of the sum of Eight Hundred Dollars, and interest at the rate of ... per cent per annum, according to the conditions of one certain promissory note..., bearing date the 2nd day of January, A. D. 1913, all mortgaged to Northwestern Mutual Savings and Loan Association heirs or assigns, certain tract... piece... or parcel... of land hereinafter particularly described, together with all the hereditaments and appurtenances thereunto belonging or in anywise appertaining, which said mortgage was afterwards, on the 27th day of January, A. D. 1913, at 4 o'clock in the afternoon, duly recorded in the Office of the Register of Deeds, in and for the County of Eddy and State of North Dakota, in Book 40 of Mortgages, on Page 353

AND WHEREAS, The said mortgage was duly assigned by an instrument in writing, duly executed and delivered by the said ... to ... dated the ... day of ..., 191..., and recorded in said office of the Register of Deeds on the ... day of ..., 191..., at ... o'clock ... m., in Book ... of Mortgages, on Page ...

AND WHEREAS, The said mortgage was duly assigned by an instrument in writing, duly executed and delivered by the said ... to ... dated the ... day of ..., 191..., and recorded in said office of the Register of Deeds on the ... day of ..., 191..., at ... o'clock ... m., in Book ... of Mortgages, on Page ...

AND WHEREAS, The said Northwestern Mutual Savings and Loan Association the Mortgagee... aforesaid, did cause due and legal notice of foreclosure by sale of said mortgaged precises to be given as required by law;

AND WHEREAS, The said M. C. Stenaby Sheriff aforesaid, on the 30th day of March, A. D. 1918, at 2 o'clock in the after noon of that day, in accordance with said notice and pursuant to the statute in such case made and provided, sold the said mortgaged premises hereinafter described, to Northwestern Mutual Savings and Loan Association the party of the second part, for the sum of Three Hundred and fifty one and 4/100 DOLLARS;

AND WHEREAS, The time has expired for the redemption of said premises, and no redemption from such sale has been made, and the said party of the second part ... the owner... and holder... of said Certificate of Sale;

AND WHEREAS, The said Certificate was assigned by an instrument thereof, duly executed and delivered by the said Northwestern Mutual Savings and Loan Association to Gilbert Christenson dated the 23rd day of January, A. D. 1919 and recorded in said office of the Register of Deeds on the 25th day of January, A. D. 1919, at 4 o'clock P. m., in Book 7 of Mcl, on Page 244

NOW THEREFORE, THIS INDENTURE WITNESSETH, That the said M. C. Stenaby Sheriff aforesaid, party of the first part, in order to complete the sale so made by him in pursuance of the power of sale contained in said mortgage, and in conformity to the statute in such case made and provided, and in consideration of the premises, has bargained, sold, released and confirmed, and by these presents does grant, bargain, sell, convey and confirm, unto the said party of the second part, the following described piece... or parcel... of land, situate in the County of Eddy and State of North Dakota, to-wit:

Lot numbered eleven (11) and twelve (12) in Block Nine (9) of Townsite of Sheyenne,

1919, trifold, sheriff's deed, including a certificate of North Dakota notary public J.V.N. Sundberg for the signature witnessing of the deputy sheriff who served the notice for the sheriff's foreclosure sale of the subject real property. There is also a perfect notarial embosser seal impression affixed to the certificate.

Chapter

10

Identifying Document Signers

STANDARDS SUMMARY

10.1 The notary should understand the importance of the proper identification of document signers.

10.2 The notary should be aware that under law the notary does not guarantee the accuracy of the identification of document signers.

10.3 The notary should be aware that the law requires the notary to exercise reasonable care to accurately identify document signers.

10.4 The notary should require each instrument signer to show one or more reliable ID documents and should closely examine those ID documents to ascertain their trustworthiness.

10.5 The notary should obtain and observe at least one present signature, and compare at least three signatures, of the document signer for each notarization.

10.6 The notary should note the method used to identify the document signer in the notarial certificate,

10.7 The notary should, if not prohibited by applicable law, request the document signer to affix a thumbprint in the notary journal entry.

10.8 The notary should note the ID document(s), and the month and year of expiration, relied upon to identify the instrument signer in the notary journal entry.

10.9 The notary should, prior to the completion of each notarization, proofread the signer identification sections of the notarial certificate and journal entry and make necessary additions and corrections.

STANDARDS EXPLANATIONS

One of the most important responsibilities of the notary public in performing document notarizations is to establish the identity of the document signers, thereby providing a heightened degree of security for documents which are notarized versus ordinary non-notarized instruments. As a further consequence of this feature of notarization, commerce is encouraged because trust can be placed in notarized documents — especially when parties to transactions are unknown to one another and/or when parties execute transactions without meeting face-to-face with one another at the time of such signings.

Historically, there have been three ways by which notaries have been authorized to identify document signers: (1) the notary's personal knowledge of the signer; (2) the notary's examination of one or more reliable ID documents of the signer; and (3) the notary's receipt of the testimony of a credible witness with personal knowledge of the signer. These three methods are still allowed by the notary law of the great majority of U.S. jurisdictions. In early times, before travel was so prevalent and before ID documents were commonplace, the identification of signers personally known to notaries and the word of credible witnesses were necessary methods of identification. But, not today.

Impersonation by document signers and resulting document frauds are frequent and serious problems for notaries, having significant financial consequences for innocent third parties as well as notaries. This irrefutable fact makes the proper identification of document signers extremely important for notaries. Indeed, notaries risk legal liability, or at least legal challenges, if they allow imposters to succeed and obtain notarizations.

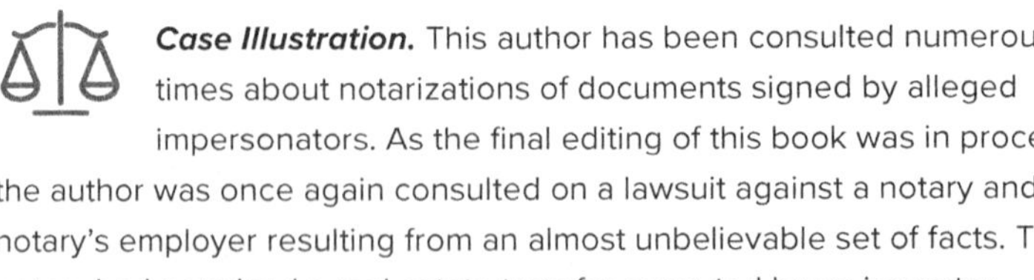

Case Illustration. This author has been consulted numerous times about notarizations of documents signed by alleged impersonators. As the final editing of this book was in process, the author was once again consulted on a lawsuit against a notary and the notary's employer resulting from an almost unbelievable set of facts. The notary had notarized a real estate transfer executed by an imposter. Remarkably, in this instance, the notary had notarized for a signer transferring land six years earlier, and the same signer reappeared six years later impersonating the landowner transferring the land back to the impersonator in her real name. The two parties to the real estate transfers had similar physical appearances, and the notary claimed not to have recognized the imposter as someone personally known to the notary six years later. So, the diligent notary requested ID from the signer and recorded it in her notary journal. Under notary law, if a notary exercises reasonable care in attempting to identify the signer but is nevertheless duped by a skillful imposter, the notary will not have legal liability for the forgery. That was my opinion of what had happened here.

Note: *Author's Rejection of Credible Witness.* In this modern era, everyone who is old enough to obtain notarial services is old enough to obtain reliable ID documents, so the use of a credible witness should not be necessary. Moreover, in the opinion of this author, the use of a credible witness shifts the responsibility for a vital feature of a proper notarization away from the impartial governmental official (the notary) to a lay witness with no legal responsibility for the notarization. In other words, the credible witness becomes a quasi-notary with regard to signer identification, and this alternative should not be tolerated. This book will not further address the use of credible witnesses, although many jurisdictions still allow this procedure.

Note: *Author's Disapproval of Notary's Personal Knowledge Test.* Whether a notary is sufficiently acquainted with another person to make the acquaintance "personally known" can be uncertain. Even parties with whom one has dealt for years may not be who they claim to be. Since everyone old enough to seek a notarization should have, or should be able to acquire, ID documents, notaries ought to require all signers to produce one or more reliable IDs. Examination of an ID document is a more objective method for use by a notary, and a method that can be objectively recorded in a notary journal entry. Furthermore, review of an ID should actually focus a notary upon the task of identification, by referencing the signer's photograph, physical description, and signature. If a notarization is challenged, the notary who has always examined signer IDs and who has always recorded those IDs in the notary journal will be allowed to prove that habit of sound practice. And, judges and juries will be favorably impressed. This book will not further address identification by personal knowledge, although all but one jurisdiction still allow this procedure.

Practice Tip: *A Ceremony-Long Process.* The process of the notary's identification of the document signer starts at the very beginning of the notarization ceremony and lasts throughout the ceremony. If at any time during the notarial ceremony, the notary recognizes objective concerns about the signer's true identity, the notary should raise and resolve those concerns and either proceed with the notarization or refuse to notarize. The notary's authority and responsibility last throughout the notarial ceremony.

10.1 The notary should understand the importance of the proper identification of document signers.

At the heart of a document notarization is the obligation of the notary public to exercise diligence and reasonable care to positively identify the document signer. Everything else about a notarization follows from the signer really being who she or he claims to be. It is the true signer who must be personally present, who must be mentally competent, who must be willing to execute the document to be notarized, and in the case of a jurat notarization, who must swear to or affirm the truth of the document's contents.

The present is a time of frequent attempts at identity theft, imposture, and document fraud. A number of circumstances present heightened risks that imposters will attempt to defeat notaries and will succeed in duping them. Those factors include one or more of the following:

(1) settings in which a notary performs a high volume of notarizations,

(2) settings in which a notary notarizes for strangers unknown to the notary,

(3) settings in which a notary notarizes for elderly, seriously ill, terminally ill, and/or hospitalized, hospice-bound, or nursing home resident signers, and

(4) settings in which a notary notarizes valuable commercial and financial instruments.

Of course, a huge contributing factor favoring imposters is a lack of knowledge and diligence by a notary, especially:

(5) where a notary improperly performs a notarization for an absent document signer,

(6) where a notary fails to insist upon careful examination of reliable documents of identification from document signers, and/or

(7) where a notary neglects to maintain a notary journal entry to record each official act.

Practice Tip: *Be a Savvy Notary.* The factors just identified will not stand alone, for almost always there will be multiple factors present, and many imposters will tend to be skillful at their wrongdoing. Some successful imposters will have done their homework and will have selected their notaries with care. Imposters will learn whether a notary closely examines IDs and whether a notary keeps a journal of notarizations. Imposters will prefer using a notary who regularly performs notarizations of valuable instruments for strangers, as this notary may treat such notarizations as routine and not detect the misconduct of an imposter. To counter the skillful imposter, the notary needs not only to be diligent and rigorous in following the notary statute and best practice standards, but also to be savvy in recognizing the kinds of situations which may present heightened risks for wrongdoer involvement. Although every notarization deserves to be taken seriously by the notary, higher-risk notarizations should be taken even more seriously.

10.2 The notary should be aware that under law the notary does not guarantee the accuracy of the identification of document signers.

The legal standard for the conduct of virtually all persons is the same. We are supposed to act with reasonable care — whether we are accountants, airline pilots, automobile drivers, bankers, lawyers, medical doctors, or notaries public. Business professionals and public officials are supposed to use the reasonable care expected of similarly situated individuals. This view is the sensible one, for it cannot be expected that people will be required to act perfectly or else face legal liability. If notaries and other business professionals were required to perform perfectly, no one would be willing to serve and face such an impossible standard.

Thus, when it comes to the task of notaries establishing the identity of document signers, the law requires them to act with reasonable care. In other words, notaries need to take steps as would be taken by other diligent notaries to allow them to identify signers with reasonable certainty. Notaries should be diligent and use their best efforts to identify document signers, but notaries cannot assure the correct identification of signers. To say it differently, notaries are not guarantors of the correct identification of document signers. If, for example, a capable imposter skillfully deceives a diligent notary, the notary will not face legal liability for negligent conduct, even if some third party affected by the falsely notarized document suffers financial injury.

10.3 The notary should be aware that the law requires the notary to exercise reasonable care to accurately identify document signers.

Rather than guaranteeing the identity of document signers, notaries are legally required to exercise reasonable care in the identification of signers. Hence, if the notary takes steps reasonably calculated to identify the instrument signer, the notary will not have legal liability if a skillful imposter succeeds in deceiving the notary and perpetrating a fraud upon an unsuspecting third party. This outcome of protecting the diligent notary from liability is appropriate because the absolutely conclusive identification of an individual at the time of a notarization ceremony is not really possible.

What constitutes reasonable care in identifying signers? Specifically, the notary should converse with the document signer, inquire about the signer's identity, and observe the body language and demeanor of the signer, all with the purpose of helping to verify the signer's identity. Further, the notary should diligently examine documents of identification and thoroughly record such ID document examinations in both the certificate of notarization and the journal entry for the notarization — as more fully explained below. As part of this identification process, the notary should obtain one or two present signatures from the document signer on the transactional document and the journal entry (discussed below). The notary should closely observe those signings. Signatures made by the rightful parties should generally be free and flowing, while those made by imposters trying to copy someone else's signature tend to be unnatural and forced. The notary should compare the three signatures on the transactional instrument, on the ID document, and in the journal entry to see if they appear reasonably similar. The notary should also request a thumbprint impression from the document signer for the journal entry, if not prohibited by law. See also the discussion of signatures in Chapter 11 and the discussion of thumbprints in Chapter 17.

Practice Tip: *Perhaps Get More Signatures.* If after observing the signing(s) and comparing the signatures, the notary has doubt about their similarity and the signer's identity, the notary should ask the signer to execute one or more additional sample signatures — using the next line or field in the notary journal (to preserve the example signatures to help demonstrate the notary's reasonable care).

10.4 The notary should require each instrument signer to show one or more reliable ID documents and should closely examine those ID documents to ascertain their trustworthiness.

This author is of the opinion notaries should insist that all instrument signers present one or more official and reliable government-issued documents of identification, and all notaries should diligently scrutinize those ID documents. Notaries should not identify document signers on the basis of personal knowledge, nor should notaries rely upon credible witnesses to identify document signers, even if those methods are allowed by the state or territorial notary statute. Notaries should certainly be encouraged to be more rigorous than allowed by statute — to protect the public and themselves. Notarization is an official, serious, and important governmental function. Treating all signers alike by requiring everyone seeking notarizations to present reliable ID documents is a professional and reasonable practice standard. After all, everyone should have reliable ID available.

Requiring all instrument signers to produce one or more reliable ID documents has significant advantages over other methods of identification. Insisting upon IDs being presented by all document signers will establish proof of a business routine or habit of reasonable care by the notary — provided that the review of IDs is recorded in the notarial certificate and in the notary journal entry for the relevant notarization. Such proof will be significant if a notarization is ever challenged. Remember, the reasonable care standard is the level of diligence and prudence required to be exercised by a notary in identifying document signers.

Next, requiring all signers to present IDs provides the notary with a number of objective and useful pieces of factual information, such as a physical description of the signer, a photograph of the signer, and an exemplar signature of the signer, to help corroborate (or to negate) the identification of the signer. Diligent notaries will closely examine each of those elements and compare each to the signer or to the signer's other signatures on the transactional instrument and in the notary journal.

Some notary statutes and notary regulations designate the specific ID documents which may be relied upon by a notary to establish by "satisfactory evidence" the identity of an instrument signer, and notaries should abide by those requirements. In other states and territories without such ID laws, notaries are generally required to have satisfactory evidence of the identity of a signer but are not usually provided further guidance about what that means. So, notaries should insist upon reviewing a reliable government-issued ID. A reliable government-issued ID should include at least five important elements: (1) the date of birth of the bearer; (2) a physical description of the bearer; (3) a facial photograph of the individual named on the ID; (4) a signature of the person named; and (5) current status of the ID or its expiration fewer than five years before the present date of the notarization. Some jurisdictions may require only a current ID or an ID that has been expired less than a specified time since the date of issue. Importantly, a notary may need to be presented with two or more government-issued IDs so that they can be read together in order to satisfy the five elements just noted. Of course, ID documents issued by some foreign governments are notoriously unreliable, and notaries should not accept such IDs from such foreign countries. Notaries would be well-advised to request signers using foreign IDs from less reliable places to produce at least two or more IDs.

Let us consider the five elements noted above. (1) Estimating people's ages from their appearances can be very difficult and unreliable. The date of birth in conjunction with the other elements of an ID can be useful to help prevent imposture by someone who appears substantially younger or older than suggested by the D.O.B. (2) The physical description should include such factors as height, weight, eye color, and hair color. But, of course, almost all of those features may change or may be changed. (3) A facial photo should be reasonably similar in appearance to the document signer who is present at the notarization, although again the facial appearance of a person may change over time or may be modified by hair styles, facial hair, shaving, injury, surgery, make-up, and accessories (such as glasses, hats, and clothing). (4) Even signatures for many people change from time to time, especially depending upon the exact form of the name that is signed. (5) Some jurisdictions require that an ID used for notarization purposes must be current or unexpired, but it seems that a notary should be able to use some discretion about this matter. Indeed, a notary should employ discretion in judging the reliability of IDs and should not hesitate to request a document signer to present more than one ID to corroborate (or to negate) an identification.

ID documents can be altered or forged, so notaries should closely examine them. Wrongdoers can create very effective altered or forged IDs, which cannot be detected as false. Notaries should look for signs of mischief, such as misspelled words, punctuation errors, photos that appear to have been added later, signatures which do not match cardholders' printed names, and birthdates or ages that do not seem to match photos. Notaries should not hesitate to question signers about information on IDs, to test signers' knowledge of the data. And, notaries should not hesitate to ask to see another ID document for comparison purposes.

Practice Tip: *Ask for Two IDs.* As has been noted, requiring all instrument signers to produce an official and reliable ID document allows the notary to ask to see one or more additional IDs if the first ID is not sufficiently reliable. This author favors asking all document signers to produce two government-issued IDs because this heightened standard would require would-be imposters to have to forge, falsify, or steal two IDs, rather than just one, in order to perpetrate mischief upon a notary, and would definitely provide heightened security as the result of the additional identification information and corroboration. This practice should also be noted in the journal entry and should help to prove the notary's exercise of reasonable care.

Note: *Problems of Names and Signatures for Certain IDs.* The names and/or signatures for some individuals on their IDs may be problematic. Names may have changed due to marriage, divorce, or legal name-change proceedings. But, IDs may not have been changed. Names on IDs may appear inconsistent with the genders for persons who have undergone or who are undergoing medical transgender procedures. But, IDs may not have changed. Individuals who sign by marks, and individuals who are permanently physically unable to sign their own names and whose signatures are executed by surrogates, may have difficulty providing satisfactory IDs bearing their signatures. But, ID signatures should match the signatures affixed to documents being notarized and to the journal entries for the notarizations. Individuals suffering from temporary illnesses or injuries may be physically unable to sign their signatures at notarial ceremonies. But, their IDs will not have been changed and will bear signatures that cannot be matched by present signatures at notarial ceremonies on either the documents to be notarized or on the related journal entries. What is the notary to do? The answer is that the notary should always place the responsibility to establish identity where it resides — with the document signer. Signers must prove their identities with reasonable certainty. A notarization should be refused if the document signer cannot positively convince the notary of the signer's true identity. See also the discussion of names and signatures in Chapter 11.

Note: *Special Concerns About IDs for Elderly Signers.* ID documents may be somewhat problematic for some elderly signers, either because elderly individuals may have few, if any, satisfactory ID documents or because their ID documents may have expired. However, these difficulties should not drive notaries to be less diligent about requiring elderly signers to properly identify themselves. After all, it is the responsibility of signers to possess and to present satisfactory ID, not the task of notaries to accommodate the elderly by accepting inadequate and unreliable IDs. Elderly persons who wish to obtain notarizations should plan ahead and acquire proper IDs. Of course, as suggested above, more than one ID document may need to be read together, especially in the case of an elderly signer, in order to satisfy the four elements noted previously. And, some documents used for corroboration of identification may not be of the type we commonly characterize as reliable ID documents — such as government-issued medical records, employment records and badges, and so forth. If elderly persons present themselves for notarizations without sufficient IDs, the notarization should be withheld until such time as the elderly individuals are able to obtain proper IDs. When notarizations are scheduled in advance, notaries should try to mitigate these problems about IDs for the elderly by reminding every signer that he or she will be asked to produce proper and current ID documents.

Note: *Transgender Signers.* Notaries should seldom encounter any issues resulting from the performance of notarizations for transgender signers. Indeed, notaries should rarely be aware that a signer is a transgender person, and notaries should not ordinarily ask the signer about his or her gender. Notaries should always conduct themselves in professional and respectful manners. The gender of the signer is not ordinarily a relevant issue in a notarization, even if a signer volunteers information revealing the transgender status. However, if a signer's name, gender designation, or photograph on the signer's ID does not appear to match the apparent gender of the signer, then the issue of the signer's identity must be addressed by the notary. It is the responsibility of the transgender signer to present reliable ID(s) to support his or her identity corresponding to the name to be executed by the signer on the transactional instrument and to be placed by the notary in the notarial certificate. Transgender persons should be well-aware of identification issues and their need to obtain new ID(s) during or after their gender reassignments. To date, a few U.S. jurisdictions have modified their driver's license and ID procedures to permit bearers to indicate other than the usual male or female choice, such as to mark an "X" in the gender box, or to select "nonbinary." Of course, if the transgender matter does become relevant to a notarization, the notary should record the relevant facts and circumstances in the journal entry.

10.5 The notary should obtain and observe at least one present signature, and compare at least three signatures, of the document signer for each notarization.

One of the most relevant and important elements in the identification of a document signer is the individual's name and corresponding signature. Such a signature can take two forms — an already existing signature and a present signature — and both are valuable for comparison purposes. Additionally, both the signer's manner of making a present signature and the appearance of the signature as a final product are valuable pieces of the identification puzzle.

A total of at least three signatures of the document signer should be examined and compared, and at least one or two of them will be present signatures: (1) the signature on the transactional instrument (which signature may have been executed previously for some acknowledgment notarizations, but which is usually executed in the presence of the notary); (2) the already existing signature on one or more of the signer's ID documents; and (3) the present signature of the signer placed in the notary journal at the time of the notarization. See also the discussion of document signer name and signature requirements in Chapter 11.

There are two ways a notary may obtain a present signature from a document signer at a notarial ceremony. (1) The document signer may, or may not, execute a present signature on the transactional instrument, but it depends on the type of notarization being conducted. There will always be a present signature by the document signer for a jurat and a signature-witnessing notarization. And, there may be a present signature for an acknowledgment notarization, although for an acknowledgment, the signer may have signed in advance of the notarization (and simply acknowledged it at the time of the notarial ceremony). (2) The notary should always obtain a present signature of the document signer in the notary journal entry. If two present signatures are executed at the notarial ceremony, the notary should compare them, and those signatures should reasonably match.

Importantly, the notary should watch the actual signing. The notary should not allow himself or herself to be distracted or allow the signer out of sight when the signing occurs. The notary should observe the signer's manner and method of signing, and the manner and method should be the same for each signature. As mentioned previously, an individual's signature over time should have become routine, natural, and flowing, in a continuous or almost unbroken motion. On the other hand, when someone is trying to copy or forge another's signature, the imposter will not ordinarily find the signing to be so smooth and easy. Instead, an imposter may sign in a slower, halting, broken, and unnatural manner.

A pre-existing signature on one or more ID documents will help the notary to identify the signer. The pre-existing signature(s) should be compared with the present signature(s), and all of the signatures should be reasonably similar. It should be recognized that an individual's signature may change over time, due to advancing age, medical conditions, and/or intentional modifications.

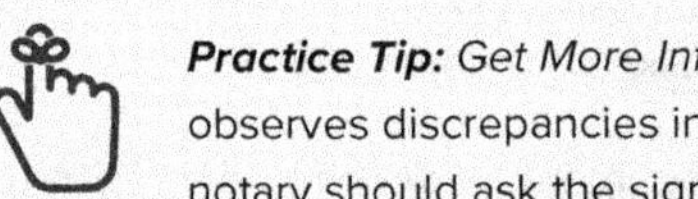

***Practice Tip:** Get More Information if Needed.* If the notary observes discrepancies in the signatures being compared, the notary should ask the signer to explain the differing appearances. The notary could ask to see other of the signer's ID documents bearing signatures for further comparison. As noted above, the notary could even ask the signer to place another present exemplar signature or two or more in the notary journal (if necessary, in the next blank area or field of the journal). If upon comparing at least three signatures, the notary finds the disparities between them are too great and cannot reconcile the differences, then the notary may either perform, or refuse to perform, the notarization. Remember, the signature is part of the whole process of identifying the signer. If there is a refusal, it should be recorded in the notary journal entry, with an explanation of one or more objective reasons for the refusal.

10.6 The notary should note the method used to identify the document signer in the notarial certificate.

Because the notarial certificate is one of the two official records of a document notarization, and because the proper identification of the document signer is a critical step of every document notarization, the certificate is an appropriate place for the notary to note the method used to identify the signer. As pointed out before, this author's view is that method should be the notary's review of one or more reliable government-issued ID documents belonging to the signer.

Although the format for some notarial certificates under state and territorial notary statutes and regulations includes reference to the method of signer identification, not all certificate forms do so. If possible, notaries should utilize forms of certificates which include the method of identification, especially forms which allow the notary to indicate that an ID document provided satisfactory evidence of identification and that the particular ID document was examined. If the form pretyped or preprinted onto the instrument to be notarized does not meet this standard, the notary should add the appropriate reference by handwriting the suggested information about the ID document.

In the notarial certificate, the notary should identify the specific type of ID document examined. It is not enough for the notary to note the general kind of ID document, such as a "passport" or a "driver's license." Rather, the notary should be specific about the ID document, such as by indicating a "U.S. passport" or a "Texas driver's license." The reality is that negligent or corrupt notaries sometimes notarize for signers who do not appear at the notarial ceremonies, or that such notaries will perform notarizations for signers without checking any of their ID documents. A notary wishing to cover up such dereliction can simply note in the certificate that a generic ID like a "driver's license" was examined, since almost every adult possesses a driver's license. Later in this chapter, a recommendation is set out directing the notary to record in the journal entry both the specific type of ID and its month and year of expiration. This detailed information will verify that a notary truly reviewed the named ID if the notary was able to confirm its month and year of expiration.

As will be recommended below, the notary should also record the method of identifying the signer in the notary journal, along with the specific type of ID document and its month and year of expiration. See also the discussion of the notary journal in Chapter 17.

10.7 The notary should, if not prohibited by applicable law, request the document signer to affix a thumbprint in the notary journal entry.

Some biometric identifiers, such as DNA, retinal scans, and fingerprints and thumbprints, are unique features of humans that can positively identify individuals. Under current technology, the only one of those biometric identifiers effectively and economically available for use by notaries is fingerprinting or thumbprinting, If state or territorial law does not prohibit a notary from obtaining and preserving a document signer's thumbprint, the notary should request the signer to provide a thumbprint in the notary journal. Indeed, a few states require notaries to obtain and preserve in their notary journals the thumbprint of document signers of certain kinds of transactions because statistics have shown that requiring thumbprints deters wrongdoers from attempting document frauds.

The principal challenge of a notary is to positively identify a document signer, or alternatively at least to exercise reasonable care to correctly identify the signer. If a notary records the thumbprint of a document signer in the notary journal, it would seem the notary has satisfied that notarial responsibility. For regardless of the name claimed by a signer and regardless of the ID document(s) presented by a signer, those things may be false, but a thumbprint is unique to each individual and constitutes positive identification of the individual. While the true name of a signer may not actually be known at the time of a notarial ceremony, if the signer's thumbprint has been recorded in the notary journal, then the notary has positively identified the signer.

Moreover, almost no imposter or identity thief will voluntarily agree to provide a thumbprint, so that will be a significant deterrent if a notary requests signers to affix thumbprint images in notary journal entries. Forgeries and identity thefts should decline in number because wrongdoers will not seek notarizations in the first place, or wrongdoers will decline to complete their attempts to obtain notarizations as soon as they are asked to submit their thumbprints.

Two aspects of this particular standard for notarizations warrant emphasis — (a) the notary should ask the signer to affix a thumbprint, and (b) the thumbprint image should be placed in the journal entry. As to (a), although very few current notary laws provide that notaries may demand signers to provide thumbprints, notaries may certainly ask signers to do so. If a document signer declines to provide the requested thumbprint, this author believes notaries can appropriately interpret declining to submit a thumbprint as grounds to insist the signer provide an additional ID document to establish the signer's identity. If the signer does not provide the requested additional ID, the notary should refuse to notarize and should journalize that refusal.

Note: *A Controversial Issue.* The matters just addressed about asking the signer to submit a thumbprint, interpreting a refusal to do so as the basis for obtaining an additional ID, and refusing to notarize for a signer who does not comply are controversial. These issues are controversial in part because almost no notary statutes and regulations deal with these points. Those who differ with this author's opinion do so in good faith, often pointing out that notaries are public servants who are supposed to perform notarizations, not to refuse to notarize. This author is of the opinion that notaries have the discretion to take the steps described as part of their duties to help protect the public against identity theft, imposture, and document fraud.

As to (b), the thumbprint should be affixed in the notary journal entry for the notarization. Importantly, the notary should protect the security of the journal at all times, as described in a later chapter. Further, the thumbprint should be protected against access unless under subpoena or under direction of the commissioning official or notary oversight agency. If there is a request for access to the relevant journal entry by a private party, and if the access is granted, the notary should redact or cover over the image of the thumbprint. See also the discussion of the journal entry in Chapter 17.

10.8 The notary should note the ID document(s), and the month and year of expiration, relied upon to identify the instrument signer in the notary journal entry.

A recurrent theme throughout this book is the insistence that notaries create official paper trails to record the steps in the notarization process. It is simply the best practice to employ to prove sound notarial performance, which in turn protects all parties who have interests in notarized instruments (including the parties to the documents, the parties who benefit from and/or rely upon the documents, the notaries who perform the notarizations, and the public).

As mentioned earlier, there are two places where notaries should record the identification of document signers — in the certificate of notarization and in the notary journal entry for the notarization. The notary should record the type of ID document examined (such as a U.S. passport or a Texas driver's license) in the notarial certificate. However, in the notary journal entry, the notary should note the specific kind of ID document, along with its month and year of expiration. By noting the month and year of expiration of the ID, the notary can corroborate that the ID was really examined, without recording anything too sensitive (such as the serial number of the ID or its exact day of expiration — which date in some jurisdictions corresponds to the birthdate of the holder of the ID). Unfortunately, some outdated notary statutes still require notaries to record an ID's serial number in the notary journal, but hopefully those laws will soon be repealed or amended. The notary should not record the serial number for the ID because of the risk to signer privacy if there were a breach of security of the notary's records.

Practice Tip: *Do Not Copy IDs.* Some conscientious notaries are tempted to make and retain photocopies or handwritten notes of signer IDs, thinking that doing so will serve as proof of the identification of the signer and of the notary's diligence. However, making photocopies or notes of IDs is unnecessary if the notary indicates both the specific type of ID and its month and year of expiration, for that information would only be known to the notary if the notary had actually examined the ID. Moreover, maintaining a file of signer ID photocopies or information places the privacy of all those signers at risk, and places those signers at heightened risk of identity theft, if there were a breach of security of the notary's file. A notary could face legal liability if the confidential ID information were accessed and a signer suffered financial injury. Hence, notaries should not photocopy or otherwise keep notes of signer ID information.

10.9 The notary should, prior to the completion of each notarization, proofread the signer identification sections of the notarial certificate and journal entry and make necessary additions and corrections.

Because the identification of the instrument signer is such a basic and important part of the notarization process and because of serious concerns about achieving accurate identifications, notaries should carefully proofread the portions of the notarial certificate and journal entry pertaining to instrument signer identification. This proofreading should be undertaken prior to the conclusion of the notarization ceremony. The matters pertaining to signer identification include the recording of ID document information, the signature of the instrument signer, and the thumbprint of the signer. Incidentally, there are two signatures of the document signer — one on the transactional instrument that is notarized and one in the notary journal entry. Certainly, the vital signature of the document signer on the notarized instrument should be reviewed at the proofreading stage, although it is not in the notarial certificate.

If modifications need to be made to matters written or imprinted (in the case of a thumbprint) in the notarial certificate or the notary journal, the notary should make such additions or corrections in order to avoid the appearance of unauthorized tampering. Material to be corrected should be stricken; replacement material should be legibly written or imprinted (in the case of a thumbprint) in the margin or other available area; and, such alterations should then be initialed and dated by both the document signer and the notary.

Timing is a key point of focus in regard to this standard, for it will be too late to correct an omission or error if it is not discovered before the notarization ceremony is concluded. Once the notarization is concluded, the notarization is finished, and it is too late to change the notarial certificate or journal entry. This conclusion is correct because the notary's authority or jurisdiction regarding a particular notarization ends when the notarial ceremony ends. See also the discussion of notary certificates in Chapter 7 and of notary journals in Chapter 17. ■

***RELEVANT MODEL NOTARY LAW**

Each notary should read, study, and abide by the notary statute and regulations, if any, of her or his commissioning state or territory.

"To always satisfy myself as to the identity of the individual appearing before me in my capacity as Notary Public ..." *Responsibility Code of Ethics* (1980).

"The Notary shall require the presence of each document signer and oath-taker in order to carefully screen each for identity and willingness, and to observe that each appears aware of the significance of the transaction requiring a notarial act. " *Notary Public Code of Professional Responsibility,* Guiding Principle III (1998).

"Requirements For Notarial Acts. A notary shall perform a notarial act only if the principal [document signer]: ... (2) is personally known to the notary or identified by the notary through satisfactory evidence ..." *Model Notary Act,* Section 5-2(2) (2010).

"Personal Knowledge Of Identity. 'Personal knowledge of identity' and 'personally known' mean familiarity with an individual resulting from interactions with that individual over a period of time sufficient to dispel any reasonable uncertainty that the individual has the identity claimed." *Model Notary Act,* Section 2-16 (2010).

"Satisfactory Evidence Of Identity. 'Satisfactory evidence of identity' means identification of an individual based on: (1) at least 1 current document issued by a federal, state, or tribal government in a language understood by the notary and bearing the photographic image of the individual's face and signature and a physical description of the individual, or a properly stamped passport without a physical description; or

(2) the oath or affirmation of 1 credible witness disinterested in the document or transaction who is personally known to the notary and who personally knows the individual, or of 2 credible witnesses disinterested in the document or transaction who each personally knows the individual and shows to the notary documentary identification as described in Subparagraph (1) of this Section." *Model Notary Act,* Section 2-20 (2010).

“Credible Witness. ‘Credible witness’ means an honest, reliable, and impartial person who personally knows an individual appearing before a notary and takes an oath or affirmation from the notary to vouch for that individual’s identity.” *Model Notary Act,* Section 2-5 (2010).

“Identification Of Individual. (a) A notarial officer has personal knowledge of the identity of an individual appearing before the officer if the individual is personally known to the officer through dealings sufficient to provide reasonable certainty that the individual has the identity claimed.

(b) A notarial officer has satisfactory evidence of the identity of an individual appearing before the officer if the officer can identify the individual: (1) by means of: (A) a passport, driver’s license, or government issued nondriver identification card, which is current or expired not more than [three years] before performance of the notarial act; or (B) another form of government identification issued to an individual, which is current or expired not more than [three years] before performance of the notarial act, contains a signature or a photograph of the individual, and is satisfactory to the officer, or (2) by a verification on oath or affirmation of a credible witness personally appearing before the officer and known to the officer or whom the officer can identify on the basis of a passport, driver’s license, or government issued nondriver identification card, which is current or expired not more than [three years] before performance of the notarial act.

(c) A notarial officer may require an individual to provide additional information or identification credentials necessary to assure the officer of the identity of the individual.” *Revised Uniform Law on Notarial Acts,* Section 7 (2010).

2010s, large, white and red, corrugated "NOTARY NOTARIO" sign. WARNING: This sign definitely should not be used, except by an attorney who is also a notary or by notaries in Puerto Rico, for it violates some statutory provisions, and it can be misleading. The sign is troublesome because it may confuse and mislead people familiar with the civil law *notario publico* of Puerto Rico and Hispanic countries, almost all of whom are also attorneys and who have much greater authority than ordinary U.S. notaries.

Chapter

11

Name and Signature Requirements for Document Signers and Notaries

STANDARDS SUMMARY

11.1 The notary should understand the importance of the names and signatures of the document signer, and the name and signature of the notary, required for each instrument notarization.

11.2 The notary should understand that a lawful signature is any mark or symbol intended and affixed by the signer for the purpose of authenticating the instrument on which it appears.

11.3 The notary should review the transactional instrument and ID document(s) to determine the form of the signer's name to be used for the notarial certificate.

11.4 The notary should, when signer names on IDs and the transactional instrument do not match, select elements common to those names as the form of the signer's name for the notarial certificate.

11.5 The notary should include the notary's name and present signature on the notarial certificate in the same form as the notary's name appears on the notary commission.

11.6 The notary should, prior to the conclusion of the notarial ceremony, proofread the names and signatures required for the notarization and make any necessary corrections.

STANDARDS EXPLANATIONS

What's in a name? Sometimes, when a name and signature are placed on a document, significant legal consequences may result depending upon the precise way the name and signature are written. After all, names and signatures constitute two of the most fundamental of all identifiers of people. An incorrect name or signature might invalidate a document or nullify what was supposed to be a legal obligation. At a minimum, an incorrect name or signature, or an inconsistency between a name and signature, may cause a lengthy and expensive legal challenge to a document and its notarization. These concerns can be particularly relevant and unsettling to notaries.

Notaries often struggle with inconsistencies between names and signatures, and between the forms in which names and signatures are expressed from document to document. Moreover, when we consider the confusion caused on documents by nicknames, titles, hyphenated names, married names, maiden names, middle names, middle initials, misspelled names, illegible signatures, changed names, aliases, and so on, it is a wonder that notaries accomplish as many unchallenged notarizations as they do. However, the best practices suggested below should simplify the notary's task and guide the notary much more easily through the seeming quagmire of inconsistent names and signatures.

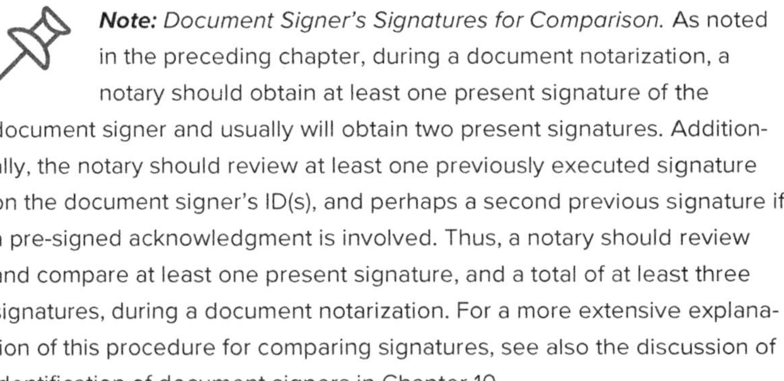

Note: *Document Signer's Signatures for Comparison.* As noted in the preceding chapter, during a document notarization, a notary should obtain at least one present signature of the document signer and usually will obtain two present signatures. Additionally, the notary should review at least one previously executed signature on the document signer's ID(s), and perhaps a second previous signature if a pre-signed acknowledgment is involved. Thus, a notary should review and compare at least one present signature, and a total of at least three signatures, during a document notarization. For a more extensive explanation of this procedure for comparing signatures, see also the discussion of identification of document signers in Chapter 10.

Note: *Signing by Mark and Physical Disabilities Affecting Signing.* The notary should know how to conduct a document notarization for a signer who uses a mark or symbol as his or her signature, and for a signer with a physical disability that affects his or her signing. Those two subjects will not be covered here but will be addressed in Chapter 16.

11.1 The notary should understand the importance of the names and signatures of the document signer, and the name and signature of the notary, required for each instrument notarization.

Not only the names and signatures of the document signer but also the name and signature of the notary public should properly appear as part of every instrument notarization. For each instrument notarization, there should typically be at least two pairs of the document signer's names and signatures presently affixed (unless an acknowledgment has been signed before the notarial ceremony, or unless the signer's name has been pretyped or preprinted on the notarial certificate). Those two pairs include the signer's name and signature in the journal entry, and the signer's signature on the transactional document and name in the notarial certificate. The notary should ask the signer to assist in making those four names and signatures match one another in substance. Additionally, the notary's name and signature will be presently affixed on the notarial certificate. So, notaries should be diligent about obtaining those six names and signatures.

One of the most basic elements provided in the notarization process involves the document signer's name and corresponding signature. It is the name and signature appearing respectively on the certificate of notarization and the notarized instrument that identify the person who is legally responsible for the document, and in whose name the document has been notarized. In an ideal world, the form of all of the signer's printed names on the transactional instrument, the ID documents, the journal entry, and the notarial certificate will match. Similarly, all of the signer's signatures on the transactional instrument, the ID documents, and the journal entry will match one another and will match the form of the signer's printed name on the transactional instrument, the IDs, the notarial certificate, and the journal entry.

But, the world of notarization is not ideal, and name and signature inconsistencies regularly arise. This is a serious matter, for inconsistencies and problems with names and signatures can cause the invalidity or rejection of the notarization and the notarized document or can at least cause uncertainties about the notarization and legal challenges to the validity of the notarization.

The reasons for the difficulties about matching names and signatures are plentiful. People who prepare transactional documents often do not ask about the form of the signer's name on ID documents prior to drafting instruments. The form of one's name on various ID documents may differ. With first, middle, and last names in play, some of those names may vary. The first name may be shortened in some fashion (Susan becomes Sue), or vice versa (Bob becomes Robert).

The first name or middle name may be shortened to a first or middle initial, or omitted altogether. The last name may become hyphenated for a married person, or legally changed. Any of these names might be misspelled, and the error not noticed. And, signatures frequently are partially or completely illegible. What is the notary to do?

Case Illustration. This author was recently confronted by complications about names and signatures when consulted on a multimillion dollar dispute about a series of seven property transfer and estate planning documents prepared for a 99-year-old individual and his spouse. One or both of the parties had signed each document, and each document had been notarized — all by the same bank notary. However, there were numerous inconsistencies in the names and signatures appearing on the documents. Sometimes the full first, middle, and last names were typed on documents, but sometimes only the first and last names were typed. Sometimes the wife's married surname was typed, and at other times her maiden surname was used. Of course, the name printed on the driver's licenses of the two people did not match some of the typed forms of their names on notarized documents, and the signed names in the majority of instances did not match either the printed name on the ID or the typed name on the notarized documents. The wife's surname had even been misspelled on one instrument, and no one had noticed the mistake. The people preparing the documents and the notary should not have allowed so many inconsistencies to arise in this extreme, but actual, example. The complicated court case involving the challenges to these imperfect notarizations was ultimately settled, but not before years of proceedings had passed and tens of thousands of dollars in attorney fees and costs had been expended.

11.2 The notary should understand that a lawful signature is any mark or symbol intended and affixed by the signer for the purpose of authenticating the instrument on which it appears.

A signature for notarization purposes must be affixed or adopted by a signer, and that signer must be present in person at the notarization ceremony to sign or acknowledge the signature. Signatures of both the document signer and the notary should be affixed at the time of the notarial ceremony, not before it, and not after it (with the exception that a document signer may sign a document requiring an acknowledgment prior to the notarial ceremony and then acknowledge that prior signature during the notarial ceremony).

It should be noted that as a general rule, the law allows individuals (called "principals") to conduct their affairs through the acts of other people (called "agents" or "employees"). So, principals can employ agents to work for them and to represent them in their absence, including to sign the principals' names on documents, such as checks, invoices, contracts, and so on. But, there are some obvious things that are too personal and too important for the law to allow to be done by agents. As examples, principals cannot have agents vote for them in government elections; principals cannot have agents stand in for them in wedding ceremonies; principals cannot have agents serve in their places in the military or to serve their sentences in jail. Similarly, a principal cannot ask an agent to stand in place of the principal at a notarization; the document signer whose signature is to be notarized must be the one to appear in person at the notarization and to sign or acknowledge the signature on the transactional document and to sign the notary journal entry (and possibly to provide a thumbprint impression). Of course, a principal could ask an agent to appear at a notarization, but the agent would have to sign the agent's name, and the agent's signature would be notarized

The law appropriately takes the view that a signature can be any mark or symbol which an individual intends to adopt in order to authenticate a document. Usually, that mark or symbol is the handwritten or scrawled signature of the individual's given name (i.e., one's "John Hancock"). Yet, even the handwritten signature may take various forms, such as a full name, a partial name, a nickname, a hand-lettered or handprinted name, or one's initials. One's signature for notarization purposes could even be a typed name, a name affixed by a signature stamp, a symbol affixed by a signet ring, or a mark such as a handmade "X" — provided the name or symbol is affixed or adopted by the individual signer to authenticate the document on which it appears. See also the discussion of signatures by mark in Chapter 16.

Moreover, a single individual may use more than one form of signature from time to time. Thus, an individual may sign one instrument with a handwritten full name, may sign the next document with her or his initials, and sign the next instrument with her or his nickname. Further, the appearance of one's signature may change from time to time, due to aging, illness, or injury. Or, one may simply choose to modify the appearance of her or his signature.

Case Illustration. This author testified in a jury trial about an elderly person who, because she had developed a shaky hand, obtained a signature stamp (a copy of her handwritten signature from before her hand began to shake), affixed her name to a document with her stamp, and had her stamped signature on the document notarized. I concluded the stamped signature and notarization were lawful, and so did the jury. Incidentally, although most jurisdictions treat signatures by mark the same way that any other signature is treated for notarization purposes, some jurisdictions have enacted laws which impose additional procedural requirements that must accompany the notarization of a signature by mark (such as witnessing by a third party — to be discussed later). Should a signature made by an individual using a stamp with a copy of the individual's hand-scrawled name be treated as an ordinary signature for notarization purposes, or should it be treated as a signature by mark for notarization purposes? In my opinion, it is a signature by mark.

Practice Tip: *Journalize Signature Issues.* Signatures are very important in the notarial context. If anything about the signing by the instrument signer is out of the ordinary and different from the usual affixing of a handwritten signature, the notary should point out the variation in the notary journal record. Perhaps the instrument signer's hand was shaky when signing, or the signer appeared to be nervous, or both. It should be noted. Perhaps there was a minor variation of the name of the signer between the ID document tendered or the preprinted name appearing on the transactional instrument and the form of the name chosen by the notary to appear in the notarial certificate. The minor variation should be noted. Perhaps the signer's name appeared differently on two or more ID documents tendered to establish the signer's identity. This discrepancy should be recorded.

11.3 The notary should review the transactional instrument and ID document(s) to determine the form of the signer's name to be used for the notarial certificate.

Happily, this best practice is the obvious and only way to proceed when the document signer's name is the same on both the transactional instrument and the ID. That name of the signer should be entered by the notary in the notarial certificate and journal entry. And happily, most of the time, the signer's name on the instrument to be notarized and on the signer's ID are the same The challenge arises when the signer's name on the transactional instrument and ID do not match.

Practice Tip: *Know Three Priorities.* Three basic points of reference for the notary regarding issues about names and signatures should be emphasized. In reverse order they are: (1) The notary's goal is to achieve two results: (a) the positive identification of the document signer, and (b) the signing of the document to be notarized in such a way as to validate that document (i.e., having the document signed by the document signer named in it.). (2) A principal task for the notary is the proper identification of the document signer as certified by the notary in the certificate of notarization. Thus, it is the form of the signer's name as it is written or printed by the notary in the notarial certificate which constitutes the critical concern. This is because the certificate is where the notary certifies the name of the individual positively identified as the document signer. (3) The notary should examine and give deference to a proper ID of the document signer which is a government-issued ID bearing a photograph of the face and head of the ID-holder along with a signature, date of birth, and, hopefully, a physical description. The key feature just mentioned is "government-issued." A government-issued ID means, in part, that the name appearing thereon constitutes an official form of the bearer's name. The notary should appreciate and take advantage of the authority and integrity associated with a name recognized by an official governmental agency.

Hence, to accomplish all three goals, the notary should place a form of the document signer's name that is taken or adapted from the signer's ID(s) in the notarial certificate. And, the form of the name selected by the notary should also be a form of the name suitable for signing by the document signer on the transactional instrument to be notarized. In the event there is inconsistency between the name appearing in the transactional instrument and the ID(s), the form of the name selected by the notary might not be the exact form appearing on one or more of the IDs, but instead may be a shorter form of the name that satisfies the name requirement for the transactional document and that matches at least one ID — as explained in the next section below.

Note: *Difference of Opinion on This Issue.* Unfortunately, notary statutes and regulations do not cover or clarify what the notary is to do when the names and signatures on the transactional document and ID(s) do not match. The key background point here is that we are talking only about the situation in which the signer's name on the transactional document and ID do not match. Not everyone agrees with this author's view to look to the document signer's name and signature as it appears on the signer's government-issued ID to establish the name and signature requirements for the notarization. The other most popular approach is to adopt the name on the transactional instrument as the name to be placed on the notarial certificate and the journal entry and to be signed by the document signer on the transactional instrument and the journal entry. This approach means the notary must decide whether the ID(s) supports the name on the transactional instrument. I think that approach has the tail wagging the dog. It makes the name of the signer appearing in the transactional instrument control the notarization because that name must be placed in the notarial certificate and because that name is not known by the notary to be a previously and governmentally verified name of the signer (as would be the case if the name appeared on a government-issued ID).

All signatures of the document signer and all other printed or written forms of the signer's name appearing on ID documents and on the transactional document should match the name printed or written by the notary in the certificate (and the journal entry). Thus, the notary should explain to the signer the importance of executing the signature in the form the notary determines to be appropriate for the notarization both in signing the transactional instrument (unless that signature has already been completed for an acknowledgment type of notarization) and in signing the notary journal entry. If the signer does not comply, the notary should refuse to complete the notarization, as the true identity of the document signer would then be in doubt.

Certainly, there will be situations in which the signer's name and signature on the transactional and ID instruments will not be consistent, and the notary has no power or authority to change what has been done on IDs prior to the time of the notarization. However, at the beginning of the notarial ceremony, the notary should review the transactional document and IDs to see if the name on the document to be notarized corresponds with the IDs and whether one form of name is clearly the name to be used for the notarial certificate. If the name already appearing in the document to be notarized is not consistent with IDs, the signer may be able to simply change the form of the signer's name appearing in the transactional document — by lining through the typed, printed, or written name, changing it to the correct form of name, and initialing and dating in the margin (perhaps, with any witnesses in attendance also initialing the changes). The signer should either know whether the form of her or his name in the transactional instrument may be modified, or should attempt to contact someone who could advise the signer whether a change in the form of the name may be made in the transactional instrument.

Note: *Ultimate Responsibility for Proving Identification.* The signer proves identity; the notary verifies identity. If an appropriate or compromised form of the signer's name can be selected by the notary to assure satisfactory identification of the signer and to allow the instrument to be correctly signed, then the notarization can proceed. If, on the other hand, there is too much disparity between the signer's name and/or signature on the transactional instrument and the ID(s), then the notarization should be refused. Although the notary should not be hypertechnical about the name and signature requirements and should attempt to resolve an inconsistency, it is the signer's obligation to establish her or his identity satisfactorily for the notary. Perhaps, the signer will have to obtain a revised version of the transactional instrument bearing the signer's name to conform to the signer's ID(s), or will have to attempt to retrieve another government-issued ID bearing a matching form of the signer's name, and return at a later time to secure the notarization of that instrument. If a notarization is refused, the notary should journalize that official refusal, including the explanation of why the notarization was declined. See also the discussion of the notary journal in Chapter 17.

11.4 The notary should, when signer names on IDs and the transactional instrument do not match, select elements common to those names as the form of the signer's name for the notarial certificate.

If there is a variation in the form of a document signer's name appearing on the transactional instrument (and if it cannot be changed or corrected at the time of the notarial ceremony) and the name and signature appearing on an ID or IDs, the notary should select to be placed in the notarial certificate a form of the signer's name that contains elements of the name appearing in both places. In other words, the name for notarization purposes in the notarial certificate should merge the signer's name from those documents and might contain less (not more) than appears in one or the other of the transactional instrument or ID(s).

For instance, if the signer's name on an ID is "Leonard Lee Lancaster," but on the transactional instrument is "Leonard L. Lancaster" (or vice versa), then Leonard L. Lancaster should be the form of the name chosen for the certificate of notarization. If "Leonard Lee Lancaster" appears on one instrument, and "L. Lee Lancaster" or "Len L. Lancaster" appears on the other, then choose "L. Lee Lancaster" or "Len L. Lancaster" (as Len is a shortened and commonly accepted version of Leonard). Further, under these circumstances, the notary should always ask to see one or more additional ID documents, in the hope that a different ID will be the solution and will fortuitously contain a form of the name and signature to match the form on the transactional instrument.

The notary should also use common sense and everyday experience in sorting out difficulties about signer names and signatures. For example, if an individual has a title (Rev. or Reverend; Prof. or Professor; Dr. or Doctor). Such a title is not part of one's name, but its inclusion would help to identify the signer and at worst is merely surplus. On the other hand, a suffix (such as Jr. or Junior; Sr. or Senior; II, III, or IV) is significant because those suffixes distinguish fathers and sons, and identify whose signature has been notarized and who has liability under a notarized document.

Practice Tip: *The Journal May Save the Day.* Most importantly, for anyone troubled about this author's suggested compromise method of selecting the form of the signer's name and signature for notarization purposes, remember this — the notary journal entry is where the disparity can and should be explained. A note can be included in the journal to describe the form of the name on the transactional and ID instruments, thus providing evidence of deference having been accorded to the official, government-issued ID. Remember too, the law requires the notary to employ reasonable care and diligence to ascertain the true identity of the document signer, and this procedure of detailing the variations in the names and signatures on the transactional and ID documents should certainly pass muster as a thorough and prudent effort on the part of the notary to accurately identify the signer. See also the discussion of notary journals in Chapter 17.

Note: *Possible Changing of the Form of the Signer's Name on the Document to Be Notarized.* As pointed out previously, there is nothing sacred about the document to be notarized, even though it may have been neatly typed or preprinted. Changes can be made to that document in the standard way any printed or typed document can be modified. Even the form of the name of the document signer can be modified. The procedure is to strike through the printed or typed name, to legibly write or print the substitute form of the name near the stricken version, and to initial and date the change in the margin. Certainly, some parties, such as some mortgage companies, banks, government agencies, and others, will not want their typed or preprinted documents to be modified. And, those parties may not accept a modified version of the transactional instrument. Yet, without the modification suggested here, the instrument would not be able to be notarized, so it would still be unacceptable to those same parties. In summary, if the form of the signer's name in the transactional document is so different from the signer's IDs that the notary is unwilling to place the transactional document's version of the name in the notary certificate and is unwilling to notarize using the document's version of the name, then either the transactional document should be modified, or the notarization should be refused.

11.5 The notary should include the notary's name and present signature on the notarial certificate in the same form as the notary's name appears on the notary commission.

One of the critical features of a document notarization is the name and corresponding present signature by the notary on the notarial certificate, for that signature and its accompanying and matching seal impression bring officiality to the paper document. After all, the notarial certificate does just as its name implies; it describes and certifies the official actions taken by the notary and, therefore, needs to bear the notary's name, signature, and seal.

When the would-be notary applies for and obtains the notary commission, the commissioning document will be printed with the name of the notary. The notary's official seal should also bear this form of the notary's name. The notary's name in both of those locations should be the same, and when conducting official business, the notary should always sign his or her name exactly as the name appears on the notary commission and the notary seal. Otherwise, there could be a challenge to the validity of the notarization on the ground of lack of authority (i.e., that the party who signed the certificate was not a duly commissioned notary). While it is unclear that a court or agency would conclude the certificate to be fatally defective on that basis, a notary should not jeopardize the notarization due to such an easy matter with which to comply.

A far more significant aspect of the duty of the notary to sign the notary certificate is the notary's obligation to execute that signature at the time of the notarization — not before, and not afterwards. There are numerous accounts of notaries who sign blank certificates in advance of notarizations simply for their own perceived convenience and ease, or more troublingly, for purposes of wrongdoing (such as to allow someone other than the notary to fill out the notarial certificate). These shortcuts cannot be tolerated. Signing before the notarial ceremony or after the notarial ceremony should constitute a fatal fault, for the certificate of notarization would be improper at the time of performance of the notarization (which time is the only time to judge the legality of the notarial act).

The notary's signature is so important that the failure of the notary to sign the certificate at all or the failure of the notary to sign the form of the name as it appears on the notary commission might constitute a fatal flaw, which would invalidate the notarization. This author believes there is another plausible conclusion as well — namely, that a notarization could be treated as valid although the notary's signature on the notarial certificate is not in conformity with the notary's name on the official notary commission or is missing entirely. After all, the nonconformity or omission of the notary's signature may be the result of a mere moment of forgetfulness — a mere technicality. If the rest of the elements of the notarial certificate are present, and if a full notary journal entry is completed, I believe the notarization should not be invalidated. Importantly, it should be remembered that most official notarial seals include the name of the notary public, so the affixing of the impression of the seal by the notary when it contains the name of the notary effects a signature of the notary.

Note: *Sample Signature of Notary on File.* The official notary commissioning certificates which many notaries hang on their home or office walls may not contain the signature of the notary, although they do contain the official form of the notary's name to be used for notarial functioning. There is a sample signature of the notary on the notary's initial application or renewal application and perhaps on a form registering the notary commission that is kept on file with the commissioning official or notary oversight agency. The sample of the notary's signature may be examined and compared with other of the notary's signatures by authorities under certain circumstances, such as in connection with the issuing of an apostille (used to authenticate the authority of the notary in some international situations) and in connection with investigations of alleged misconduct of notaries or forgeries of notarizations.

Signing and sealing by the notary carry with them added legal significance, in that those steps are prima facie evidence of the authority of the notary, making the notarization presumptively admissible as evidence. The best practice is for the notary to sign and seal the notarial certificate as the final steps in the notarization process, prior to proofreading the journal entry and notarial certificate (meaning that the notary journal entry will have been finished prior to the completion of the notarial certificate, and meaning that proofreading naturally comes after the sealing and signing by the notary). See the section about proofreading immediately below. See also the discussion of notary journal entries in Chapter 17.

Note: *Avoid Signing as Notary and Lay Witness.* While in most situations the law is not perfectly clear on the issue of whether a notary may serve as both a witness to a transactional document and as the notary public who will notarize that same document, this author strongly advises against doing so, for a number of reasons which are more fully set out just below in Chapter 12. There is no sound reason to ask notaries to serve as witnesses on the very documents they are notarizing. Almost never is there a shortage of notaries or of individuals available to serve as witnesses to documents, so there is no need for the dual notary-witness role. Having a notary serve also as a witness constitutes a lazy and unprofessional method of filling in a document. When a notary also serves as a witness, there appears to be a conflict of interest. The general rule is that a notary should not notarize a document to which the notary is a party in interest or in which the notary is named. This dual status as witness and notary appears unseemly. See the more complete discussion of this conflicted practice in Chapter 12.

11.6 The notary should, prior to the conclusion of the notarial ceremony, proofread the names and signatures required for the notarization and make any necessary corrections.

There are far too many avoidable mistakes in notarizations resulting from neglect about the basic matter of names and signatures. With some frequency, one or more signatures are simply, accidentally omitted. Or, names and signatures do not match, when it would have been so easy to assure that they did. Because the names and signatures constitute such important and fundamental elements of all document notarizations, prior to the close of the notarial ceremony, a diligent notary should review those names and signatures to make sure that all required names and signatures are present and are in proper form.

There should be three sets of names and signatures in three distinct locations. (1) The notary's name should appear, and the notary should have signed on the certificate of notarization, and both the name and signature should match how they appear on the notary commissioning document on file with the commissioning official or notary oversight agency. (2) The document signer should have signed the transactional document (the affidavit, contract, deed, mortgage, etc.), and the signer's name should legibly appear in the notarial certificate. Both should match in substance. (3) The document signer's name should appear in, and the signer should have signed, the notary journal entry. And hopefully, the signer's names and signatures in those four locations should match.

If the notary discovers any fault with any of the names and signatures during the proofreading step as the notarial ceremony is concluding, there is time to correct the fault(s). A missing or corrected name or signature can be executed at that time. The clearest and safest method to make a change in an existing name or signature is to strike through the first incorrect name or signature and to correct the name or obtain a signature anew in the correct form. In addition, the document signer and notary public should date and initial the stricken name or signature, and the notary should include a note explaining the correction in the notary journal entry. Hence, the omission or fault will have been corrected, and the notarization will have been saved from possible challenge due to name or signature problems. ■

***RELEVANT MODEL NOTARY LAW**

Each notary should read, study, and abide by the notary statute and regulations, if any, of his or her state or territory of commissioning.

"'Sign' means, with present intent to authenticate or adopt a record: (A) to execute or adopt a tangible symbol ..." *Revised Uniform Law on Notarial Acts,* Section 2(11) (2010).

"A notary shall perform a notarial act only if the principal [document signer]: (5) signs using letters or characters of a language that is understood by the notary ..." *Model Notary Act,* Section 5-2(5) (2010).

"'Official signature' means a handwritten signature made by a notary that uses the exact name appearing in the notary's commission and is signed with the intent to perform a notarial act." *Model Notary Act,* Section 2-14 (2010).

“Notarial Act In This State. (a) A notarial act may be performed in this state by: (1) a notary public of this state; [or] (2) a judge, clerk, or deputy clerk of a court of this state [; or] [(3) an individual licensed to practice law in this state] [; or] [(4) any other individual authorized to perform the specific act by the law of this state].

(b) The signature and title of an individual performing a notarial act in this state are prima facie evidence that the signature is genuine and that the individual holds the designated title.

(c) The signature and title of a notarial officer described in subsection [(a)(1) or (2)] [(a)(1), (2), or (3)] conclusively establish the authority of the officer to perform the notarial act.” *Revised Uniform Law on Notarial Acts,* Section 10 (2010).

“A notary may certify the affixation of a signature by mark by a principal [document signer] on a document presented for notarization if: (1) the mark is affixed in the presence of the notary and 2 witnesses disinterested in the document; (2) both witnesses sign their own names beside the mark; (3) the notary writes below the mark: “Mark affixed by (name of signer by mark) in the presence of (names and addresses of 2 witnesses) and the undersigned notary pursuant to Section 5-3 of [Act]”; and (4) the notary notarizes the signature by mark through an acknowledgment, jurat, or signature witnessing.” *Model Notary Act,* Section 5-3 (2010).

“Signature If Individual Unable To Sign. If an individual is physically unable to sign a record, the individual may direct an individual other than the notarial officer to sign the individual’s name on the record. The notarial officer shall insert ‘Signature affixed by (name of other individual) at the direction of (name of individual)’ or words of similar import.” *Revised Uniform Law on Notarial Acts,* Section 9 (2010).

State of California

Executive Department

Know all men by these Presents:

That I, Harold J. Powers, Acting Governor of the State of California, in the name and by the authority of the People of the State of California, do, by these presents, appoint and commission

ALLEN C. CLARK

A Notary Public

in and for the County of Contra Costa

for the term commencing May 13, 1956.

In Witness Whereof, I have hereunto set my hand and caused the Great Seal of the State to be affixed at Sacramento, this tenth day of May, one thousand nine hundred and fifty- six.

Harold J Powers
Acting Governor of the State of California

By the Acting Governor:

Frank M. Jordan
Secretary of State

By
Deputy

1956, official State of California notary commission for Allen Clark, bearing the large, 3.5-inch diameter, official state gold seal. Notice that at the time, there was an Acting Governor Harold Powers in California who appointed and commissioned notaries.

Chapter

12

Notary as Public Official, Not a Lay Witness

STANDARDS SUMMARY

12.1 The notary should understand the differences between signing a document as a lay witness and a notary public.

12.2 The notary should not serve as both notary public and lay witness in regard to the same transactional document.

STANDARDS EXPLANATIONS

The topic of this chapter is one of the many subjects relating to notarial practice about which there is a good deal of uncertainty and confusion, and not surprisingly, about which there is little or no guidance in notary statutes and regulations or in court opinions. The question is whether a notary may, or should, also serve as a lay witness on an instrument which the notary will then notarize.

The vast majority of states and territories have no statutes addressing the subject of this chapter. Statutes in only a few states require two witnesses for certain kinds of documents and expressly permit one of the two witnesses to be the notary who notarizes the document. However, just because notaries in those few states are allowed to serve as both lay witness and notary does not mean that notaries there should do so.

In the legal arena, when authority to do a thing is unknown or not expressly provided for, the prudent course is usually to decline to do the thing. Especially in the notarial field, it is prudent not to do a thing that is not expressly provided for, so as not to put the notarized transaction and the parties involved at some sort of risk — such as the invalidity of the notarization, or at least a challenge to its validity. In this author's opinion, it is quite clear, even without expressly being prohibited in statutes, regulations, or court decisions that a notary should not serve in both positions for the same instrument. I hope those few states that allow the dual service will reconsider their position, and reverse it.

12.1 The notary should understand the differences between signing a document as a lay witness and a notary public.

Some confusion stems from frequent partial references in definitions and descriptions of the "notary public" as a "disinterested witness" or "impartial witness." But that partial description should not be taken out of context, for the more complete definition would include more details about what the notary does in the official notarial capacity — i.e., the notary public serves as a government officer and disinterested witness to identify the document signer, to assess the signer's willingness and competence to sign, and to observe the acknowledging or signing of the document to be notarized. Thus, the notary's presence at a notarial ceremony is strictly as a government official. The reference to the notary's task to "witness" is really a synonym for the task to "observe." The notary must observe the signer and the signing as part of the notary's official function, which includes the exercise of a degree of discretion and judgment in determining whether all legal requirements have been satisfied. Generally, lay witnesses are neither authorized nor trained to exercise discretion.

Consider that notaries already occupy two posts at the same time, in that most of them occupy both a position as a private party and a position as a public official (although some notaries occupy two roles as public officials — for instance, as a court clerk and notary public, or as a recorder of deeds and a notary public). The circumstances should not be made even more complicated by allowing notaries to occupy three positions simultaneously — private citizen, lay witness, and notary public.

Additionally, when a private person is asked by someone to serve as a lay witness, the would-be witness is not in an official neutral position and undoubtedly feels some pressure to support the party requesting the witness's service and the instrument being signed. Whereas, when asked to perform a notarization, a notary is a government officer who is required and trained to act as a disinterested party, who must exercise judgment as to the legal requirements for the notarization, and who should feel no pressure whatsoever to perform the notarization unless all legal conditions have been satisfied.

Hopefully, even a private individual serving as a lay witness will scrupulously observe the signing of a document, and as a result, the document will be more secure and more likely to be above reproach. This outcome ought to occur almost always because a lay witness simply observes the objective facts about the signing without exercise of any discretion as to legal factors. But, a lay witness is not a commissioned governmental official.

Incidentally, one key similarity between a lay witness and a notary public is that both will sign the transactional document or notarial certificate. So, the notary will first sign as lay witness and will then sign as a notary public.

12.2 The notary should not serve as both notary public and lay witness in regard to the same transactional document.

In this author's opinion, notaries should not serve as both lay witness and notary public on the same transactional document for a number of important reasons. (1) When the notary serves as a lay witness on the same transaction, this dual service results in one person in two roles with the result that one less person is involved in the documentation of the instrument. Dual service by the notary as a lay witness deprives the document of the support of a separate individual who could have been called upon to testify to its signing. This result is a tactical mistake that should not be practiced upon the instrument signer (even if the instrument signer may have been the one to have exercised poor judgment by asking the notary to serve in the dual roles). With more than 4,450,000 notaries, and with countless millions of lay witnesses in this country, why would someone choose to have the same person act in these dual roles? This picture causes me to be suspicious from the outset.

(2) There is an appearance of impropriety when the notary notarizes a document in which the notary's name appears in a private capacity and which the notary has already signed as a lay witness prior to the performance of the notarization. A notary should not notarize a document in which the notary's name appears as a party. A lay witness could be considered a party in interest to some extent to a document. After all, the name and signature of the lay witness appears on the document, and the name and signature of the lay witness are affixed prior to the conduct of the notarization. Further, before the notarization is performed, the lay witness has already lent his or her support to the instrument to be notarized by agreeing to serve as a witness and by signing it. The notary must remain impartial throughout the notarial procedure. Consider this example. In the case of notarization of a will where there is an

accompanying self-proving affidavit, the notary should not notarize his or her own signature on the self-proving affidavit.

(3) This issue has been around for a very long time, and the failure of the vast majority of states and territories to address the subject suggests notaries should abstain from the practice. The reason for this view is that on this topic, there should at least be some doubt about whether a notary may undertake the dual roles as to a single transactional instrument. If there is doubt, the notary should not serve as both notary and lay witness on the same document. Indeed, as a fiduciary of the public, a notary owes document signers the duty to avoid placing the notarization at risk. ■

***RELEVANT MODEL NOTARY LAW**

Each notary should read, study, and abide by the notary statute and regulations, if any, of her or his commissioning state or territory.

"The Notary shall, as a government officer and public servant, serve all of the public in an honest, fair and unbiased manner." *Notary Public Code of Professional Responsibility,* Guiding Principle I (1998).

"The Notary shall act as an impartial witness and not profit or gain from any document or transaction requiring a notarial act, apart from the fee allowed by statute." *Notary Public Code of Professional Responsibility,* Guiding Principle II (1998).

"The Notary shall give precedence to the rules of law over the dictates or expectations of any person or entity." *Notary Public Code of Professional Responsibility,* Guiding Principle V (1998).

"Disqualification. (a) A notary is disqualified from performing a notarial act if the notary: (1) is a party to or named in the document that is to be notarized ..." *Model Notary Act,* Section 5-5 (2010).

"Authority To Perform Notarial Act. ... (b) A notarial officer may not perform a notarial act with respect to a record to which the officer or the officer's spouse [or civil partner] is a party, or in which either of them has a direct beneficial interest. A notarial act performed in violation of this subsection is voidable." *Revised Uniform Law on Notarial Acts,* Section 4 (2010).

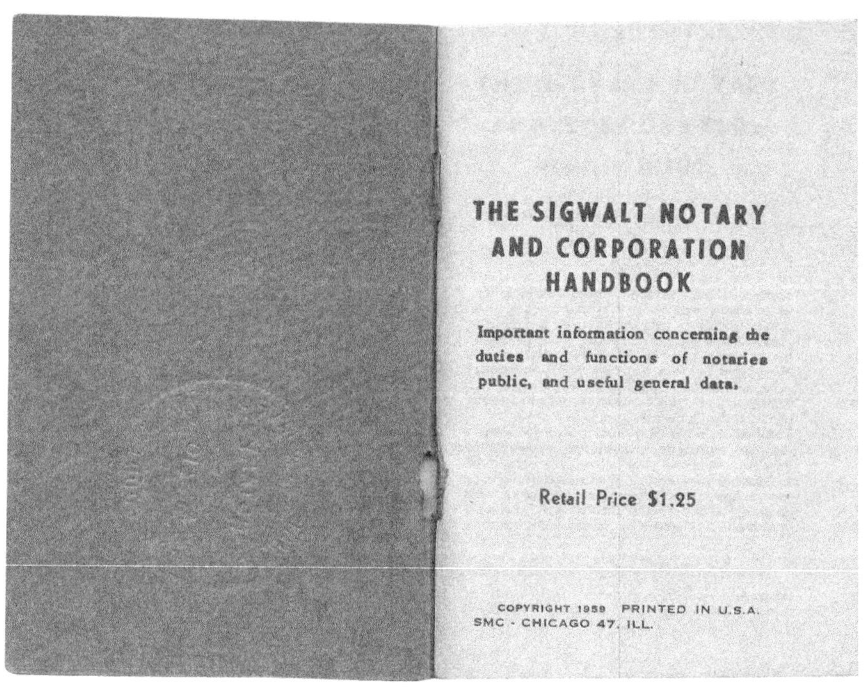

1959, miniature *The Sigwalt Notary and Corporation Handbook*, with 78 pages (of which, some 53 pages deal with notaries). This helpful, little book was pocket-size for the notary who traveled and performed notarial services from place to place.

Chapter

13

Assessing Document Signer Mental Competence

STANDARDS SUMMARY

13.1 The notary should be aware that the signer must possess mental competence in order to execute a document and to obtain its notarization.

13.2 The notary should be prepared to respond properly when a document signer is a minor.

13.3 The notary should take steps reasonably calculated to assess mental competence by observing, conversing with, and questioning the document signer.

13.4 The notary should note the mental competence assessment process in the journal entry for the notarization.

13.5 The notary should proofread the journal entry relating to the signer competence assessment and make any necessary corrections prior to completion of the notarial ceremony.

STANDARDS EXPLANATIONS

Whether notaries have the responsibility to assess the mental competence of document signers has been debated within the notarial community for decades. Only a few notary statutes, regulations, and court decisions from around the country have expressly permitted or directed notaries to consider signer mental competence. But, with changing times and greater concerns about document fraud and security, and increased attention to the competence and financial abuse of signers with dementia, of terminally ill signers, and of elderly signers, there has been an expanding view that notaries should consider the mental competence of all document signers as part of the notarization procedure.

Until at least the year 2010, few states imposed upon their notaries any kind of duty to determine the mental competence of document signers. Such a duty was generally thought to be beyond the role and the expertise of notaries, for whom there are no substantial general education requirements and who are generally neither educated nor experienced in the subjects of mental health and competency. It was not until 1998 that a major notary ethics and procedure model, the *Notary Public Code of Professional Responsibility*, suggested a duty of notaries to assess the mental acuity of document signers, followed by other recommendations of similar responsibilities of notaries to assess signer mental competence in the *Model Notary Acts* of 2002 and 2010. In the *Revised Uniform Law on Notarial Acts* of 2010, a notary is authorized to refuse to notarize if the notary is not satisfied the document signer is mentally competent. There has been a continuing debate about whether notaries should possess a right or, instead, a duty to consider the mental capacity of document signers, and if so, what the mental competence standard should be for document signers.

Several additional jurisdictions have now adopted statutory provisions permitting their notaries to judge the mental capacity of document signers as a condition to the performance of notarizations. This seems to be the trend, which is intended to promote the increased security of notarized documents and to heighten the role and status of the notary (moving the notary toward a more professional position in connection with commercial and governmental transactions, and involving the exercise of heightened discretion in judging the competence of signers). While both goals are admirable, the only outcome absolutely certain if the country continues to move in this direction is that the stakes will be raised for notaries. Notaries will have a much greater obligation to carry out an extremely difficult task and may face heightened liability risks for faulty performance of this new task.

Parenthetically, the next chapter, dealing with the subject of the voluntariness of signing, is closely related to the issue of mental competence. Clearly, a signer suffering from diminished mental capacity may be more susceptible to coercion and undue influence, and the pressure, depression, and anxiety caused by coercion and duress may hasten emotional difficulties and mental incapacity. See Chapter 14 dealing with assessment of the signer's willingness to execute the transactional document and to have it notarized.

Practice Tip: *A Ceremony-Long Process.* The notary's assessment of the signer's mental competence to execute the document to be notarized starts at the very beginning of and continues throughout the notarial ceremony. If at any time during the ceremony, the notary develops objective concerns about the mental competence of the signer, the notary should raise and resolve those concerns, and either proceed with the notarization or refuse to notarize. It is not too late until the ceremony is finished.

Finally, it must be clarified in the strongest terms that individuals with physical disabilities — as opposed to mental infirmities — possess the same legal right to obtain the notarization of their documents as possessed by other persons, provided that those documents themselves are in proper order. This chapter is about mental competence to sign, not about physical capacity to sign. If someone is physically unable to sign, there are ways to accommodate such a physical disability, and that subject is discussed in Chapter 16.

13.1. The notary should be aware that the signer must possess mental competence in order to execute a document and to obtain its notarization.

This author's opinion has changed over the past several years about the issue of whether notaries should consider the mental competence of document signers. I now agree with the growing number of others in the notary field who support the view that notaries have the ethical and legal responsibility to do so, and this chapter will proceed accordingly. It must be kept in mind that most jurisdictions do not yet have statutes, regulations, or court decisions expressly permitting or requiring their notaries to assess signer mental competence.

Note: *Reasons Notaries Should Assess Signer Mental Competence.* Briefly, the key reasons notaries should assess signer mental competence include that such an assessment is part of the process for individuals to undertake other kinds of legal action, such as the making of contracts, powers of attorney, and wills. The important legal procedure of notarization should be no exception. Furthermore, notaries have always been obligated to assess whether document signers are acting willingly, and the voluntariness assessment is closely related to the mental competence issue. That is, one who suffers from diminished mental capacity is more susceptible to coercion and fraud, and one who is subjected to coercion and undue influence is more likely to suffer resulting mental stress and anxiety. Hence, in an era of increased concerns about document fraud and financial abuse, and when a disinterested public official is presiding over each notarization, it simply is the right thing to do — to ask notaries to consider the mental competence of document signers.

In regard to property and financial matters, the law of contracts appropriately announces the test for mental competence to be whether one is able to understand in a reasonable manner the nature and consequences of the instrument or transaction involved. In the estate planning field, the test is whether the individual executing a will or other estate instrument is of sound mind and memory. These tests of mental capacity are similar to the existing standards for notaries in assessing signer mental awareness and, thus, should form the basis for what a notary should be expected to do.

Hence, the test for document signer mental competence for notarial purposes should be whether the signer reasonably understands the nature of the transactional document and the consequences of notarization of the transactional document, or whether the signer is of sound mind and memory. In other words, the signer should appreciate the general nature of both the transactional document and the act of notarization. Individuals should realize basically what they are doing and why they are doing it.

Importantly, it should be noted that notaries are not required to be amateur psychologists or psychiatrists. Neither are they required to always be correct in their assessments of the mental competence of document signers. Instead, the law of negligence requires notaries to exercise reasonable care to determine whether signers possess mental capacity. Notaries will have acted reasonably if they exercise diligence and prudence in attempting to arrive at the correct assessment. Notaries do not have to be correct in the assessment in order to have acted reasonably. After all, notaries spend only a few short minutes with document signers during notarial ceremonies, so their diligence and reasonableness will be measured with that important fact in mind.

Furthermore, the judgment about whether a particular notary has acted reasonably is based upon how other similarly situated notaries would handle the matter of assessing signer competence. This approach to the law of negligence presumes that the members of an established vocation or profession will have developed an appropriate standard for dealing with such an issue. Of course, diligence and prudence will always be a central part of the way a standard of care develops. Thus, notaries will not face liability for damages arising due to notarizations performed for signers who are in fact mentally incapacitated, if the notaries use diligence and due care in their attempts to assess signer competence. Nor will notaries face liability for damages when they refuse to notarize for signers they have erroneously found to be mentally incompetent, if the notaries use reasonable care in their assessment efforts.

Although the document signer competence standard is relatively easy to express (one way or another), it is the application of the standard that can be far more difficult, particularly in cases in which signers are neither clearly competent nor clearly incompetent. Moreover, an individual may experience intervals of mental competence, with periods of mental incapacity in between. During the short span of minutes in a typical notarial ceremony, there can hardly be a full opportunity to learn with certainty the true state of one's mental condition, at least in those instances that are not immediately and abundantly clear. Signers should be presumed competent, unless circumstances and evidence indicate otherwise. Thankfully, most persons are mentally competent, but notaries should not merely accept that everyone is. The test should be similar to the evidentiary test that controls the outcome in civil lawsuits — the preponderance of the evidence. If the preponderance of the facts suggests to the notary that the signer is competent, the notarization should be performed. However, if the preponderance of all the facts indicate that the signer is not competent, the notarization should not proceed.

Not surprisingly, because of the many circumstances that impact mental capacity, each individual's situation is unique. Moreover, most notaries are not trained in law or psychiatry, and, therefore, notaries confront the issue of mental competence from a layperson's perspective. Unless a document signer has been declared incompetent by a court and the notary is aware of that finding, the notary will have to take steps to judge the mental capacity of all document signers who present themselves to obtain notarizations. Most people are clearly competent; and among persons who are not competent, many of the most profoundly afflicted will be readily identifiable. The remaining group of document signers present a potentially difficult and uncertain challenge for notaries, particularly because individuals commonly experience diminished capacity without suffering from full-scale mental incapacity.

As individuals age and become senior citizens and/or become afflicted with terminal illnesses, their circumstances often tend to change. Many terminally ill and elderly individuals show signs of effects on their mental faculties to various degrees, and for many the decline is progressive. They may lose some of their memories, and they may suffer from anxiety, depression, and fear, especially if they are alone, disabled, medicated, and/or financially challenged. Over time, the effects of illnesses and medications may take their toll on the mental competence of elders. Although notaries should be especially careful in their assessment of the mental capacity of terminally ill and elderly signers, notaries should realize that the same legal standard for mental competence applies to all signers. Notaries should also be equally careful not to deprive elders and terminally ill persons of their rights to obtain notarizations when they are competent to execute instruments.

Practice Tip: *Intoxicated Signers.* No business professional, including a notary public, should have to deal with intoxicated persons. Intoxication, by definition, diminishes one's mental competence, and notaries should not have to try to distinguish whether a drunken would-be signer is too intoxicated or not. Alcohol impairment should not be tolerated by notaries, and notaries should not have to accept the risk of notarizing for someone who may be incompetent. Notaries should not hesitate to refuse to notarize for an intoxicated party and should record the refusal in a journal entry, taking care to record the objective reasons which led to the conclusion the person was intoxicated or impaired — such as slurred speech, disheveled appearance, bloodshot eyes, unsteadiness while walking or standing, incoherent communication, alcohol odor on the breath, and so on.

Note: *Alternative Legal Protection for Mentally Incompetent Signers.* Significantly, notaries should be aware that they are not the only disinterested and official parties with the opportunity to protect incompetent individuals from signing instruments and being bound by those transactions. Even after a document has been notarized, the notarization and/or the transaction itself could be challenged in court, on the basis that the document signer lacked the mental competence to execute the instrument. Thus, the notary may not be the final arbiter on the issue of signer mental competence. Yet, the notary is an important gatekeeper who has the authority to prevent the faulty signing and notarization of the document in the first place.

13.2 The notary should be prepared to respond properly when a document signer is a minor.

If a would-be document signer seeks notarial services and appears to be very young, the notary should ask the signer's age and then verify that the signer is an adult. For, if the signer is not an adult, a notarization of the signer's document could be jeopardized.

Notaries are not often faced with juveniles or minors who present documents for notarization, but it could happen. While U.S. jurisdictions have not enacted statutes setting a minimum age at which individuals may obtain notarial services, all states and territories have enacted laws designating the age at which juveniles or minors reach the age of majority. That age is 18 years in the vast majority of jurisdictions, with 48 states and the District of Columbia having set the age at 18 years, and with Alabama and Nebraska selecting 19 years as the age of majority. The general view is that individuals who are minors have not become old enough, mature enough, and thus mentally capable enough to engage in contractual and other legal transactions for which they can generally be held personally responsible. Thus, it is unlikely a minor would present and sign a commercial document, or even other financial or estate planning documents, for notarization.

Because no minimum age for notarial services is expressly set by statute or other law, notaries must use their discretion in determining for which minors to perform notarizations. First of all, the notary should require the minor to be accompanied to the notarial ceremony by an adult parent or guardian, who approves of the request for notarial services and who is not a party to or a beneficiary of the instrument to be notarized. If the parents and guardian are disqualified, an attorney for the minor (and not representing the parents or guardian) should be required to attend with the minor.

Then, the notary should consider the minor's age, the level of maturity and mental acuity of the minor, and the type of document to be notarized (as some documents are more important than others). Interestingly, the law permits very young children to take oaths or affirmations and to testify in legal proceedings if the child is perceived as being able to distinguish right from wrong or to understand the duty to tell the truth. Thus, the more likely scenario a notary may confront is the case of a minor who is to sign (and swear or affirm to) an affidavit of some kind. Again, the notary should exercise thoughtful discretion to decide whether to notarize. If the notary refuses to notarize, that official act of refusal should be recorded in a notary journal entry.

Importantly, if the notary proceeds to notarize for a minor signer, all of the steps in the typical notarization procedure for an adult signer should be followed. Thus, among other things, the minor should be positively identified with reasonable certainty and should be acting willingly. Identifying the minor may be problematic, but minors who wish to obtain notarial services should be prepared to establish identity and age by presenting appropriate documents, such as passports, driver's licenses, or state or tribal IDs.

Depending on the circumstances, the notary may wish to exclude the parent or guardian from the room for part of the notarial ceremony while making the willingness assessment of whether to notarize for the minor. The notary should record in the notary journal entry the age of the minor signer and the name and relationship of anyone attending with the minor at a notarial ceremony. Additionally, the notary should record the information elicited to make the determination of whether to proceed. The notary should obtain the signature of both the minor and the accompanying parent, guardian, or attorney in the journal. See the discussion of notary journal entries in Chapter 17.

Practice Tip: *Noting the Minor Signer's Age.* A sound practice for notaries when providing a notarization for a minor is to ask the minor to sign the document and the notary journal using both his or her name and age. If an acknowledgment has already been signed before the notarial ceremony, the notary should ask the minor to add the age close to the signature on the instrument. Thus, in any case, the signature of a minor would appear along with the age (i.e., "Pat Smith, age 15"). Although not everyone would agree with this piece of advice, the notary should also note the minor's age next to the signer's name in the notarial certificate. This procedure of noting the age on the instrument and the journal entry should serve to alert third parties receiving and relying on the transactional document to the fact that it was signed by a minor. The notary should also note the method used to verify the minor's age in the notary journal entry.

In this author's opinion, teenage minors in their mid-teens (about age 15–16) or older generally should be allowed to sign documents and to obtain notarizations, if there are no other problems, as they should then be old enough and mature enough. Obviously, there is a point at some early age when a minor is just too young to be mentally competent to sign and to obtain a notarization. A notary will have to use his or her reasoned discretion in each individual case to draw the line.

13.3 The notary should take steps reasonably calculated to assess mental competence by observing, conversing with, and questioning the document signer.

As pointed out above, the key for notaries in assessing the mental competence of document signers is to be reasonable, diligent, and careful in making the notarial determinations. This process suggests that notaries should (a) take steps to do proper assessments and (b) document those steps to be able to later prove the notaries had in fact acted reasonably and diligently.

For every document notarization, the notary should undertake certain basic steps to determine the mental alertness, awareness, and understanding of the signer. Those steps include: (a) to engage the signer in general conversation; (b) to question the signer about the type of transactional document to be presented and about its general nature; (c) to ask the signer why the document is to be notarized; and (d) to observe the body language, facial expressions, and demeanor of the signer. Certainly, the notary should not conduct an intense interrogation of the signer, but rather a courteous and professional questioning. This author actually explains to document signers my duties as a notary, and the reasons for the questions which I ask. Nor should the notary read or pry into the details of the contents of the transactional document, for that information is beyond what the notary needs to know. Instead, the notary should talk briefly with the signer at the beginning of the notarization process to establish that the signer is grounded in the reality of the moment, can communicate with the notary, is possessed of a sound basic memory, and appears initially competent. Then, the notary should ask about the general nature of the transactional document and the purpose of obtaining a notarization of it. If the signer's answers are sound and the signer appears competent, the notarization should proceed.

Note: *Types of Mental Conditions.* Thankfully, most of the time for notaries, the assessment of signer mental competence or understanding is uncomplicated and clear. The vast majority of signers are sufficiently alert and competent to execute their documents and to obtain notarizations. However, in some instances, mental afflictions and competence issues can be extremely complex. There are many variations in kinds and degrees of conditions. Further, the severity of mental impairments can differ markedly from time to time, and even from moment to moment, depending on factors such as medication usage or nonusage, life conflicts, and all sorts of surrounding circumstances.

Importantly, people afflicted with a diagnosed mental illness may well be competent to conduct their affairs, and may be competent to obtain notarizations, if the diagnosed condition does not impair one's ability to understand property and financial transactions. Even someone involuntarily confined in a mental ward of a hospital or other institution may be competent to execute instruments and obtain notarizations. The test for such involuntary confinement is whether an individual is a physical threat or danger to oneself or to others, and that status should be unrelated to the question of whether one understands the nature and consequences of his or her transactions that are presented for notarization. For example, there is a well-known case of a man who was involuntarily confined in a mental institution because he had done serious bodily injury to himself on a number of occasions, but he very capably managed the entire operation of the institution's commissary. So, he would undoubtedly have been mentally competent to obtain a notarization.

Practice Tip: *Types of Questions to Be Asked.* Throughout the assessment process, the notary should not ask questions which can be answered with "yes" and "no" responses. "Yes-no" questions might result in leading the signer, and at a minimum, such questions give the signer a 50-50 chance of guessing at the correct answers. Rather, the notary should ask open-ended and probative questions which require the signer to describe or explain the answers. It is the notary's observation of both the manner and substance of what the signer says during the notarial ceremony that will provide the basis for the mental competence assessment.

If at any point during the notarization ceremony, the notary becomes concerned about the mental competence of the signer, the notary should delay the notarization procedure and should focus further attention on the competence issue. Additional conversation and observation are the methods available to the notary, perhaps including returning to some of the same matters already addressed to see whether the signer's comments and behavior are consistent. The notary should resolve the concern before proceeding to complete the notarization, or decline to proceed and record one or more objective reasons for the refusal to notarize in the notary journal entry.

***Practice Tip:** When Others Are Present at the Notarial Ceremony.* If the signer has been accompanied to the notarial ceremony by anyone else, the notary should be alert to the signer's comments and attitude to notice any reluctance of the signer to converse. Although the notarial ceremony is not the place for discussion of very personal and private information, still the signer may not really wish the accompanying party to hear the conversation. The notary should temporarily excuse the party accompanying the signer, unless the signer speaks up and wishes the accompanying party to remain. It is better for the notary to err on the side of protecting the signer's privacy and possibly obtaining information the signer was reluctant to volunteer with someone else present. Then, the notary will hear what the signer is comfortable saying and will see how the signer behaves. The notary is expected to carry out a layperson's assessment of the signer's mental competence, and nothing more than that level of performance. The test for the notary is whether the signer has a sufficient alertness and understanding of the nature of the transactional instrument at the time of the notarization (which is almost always also the time of the signing of the instrument), and this analysis is expected of the notary after spending only a few minutes with the signer.

Mere diminished mental capacity is not the same as mental incompetence. Many people suffer periodically or chronically from various degrees of emotional or mental strain and distress — short of being mentally incapacitated. Some mental distractions, some lack of short-term or long-term memory, some emotional upsets, and some nervousness, depression, or anxiety afflict many individuals. Indeed, long ago, my graduate school psychology professor quipped: "Everyone is crazy, and only the matter of its degree separates one of us from another." Although he obviously exaggerated for effect with his description of people being "crazy," his basic point was correct — just about all of us are afflicted somehow, although we fall within the broad normal range on the mental competence scale.

It should be noted that notaries may face claims for legal liability due to their allegedly erroneous mental competence assessments of document signers. However, such claims against notaries should have no chance of success if the notaries have acted with diligence and reasonable care, even if their assessments are incorrect. See the discussion about legal liability in Chapter 20.

Practice Tip: *Asking Whether the Signer Has Read the Instrument.* There may be a temptation for a notary in speaking with a document signer in order to determine mental competence to ask whether the signer has read the document. In my opinion, notaries should not, not, not do so (unless the signer is blind or seriously visually impaired). First of all, there is no need to ask if the signer has read the instrument, for the law itself does not require a signer to have read a document. Instead, the law presumes that an individual who signs a document has read it and understands it. Certainly, the signer should have read the document, but the signer has the right not to do so. Secondly, the failure of a signer to have read a document demonstrates not mental incompetence but rather only poor judgment. Next, there are the serious problems which arise if the signer were to admit to having not read the document to be notarized. What should the notary do then? The notary cannot refuse to notarize, for the law does not require a signer to read the document. Should the notary suspend the notarization and insist that the signer read the instrument? Some documents are long, and it would take a very long time for signers to read them. Must the notary monitor the signer to assure the signer reads the document, or test the signer by asking specific questions about the document? Would the notary also need to ask about the actual understanding of what the signer has read? Then, the notary would have to read the document too, and we most assuredly do not want to go so far. Some documents are quite complex, and their complexities may be beyond the ability of some notaries to comprehend. Notaries should not, and cannot, become document police.

Practice Tip: *Blind or Visually Impaired Signers.* If the notary observes or learns that the document signer is blind or seriously visually impaired, the circumstances have changed and the above practice tip does not apply. The notary should ask whether the signer has had the opportunity to have the instrument read to her or him. In some states, statutes require the document to be read to a blind signer prior to completion of the notarization. Of course, the notary journal entry should record the relevant circumstances about the handling of a notarization for a blind or seriously visually impaired signer.

13.4 The notary should note the mental competence assessment process in the journal entry for the notarization.

The mental competence assessment of the document signer is quite important to the security of the notarized document and to the integrity of the notarial process. On the face of the standard-form notarial certificate alone, there is no way of knowing whether the notary has actually considered the mental capacity of the document signer. The notary's assessment of the mental competence of the document signer is not a matter that appears in the usual format of the certificate of notarization. Thus, there would be no written record confirming that the mental assessment has been conducted unless the notary enters a note about it in the journal entry for the notarization.

The notary should place some type of notation in the journal entry to confirm that the mental competence assessment was undertaken. Obviously, the notary should state whether the signer was competent, or incompetent. Especially in the case of any uncertainty about mental competence of the document signer (perhaps, for instance, in the case of an elderly or terminally ill signer), the notary should include as much information as necessary to assist the notary to recall what steps were taken to assess mental competence.

Practice Tip: *Making More Room in the Journal Entry.* In order to accomplish the step of recording a notation about the mental competence assessment, it may be necessary to use additional space or additional lines in the journal record book — and, if necessary, so be it. For instance, the notary might note that the document signer was engaged in general conversation and that the notary questioned the signer about the nature of the transactional document and about the notarization of it. However, these general remarks could apply for every notarization. One or more specifics about the particular notarial ceremony should be included to provide proof that the process was really undertaken. It is far more important to make a solid record about the assessment than to be neat about it by staying within the spaces or lines of the journal format.

Hopefully, the publishers of notary journals will revise their formats to include a section or column referencing mental competence. Perhaps, a box or other icon could be marked to indicate the notary's determination about signer competence, and perhaps space could be provided to note how the assessment was conducted. Of course, there should always be a column or space for additional or other information, which could be used in connection with the mental competence assessment.

If the notary were to decide to refuse to notarize due to the mental incapacity of the signer, such denial would constitute an official act that should be recorded in the journal. Again, the notary should include a notation briefly describing the reasons for concluding the signer was mentally incompetent. Importantly, the notary should be able to refer to objective factors that can be articulated in order to conclude someone is incompetent and to refuse a notarization. The decision about mental competence cannot be based upon hunches, suspicions, or guesswork.

13.5 The notary should proofread the journal entry relating to the signer competence assessment and make any necessary corrections prior to completion of the notarial ceremony.

Everyone makes mistakes, even about commonplace matters. Sometimes mistakes occur because some matters become routine, and those matters are taken too lightly and too routinely. The mental competence requirement for document signers and the notary's assessment of it are critical features of every document notarization, and they deserve full attention. Proofreading should reveal any errors and omissions in the mental competence assessment and provide the notary with the opportunity to correct mistakes in a journal entry before the conclusion of the notarial ceremony — after which it is too late to make changes in the journal entry. ■

***RELEVANT MODEL NOTARY LAW**

Each notary should read, study, and abide by the notary statute and regulations, if any, of his or her commissioning state or territory.

"To always be satisfied that the individual appearing before me understands the contents of the document to be executed or oath to be administered before proceeding ..." *Responsibility Code of Ethics* (1980).

"The Notary shall require the presence of each document signer and oath—taker in order to ... observe that each appears aware of the significance of the transaction requiring a notarial act." *Notary Public Code of Professional Responsibility,* Guiding Principle III (1998).

"A notary shall perform a notarial act only if the principal [document signer]: (3) appears to understand the nature of the transaction requiring a notarial act ..." *Model Notary Act,* Section 5-2(3) (2010).

"A notarial officer may refuse to perform a notarial act if the officer is not satisfied that: (1) the individual executing the record is competent or has the capacity to execute the record ..." *Revised Uniform Law on Notarial Acts,* Section 8(a) (2010).

Cover of *Notary Public Encyclopedia*, an outstanding 2001 notary book with 468 pages and authored by Peter Van Alstyne, a lawyer, founder of the Notary Law Institute, and one of the nation's leading authorities on notarization. I have known Peter and his superior notary work for many years, and I once had the pleasure to teach a notary program with him — at which time, I learned he was also an exceptional notary instructor.

Chapter

14

Assessing Document Signer Willingness

STANDARDS SUMMARY

14.1 The notary should be aware that the signer must act willingly to execute a document and to obtain its notarization.

14.2 The notary should take steps reasonably calculated to assess willingness by observing, conversing with, and questioning the document signer.

14.3 The notary should note the signer willingness assessment process in the journal entry for the notarization.

14.4 The notary should proofread the journal entry relating to the signer's willingness assessment and make any necessary corrections prior to completion of the notarial ceremony.

STANDARDS EXPLANATIONS

Historically, it is undisputed that notaries have been obliged to determine whether document signers are acting voluntarily in signing instruments to be notarized. In regard to acknowledgment notarizations in particular, the earliest statutes have prescribed certificate forms which state that signers have signed voluntarily or of their own free will for the intended purpose of the document. But of course, all notarizations of all types must have been entered into willingly by their document signers — regardless of whether the notary statutes or notary certificates expressly refer to it. Especially in the current era of increased financial fraud, undue influence, and economic coercion, including heightened concerns for the protection of elderly and terminally ill signers from financial abuse, notaries should assess the voluntariness or willingness of all document signings that are to be notarized.

Case Illustration. The author was recently consulted as a notarization expert in regard to a lawsuit in which an acknowledgment certificate did not include the usual language that the acknowledgment had been "signed voluntarily for its intended purpose," but instead recited only that it had been "duly executed." One of the parties to the suit argued that the acknowledgment was void due to the omission of language referencing the voluntariness of the signing. I expressed the opinion that since all of the other elements of the certificate were correctly set out, since exact words should not be required, and since all document signings and their notarizations must be voluntarily undertaken, the acknowledgment did not require an express reference to the voluntariness of signing and was therefore valid. I also cited the definition of "acknowledgment" in the *Revised Uniform Law on Notarial Acts* (included at the end of this chapter), which does not contain reference to signer willingness.

The subject of this chapter, the assessment of signer willingness, is closely related to and overlaps the topic of the preceding chapter, the assessment of signer mental competence. Individuals who are subjected to undue influence and duress are more likely to suffer resulting mental capacity effects, such as anxiety, depression, and stress. Similarly, individuals who suffer from diminished mental capacity or who are mentally incompetent are more likely to be susceptible to coercion and undue influence. See also the discussion of assessment of mental competence in Chapter 13.

***Practice Tip:** A Ceremony-Long Process.* The process of the notary's assessment of the signer's willingness to execute the document to be notarized starts at the very beginning of and continues throughout the notarial ceremony. If at any time during the ceremony, the notary develops objective concerns about the willingness of the signer, the notary should raise and resolve those concerns and either proceed with the notarization or refuse to notarize. As the old saying goes: "It isn't over, 'til it's over."

14.1 The notary should be aware that the signer must act willingly to execute a document and to obtain its notarization.

Willingness or voluntariness is fundamental to document integrity and security. In order for a document to be genuine and to be notarized, its signer must willingly or voluntarily execute it. That is, a signer should not be victimized by duress or undue influence from someone else.

The notary serves as one of the key gatekeepers to protect against coerced and, therefore, fraudulent or faulty transactional documents. However, one of the most difficult of tasks can be the assessment of whether an individual is truly willing to sign. It is comparable in difficulty to the challenge of deciding in a legal case whether a witness is telling the truth or telling a lie. Fortunately, it is highly unusual that document signers will be coerced to sign documents against their free will. Yet, duress can occur, and signers can be coerced or unduly influenced.

Notaries should apply their common sense understanding of the real world and of human nature, including the understanding that an individual may feel pressure to sign a document due to financial difficulties, illness or injury, emotional upset, and/or urging by family, friends, or associates. Such sources of pressure, though unfortunate and unsettling for the signer, are usually commonplace influences, are not significant enough to truly rob an individual of free will, and are not typically improper or unlawful. It is not denial of free will for notarization purposes for signers to have gotten into difficulties of their own creation and their own fault. If signers have caused their own troubled circumstances, or have simply been unlucky and unfortunate, thereby subjecting them to pressures that otherwise would not have influenced them, there has been no denial of free will under the law. Denial of free will for notarization purposes is really about undue or improper influence being exerted by one or more persons to the degree of constituting duress upon the document signer (forcing the signer to sign when he or she would otherwise not have signed). The law of notarization is not expected to protect signers from themselves or from their own poor judgment.

The notary should be aware that a possible source of coercion or undue influence would be individuals closely connected to document signers, such as family members, friends, business associates, caregivers, and service providers (like accountants, stock brokers, bankers, financial planners, lawyers, insurance agents, and so on). Obviously, someone close to the signer may know information about the signer's property and financial affairs, may have achieved a position of trust and confidence with the signer, may be able to exert influence over the signer, and may be able to take advantage of the signer. If anyone accompanies a signer to the notarial ceremony, that person will almost assuredly be on the list of those people closely connected to the signer. Signers would rarely be accompanied to notarizations by casual acquaintances or strangers. Thus, the notary should be on the alert if anyone attends the ceremony with the signer.

Note: *Alternative Legal Protection Against Coercion and Undue Influence of Signers.* The point made here is like the note appearing in the preceding chapter relating to the notary's mental competence assessment. Notaries public are not the only guardians protecting signers of notarized documents from those who would deprive signers of their genuine willingness to sign. Even after the notarization has been performed, a legal challenge based upon coercion or undue influence might be raised and might invalidate the notarization and/or the underlying transaction. Therefore, the notary should appreciate that the notary's role is extremely important because the notary is an unbiased public servant with the first official opportunity to prevent coercion or undue influence from affecting a transaction, and there may not be a second chance to undo the signing.

14.2 The notary should take steps reasonably calculated to assess willingness by observing, conversing with, and questioning the signer.

At the notarization ceremony, the notary should ask the signer a number of basic questions on the subject of voluntariness and possible coercion. Have you signed or are you signing of your own free will? Has anyone instructed, demanded, or asked you to sign the transactional document? If the answer to that question is "yes," the notary should then ask further questions to elicit the details about why someone has done so, and under what circumstances. The notary should ask whether the signer would like to consult an attorney before continuing. If the answer is "yes," the notarization ceremony should be discontinued (and a journal entry should be prepared to reflect that outcome).

Throughout the notarization ceremony, the notary should observe the signer's facial expressions, body language, and demeanor, and look for any evidence of coercion or undue influence. The notary should look for signs of anxiety or nervousness, fear or intimidation, reluctance, uncertainty, or displeasure. If any are observed,, the notary should ask further questions to clarify the signs observed by the notary. If anyone has accompanied the signer to the notarization ceremony, that person or persons should be observed as well, in order to see whether they are attempting to coerce the signer.

Practice Tip: *Temporarily Excluding Non-Signers from the Ceremony.* Whenever notarizing a document involving estate, financial, health care, or property matters, the notary should ask any witnesses or observers accompanying the signer to leave the room at least temporarily in order to allow the notary to speak privately with the signer about the issue of willingness to sign the transactional document. The reason to employ this tactic should be obvious. Coercion and duress will originate from some third party other than the signer or the notary, and that third party may want to attend the notarization ceremony to assure the coercion succeeds in effecting a signing and notarization. If the notary removes the possible source of duress from the room, there is greater likelihood that questioning of the signer by the notary will reveal the treachery. It is possible that the signer would really prefer that the accompanying person were not present in the first place. Furthermore, the signer may simply be reluctant or embarrassed to talk about the coercion or undue influence in front of another person, especially someone known to the signer. Importantly, see the continuation of this tip immediately below. Certainly, removing someone from the notarial ceremony will not necessarily make coercion or duress go completely away, for threats and pressure already exerted toward the signer may still loom large. The notary will have to exercise the discretion and judgment whether to proceed with the notarization or to refuse to notarize (and to record one or more objective reasons for the refusal in the notary journal entry).

Practice Tip: *Have the Signing Occur When Only the Notary and Signer Are Together.* If there is no need for a witness or witnesses to observe the actual document signing, then after the notary has temporarily excluded any guest(s) accompanying the signer, there is a significant reason to have the present signing of the document at that time — while only the notary and signer are together. Court opinions have rightly observed that when the signer executes a present signature of the document to be notarized in the presence of the notary, such signing is willingly made, and the notary need not ask if the signing is being voluntarily done, and need not declare in the notarial certificate that the signing was voluntarily done. This observation is even more compelling in instances when there are no other parties present except for the notary and the signer.

Note: *Intoxicated Signers.* Signers who are intoxicated, or to a lesser extent affected, as the result of alcohol and/or drug consumption may be more likely to be taken advantage of, coerced, or subjected to undue influence or duress. Besides, notaries should not have to deal with anyone who has been drinking or doing drugs, nor should they have to accept the extra, avoidable risk of assessing signer willingness for someone who is impaired by alcohol or drugs. If a would-be signer is not fully sober, the notary should refuse to service the individual, and the notary should record the refusal in a journal entry. The journal entry should include the objective evidence that the individual was intoxicated — such as slurred speech, bloodshot eyes, disheveled appearance, alcohol or drug odors, and the like.

Note: *Elderly and Terminally Ill Signers.* The elderly and the terminally ill populations in this country are large and special groups worthy of separate mention in connection with notarizations and the willingness issue. As life expectancy increases and the elderly population grows, and as so many individuals face terminal illnesses, there are more and more potentially vulnerable people. As people grow older, two conflicting circumstances take place with more frequency. On the one hand, as many people grow older or become terminally ill, they may undertake increased numbers of transactions that may involve notarized documents. Such people often have considerable wealth. They may buy and sell homes. They may engage in advance health care decision-making involving living wills, advance directives, and powers of attorney for health care. They may wish to sign life-care contracts, powers of attorney for financial matters, and residential nursing care agreements. They may wish to engage in estate planning to dispose of their assets upon their deaths (including the making of wills) and for funeral arrangements.

Simultaneously, on the other hand, as many people grow older or become terminally ill, they suffer the effects of diminished physical and mental health.

Even physical ailments and injuries can take a great toll on the elderly, causing distractions and doubts, and sometimes creating the need for personal care providers. At some point, many people become terminally ill, and that reality complicates everything in one's life. A range of mental health issues may afflict such people, like memory loss and dementia. Such individuals may lose many of the trustworthy people in their circles of family and friends. They may need the assistance of others in matters of daily living and long-term financial planning. Moreover, each of us grows older only once, and one becomes terminally ill only once. No matter how many other people we have observed go through the process, our own individual experience of aging or dealing with a terminal illness is novel and mostly unfamiliar. Dealing with family members and friends as they grow older or face a terminal illness does not fully prepare us for our own personal experiences in aging or dealing with a fatal illness.

So, many elderly and terminally ill persons are vulnerable and ideal targets for unscrupulous individuals and groups. Notaries must be aware of this general area of concern, and notaries should recognize the need for heightened care and scrutiny in dealing with elderly and terminally ill signers.

Case Illustrations. Over my more than 20 years of service as an expert consultant and expert witness in notary disputes, at least 75% of those cases have involved elderly document signers, some of whom have also been terminally ill at the times of the challenged notarizations. And, I have performed notarizations for terminally ill, elderly signers in hospice settings. Notaries should be savvy enough to recognize the heightened risk of notarizing for elderly and terminally ill signers. Notaries should take prudent steps to protect such signers and to protect themselves. Notaries should engage those signers in enough conversation to assure they are mentally capable and likely able to resist efforts of others to unduly influence them. Notaries should be sure such signers understand the importance of notarizing documents and understand the general nature of the documents to be notarized and the transactions involved. This conversation should also include some discussion about their current health conditions and about medications they are taking. As noted above, notaries should ask those accompanying such signers to temporarily leave the rooms of the notarizations so that notaries can talk with the signers alone for a while, to assure that those accompanying them have not coerced them into signing the documents to be notarized and to assure some privacy to the signers when discussing personal matters. As noted above, the signer may not really want the individual present for the notarization anyway. The notary should complete a thorough journal entry to record each such notarization. Lastly, we do not want to err on either side of this difficult issue, by depriving elderly or terminally ill signers of the opportunity to obtain notarizations when they are acting of their own free wills, or by notarizing their documents which have been signed because they were coerced or unduly influenced.

It should be noted that notaries may face legal claims and liability for faulty assessments of signer willingness. See the discussion of legal liability in Chapter 20.

14.3 The notary should note the signer willingness assessment process in the journal entry for the notarization.

As explained above in connection with the assessment of signer mental competence in the previous chapter, on the face of the notarial certificate, there is no way of knowing whether the notary actually conducted an assessment of signer competence or willingness. Thus, after the notary has conducted the willingness assessment, the notary should record that the process was carried out by entering an appropriate notation in the notary journal.

Ideally, the format of both notarial certificates and notary journals should accommodate a reference to the willingness assessment. A box or a space could be designated where the notary can place an "X" or a checkmark to denote that the assessment of voluntariness was conducted, as well as the outcome of the assessment (such as "voluntary").

The notary should note that the notary questioned the signer regarding the willingness to sign the document, and the notary should note the result. Also, the notary should mention any other steps that were taken — such as having other parties leave the room to allow the notary and signer to talk privately about the transaction.

The more significant and valuable the transactional document, the more important it is for the notary to have a complete and thorough record of the willingness assessment. If needed, the notary should use additional space in the notary journal to fully record the relevant information. It is better to have more information than less.

14.4 The notary should proofread the portion of the journal entry relating to the signer's willingness assessment and make any necessary corrections prior to completion of the notarial ceremony.

In many years of service as an expert consultant and witness in notary cases, this author has reviewed thousands of notary journal entries performed by notaries from around the country. I have observed hundreds of errors in those journal entries which should have been discovered if the notaries preparing the entries had simply proofread them. Of course, it has been recommended that notaries proofread the entirety of their notarial certificates and journal entries, but in this context the recommendation is set out separately for the purpose of emphasis.

Because of the importance that signers willingly execute the documents to be notarized, the portion of the journal entry relating to that key element should be proofread prior to the completion of the notarial ceremony. By doing so, the notary will have the opportunity to make timely additions or corrections, whereas after the notarization is finalized it is this author's view there can be no modifications to the journal entry. ■

***RELEVANT MODEL NOTARY LAW**

Each notary should read, study, and abide by the notary statute and regulations, if any, of her or his commissioning state or territory.

"The Notary shall require the presence of each document signer and oath-taker in order to carefully screen each for identity and willingness ..." *Notary Public Code of Professional Responsibility,* Guiding Principle III (1998).

"A notary shall perform a notarial act only if the principal [document signer]: (4) appears to be acting of his or her own free will ..." *Model Notary Act,* Section 5-2(4) (2010).

"A notarial officer may refuse to perform a notarial act if the officer is not satisfied that: ... (2) the individual's signature is knowingly and voluntarily made." *Revised Uniform Law on Notarial Acts,* Section 8(a) (2010).

"'Acknowledgment' means a notarial act in which an individual at a single time and place: ... (3) indicates to the notary that the signature on the document was voluntarily affixed by the individual for the purposes stated within the document ..." *Model Notary Act,* Section 2-1 (2010).

"'Acknowledgment' means a declaration by an individual before a notarial officer that the individual has signed a record for the purpose stated in the record ..." *Revised Uniform Law on Notarial Acts,* Section 2(1) (2010).

Baltes' Oregon Blank No. 17MN—MORTGAGE—Printed and Sold by F. W. Baltes and Company, Portland

This Mortgage, Made this Second day of May, 1911, by W. Clyde Hood and Jennie B. Hood, husband and wife Mortgagors, to H. Van Auken Mortgagee,

WITNESSETH, That said mortgagors, in consideration of One Hundred and Fifty ($150.00) Dollars, to them paid by said mortgagee, do hereby grant, bargain, sell and convey unto said mortgagee, his heirs, executors, administrators and assigns that certain real property situated in Multnomah County, State of Oregon, bounded and described as follows, to wit: All of Lot numbered Four (4), in Block numbered sixteen (16), in WOODLAWN, according to the duly recorded plat thereof all of which is now a part of the incorporated City of Portland, county and state aforesaid.

together with the tenements, hereditaments and appurtenances thereunto belonging or appertaining.

TO HAVE AND TO HOLD the said premises with the appurtenances unto the said mortgagee, his heirs, executors, administrators and assigns forever.

This mortgage is intended to secure the payment of a promissory note of which the following is a substantial copy:

C O P Y.

$150.00 Portland, Oregon, May 2nd 1911

On or before two years after date without grace, I promise to pay to the order of H. Van Auken at Portland, Oregon

ONE HUNDRED AND FIFTY ($150.00) DOLLARS,

in Gold Coin of the United States of America, of the present standard value, with interest thereon in like Gold Coin at the rate of six per cent. per annum from Date until paid, for value received. Interest to be paid semi-annually and if not so paid, the whole sum of both principal and interest to become immediately due and collectable, at the option of the holder of this note. And in case suit or action is instituted to collect this note, or any portion thereof I promise and agree to pay, in addition to the costs and disbursements provided by statute, such additional sum, in like Gold Coin, as the Court may adjudge reasonable, for Attorney's fees to be allowed in said suit or action.

W. Clyde Hood

Jennie B. Hood

No.

IRON CLAD NOTE. THE J. K. GILL CO., PORTLAND

which may be hereafter erected on the premises insured in favor of the mortgagee, against loss or damage by fire in the sum of $, in such company or companies as the mortgagee may designate, and will have all policies of insurance on said property made payable to the mortgagee as interest may appear and will deliver all policies of insurance on said premises to the mortgagee as soon as insured; that they will keep the buildings and improvements on said premises in good repair and will not commit or suffer any waste of said premises.

Now, therefore, if said mortgagors shall keep and perform the covenants herein contained and shall pay said note according to its terms, this conveyance shall be void, but otherwise shall remain in full force as a mortgage to secure the performance of all of said covenants and the payment of said note; it being agreed that a failure to perform any covenant herein shall give the mortgagee the option to declare the whole amount unpaid on said note or on this mortgage at once due and payable, and this mortgage may be foreclosed at any time thereafter. And if the mortgagors shall fail to pay any taxes or charges or any lien, encumbrance or insurance premium as above provided for, the mortgagee may at his option do so, and any payment so made shall be added to and become a part of the debt secured by this mortgage, and shall bear interest at the same rate as said note—without waiver, however, of any right arising to the mortgagee for breach of covenant. And if suit be commenced to foreclose this mortgage, the attorneys' fees provided for in said note shall be included in the lien of this mortgage.

Each and all of the covenants and agreements herein contained shall apply to and bind the heirs, executors, administrators and assigns of said mortgagors and the successors and assigns of said mortgagee respectively.

1911, trifold mortgage, including an acknowledgment certificate prepared by Oregon notary Clinton Ambood and an embosser impression of his notary seal.

Chapter

15

Oaths and Affirmations for Jurat (Verification) Notarizations

STANDARDS SUMMARY

15.1 The notary should understand the differences between an oath and an affirmation but understand they have the same legal effect.

15.2 The notary should understand the purposes of an oral oath or affirmation, including subjecting the document signer to the law of perjury.

15.3 The notary should understand that a jurat notarization requires the administration of an oral oath or affirmation to the document signer.

15.4 The notary should understand the oath or affirmation requires the signer to pledge that the contents of the transactional document are correct and true.

15.5 The notary should formulate appropriate language for administration of the oral oath or affirmation to the document signer and consistently use that language for each jurat.

15.6 The notary should conduct the oral oath or affirmation in an appropriately solemn manner, in part by consistently incorporating corporal elements for each jurat.

15.7 The notary should note the administration of the oral oath or affirmation in the jurat certificate.

15.8 The notary should note the administration of the oral oath or affirmation in the journal entry.

15.9 The notary should, prior to completion of the notarial ceremony, proofread the portions of the notarial certificate and journal entry relating to the oath or affirmation and make any necessary corrections.

STANDARDS EXPLANATIONS

Historically, oral oaths and affirmations have been required as important and necessary elements in numerous religious, organizational, commercial, and governmental ceremonies. These include the testimony of witnesses, the membership process in private organizations, the installation of elected and appointed public officials, the licensure of attorneys, and so forth. Not just anyone can administer an oath or affirmation; rather, only specified individuals are authorized to administer them. Often, government officials, such as judges, court clerks, and notaries public, are authorized by law to administer oaths and affirmations.

Unfortunately, it appears that the great majority of practicing notaries around the country do not actually administer oral oaths or affirmations which comprise a critical requirement of jurat (verification on oath or affirmation) notarizations. Indeed, this author has regularly opined that there is an appalling failure rate regarding notarial oaths and affirmations and that in at least 80–90% of jurat notarizations, notaries fail to administer oral oaths or affirmations. This is a serious problem regarding the general performance of notaries, and specifically regarding the integrity and trustworthiness of jurat notarizations. The author has arrived at this estimated failure rate from several sources, including (1) some 25 years of anecdotal accounts from fellow notaries, state notary regulators, and other notary authorities, (2) a paper survey which I administered to hundreds of law students in three states (published in a *Buffalo Law Review* article cited in the bibliography at the end of this book), and (3) my examination of documents, notary journals, and testimony in numerous notary legal cases with regard to which I have served as expert consultant and/or expert witness (representing thousands of notarizations that I have reviewed).

Case Illustration. In one case alone in which this author testified as an expert and in which I reviewed more than 1,000 notary journal entries, a single notary had neglected to administer oral oaths or affirmation for hundreds of jurats. In fact, that notary had never administered an oral oath or affirmation in several years of active service as a notary. In this author's opinion, all of those jurat notarizations would have been found to be invalid if they had been challenged.

Note: *Scope of This Chapter.* This chapter covers oaths and affirmations administered in conjunction with jurat document notarizations, or what are also called verifications on oath or affirmation. Thus, the chapter does not deal with other settings in which notaries may administer oaths or affirmations, such as oaths of office. Nor does this chapter deal with oaths or affirmations administered by notaries to credible witnesses because this author disapproves of the credible witness method of identification of document signers, and the book does not cover that subject.

15.1 The notary should understand the differences between an oath and an affirmation but understand they have the same legal effect.

Oaths and affirmations are similar, but different too. An oath is a solemn pledge of truthfulness which, as part of the aura of the pledge ceremony, involves swearing by the oath-taker, most often to God or some deity. Thus, in the notary context, the language of a jurat certificate will usually recite "sworn to" before the notary, who is a public official authorized to administer oaths. Often the oaths end with the words "so help me God."

However, some people are not religious and/or object to swearing, so an alternative to the oath, called an affirmation, was developed. An affirmation does not require the affirmation-taker to swear, but rather to "affirm," that the relevant statements made are correct and truthful. An affirmation does not invoke a pledge to a god or deity, Hence, affirmations should not conclude with the words "so help me God."

In other respects, an oath and an affirmation are alike. A notary can administer both, and both are solemn promises to tell the truth. Incidentally, jurat certificates should now recite that they have been "sworn to or affirmed by" the instrument signer. See also the discussion of jurats in Chapter 5.

15.2 The notary should understand the purposes of an oral oath or affirmation, including subjecting the document signer to the law of perjury.

Historically, especially in ancient times when few people outside the clergy and the nobility could read and write, the principal reason oral oaths were so commonly used was that participants in ceremonies involving oral oaths did not have to be literate to appreciate what was going on, to recognize the importance of the occasions, and to submit to the oaths. In modern times, this purpose of the oral oath and affirmation has been lost to the wide sweep of literacy.

Since early eras, there were also two other symbolic reasons for the popularity of oral pledges, for they brought solemnity and officiality to ceremonies. Solemnity and officiality go hand in hand; they are interdependent. Solemnity is fundamental to notarization, because the procedure for notarizing documents should be taken quite seriously. A notarized document is special. It is not simply a written promise; it is a legally recognized pledge, with rights and duties attaching to it. Hence, the signing ceremony should also be special, and it is made special by the incorporation of the oral oath or affirmation.

Additionally, officiality is fundamental to notarization. Only public officials [such as notaries] are authorized to perform notarizations, and only certain public officials [including notaries] are authorized to administer oral oaths and affirmations which create the legal obligation to be truthful. Officiality is enhanced by the oath-taking or affirmation-taking ceremony which, unlike a modest document signing, includes oral and usually corporal components (such as standing up and raising the right hand).

Importantly, the other key purpose of the oral oath or affirmation is to invoke the law of perjury. When one swears to tell the truth in the presence of a public officer empowered to administer an oath or affirmation, the legal result is that the law of perjury applies, and that a person who knowingly lies under the oral pledge commits the crime of perjury. Perjury is a serious offense, and a perjurer can be punished by imprisonment and/or fine.

A couple of important reservations about perjury should be emphasized. First, perjury results from a knowing or intentional lie. An innocent or accidental false statement is not perjury. Second, perjury is reserved for material or important false statements. Falsehoods about trivial or unimportant matters are not perjury.

Case Illustration. This author recently served as expert consultant on a case in which two notaries working at the same business had performed two separate jurat notarizations signed by their boss, the owner of the company. The notaries had not administered an oath or affirmation to their boss. The boss had lied in both of the documents which were publicly filed, and the falsifications by the boss were discovered. Prosecutors charged the boss with two counts of felony perjury, but then found out that the notary-employees had not actually administered oral oaths or affirmations to the employer. This situation became extremely uncomfortable for the two notaries. The notaries were threatened with prosecution, but were eventually granted immunity from criminal prosecution in exchange for their testimony against their employer. Of course, the immunity from prosecution covered only criminal liability of the two notaries. It did not affect possible administrative sanctions faced by the notaries from the state notary regulatory agency. And, the immunity from prosecution would not make the workplace atmosphere any better either. By the way, in my capacity as expert consultant, I expressed the opinion that the boss could not be guilty of perjury in the absence of taking an oral oath or affirmation. The prosecutor dismissed the perjury charge.

15.3 The notary should understand that a jurat notarization requires the administration of an oral oath or affirmation to the document signer.

Each type of document notarization is unique, in order to allow each to achieve its central purpose. The central purpose of a jurat is to provide the highly desirable element of the trustworthiness of the notarized document's contents. No other kind of document notarization includes such a pledge by the document signer of the correctness and truth of the document's contents, especially a pledge which, if it is broken, can lead to a criminal charge and a conviction and punishment of the signer for perjury.

Notary statutes require the administration of an oral oath or affirmation as part of the procedure for a jurat notarization, as also indicated by the standard form language of a jurat which historically has most commonly stated it was "sworn to." The synonym for jurat is "verification on oath or affirmation," which might be the better name as it emphasizes the need for an oral pledge. Indeed, because the oath or affirmation is an essential element of a jurat, the notarial certificate requires notation of or reference to the administration of the oath or affirmation.

Unfortunately, as noted earlier, the most frequent fault in U.S. notarizations is the overwhelming failure of notaries to actually administer the required oath or affirmation for jurat notarizations. This neglect arises even though the relevant notarial certificates state that an oath or affirmation was administered, or that the certificate had been "sworn to" or "affirmed." This failure of the notary to actually administer the oath or affirmation raises a number of possible serious and adverse consequences for all parties with interests in those faulty notarizations.

First, if no oath or affirmation is administered to the document signer, then the signer should not be subject to the law of perjury. The signer could lie and falsify statements in the document with impunity from criminal prosecution.

Second, if there is no oath or affirmation taken by the document signer, the notarization may be invalidated. After all, the oath or affirmation is a key element of a jurat. In turn, the transaction underlying the invalid jurat notarization may be invalid as well.

Third, the failure of the notary to follow the jurat procedure of administering an oath or affirmation may cause adverse consequences for the notary. If the notary's neglect invalidates the notarization, and if financial injury is suffered by either the document signer or a third party relying upon the document, the notary could face a civil claim for damages. The notary could also face a criminal charge for official misconduct for failing to administer the required oath or affirmation. Finally, the notary may be sanctioned by the state or territorial agency that regulates notaries, possibly including suspension or cancellation of the notary commission and/or a fine. See the discussion of notary liability concerns in Chapter 20.

Fourth, when any notaries fail to fully perform their duties, this neglect casts doubt on all notaries. It is dishonest, unlawful, disrespectful, and unprofessional. Most importantly, this neglect jeopardizes the interests of document signers whose notarizations may be invalid. The cardinal rule for both doctors and notaries should be: "Do no harm."

Note: *A Split of Court Decisions*. Although in a substantial number of instances, notaries do not really administer oral oaths or affirmations as part of jurat notarizations, there have been only a small number of court cases involving those situations. The few legal cases which have considered the issue of the effect on the law of perjury resulting from the notary's failure to administer an oral oath or affirmation have split on the outcome. A couple of courts have concluded that without an oral oath or affirmation, the law of perjury has not been invoked — the position with which this author agrees. But, a couple of other courts have reached the opposite conclusion, relying upon the recital in the notarial certificate that it has been "sworn to" by the document signer. These courts have taken the view that the document signer is bound to the truth because the notarial certificate states the signer was sworn. This author disagrees with that view because the signer does not typically read and does not sign the notarial certificate, but rather signs the transactional instrument. Importantly, regardless of the outcome, the failure of the notary to actually administer the oral oath or affirmation will put the law of perjury at risk of not applying and will risk a long and costly legal battle that could have easily been avoided. Incidentally, those few court cases did not address the issue of whether the transactional instrument would be valid for other purposes. Most certainly, the notary should not jeopardize the validity of a jurat by failing to do something as easy as administering the prescribed oral oath or affirmation.

15.4 The notary should understand the oral oath or affirmation requires the signer to pledge that the contents of the transactional document are correct and true.

Too often, notaries are unsure about just what the document signer must pledge in the oath or affirmation. Does the signer promise that his or her claimed identity is true, or does the signer promise that the content of the document to be notarized is true, or both? This confusion stems from a number of factors. Notary statutes do not describe precisely what the pledge must be and do not tend to provide suggested language for the oath or affirmation. Few jurisdictions require notaries to attend live notary training programs or real-time online notary education sessions during which notaries could be told more about the oath and affirmation, or could ask about the nature of the pledge. Further, the standard form jurat certificates simply recite "subscribed and sworn to or affirmed by" the named document signer, without explaining what the phrase really means.

Some notaries mistakenly believe that the oath or affirmation is merely the pledge by the document signer that the signer's claimed identity is true and correct. But, that is only part of what the signer promises is correct and true. The pledge in the oath or affirmation should be that the contents of, or statements made in, the transactional instrument are correct and true. The great value of a jurat is the heightened assurance of the accuracy of the notarized document's contents resulting from the pledge contained in the oath or affirmation. That pledge would, of course, also include the promise that the individual's claimed identity is truthful, for the individual's claimed name appears in the transactional document, in the form of a written or printed name, and a signature. And, that claimed name or identity is also corroborated by the written or printed name of the signer included by the notary in the notarial certificate. So, the answer to the question at the beginning of this section is "both." The signer promises that he or she is who he or she claims to be, and that the contents of the document to be notarized are correct and true. This author's suggested form of an oath or affirmation appears immediately below in the next section.

15.5 The notary should formulate appropriate language for administration of the oral oath or affirmation to the document signer and consistently use that language for each jurat.

Exact or magic words are not required in order for a statement to constitute an oath or affirmation and to subject the oath-taker or affirmation-taker to the law of perjury. The key requirement of an oath or affirmation is to place the oath-taker or affirmation-taker clearly on notice that she or he is undergoing a formal legal process resulting in the need to be accurate and honest in regard to the content of the notarized instrument and subjecting the oath-taker or affirmation-taker to the risk of criminal prosecution and criminal punishment for perjury committed in the notarized instrument. The words and procedure employed by the notary must clearly convey this meaning. To put it differently, the main thing with which the signer must be aware is that she or he is being put under oath or affirmation. Incidentally, one of the methods by which to make clear to signers that they are being placed under oath or affirmation is to incorporate corporal elements — to be addressed in the next section.

There are basically two different formats by which to administer an oral oath or affirmation. One method is for the notary to recite the oath or affirmation and to have the jurat signer repeat those words aloud. The other is for the notary to recite the language of the oath or affirmation in the form of a question and to have the jurat signer answer in the affirmative (such as with the words "I do").

This author, as an arbitrator and as a notary, has, over the course of many years, administered hundreds of oral oaths or affirmations to arbitration witnesses and document signers, using very similar language in both venues. I have used the following language in the form of a question in administering an oath or affirmation in a jurat notarization: "Do you solemnly swear or affirm, subject to the law of perjury, that the statements contained in this document are true and correct?" There are a number of important advantages to this language. First, the reference to "swear or affirm" indicates it constitutes either an oath or an affirmation, without offending any document signer. Second, the references to "solemnly" and "subject to the law of perjury" helps to emphasize the legal seriousness of the oral pledge to the document signer. Third, the reference to the law of perjury makes clear that the document signer will be subject to the law of perjury in regard to the contents of the document. Fourth, this formal, though brief and understandable, language should unquestionably inform the signer that he or she in being subjected to a legal pledge.

Especially if the notary only infrequently performs jurat notarizations that require the administration of oral oaths or affirmations, the notary may want to write or type the words to be used on a small slip of paper and perhaps to laminate it and keep it in close proximity to the notary's seal and journal for quick reference when needed. This practice is much like that of many police officers, who carry a card printed with the words of the Miranda warning to be read to suspects who are interrogated in connection with criminal investigations.

Regardless of the language and format selected by the notary for the oath or affirmation, the notary should use the same form and wording consistently, so that the administration of the oath or affirmation will become a regular business practice of the notary. Then, if ever there is a challenge to a jurat, the notary will be able to testify to her or his established professional practice in the administration of the oaths and affirmations.

Practice Tip: *A Written Reminder.* The notary should write the language of the oath and affirmation to be consistently used in the front cover of the notary journal (and date it), so that it will be readily available, if needed, to assist the notary's recollection for the administration of oral oaths and affirmations, and so that it will be recorded as possible written evidence for presentation in a hearing, arbitration, or trial to show the notary's professional practice.

15.6 The notary should conduct the oral oath or affirmation in an appropriately solemn manner, in part by consistently incorporating corporal elements for each jurat.

Because notarization is a serious matter and because an official oral oath or affirmation invokes application of the law of perjury, a jurat notarization is an especially important and serious event. The notary has the responsibility to create the atmosphere for the notarial ceremony, a serious atmosphere from beginning to end. That obligation does not mean there is no room for humorous or lighthearted moments, but the overall atmosphere should be appropriately serious and solemn.

As previously said, essential features of administering a proper oath or affirmation include assurance that the individual is aware she or he will be placed under oath or affirmation and that the oath-taker or affirmation-taker is clearly aware of the legal importance of the oath or affirmation, subjecting the individual to the obligation of truthfulness or else to the threat of criminal prosecution for perjury. Because the notary is the public official who controls the notarial ceremony, the notary must take charge and guide the participant(s) in such a manner as to maintain the necessarily serious tone and to assure the signer's awareness of the fact that a notarization is being conducted.

Since ancient times, corporal elements have been part of many formal ceremonies in public, private, and religious settings. Such actions as standing up and raising the right hand have brought an air of dignity, officiality, and seriousness to ceremonial events. These corporal elements have stood the test of time as traditional features of notarial oaths and affirmations that lend a solemn atmosphere to the official business at hand. When administered thoughtfully and skillfully, the corporal elements play a substantial role in making oath-takers and affirmation-takers aware of the notarial purpose and of the legal significance of the ceremony.

Although not required to do so as part of the administration of a notarial oath or affirmation, the notary should employ a number of nonreligious corporal elements in order to emphasize to the signer of a jurat the significance of the oath or affirmation. The notary should stand along with the jurat signer; both parties should raise their right hands; and, the notary should either orally pronounce the words of the oath or affirmation with the jurat signer repeating the same language aloud, or the notary should state the oath or affirmation in the form of an oral question with the jurat signer answering the question aloud and in the affirmative. By standing and raising the right hand, the notary will make the point that the notary is serious about the oath or affirmation, and by insisting on the signer's compliance with these corporal acts, the notary will convey to the signer a similar message.

The notary should follow the same pattern in conducting notarization ceremonies for all jurat notarizations, using the same language for the oath or affirmation and the same corporal elements. Religious references in the language and the use of religious objects (such as bibles or texts) should be avoided so as not to embarrass or offend anyone. Remember, the notarization ceremony is part of the official function of a public officer commissioned by the state or territory, so the separation of church and state should be honored. Furthermore, if used consistently, these sound practices will become professional habits about which the notary could testify generally in court if a challenge to a notarization were to arise.

15.7 The notary should note the administration of the oral oath or affirmation in the jurat certificate.

Customarily, jurat certificates recite that the transactional instrument has been "subscribed and sworn to or affirmed by" the document signer (or words to that effect). We should remember that the certificate is an official certification by the notary as to what steps were taken during a notarization. This practice and language like that just cited should continue for jurats, but, hereafter, notaries should mean what they say in those certificates. Notaries should actually administer oral oaths or affirmations for jurats because notaries, as public officials, are certifying that they have done so.

The accuracy and trustworthiness of the notarial certificate is a serious matter, a matter for which the notary is fully and exclusively responsible. Consider that the notary's falsification of the notarial certificate (by stating that an oath or affirmation was administered when that did not happen) constitutes obstruction of justice (falsifying evidence or covering up misconduct) and official misconduct.

15.8 The notary should note the administration of the oral oath or affirmation in the journal entry.

The basic purpose for a notary journal is corroboration. The journal corroborates what occurs at a notarization, even if the memories of the participants fade or fail, and even if the notarial certificate is unavailable or differs in some respects from the journal entry. So, even though the certificate (which is attached to the transactional document) should state that an oath or affirmation was administered to the document signer, the journal entry is a backup record (that stays in the possession of the notary) to corroborate that element.

Due to the importance of the oral oath or affirmation for a jurat notarization and due to the peculiarity of the oath or affirmation in the notarial setting (as no other document notarization requires an oath or affirmation), the administration of the oral oath or affirmation should always be noted in the journal entry for a jurat. Additionally, since it is the oral oath or affirmation that invokes the law of perjury, a notation about the oath or affirmation is warranted. Moreover, in light of the fact that so frequently the oral oath or affirmation is not in fact administered, even though the notarial certificate recites to the contrary, the notary would be well-advised to record the administration of the oath or affirmation in the journal entry. Such a notation would help to prove that the oral oath or affirmation had really been administered. Of course, the notary need not record the words of the oath or affirmation in the notary journal — but simply a notation that it was administered.

The formats of notary journals vary. Some include a column or location where the notary can check a box or otherwise indicate that an oath or affirmation was administered, while some others have no designated space pertaining to an oath or affirmation. In virtually all notary journals, there is a column or location for "other information" or "additional facts." Certainly, the notary could use the "other information" or "additional facts" area of the journal entry to record the administration of the oath or affirmation. If there is no designated location about the oath or affirmation in the particular journal being utilized, and no area for additional or other information, the notary should simply continue into the next entry field or area and write in the necessary information about the oath or affirmation (disregarding the strict format of the journal for the greater good of recording the relevant and important information). This author strongly recommends the use of a journal format with a designated column or area for noting the administration of an oral oath or affirmation.

15.9 The notary should, prior to completion of the notarial ceremony, proofread the portions of the notarial certificate and journal entry relating to the oath or affirmation and make any necessary corrections.

A recurring theme of this book is the value of diligence and proofreading. If notaries would only proofread their notarial certificates and journal entries for every notarization, almost all notarial errors would be avoided, or discovered and cured. Since the oath or affirmation is critical to a jurat notarization, the notary should proofread both the notarial certificate and the journal entry to assure that they document the oral oath or affirmation was in fact administered. The proofreading needs to be done before the completion of the notarial ceremony because after the notarial ceremony is concluded, it is too late for the notary to make changes in the certificate or journal entry. ■

***RELEVANT MODEL NOTARY LAW**

Each notary should read, study, and abide by the notary statute and regulations, if any, of his or her commissioning state or territory.

"To always be satisfied that the individual appearing before me understands the contents of the document to be executed or oath to be administered before proceeding ..." *Responsibility Code of Ethics* (1980).

"The Notary shall require the presence of each signer and oath—taker [and affirmation—taker] in order to carefully screen each for identity and willingness, and to observe that each appears aware of the significance of the transaction requiring a notarial act." *Notary Public Code of Professional Responsibility,* Guiding Principle III (1998).

"Jurat. 'Jurat' means a notarial act in which an individual at a single time and place: ... (4) takes an oath or affirmation from the notary vouching for the truthfulness or accuracy of the signed document," *Model Notary Act,* Section 2-7 (2010).

"'Oath' means a notarial act, or part thereof, which is legally equivalent to an affirmation and in which an individual at a single time and place: (1) appears in person before the notary; (2) is personally known to the notary or identified by the notary through satisfactory evidence; and (3) makes a vow of truthfulness or fidelity on penalty of perjury while invoking a deity or using any form of the word 'swear.'" *Model Notary Act,* Section 2-11 (2010)

"'Affirmation' means a notarial act, or part thereof, which is legally equivalent to an oath and in which an individual in a single time and place: (1) appears in person before the notary; (2) is personally known to the notary or identified by the notary through satisfactory evidence; and (3) makes a vow of truthfulness or fidelity on penalty of perjury, based on personal honor and without invoking a deity or using any form of the word 'swear.'" *Model Notary Act,* Section 2-2 (2010).

"Official Misconduct. 'Official misconduct' means: (1) a notary's performance of any act prohibited, or failure to perform any act or duty mandated, by this [Act] or by any other law in connection with a notarial act; or (2) a notary's performance of an official act or duty in a manner that is negligent, contrary to established norms of sound notarial practice, or against the public interest." *Model Notary Act,* Section 2-2 (2010).

"'Verification on oath or affirmation' means a declaration, made by an individual on oath or affirmation before a notarial officer, that a statement in a record is true." *Revised Uniform Law on Notarial Acts,* Section 2(15) (2010).

Vintage 1950s–60s, brass notary public sign.

Chapter

16

Signing by Mark and Physical Disabilities Affecting Signing

STANDARDS SUMMARY

16.1 The notary should, as a public official and public servant, treat all persons with dignity and respect.

16.2 The notary should be aware that every mentally competent individual possesses the legal right to execute a signature in some fashion which is entitled to be notarized.

16.3 The notary should take reasonable steps to accommodate document signers who wish to sign by mark.

16.4 The notary should take reasonable steps to accommodate document signers who are physically unable to execute their own signatures.

16.5 The notary should note in the notary certificate and the journal entry any accommodation used to assist a document signer in the execution of a signature.

16.6 The notary should, prior to completion of the notarization, proofread the portions of the notary certificate and journal entry noting accommodation of the signer and make any necessary corrections.

STANDARDS EXPLANATIONS

Notaries are commissioned or licensed public officials who, therefore, have the responsibility to provide public services without unlawful discrimination or prejudice. We live in the age of the Americans with Disabilities Act, and thankfully in an age in which people with physical challenges and disabilities must be accommodated. Some states and territories have enacted notary statutes which address and allow document signers to sign by mark and/or which address and provide a procedure for a surrogate to sign on behalf of a disabled signer. Notaries are expected to perform their functions appropriately in this enlightened context.

16.1 The notary should, as a public official and public servant, treat all persons with dignity and respect.

Public officers, including notaries, bear the official responsibility to treat all members of the public whom they serve with basic respect and with equal dignity. This standard is especially true when officials deal with individuals who are illiterate or suffer from physical challenges and disabilities, for such persons may need additional assistance that other parties should not need. Additionally, public officers, such as notaries, are public servants whose primary duty is to serve the interests of the public. This public service includes the obligations to treat everyone in a professional manner and to take the usually simple steps necessary to provide the extra assistance needed by people who are illiterate or physically challenged or disabled.

The notary should be aware that some individuals execute their signatures by mark, rather than by a traditional hand-scrawled signature. The most common method for signing by mark is for the signer to execute an "X," although some other mark could be made. Furthermore, other marks in the form of symbols could be used, or a signer could use a signature stamp with the image of his or her handwritten or printed name or symbol on it.

16.2 The notary should be aware that every mentally competent individual possesses the legal right to execute a signature in some fashion which is entitled to be notarized.

All persons of sound mind have a right of access to notarial services, including individuals who are illiterate or have physical challenges and disabilities. This rule applies in particular to individuals who, because of such conditions, are unable to execute traditional hand-scrawled signatures. There are a number of variations on the degrees of disabilities that would-be document signers may have, and there are a variety of ways in which individuals may be assisted in order to reasonably accommodate their disabilities so as to allow them to execute lawful signatures which can then be notarized.

A legal signature is any mark or symbol which an individual adopts and intends to serve as her or his signature. The mark or symbol must be affixed by the signer and must be intended to authenticate the instrument on which it appears to be the signer's document. Hence, the commonly cited example of an "X" can be a signature by mark. In ancient history, a signet ring bearing a symbol served as a signature when it was impressed into molten wax on a document and thereafter left a wax image of the symbol. As we will see in sections appearing below, an individual who is physically unable to sign a traditional signature or a mark can be accommodated by a surrogate who will execute a signature on behalf of the person physically unable to sign, and that surrogate-executed signature can be notarized.

Some individuals with diminished physical abilities might be able to barely create a mark or to execute a hand-scrawled signature. Such individuals may not wish to struggle to sign or to be embarrassed by the illegible or barely legible results. People should not have to prove their inability to sign. People should not have to suffer embarrassment by having to struggle to sign or create a mark. Our society and our laws are more compassionate than that.

Case Illustration. Interestingly, this author testified in an unusual and complicated case involving signatures by mark. In that case, an elderly and terminally ill cancer patient in a hospital had acquired a signature stamp with an image of her hand-scrawled signature on it. Although the lady had the ability to perform a signature, she had a shaky hand and was embarrassed by the illegible signature that resulted. So, she used a signature stamp to sign three documents, each of which were notarized by the same notary over a period of a few weeks. The notarized documents transferred valuable assets from the signer to a friend of hers. The state in which this case arose had adopted a statute which required a special signature-by-mark procedure, involving a witness in addition to the notary and directing the notary to record the special circumstances of the signature by mark. But, the notary did not abide by either of those requirements, and the notary was later alleged to have colluded with the signer's friend (who acquired the valuables) to defraud the signer. The signer died in the hospital shortly after the third and final notarization. This author testified that a signature by a signature stamp was permissible and was a signature by mark. I also testified in support of the validity of the technically faulty notarizations because there was convincing evidence in the notary's journals of the notary's diligence and trustworthiness, and there was no evidence of any corruption in connection with the notarizations and the transfers of valuables. The judge and jury agreed and upheld the notarizations.

16.3 The notary should take reasonable steps to accommodate document signers who wish to sign by mark.

Practice Tip: *Explaining the Mark on the Instrument to Be Notarized.* When the document signer places a mark of some kind on the instrument to be notarized, some kind of notation is needed to identify and explain the mark at that location. Usually, there is a typed or printed form of the signer's name appearing under or next to a signature line. If no such name appears, someone should write the signer's name or a short note near the mark to identify it. The note might say: "Pat Smith," or "This mark made by Pat Smith." The signer is unable to write this notation, and the notary should not write on the document (unless there is absolutely no one else available to do so, in which case the notary may need to depart from the usual best practice of not writing anything on the instrument to be notarized).

Historically, the widespread illiteracy of the general population was a significant reason for the creation of the office of notary in ancient times and for the continuing need for notary services in early America. Notaries were needed because they were literate and could record and maintain written records and documents. Today, individuals in this country appearing before notaries will seldom be illiterate. But, notaries should nevertheless be prepared to deal with the circumstance if an illiterate individual seeks a document notarization.

Of course, it may be that an illiterate individual will appear and obtain a notarization without ever revealing to the notary that he or she is illiterate. If an illiterate individual has learned how to write his or her signature, the illiteracy may not even come to light during a notarization. In this author's opinion, the notary should not ask the potentially embarrassing question whether an individual is literate, or illiterate. If the signer does not want to reveal this fact, it is not the duty of the notary to inquire. If a signer reveals that he or she is illiterate, and indicates that he or she wishes to sign by mark, the notary should allow the signer to do so — if the other requirements for a document notarization are satisfied, including proper identification of the signer (to be addressed later in this section).

Many document signers with physical challenges and disabilities, including temporary ailments and injuries, can nevertheless execute signatures on their own. For instance, an individual with a physical challenge or disability may want to sign with a mark. A signer with a physical challenge or disability may need extra time to complete the signing process, especially because the signer will usually need to execute two signatures, i.e., to sign both the transactional document and the notary journal entry. Importantly, when signers are able to sign for themselves, whether by use of a mark or signature stamp, most jurisdictions treat such circumstances the same way that ordinary signings are handled by notaries — as should be the case, in this author's opinion. Furthermore, we should prefer that signers directly control their own fates by signing their own signatures and that they benefit from the self-esteem which should accompany the signing process.

Some other jurisdictions have enacted notary laws which treat signatures by mark as special enough to warrant additional notarial procedures to assure the legitimacy of the signers' desires to obtain notarizations. For example, there may need to be one or two witnesses to the signing by mark, and their names and signatures may need to appear on the transactional document or certificate of notarization The notary may need to include appropriate language in the certificate to describe the signing by mark. Finally, the law may require the notary to record the names and signatures of the signer by mark and witnesses in the journal entry. Of course, regardless of whether required by law, a journal entry should be created to record the circumstances of every notarization, including descriptions signatures by mark and notations and signatures of any witnesses who are present.

If any individual wishes to sign by mark, he or she should be allowed to do so. As suggested earlier, individuals should not have to prove they have a physical challenge or disability in order to sign by mark. It might be embarrassing and disrespectful for the notary to insist on evidence of disability. It is enough if that someone wishes to sign by mark or symbol because the law says that a signature can be a mark or symbol adopted by an individual for the purpose of authenticating his or her document. It is one's legal right to sign by a mark, if the signer can be satisfactorily identified and if the other requirements for a document notarization are also satisfied.

Note: *Caution About Identification of Signers by Mark.* One serious concern that may arise in cases of signers wishing to sign by mark relates to identification of those signers. This issue will become apparent early in the notarial ceremony when the notary obtains the present signature of the signer in the journal entry and reviews the signer's ID. Every signer should be asked to present a satisfactory ID, which, in this instance, presumably will include an image of the signature by mark the signer executes in the journal entry and will execute as the signature on the instrument to be notarized. If the tendered ID does not bear the signature by mark of the signer, the notary should inquire. This disparity is a serious deviation from the normal and proper elements of the identification of a document signer. Why might the ID display some other signature? A possible answer is that the physical challenge or disability causing the signer to wish to sign by mark is of very recent origin or is a temporary condition due to illness or injury. For instance, the signer may have broken the wrist or arm of the signer's writing hand. Regardless of the reason for the discrepancy between the ID signature and the signature by mark, the notary should be on the alert. If the ID signature does not match the signature by mark, this author recommends requesting at least two IDs from the signer and a satisfactory explanation for the disparity, all of which should be fully detailed in the journal entry.

Case Illustration. Earlier in this section, a case was described in which an elderly and terminally ill patient had used a signature stamp to sign instruments because she was embarrassed by her trembling hand and the resulting illegible signature. Those instruments were then notarized. I testified that it was entirely appropriate for the patient to sign by signature stamp and that it was proper for the notary to have notarized the stamped signature. The judge and jury agreed. However, although the notary maintained a journal, the notary made the big mistake of neglecting to note the use of the signature stamp in the journal entry, and this omission made it seem the notary was concealing use of the signature stamp. Any important and relevant circumstance which is unusual should be noted in the journal entry.

16.4 The notary should take reasonable steps to accommodate document signers who are physically unable to execute their own signatures.

If individuals with disabilities are rendered physically unable to sign for themselves, they nevertheless have the legal right to obtain document notarizations — by having designated surrogates sign the names of the individuals unable to sign in the presence of notaries and having the notaries then perform proper document notarizations. In some places, the notary may even be allowed to sign for the disabled party. The state and territorial statutes vary somewhat about the exact procedure to follow to achieve such notarizations, but the laws usually require one or more witnesses in addition to the notary and require the notarial certificate to indicate the signing by a surrogate. The other requirements for standard document notarizations must be satisfied. The notary should review the applicable notary statute to determine if the notary's state or territorial statute sets out a special procedure, and such a procedure should then be followed.

If the state or territorial notary statute does not include a procedure for signing by surrogate for a signer physically unable to execute his or her own signature, the individual unable to sign nevertheless has a legal right to obtain a signature by a surrogate and to have it notarized. The notary should be guided by the procedure of the *Model Notary Act* (set out below), of the *Revised Uniform Law on Notarial Acts* (set out below), or of the notary laws of other states or territories. Basically, a proper and safe procedure would be to have two disinterested witnesses attend the notarial ceremony, to assure that the individual unable to sign approved of one of the witnesses signing the name of the person unable to sign, to have one of the witnesses sign the name of the individual unable to sign, to have the witnesses sign both the notarial certificate and the notary journal entry, to have the notary certify to the procedure in the notarial certificate, and to have the notary record the circumstances in the journal entry.

Practice Tip: *Surrogate Signature on the Instrument to Be Notarized.* When the instrument to be notarized is signed by a designated surrogate on behalf of the document signer who is physically unable to sign, the document signer's name should not simply be signed by the surrogate with no reference to the surrogate-signing circumstance. Rather, the signer's name should be signed with a notation of who signed it on the signer's behalf, i.e., "Pat Smith, by Sam Jones." The same procedure should be followed for the signing of the journal entry for the notarization. It is the notary's responsibility to perform a document notarization only if all legal requirements for such a notarization have been satisfied, including the determination that a proper signature appears on the instrument to be notarized and in the journal entry. After all, both the disabled signer and the notary should wish the proper steps to be followed to protect the integrity of the notarization and to disclose for third parties who receive and/or rely upon the notarized instrument that it was signed by a surrogate. This situation is so unusual that the surrogate will probably never have served as a surrogate before. Thus, the notary and the surrogate should confer before the signing of the instrument to be notarized and the signing of the journal entry so that the surrogate employs an appropriate form of signing.

***Note:** Identification of a Document Signer Unable to Personally Execute a Signature.* As discussed in the preceding section about signers who sign by mark and who may have difficulty providing satisfactory ID, the same concern may arise for a signer who is physically unable to execute a signature, because such a signer needs to have one or more reliable government-issued IDs bearing a signature of some sort. The name and signature on the ID should match the name on the notarial certificate and the signature on the instrument to be notarized. The signer has the responsibility to establish her or his identity with reasonable certainty, and that task may be more challenging for such an individual.

16.5 The notary should note in the notary certificate and the journal entry any accommodation used to assist a document signer in the execution of a signature.

Whenever a notarization is performed upon a signature by mark or upon a surrogate signature, the signature on the notarized instrument will be different and will appear different than the standard signature. Therefore, the notarial certificate should explain the difference and certify the procedure employed to assure the integrity and security of the notarization.

When anything outside the normal routine occurs during a notarial ceremony, the notary should record the circumstances in the notary journal. This procedure would include noting unusual aspects about the method of document signing, such as signing by mark and accommodating disabled signers. Such a notation will not only assist the notary to later recall the circumstances but will also provide evidence of the reasonable accommodation of the document signer. Most importantly, the notation will record the steps taken to assure the integrity and security of the notarization. The usual format of a notary journal will include an area for additional or other information, which is where notes about signing by mark and accommodating signers can be placed. If even more space is needed, the notary should simply continue the record for the relevant notarization onto the next lines or columns, utilizing as much room as necessary to fully record the circumstances. Unquestionably, any fact out of the ordinary about the execution of the signature to be notarized should be included in the journal entry in detail because the signature is among the most important elements in the notarization process.

Interestingly, when a document signer with a disability has been accommodated (with assistance in the execution of the transactional document or to have a surrogate execute the document), the notary journal entry for the notarization also must be signed by the individual who has been accommodated. The same accommodation should be utilized to achieve the signing of the journal entry. The journal entry could be signed by mark or could be signed by the surrogate who signed the transactional document.

16.6 The notary should, prior to completion of the notarization, proofread the portions of the notary certificate and journal entry noting accommodation of the signer and make any necessary corrections.

As mentioned elsewhere in this book, proofreading of the signature area of the transactional document, the notarial certificate, and the notary journal entry is so important to help avoid simple errors and omissions that should not be allowed to undermine a notarization. When the proofreading is undertaken before the notarial ceremony is concluded, there is still time to make corrections to cure and avoid defects. Proper signatures are critical, so notaries should be diligent about handling signatures appropriately and about recording signature-related circumstances. The notary should proofread the signature area of the transactional document being notarized and the journal signature, as well as the portions of the notarial certificate and journal entry relating to accommodation of the signer by mark, and make necessary additions and corrections. ■

***RELEVANT MODEL NOTARY LAW**

Each notary should read, study, and abide by the notary statute and regulations, if any, of her or his commissioning state or territory.

FLORIDA JURAT FOR SIGNER WITH DISABILITY
F.S. 117.05(14)(E)

State of Florida
County of Orange

Sworn to (or affirmed) before me this 12th (Day) day of November (Month), 2016 (Year),

by Donald Jenkins (Name of Person Swearing or Affirming), and subscribed by Pat R. Jones (Name of Notary)

at the direction of and in the presence of Donald Jenkins (Name of Person Swearing or Affirming), and in

the presence of these witnesses: Donna Nunez (Name of 1st Witness),

Michael T. Smith (Name of 2nd Witness)

Pat R. Jones
Signature of Notary Public — State of Florida

Pat R. Jones
Name of Notary Typed, Printed or Stamped

PAT R. JONES
Notary Public – State of Florida
Commission # 12345678
My Comm. Expires Jan 30, 2020

Place Notary Seal and/or Stamp Above

☐ Personally Known or ☒ Produced Identification

Type of Identification FL Driver's License

Any Other Required Information
(Name(s) of Credible Witness(es), etc.)

OPTIONAL

Completing this information can deter alteration of the document or fraudulent reattachment of this form to an unintended document.

Description of Attached Document

Title or Type of Document: Affidavit of Loss

Document Date: 11/9/16 Number of Pages: 1

Signer(s) Other Than Named Above: No other signers

Sample jurat for signer with disability

SIGNATURE BY MARK ACKNOWLEDGMENT

State/Commonwealth of Arizona }
County of Maricopa } ss.

On this the 18th (Date) day of January (Month), 2017 (Year), before me, the undersigned Notary Public, personally appeared Samuel Curran,
Name of Individual Signing by Mark

X personally known to me – **OR** –
☐ proved to me on the basis of satisfactory evidence

to be the person who made and acknowledged making his/her mark on the within instrument in my presence and in the presence of the two persons indicated below, who have signed the within instrument as witnesses, one of whom, Steven J. Richards,
Witness Writing Marker's Name

also wrote the name of the signer by mark near the mark. WITNESS my hand and official seal.

Pat R. Jones
Signature of Notary Public

January 30, 2020
Any Other Required Information (Residence, Expiration Date, etc.)

PAT R. JONES
Notary Public – Arizona
Maricopa County
My Comm. Expires Jan 30, 2020

Place Notary Seal/Stamp Above

Steven J. Richards 123 Lemon Lane, Maricopa, AZ
Name and Address of Witness 1

Samuel Curran 456 Sun Street, Maricopa, AZ
Name and Address of Witness 2

OPTIONAL

This section is required for notarizations performed in Arizona but is optional in other states. Completing this information can deter alteration of the document or fraudulent reattachment of this form to an unintended document.

Description of Attached Document

Title or Type of Document: Grant Deed Document Date: 1/14/17

Number of Pages: 3 Signer(s) Other Than Named Above: No Other Signers

©2017 National Notary Association

Sample signature by mark acknowledgment

"To uphold the trust placed in me by the public I serve;

To maintain a professional manner suitable to the office I hold;

To treat each individual fairly and equally, with kindness and respect ...

To always conduct myself and perform my duties in a manner which will bring credit to myself, my office and the [American] Society [of Notaries]." *Responsibility Code of Ethics* (1980).

“The Notary shall, as a governmental officer and public servant, serve all of the public in an honest, fair and unbiased manner.” *Notary Public Code of Professional Responsibility,* Guiding Principle I (1998).

“Refusal To Notarize. A notary shall not refuse to perform a notarial act based on a person’s race, advanced age, gender, sexual orientation, religion, national origin, disability, or status as a non-client or non-customer of the notary’s employer.” *Model Notary Act*, Section 5-6(a) (2010).

“Signing For Principal Unable To Sign. A notary may sign the name of a principal [document signer] physically unable to sign or make a mark on a document presented for notarization if: (1) the principal directs the notary to do so in the presence of 2 witnesses disinterested in the document; (2) the notary signs the principal’s name in the presence of the principal and witnesses; (3) both witnesses sign their own names beside the signature; (4) the notary writes below the signature: “Signature affixed by the notary at the direction and in the presence of (name of principal unable to sign or make a mark) and also in the presence of (names and addresses of 2 witnesses) pursuant to Section 5-4 of [Act]”; and (5) the notary notarizes the signature through an acknowledgment, jurat, or signature witnessing.” *Model Notary Act,* Section 5-4 (2010).

“Signature If Individual Unable To Sign. If an individual is physically unable to sign a record, the individual may direct an individual other than the notarial officer to sign the individual’s name on the record. The notarial officer shall insert ‘Signature affixed by (name of other individual) at the direction of (name of individual)’ or words of similar import.” *Revised Uniform Law on Notarial Acts,* Section 9 (2010).

Scarce, unused, self-adhesive official seal of *notario publico* Mauricio Guerra of Puerto Rico, c. early 1900s. Such seals could be individually numbered (in the blank space) and readily affixed to documents. The civil law notaries of Puerto Rico maintain detailed notary records, which describe the document to which the numbered seal is attached. Notice that the seal actually reads "Notario Archivero" because civil law notaries maintain archives of the instruments with which they deal.

Chapter

17

Notary Journal Records

STANDARDS SUMMARY

17.1 The notary should understand the values of record-keeping in general.

17.2 The notary should understand the benefits of official record-keeping pertaining to document notarizations in particular.

17.3 The notary should acquire and maintain one, or if not prohibited by law possibly two, active notary journals to record official acts.

17.4 The notary should use only a securely bound and commercially printed notary journal.

17.5 The notary should complete a contemporaneous and sequential journal entry for each official act.

17.6 The notary should complete the journal entry for each document notarization before completing the certificate of notarization.

17.7 The notary should record no fewer than 13 informational items in the journal entry for each document notarization, including the present signature of the document signer.

17.8 The notary should, if not prohibited by law, request each document signer to affix a thumbprint in the journal entry.

17.9 The notary should record each refusal to perform a document notarization in a separate journal entry.

17.10 The notary should proofread the journal entry and make any necessary corrections prior to completion of the notarization ceremony.

17.11 The notary should, if a material error is later discovered in a completed notarial certificate, not alter the related journal entry, but should prepare an additional journal entry to reflect the new information.

17.12 The notary should, if a material error is later discovered in a completed journal entry, not alter that entry, but should prepare an additional journal entry to reflect the new information.

17.13 The notary should keep the journal under the exclusive control of the notary at all times and, when not in use, under lock and key within the exclusive control of the notary.

17.14 The notary should preserve and safeguard the journal for a period of at least 10 years after the date of the last entry, unless directed otherwise by law.

17.15 The notary should understand that the notary journal is an official public record that is accessible by other parties under limited circumstances.

17.16 The notary should understand the confidential and private nature of certain contents of a journal entry and limit access accordingly.

17.17 The notary should record each request for access to journal information and its disposition in a separate journal entry.

STANDARDS EXPLANATIONS

This chapter is one of the book's most important. It is also the book's longest chapter. The notary's most important tool of the trade is the notary journal. When the journal is maintained meticulously, it is critically helpful for the notary, which is why every notary should steadfastly keep a journal the right way — as described here.

Unfortunately, while numerous U.S. states and territories by statute require their notaries to keep and preserve journals of their official acts, most jurisdictions do not. Significantly, no U.S. jurisdiction prohibits its notaries from maintaining journals of their official acts. So, every notary should take advantage of this opportunity to journalize each of their official acts.

Regrettably, most U.S. notaries do not retain records for themselves of the document notarizations they perform. When notaries perform document notarizations, the notaries complete written notarial certificates, but those certificates are attached to the transactional instruments that are notarized. At the conclusion of those document notarizations, in most instances, those certificates then leave the possession of the notaries when the transactional instruments are taken away by the document signers. If notaries do not create and preserve journals of their official acts, serious adverse consequences — including the reduced likelihood notaries will recall details of their document notarizations, the heightened prospect that notarizations can be successfully challenged, the diminished security of notarizations, and the continued appearance of notaries as inconsequential and unprofessional bureaucrats — may result.

Note: *The Expert Witness Perspective.* When this author is initially contacted by lawyers or parties soliciting my expert services about a disputed notarization, one of my first questions is whether the notary who performed the challenged notarization kept a notary journal. As an expert who cares about notary practice standards, about obtaining the fair and just result in a notary dispute, and about maintaining my own credibility and reputation as a capable expert, I will only serve the party which I believe to have the law on its side in a case — whether I take a position in support of the notary and the validity of the notarization, or against the notary and the validity of the notarization. If there is a notary journal entry for the disputed notarization, I can almost always tell who should prevail by examining the notarial certificate, the whole notary journal, and the journal entry for the disputed notarization. And, if a notary has maintained a detailed notary journal, the chance is that I will favor the notary's actions because most notaries who maintain sound journals are diligent and prudent in performing notarizations. Good notaries tend to keep journals, whereas less diligent and less capable notaries do not. Most importantly, my position, whether for or against the notary and the notarization, will be much more certain and much stronger if there is a notary journal. It will almost certainly provide great help in arriving at my conclusion and, in turn, in providing documentary evidence to support my conclusion.

Although this chapter is the longest in this book, for a more complete discussion of the notary journal there is a 230-page article with more than 900 footnotes. See Closen & Faerber, "The Case That There Is a Common Law Duty of Notaries Public to Create and Preserve Detailed Journal Records of Official Acts" — cited in the bibliography at the end of this book.

Practice Tip: *The Notary Journal as Legal Evidence.* If a complaint is filed with the state or territorial commissioning official or notary oversight agency against a notary for misconduct, or if a legal case against a notary is filed in an arbitration or a court, the notary journal will be admissible in evidence. Not only is the notary journal a type of public record, it is the notary's record kept in the regular course of business as a notary. Significantly, the entire journal showing all recorded notarizations will be admitted into evidence, not simply the entry or entries for specifically questioned notarizations. If the notary has filled more than one journal, earlier retired journals, as well as current active journals, will be admissible. Years of journal entries may be admitted into evidence in a legal proceeding. Hence, as the notary creates each journal entry, the notary should be mindful that every journalized entry can be important to the overall impression of the notary's performance and diligence. Consequently, a detailed and thorough journal will contribute to a favorable impression of the notary with arbitrators, investigators, judges, and jurors.

Case Illustration. In one court case alleging notary malpractice in which this author testified as an expert witness, the notary had served for a number of years and had filled three journals and was using a fourth journal at the time the lawsuit was filed. The notary had recorded a total of more than 1,200 document notarizations in the four journals. All four journals were admitted into evidence. This author testified about the 1,200 plus recorded notarizations, and the journals were examined by the jury during its deliberations. I was impressed by the thorough journal entries, and I explained my reasons to the jury. The jury concluded the notary had acted with reasonable care and was not guilty of malpractice.

Scope Note: *Electronic Notary Journals Excluded.* It should be noted that in the U.S. jurisdictions which require their notaries to maintain notary journals, if permitted by statute to do so, a notary could choose to maintain an electronic journal — even to record traditional paper document notarizations. In most U.S. jurisdictions which have no statutes at all regarding notary journals, notaries could choose to keep electronic notary journals for paper document notarizations. Paper and electronic journals should be identical in substance, the difference is just in their format. However, just as this book does not address electronic notarizations, nor does it deal with electronic journals — this chapter, then, focuses exclusively on bound, paper journals.

17.1 The notary should understand the values of record-keeping in general.

Every adult ought to recognize the need for, as well as the benefits of, record-keeping in connection with business and governmental dealings. Every responsible adult should appreciate the need for keeping important records for commercial, governmental, and family purposes. Otherwise, important matters are left to the uncertainties and inadequacies of people's memories, including the corrupting influences of the passage of time, changing circumstances, family and other relationships, financial interests, and personal prejudices and ambitions.

For nearly 30 years, this author taught contract law and practice to first-semester law school students and emphasized to them in their early days in law school the importance of creating and preserving a paper trail of important transactions. It is simply prudent practice in business, in government, and in law. And, everyone — not just law students — should have learned this lesson. The second part of the lesson to my law students was to preserve important records for a long period of time — at least several years. Notary journals should be kept and secured for at least 10 years, and preferably longer, as will be discussed below.

Case Illustration. This author was consulted about the case of a 99-year-old millionaire who suffered from a number of serious chronic health ailments and was taking several medications. This millionaire was driven to a local bank by his much younger wife and, while sitting with his wife in their car in the bank parking lot and with a bank notary present at the open car door, he allegedly signed a document transferring several millions of dollars to his wife. It was also alleged that the notary then returned to the bank building and prepared the notarial certificate and affixed the notary seal while inside the bank — without returning to the parking lot. The notary delivered the notarized document to the wife, and that document reversed the prenuptial agreement the spouses had executed years earlier limiting the wife to just $1 million from the husband's estate. The husband died a few months later. The state where this happened did not require its notaries to maintain journals, and the bank notary did not maintain a journal. If ever there was an extraordinary situation in which a notary should have journalized a notarization, this was that case. A written account of what had happened would have clarified several aspects of this dubious notarization. Incidentally, the lawsuit that had been filed was eventually settled.

Case Illustration. This author testified in a trial involving a situation that seemed ordinary at the time. A notary working at an office copy store notarized a real estate transaction, but the signer was actually an imposter who forged the owner-seller's name on a deed conveying the property. Although the notary maintained a journal of sorts (it was homemade and incomplete), the notary changed jobs a few months after the notarization and left the unsecured notary journal behind at the workplace. The journal was discarded and destroyed. The forgery on the notarization was discovered several years later, and the notary could not remember much at all about the notarization by then. This author's day of testimony at the trial occurred almost exactly 10 years after the date the notarization was performed. Two lessons should be evident from this case. (1) Written records are important. Every document notarization should be journalized, for one cannot know for sure whether a notarization has really been ordinary. (2) Records should be secured and preserved for a long time, at least 10 years for notarial journals.

17.2 The notary should understand the benefits of official record-keeping pertaining to document notarizations in particular.

Several benefits derive from the keeping of a detailed journal record for each document notarization. There are so many benefits associated with notarial record-keeping to truly make the notary journal the most significant, but least known and least appreciated, feature of a document notarization. The beneficiaries include the document signer, parties receiving and relying on the document, the notary, the notary's employer, notary commissioning officials and agency oversight investigators, lawyers handling notary cases, expert witnesses, and the general public.

Note: *The Impression on Judges and Jurors.* As an expert witness in lawsuits challenging the validity of document notarizations, this author has testified in bench and jury trials and observed firsthand the favorable reactions (facial expressions, reserved smiles, and nodding of heads) of jury members and even a seasoned trial judge when I described the benefits of thorough journalizing and preserving of the journal entries for document notarizations.

***Practice Tip:** Prepare the Journal Entry Before Completing the Notarial Certificate.* For reasons to be explained throughout the rest of this chapter, the notary should prepare the journal entry prior to completing the certificate of notarization. Entering the several pieces of information needed for the journal entry will guide the notary through the notarization process to the final steps involved in completing the notarial certificate. See especially section 17.6 of this chapter.

Here are 15 good reasons why a notary should prepare and preserve a journal entry for every document notarization:

1. **Instilling a procedure and a habit of diligence.** Shortly, we will see that a proper, detailed journal entry includes numerous separate pieces of information to be chronicled by the notary. The methodical recording of all of that information for each notarial act is a substantial process. In commerce and law, this type of repeated procedure constitutes a routine business practice or habit that can appropriately be admitted into evidence. It reliably and accurately reflects how the maker of the record behaves under similar circumstances. For a notary, the process of repeatedly capturing so much information requires care and diligence, and the legal standard for the performance of a notarization is reasonable care. It follows that a notary who exercises reasonable care in preparing such a detailed journal entry will likely have exercised the same care in conducting the rest of a notarization, in part because the journal also records how well the notarization was performed. See also the discussion of legal liability in Chapter 20.

2. **Proving reasonable care and avoiding liability.** This point is related to, but different from, the preceding one. It is separately stated to emphasize a critical value of the notary journal. The preceding point explained that keeping a detailed journal forces the notary to be habitually diligent about document notarizations. The point here is that this written record in the journal can then be presented to investigators, judges, arbitrators, and juries as direct and tangible proof of the notary's due diligence or reasonable care. Thus, the journal not

	Date and Time of Notarization	Kind/Type of Notarization/Certificate	Address Where Notarization Performed	Document Kind/Type and Date	Name and Address of Signer
1	March 2, 2017	Acknowledgment	510 Doheny Drive	Grant Deed	John R. Allen
	3:00 p.m.		Beverly Hills, CA 90409		510 Doheny Drive
				Date of Document: March 1, 2017	Beverly Hills, CA 90409 (310) 555-2386
2	March 2, 2017	Acknowledgment	510 Doheny Drive	Grant Deed	Mary S. Allen
	3:00 p.m.		Beverly Hills, CA 90409		510 Doheny Drive
				Date of Document: March 1, 2017	Beverly Hills, CA 90409 (310) 555-2386
3	March 14, 2017	Jurat	123 Main Street	Affidavit of Forgery	Samuel Curran
	10:45 a.m.		Beverly Hills, CA 90409		625 Park Ave.
				Date of Document: March 14, 2017	New York, NY 10642 (212) 555-7533

Example of standard journal entries.

only drives the notary to be diligent and careful but also proves the notary has actually performed with reasonable care. When a notary has acted with reasonable care, the notary will not have legal liability — even if an error or omission has accidently occurred and even if a document signer or someone relying on a notarized document has suffered financial injury. The law does not require a notary to act perfectly, but it does require the notary to act with reasonable care. See also the discussion of legal liability in Chapter 20.

3. Guiding the notary through notarizations and preventing errors. The recording of a detailed notary journal entry before the preparation of the notarial certificate serves as a guide or road map for conducting the notarization and increases the likelihood of accuracy in completing both of those documents. If this procedure is followed, the critical assessments of the signer's identity, willingness, and mental competence will be undertaken and usually resolved before the notary begins to fill in the notarial certificate. Further, virtually all of the information needed for the notarial certificate will have already been included in the journal entry. The journal entry in a detailed format will serve as a checklist for the notary to follow in completing a thorough notarization, which is then concluded with the preparation of the notarial certificate. This process will help assure and, if necessary, resolve the all-important consistency of the names and signatures of the signer on the various documents involved (the certificate, the journal, the notarized instrument, and the IDs). See also the discussion of the notarial certificate in Chapter 7 and of name and signature issues in Chapter 11.

The fact is that among the hundreds of published court decisions about challenges to the validity of notarizations, there are virtually no cases in which notaries had kept detailed and proper notary journals of their official acts. The reason seems obvious. When notaries have kept detailed journal entries of their notarizations, those notaries have not committed errors or omissions

Identification of Signer	Additional Information	Notary Fee	Signature of Signer	Right Thumbprint of Signer	
☐ Personally Known by the Notary ☒ ID Cards — Describe each card below ☐ Credible Witness(es) — Include signature of each witness CA Driver License - DMV R7123066 Expires 9/23/21	Signers are husband + wife. certificate form stapled to document.	$10	John R. Allen	Top of thumb here	1
☐ Personally Known by the Notary ☐ ID Cards — Describe each card below ☒ Credible Witness(es) — Include signature of each witness Michael Smith Michael Smith (personally known)	address of credible witness: 345 S. Westlake Ave. L.A., CA 90057	$10	Mary S. Allen	Top of thumb here Right Ring Finger	2
☐ Personally Known by the Notary ☒ ID Cards — Describe each card below ☐ Credible Witness(es) — Include signature of each witness NY Driver License - DMV 123 456 789 Expires 4/22/21	Signer was wearing a cast on left leg and using crutches.	$10	[illegible]	Top of thumb here	3

of consequence in the performance of those notarizations, and those notarizations have not been challenged.

4. Establishing signer presence at notarial ceremonies. The personal presence of the document signer at the notarization ceremony is the most fundamental requirement for a valid notarization. This book has already explained that too many notarizations are falsely performed by notaries without the document signers really appearing at the notarial ceremonies, and that this fatal fault can be covered up by the pre-signed signature of the signer on the transactional document. The notarial certificate, on its face, will appear to be in proper order. However, if a journal entry has been prepared in a bound, contemporaneously completed, chronologically sequential format bearing a signature of the document signer (and perhaps a thumbprint of the document signer), it becomes almost certain the signer actually appeared for the notarial ceremony.

The value of this confirmation cannot be overstated. It should prevent those cases in which notaries are suckered into allowing individuals with sympathetic stories about why document signers cannot appear to present other people's documents for notarization. It should prevent those cases in which document signers later become afflicted with transactional remorse and seek to invalidate the notarizations of their instruments by falsely claiming they did not appear and sign the notarized instruments. It is solid, tangible proof of due diligence by the notary. See also the discussion of signer personal presence in Chapter 9.

5. Assisting in assessment of signer identity, willingness, and mental competence. The completion by the notary of the journal entry necessitates a conversation between the notary and the document signer, during which the information included in the entry is acquired. This discussion is crucial because it is related to the subject matter in question (i.e., the notarization of the document presented), and because the communication should provide the notary with the opportunity to assess the signer's identity, willingness, and mental competence. As already explained in this book, the assessment process for these issues begins as soon as the signer requests notarial services and continues throughout the notarization ceremony. The notary should be trying to observe and gauge the "big picture" that is the signer — including the signer's words, body language, facial expressions, and demeanor. Specifically, observation of the manner in which the signer performs the signature in the journal entry and the manner in which the signer responds to the notary's request for the signer's thumbprint should serve as important impressions for the assessments under consideration. See also the discussion of signer identification in Chapter 10, of signer willingness in Chapter 14, and of signer mental competence in Chapter 13.

6. Reminding the notary to administer oral oaths or affirmations to signers, if required, and confirming such administrations. Undoubtedly the most frequent fault committed by U.S. notaries is their failure to administer the oral oath or affirmation required as part of jurat notarizations, or verifications on oath or affirmation. These omissions represent serious faults undermining the key purpose of a jurat or verification on oath or affirmation, which is to obtain the legal pledge of the document signer that the contents of the document are true. Without an oath or affirmation, the law of perjury is not invoked, and the document signer cannot be prosecuted if known falsehoods appear in the document. In other words, the jurat or verification on oath or affirmation is rendered invalid due to the absence of the oath or affirmation. Significantly, when a notary fails to administer the required oral oath or affirmation but certifies in the notarial certificate that the signer was "sworn," the notary has falsely certified and has committed the crime of official misconduct.

Notary journals should include a section which references the administration of an oral oath or affirmation. If the notary uses such a journal, it will remind the notary to consider whether the notarization requires administration of an oral oath or affirmation. And, when an oath or affirmation is administered, that vital fact should be noted in the journal entry. See also the discussion of oaths and affirmations in Chapter 15.

7. Corroborating the integrity of notarizations. As commissioned public officials, notaries owe legal, fiduciary duties to the public. Further, the signers for whom notaries perform document notarizations rightly expect that those notarizations will be carried out correctly so that notarizations are legally valid.

As well, third parties regularly rely upon the validity of notarized instruments in conducting commercial and governmental business. Thus, notaries owe document signers, third parties affected by notarizations, and the general public the obligation to get the notarization right. These legal responsibilities should be taken seriously, for time-consuming and expensive procedures and legal liabilities can result from notary errors, omissions, and wrongdoing.

The best way for notaries to protect themselves, the document signers for whom they perform notarizations, the third parties who rely upon those notarizations, and the general public for whom they serve as public officials is for notaries to keep detailed notary journals of all of their official acts. This author has observed time and time again that the notaries targeted in legal cases involving administrative proceedings, criminal prosecutions, and civil court litigations have not kept notary journals. When notaries have kept detailed journal records, they either do not get investigated and sued in the first place, or they are exonerated if they are investigated and/or sued.

8. Refreshing the memory. Almost all challenges to the validity of notarizations occur at least several months or even several years afterwards. Thus, it is quite difficult for notaries to recall the details about notarizations. If the notary is unable to recall aspects of the notarial ceremony, the journal entry can serve to refresh the recollection of the notary and possibly of the document signer as well (because the signer will also get to see the journal entry). After all, most notarial ceremonies are fairly routine and ordinary at the time they are performed, so recall of them undoubtedly fades rapidly. In the reported and published legal cases of challenges to the validity of notarizations in which notaries have not prepared journal entries, the notaries virtually always testify that they have no recollection whatsoever of the particular notarizations.

Therefore, the notary should thoroughly record the detailed information describing the notarization because the notary almost certainly will not independently recall the facts. Further, the notary should note something unique about the circumstances in the "other information" or "additional information" section of the entry to jog the notary's memory if needed at some point in the future — perhaps something about how the signer was dressed, or something about the signer's background.

9. Curing defects discovered in completed notarial certificates. In the early 1800s, the U.S. Supreme Court decided a case about a detailed notary journal that had been meticulously prepared and preserved. Due to the high reliability of such a thorough notary journal, the Supreme Court decided that, although the notary who created it had died and although the journal entry was hearsay, it was entitled to be admitted into evidence.

The reliability of a detailed journal entry has value if there are defects in a completed notary certificate, such as omitted, illegible, or incorrect information. The journal entry can be used to cure the defects. For instance, if the date of the notarization is omitted or incorrect, the journal entry can provide the accurate date (and since each journal entry is dated and kept in chronological order, there may be even further corroboration of the correct date). Remember, the notary journal is a public officer's record of official acts. It deserves to be treated as such. The content of a notary journal should be accorded deferential treatment and substantial weight. Additionally, since the journal entry is signed by the document signer, the signer has authenticated the journal entry. The law favors upholding notarizations, in large part because the intention of both notaries and document signers is always to obtain lawful and valid notarizations. If the content of all the entries in a notary journal shows the notary to be thorough, honest, and diligent, there is likely to be a strong inclination to favor the journal and, in turn, to interpret the journal to support the notarization.

In the more extreme case in which the completed notarial certificate is later damaged, lost, or destroyed, the notary journal entry can serve to cure defects in the certificate or to effectively substitute for the certificate. Thus, reliability of the journal record should not be in doubt. See also the discussion of notarial certificates in Chapter 7.

10. Deterring imposters and other wrongdoers. If imposters, identity thieves, and other wrongdoers wish to obtain notarizations to help validate fraudulent documents, those imposters and wrongdoers may be deterred from attempting their misdeeds by notaries who keep detailed notary journals, especially when notaries obtain present signatures and request document signers to provide thumbprints in the journal entries. Imposters and wrongdoers do not want their IDs scrupulously examined and recorded, do not want to provide addresses and phone numbers, and do not want to leave signatures and thumbprints at the scenes of their frauds and crimes (the notarial ceremonies).

Case Illustration. When some of the 911 terrorists wished to obtain fraudulent identification, they sought notarizations of documents to help them apply for IDs. Not surprisingly and not accidentally, those terrorists sought service from a notary in a state that did not require its notaries to maintain journals and from a notary who in fact did not maintain a journal of notarizations.

Practice Tip: *Signer Photos.* In this age of advanced technology, notaries should consider taking smartphone photographs of document signers, maintaining separate electronic files of those signer photographs, assigning numbers to signer photos, and noting the numbers in corresponding journal entries — unless taking and preserving such photos is prohibited by applicable law. Certainly, imposters and wrongdoers do not want their photos to be left at the scenes of their frauds and crimes. See also the discussion of signer confidentiality and privacy issues in Chapter 18.

11. Dispelling concerns the notary has engaged in the unauthorized practice of law. The unauthorized practice of law (UPL) by non-attorneys is prohibited in all U.S. jurisdictions, and numerous notary statutes and regulations expressly forbid it. Additionally, non-attorney notaries are regularly warned to avoid the UPL because, in the course of their official functions, notaries often become involved with law-related documents, are tempted by document signers to answer questions about documents to be notarized, or volunteer comments or opinions about those documents.

Notaries can take several steps in the preparation of journal entries to significantly diminish the chances they would commit the unauthorized practice of law, or would even be accused of doing so. Notaries should note both the starting time and ending time of the notarial ceremony, as the time frame will be only a few minutes in duration — not long enough for the notary to have offered much legal advice or consultation. The notary should record the amount of the fee charged and paid by the document signer — a paltry sum in comparison to the amount charged by lawyers for legal advice and consultation. If the notary is asked questions by the document signer about the document to be notarized, the notary should decline to answer and should make note of theses circumstances in the journal entry. At that point, the notary should also suggest that the signer may wish to delay the notarization and to seek the advice of a licensed attorney. The notary should then note this suggestion in the journal entry.

If a document signer presents an instrument for notarization without an accompanying notarial certificate and asks the notary to select the form of notarization to be performed, the notary should decline and should provide the signer with samples of the kinds of notarial certificates (for an acknowledgment, a jurat, and/or a signature witnessing) allowed by law in the commissioning jurisdiction. The notary should inform the signer that the signer could either select the form of certificate to be used for the notarization from the samples, or that the signer could delay the notarization and seek the assistance of a licensed attorney in selecting the type of notarization. If any of these circumstances arise, the notary journal should record those facts. See also the discussion of the unauthorized practice of law in Chapter 26.

12. Recording of notarial fees, if any. Complaints about excessive notary fees, including the assessment of costs for travel and incidentals, such as photocopy services, are among the most common formal complaints filed against notaries with notary commissioning officials and oversight agencies. Additionally, part of the difficulty for notaries when complaints are filed is often the lack of documentation about fees, including the lack of receipts and itemized statements as to fees and reimbursed expenses.

Maximum notary fees are established by statute in many jurisdictions. If notaries charge and collect fees for their notarizations, what better place is there to record those fees and to preserve that record than in the notary journal? A simple notation in the journal would cover the typical case of a single fee for a document notarization and would corroborate the fee. If other fees for travel or collateral services are involved, then a journal notation itemizing the fees would suffice. Of course, the notary should also provide a receipt to each document signer when fees are assessed and paid. Because notary fees constitute taxable income, a notation about fees in the journal should also satisfy the recording of such fees for taxing authorities. See also the discussion of notary fees in Chapter 28.

13. Creating public records that can be appropriately accessed. There are heightened concerns about transparency today. Because the notary is a public official and the notary journal records are official acts of the notary, the journal is a kind of public record. It follows that a public record will be available for access by members of the public and many other parties (such as government officers, notary commissioning officials and oversight agency investigators, journalists, insurance and surety company personnel, and lawyers) under appropriate conditions. See the discussion later in this chapter about access to the journal. See also the discussion of signer confidentiality and privacy issues in Chapter 18.

14. Promoting the professional status of notaries. Notaries may be the least appreciated public officials. Yet, notaries really possess considerable authority with respect to many of our most important commercial, financial, and governmental transactions. When notaries neglect or refuse to journalize their document notarizations, they jeopardize still further their own standing.

Consistent and thorough record-keeping is a fundamental practice in all true professions, whether for accountants, architects, bankers, doctors, engineers, lawyers, and others. The significant merits of creating and preserving a solid record trail of documents and transactions constitute the reasons for the adoption of detailed record-keeping in the professions and in governmental activity as well. Notaries should welcome and embrace the journaling task as a function that will promote their responsibilities and their credibility.

15. Aiding investigators, lawyers, and experts. A notary journal entry can become a valuable investigative tool for expert witnesses, lawyers, notary commissioning officials and oversight agency personnel, police, and prosecutors if complaints or legal cases arise involving notarized documents or the signers of those documents. The information recorded in a journal entry should include such helpful items as the document signer's exemplar signature, purported name and address (and maybe a phone or cellphone number), and possibly a thumbprint. For example, if a handwriting expert becomes involved in a dispute to opine whether the signature on the notarized document is a forgery, the signature appearing in the journal entry will be relevant and helpful for comparison purposes. There is even a chance that a diligent notary will have noted useful incidental matter in the "other information" or "additional information" section of the journal entry, or that the thorough journal entry will trigger recall by the notary of additional worthwhile information about the document signer and the notarial ceremony.

The entire notary journal will be valuable if a complaint about the notary is filed with the notary commissioning official or oversight agency or if a legal challenge to a notarization is filed in court. In those instances, the overall performance of the notary will become relevant. That is, the question of the notary's exercise of due diligence or reasonable care over an extended period of time, as demonstrated by the entire array of journal entries, will paint the true picture of the notary's quality of performance.

17.3 The notary should acquire and maintain one, or if not prohibited by law possibly two, active notary journals to record official acts.

In order for notary journal entries to be valuable, their integrity must be assured. One method insisted upon to guarantee the accuracy and trustworthiness of journal entries is to record them in chronological order on numbered pages in securely bound journal books or ledgers. In each notary journal, notarizations appear in chronological order, and notarizations cannot be removed or inserted out of order without the tampering being noticeable. Consequently, some notary authorities recommend, and a few notary statutes direct, notaries to maintain only one active notary journal at a time.

However, some notaries prefer to have two separate journal books — one which they keep at their place of business, and one at home. This way, those notaries can perform notarizations both at work and at home without the need to carry their one-and-only journal back and forth. Besides, transporting the journal between home and office risks loss, theft, or damage to the journal. Incidentally, when a notary wishes to conduct notarial activities in this manner, the notary is also faced with the issue of the security of the notary seal. Hence, the notary must either carry the notary seal back and forth between home and business, or the notary must acquire two seals in order to house one at each location. Hence, if not prohibited by law, notaries who wish to do so could acquire and use two active journals and two official seals — with one of each at the home and office.

Note: *Author's Personal Experience.* In fact, when the author served as an Illinois notary, I worked in downtown Chicago and commuted by car and train more than an hour each way between my suburban home and my Chicago office for more than a dozen years. I elected to maintain two separate seals and journals so that I did not have to transport a seal and journal for some two hours a day, for more than 300 days each year. Thus, I avoided carrying the seal and journal around for the more than 7,000 hours that they would have been at risk of loss, theft, and damage. I believed that I was acting responsibly with my notary seals and journals securely housed at my home and office so that I had my tools of the trade available to render the public service of performing notarizations in both areas.

Note: *A Controversial Issue.* It must be emphasized that whether a notary may maintain more than one active journal is controversial. As previously noted, some people favor a "one notary, one journal" rule. Some notary advocates and experts and a few U.S. notary statutes (including the *Model Notary Act*, Section 7-1(c) (2010), which this author opposed as a member of the drafting committee for that model law) have taken the position that a notary may have only one active notary journal at a time. The rationale is that there will be an opportunity for fraud if notaries have two active journals. Apparently, those advocates of only one journal believe a dishonest notary could defeat the chronological ordering of entries by choosing in which journal to place the entry. But of course, that scenario

> is highly unlikely. Falsifying of dates is not an especially prevalent notarial problem. Alternatively, there is a creative way to allow notaries to avoid needing to carry their journal back and forth between home and office. A very simple format change should satisfy the "one notary, one journal" limitation advocated by some parties and adopted by a few notary statutes. That is, a notary could have two separate journal books — but with the individual entries within the two books numbered in order as a single, sequential record. I believe that procedure would preserve internal journal security, as all sequentially numbered notarial entries would appear in chronological order on permanently bound pages.

It seems that many notaries and the public would benefit if notaries kept both a seal and a journal at work and at home. That arrangement would heighten the security of seals and journals (if they are handled properly at both locations and if the seals and journals do not have to be transported around with some frequency), and that arrangement would often provide increased notarial services for the public by facilitating such services in both locations. Certainly, notaries should not be required to keep a seal and journal at both locations, for, of course, notaries are not required to have their seals and journals with them at all times and are not required to accommodate requests for notarial services at all hours of the day and night. Notaries should be allowed to maintain one or two active journals at a time, but not more than two such journals.

17.4 The notary should use only a securely bound and commercially printed notary journal.

Not all notary journals are the same. Most have been professionally or commercially published, while occasionally some have been homemade. The notary should acquire a commercially printed journal in a bound book format. The bound book format is critical to journal security so that pages cannot be removed or added without being detected. The journal should be commercially printed so that it will have most of the important elements labeled for easy use. This author uses the commercially printed journal which contains the most information headings or labels so that each entry captures the most information.

Yet, the notary should not be reluctant to make desired modifications to the headings, and the notary should especially not hesitate to expand the headings by using two sets of lines or entries if more space is needed (such as to include references to assessment of signer willingness and signer mental competence, to include administration of an oath or affirmation to the document signer, and to include a space to capture a thumbprint of the document signer). Most journals include a heading or section for "additional information" or "other information," which is a flexible and useful area of a journal entry.

17.5 The notary should complete a contemporaneous and sequential journal entry for each official act.

The journal entry must be created contemporaneously with the notarial ceremony if it is to be most useful, and if it is to capture the present signature and possibly the thumbprint of the document signer. The journal entry is a critical part of a notarization so that if it were created either before or after the time of the notarial ceremony, it might not result in a truly sequential record and might not accurately reflect what actually transpired at the notarization. Journal entries that are sequential and chronological establish their authenticity and prevent their forgery or alteration. A contemporaneous journal entry should always include a present signature and possibly a thumbprint of the document signer, which signature and thumbprint should assure the signer was really present at the time of the notarization (as the absence of document signers at notarizations is among the most frequent and most serious of all notarial faults committed by notaries).

To emphasize that key point, a proper journal entry should appear in both sequential and chronological order in the journal — after the notary's immediately previous notarization, and before the notary's immediately subsequent notarization. Additionally, to further prove the veracity of the entry chronology, the journal entry should include both the present date and time of the notarial ceremony. This step will result in all entries appearing in date and time order.

Note: *Delayed Completion of Journal Entries.* Busy notaries sometimes defer the completion of journal entries until later times, but that practice is improper and may result in an invalid journal entry. The notary has authority over a notarization only during the notarial ceremony, not afterwards. This proposition is about accuracy and document signer protection. If the completion of the journal entry could be deferred, for how long could it be delayed — an hour, a day, a week, a month, or longer? The document signer has a right to be present and to be assured that the journal entry is correctly completed to corroborate the notarization. Just as a notary would have no authority to alter or correct a journal entry after the conclusion of the notarial ceremony, so too the notary would have no authority to prepare or finish the journal entry afterwards. Indeed, as suggested just below, the best practice is for the journal entry to be completed prior to preparation of the notarial certificate.

17.6 The notary should complete the journal entry for each document notarization before completing the certificate of notarization.

Importantly, the journal entry for a notarization should be recorded prior to the preparation or completion of the notarial certificate, and not the other way around. The reasons follow. First of all, the journal entry should serve as a road map to guide the notary through the accurate filling in of the notary certificate, as nearly all of the information to be placed in the certificate will have already been placed in the journal entry. Secondly, completion of the journal entry first should result in the notary making the necessary judgments about the signer's identity, willingness, and competence before completion of the certificate — which certificate signals the notary's approval of the signer and which, on the other hand, should not be completed if the notarization is to be refused.

Third, if the certificate were completed first, there is a risk that a document signer may simply take hold of it and leave the scene without completing the journal entry. This surprise departure might deprive the notary of the only present signature of the document signer and would deprive the notary of the opportunity to request and obtain a thumbprint in the journal entry (if such thumbprinting is not prohibited by law). Further, if a fee is to be assessed for the notarization, that fee should be discussed with the signer and should be noted in the journal entry, so there should be no chance of surprise or confusion about the need for payment of the agreed fee after the notarial certificate has been finalized. The fee should be assessed, paid, and noted in the journal at about the same time so that when the certificate is prepared, the last two steps of a notarization are the notary's signature and the affixing of the official seal impression on the certificate. See also the discussion of notary fees in Chapter 28.

17.7 The notary should record no fewer than 13 informational items in the journal entry for each document notarization, including the present signature of the document signer.

The notary's preparation of a detailed notary journal entry should corroborate fulfillment of the notarization procedure, should have a valuable deterrent effect on would-be wrongdoers, and should enhance document security. A thorough journal entry will help substantiate that the steps in the notarial process really happened, including that the document signer actually appeared at the notarization ceremony. Thus, this author's opinion is that the signer's signature constitutes the most valuable item in a journal entry. Wrongdoers should feel quite threatened by diligent notaries who closely examine ID(s), who closely compare names and signatures, who request thumbprints (if not prohibited by law), and who thoroughly record those steps in notary journals. Hence, fewer wrongdoers will be likely to attempt their mischief with prudent notaries, and wrongdoers who make such attempts should more frequently be discovered. Subsequent alteration or tampering with a notarized instrument is less likely when there is a detailed journal entry that may reveal the mischief.

Note: A Frequent Notary Fault. In those jurisdictions which require notaries to prepare and preserve journal entries, a common complaint lodged against notaries with notary commissioning officials and oversight agencies concerns neglect to journalize at all or to record entries incompletely. If document signers or third parties receiving or relying on notarized instruments request access to journal entries, those parties may discover that the journal entries are absent or incomplete, and report the violations. Or, agency personnel may discover journal deficiencies in the course of their interactions with notaries. Inadequate journal keeping in jurisdictions which require it is a serious violation of notary law and sound notarial practice.

Here are at least 13 pieces of information that should be recorded in a thorough journal entry for a document notarization:

1. Present Date and Time of Start and End of Notarization. The date of a notarization is always the present date. Notarizations may never be predated nor postdated. Regardless of what date appears on the transactional document, and regardless of on what date the transactional document was signed by the document signer (which in the case of an acknowledgment could be a date prior to the notarial ceremony), the notarization must always bear the present date. The date of the notarial certificate and of the notary journal entry must be the same date. See also the discussion of notarial certificates in Chapter 7.

The time of day of the notarial ceremony should also be noted in the journal entry. Once in a great while, the time of the notarization can become relevant.

For instance, if a transactional document is time-sensitive, the notarization may need to have been completed before a time deadline. This author recommends noting both the start time and the end time of the notarization. For example, if it were alleged the notary had engaged in the unauthorized practice of law during the notarial ceremony, and if the start and end times showed the notarial procedure lasted only a few minutes (as notarizations almost always do), not much unauthorized legal advice or consultation could have occurred in such a brief period. See also the discussion of the unauthorized practice of law in Chapter 26.

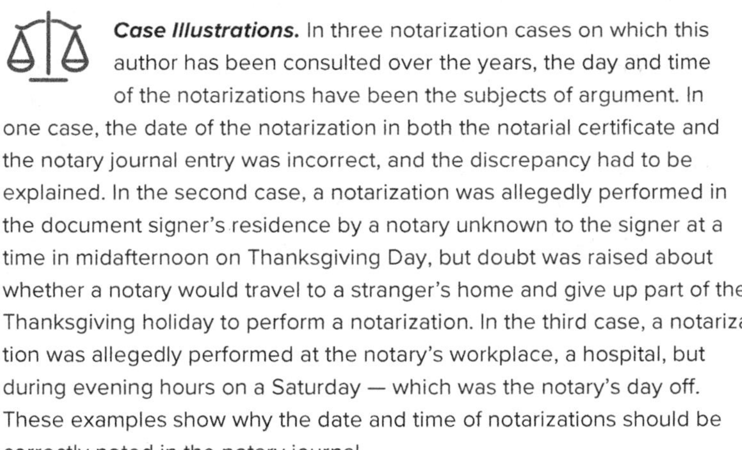

Case Illustrations. In three notarization cases on which this author has been consulted over the years, the day and time of the notarizations have been the subjects of argument. In one case, the date of the notarization in both the notarial certificate and the notary journal entry was incorrect, and the discrepancy had to be explained. In the second case, a notarization was allegedly performed in the document signer's residence by a notary unknown to the signer at a time in midafternoon on Thanksgiving Day, but doubt was raised about whether a notary would travel to a stranger's home and give up part of the Thanksgiving holiday to perform a notarization. In the third case, a notarization was allegedly performed at the notary's workplace, a hospital, but during evening hours on a Saturday — which was the notary's day off. These examples show why the date and time of notarizations should be correctly noted in the notary journal.

2. Location of Notarial Ceremony. There are occasional instances in which notaries purport to perform notarizations in locations where they are not commissioned and where their notarizations are, therefore, invalid. Thus, the location where the notarization is conducted is actually quite significant. It is essentially the confirmation of the jurisdiction and authority of the notary to perform the document notarization. In the notarial certificate, this information is called the venue, and it includes the county or parish and the state or territory where the notarization is performed. The location identified in the notary journal should show the street address, city, or county and state or territory where the notarization is performed, and this information should place the notarial ceremony in the state or territory that issued the notary's commission.

Incidentally, a few small western states, by reciprocity, allow notaries of an adjacent jurisdiction to perform notarizations in the neighboring state, and again, the information in the venue section of the notarial certificate and in the location section of the journal entry should confirm where the notarization was performed. See also the discussion of jurisdiction and venue in Chapter 2 and of notarial certificates in Chapter 7.

3. Type of Document and Number of Pages. Noting the title or type of document and its number of pages helps to provide the background information for the notarization and serves to verify the kind of transactional document (a contract, affidavit, power of attorney, will, deed, or so on) to be notarized. It is also are relevant for security purposes to help prevent the substitution of a different document or the addition or removal of pages after the notarization has been completed. Hopefully, whoever drafted the document will have taken other common steps to provide security, such as numbering the pages, including designated spaces for initialing of the pages by the document signer at the time of the execution of the document, and carrying over language from one page to the next (so that the pages must be read in sequence in order to make full grammatical and substantive sense). In teaching contract law for many years, this author recommended to students that when drafting instruments, they should not end an internal page of a multipage document with a period, but instead should continue a sentence from one page onto the next page — to make the unauthorized removal or addition of a page more difficult.

Practice Tip: *Be a Savvy Notary.* This author believes it is inherently insecure to format the last page of a document with only the notarial certificate appearing there, or with only the document signer's signature and the notarial certificate appearing there. This format invites mischief, for it would be so much easier for a wrongdoer to switch the last page or to remove the last page and attach it to a different document. Although notaries should not have drafted the documents they notarize, notaries would be well-advised to note such a fact in their journal entries. Notaries may be called upon to revisit and remember the notarizations of such documents in later controversies or legal challenges to the transactions involved.

4. Type of Notarization. In this section, one of three possible document notarizations should be identified — an acknowledgment, a jurat (verification on oath or affirmation), or a signature witnessing. The obvious importance of the correct identification by the notary of the type of document notarization performed is it signals that the notary should know the steps to follow in order to properly conduct such a notarization and that the required steps were followed to perform the designated type of notarization. See the discussion of the three types of document notarizations in Chapters 4, 5, and 6.

Case Illustration. Previously in this book, I described a case in which I testified and which challenged an acknowledgment notarization performed by a notary who had conducted more than 1,000 notarizations which she had meticulously recorded in her journals over several years of service. Of course, each of her retired journals and her current journal were admitted into evidence in the lawsuit. Incredibly, all 1,000+ journal entries routinely identified the type of notarization performed as an "acknowledgment." However, it was statistically impossible that a notary serving the general public would have performed only "acknowledgment" notarizations more than 1,000 times. In fact, the information in the journal entries revealed that many of the notarizations performed were actually jurats (as the "type of document" section of her journals revealed a jurat would have been needed, such as for the numerous "affidavit" instruments with which she had been presented). This basic mistake must have caused a negative impression about her performance in the minds of the trial judge and jurors. Even though the notarization in question was an acknowledgment, the notary's mistaken identification of many other notarizations as "acknowledgments" was pointed out to the judge and jury. The lesson here: Everything noted in a journal entry matters. Notaries cannot afford to allow things to become routine. Accuracy matters.

5. Document Signer's Name and Contact Information. This information is both basic and helpful if the document signer should need to be contacted regarding the transactional document or its notarization. The signer's name should match the form of the name appearing in the notarial certificate. The contact information should include the complete home or office address for the signer (which information should be verified by taking it from an appropriate ID), as well as a phone number and email address, if possible. In these days of stalking, domestic violence, identity theft, and other concerns, some signers may wish to use business or mailing addresses, rather than residence addresses, and such preferences should be honored. See also the discussion of names and signatures in Chapter 11.

6. Method of Document Signer Identification. One of the notary's primary responsibilities is to correctly establish the document signer's true identity. Thus, the features of the journal entry which are most relevant to that notarial duty should be particularly important to the notary. The notary should take the process of correctly identifying the document as a very serious duty and not simply a matter of cavalierly recording specified data in the notary journal. Every signer should be asked to present proper identification, which should be noted in the journal entry in sufficient detail to corroborate which ID has been presented (namely, the particular type of ID and its month and year of expiration). The month and year of expiration of the signer's ID should indicate the notary has actually reviewed the ID, but will not reveal the signer's date of birth if that day coincides with the ID's expiration. See also the discussion of identifying document signers in Chapter 10.

Incidentally, the notation of the method of identifying the document signer through IDs will help to confirm the attendance of the signer at the notarial ceremony. Noting an ID's month and year of expiration will verify the ID was presented at the notarial ceremony, as ordinarily the signer will have possession of her or his own ID.

7. Oral Oath or Affirmation Administered. The most frequent of all notary mistakes or omissions is to neglect to administer oaths or affirmations when they are required. For a jurat notarization (verification on oath or affirmation), the notary is required to administer an oral oath or affirmation to the document signer. The fact that an oral oath or affirmation has actually been administered should be noted in the journal entry. Some journals will include a space or column where the notary can check a box or place an "X" or other mark to indicate the administration of the oath or affirmation. If the journal format does not provide a reference about the oath or affirmation, the notary should simply write a note in the journal entry to reflect the oath or affirmation was administered — perhaps in the "other information" or "additional information" section, or onto the next lines or spaces even if a second journal entry field needs to be utilized.

The language of the oath or affirmation should not be written in the journal entry, although it would be a good idea to record the words of the oath and affirmation used consistently by the notary on the inside cover of the journal (so the notary could make quick reference to the language, and so the wording would be recorded in writing for possible use as evidence, if needed). See also the discussion of oral oaths and affirmations in Chapter 15.

8. Signer Willingness Assessment. The willingness of a document signer to execute the transactional instrument and to obtain its notarization is an essential element of a valid notarization, and such willingness should be assessed by the notary. Thus, the willingness assessment should be recorded in the journal entry. The journal format might provide a box or space to be marked, thereby indicating the willingness assessment was conducted, and the signer was found to be acting voluntarily. Or, if the journal format does not include a reference to the voluntariness assessment, the notary should write a note about it — indicating that the assessment was considered and that the signer was acting willingly. The notation could be placed in the "other information" or "additional information" area of the entry format, or the notary may need to write the desired information on additional lines or into the next entry field. See also the discussion of document signer willingness in Chapter 14.

9. Signer Mental Competence Assessment. The mental competence of a document signer to execute the transactional instrument and to obtain its notarization is an essential feature of a valid notarization, and such mental competence should be assessed by the notary. Hence, completion of the mental competence assessment should be recorded in the journal entry. The journal format might provide a box or space to be marked, thereby indicating the competence assessment was conducted, and the signer was found to be mentally competent. But, if the journal format does not include a reference to mental competence, the notary should write such a notation, indicating that mental competence was assessed and that the signer was competent. The notation can be placed in the "other information" or "additional information" area of the journal entry, or the notary can write the needed information on additional lines or into the area for the next entry. See also the discussion of mental competence in Chapter 13.

10. Signer's Present Signature. One of the most important steps of the notarial ceremony and the most important element of the journal entry is the present signing by the document signer. The present signing by the document signer constitutes a significant part of the process of identification of the document signer and establishes that the signer was really present at the notarial ceremony. Every signer should be asked to execute a present signature in the journal, and the notary should closely observe the signing. The notary should assess whether the signing is a normal fluid signature (as opposed to a jerky, halting, or unnatural process) and whether the present signature matches the name and signature appearing on the ID(s). If the notary has any concern in either regard, the notary should ask the signer for an explanation (which might include illness or injury or other adverse effect upon the signer's ability to sign) and the notary should not hesitate to ask for additional ID(s) and even for additional present signatures to be placed in the journal (in the "other information" or "additional information" area). The signer's signature (either a previous signature for an acknowledgment or a present signature) on the transactional instrument that is being notarized should also be compared to the present signature in the journal entry. See also the discussion of the signer's personal presence in Chapter 9 and of names and signatures in Chapter 11.

11. Signer's Thumbprint (If Not Prohibited by Law). Because this topic is somewhat unclear and somewhat controversial, it is addressed separately in the section immediately below. This author will suggest that notaries should request document signers to affix a thumbprint in journal entries, unless prohibited by law from doing so.

12. Notary Fee. Or No Fee. One of the unique attributes of the position of notary public in the U.S. is that the notary is a commissioned public official but is allowed to charge and personally retain fees collected for services rendered as a public officer. No other public official is permitted to do so (although in earlier U.S. history, justices of the peace were allowed to retain a portion of the fines and fees they collected as the method of compensation for their services as public officers). Notaries are not required to charge for notarial services, but when notaries do charge fees, the charging and collecting of fees is an official act that must be recorded in the journal. Notary fees collected by the notary constitute taxable income that must be properly reported for state, territorial, and federal income tax purposes. The best place to record this income is the notary journal, for the journal should record other pertinent information, including the date of service and payment, the type of service, the source of payment, and the amount of payment. See also the discussion of notary fees in Chapter 28.

If no fee is assessed or collected, that fact should be noted in the journal entry. For instance, if a notary were to be accused of engaging in the unauthorized practice of law, the fact that no fee or only a nominal fee had been charged would be useful. After all, licensed attorneys tend to assess substantial fees for their professional services. See also the discussion of the unauthorized practice of law in Chapter 26.

13. Additional or Other Information. Virtually every commercially printed notary journal includes a very helpful space for "additional information" or "other information." Furthermore, there is nothing sacred about the lines or boxes in a journal entry. If more space is needed for information that the notary wishes to record, then the notary should use the next blank line in the journal to record this information. The important thing is to fully record information about the document notarization, not to have a neat and tidy journal entry. The notary might draw arrows, use underlining, make an asterisk — do whatever is necessary to record and emphasize the unusual or any other matter the notary wishes to include.

Diligent notaries should not be afraid to record the details of what they do — to help them remember the notarizations they perform. It will help them, not hurt them. They should use the "other information" or "additional information" section of the journal, or the next line in the journal, to record anything unusual about the notarization. The notary should note who, if anyone, accompanied the document signer to the notarization. The notary might note what was talked about to establish the general competence of the signer. The notary should note anything out of the ordinary about the appearance or the comments of the document signer. As examples, the signer might have smelled of alcohol (but was not intoxicated); the signer's hand might have shaken from palsy while signing the transactional instrument and the journal entry (but not from fear or nervousness about the signing); the signer might have explained in great detail the content of the document to be notarized (although the notary cautioned that such detail did not need to be disclosed); or, the signing may have occurred in a hospital or nursing home where the signer was bedridden (but coherent and articulate).

Practice Tip: *Do Not Leave an Entry Space Blank.* Every notary should fill in each column or space in a journal entry to obtain as much information as possible to help future recall. The notary should use the "additional information" or "other information" location (or else the next line in the journal) to record some kind of extra reminder information about each notarization. The reason for this suggestion is that probably 99% of notarizations seem routine and unremarkable at the time they are conducted. Challenges to notarizations do not commonly arise until many months or years later, when notaries will undoubtedly have little or no independent recollection about them. In fact, this lack of recollection has been reported in almost all of the many published court decisions about notarizations around the country. And, this absence of recall does not help the notaries' causes. Indeed, it may be countered by possible documentary evidence and by testimony of the recollections of the parties and witnesses to the notarizations (for whom the notarizations were not as commonplace and routine). So, the notary should record something to help the notary remember each particular notarization.

17.8 The notary should, if not prohibited by law, request each document signer to affix a thumbprint in the journal entry.

As is well-known, an individual's fingerprints and thumbprints are unique to that individual, so one's thumbprint is a reliable method of identification. Furthermore, the thumbprint of the document signer in the journal entry shows that the signer actually appeared at the notarial ceremony. While only two states presently require document signers to provide a journal thumbprint for certain kinds of notarizations, biometric identifiers are being increasingly utilized. Few states or territories prohibit their notaries from requesting document signers to submit to thumbprinting. If not prohibited by applicable law, the notary should request the signer to affix a thumbprint in the journal entry. The notary should be careful to obtain a full and clear print of the signer's right thumb, or if the right thumb is unavailable, then the left thumbprint (or then a fingerprint). As noted elsewhere in these materials, even if the signer were to successfully misrepresent his or her identity, a thumbprint accurately and absolutely identifies the signer, regardless of the name claimed by the signer — and the positive identification of the signer is the ultimate goal of the notary.

Note: *Difference of Opinions.* There is a difference of opinion regarding the question of whether a notary is authorized to condition the performance of a document notarization on submission by the document signer to thumbprinting for the notary journal, when the law does not require the signer to do so and when the law does not prohibit thumbprinting of the signer. In that situation, notaries cannot insist signers submit to thumbprinting as a condition to the performance of a notarization. However, this author has joined others who have concluded the notary should request the signer to affix a thumbprint in the journal entry (if not prohibited by law). Fingerprinting and thumbprinting have been around for more than 100 years as reliable identification methods and as significant deterrents to imposters and criminals. Fingerprinting and thumbprinting are now widely required in countless commercial and governmental settings, and many people voluntarily provide fingerprints and thumbprints for a variety of applications. The security and confidentiality of the journal thumbprint could be appropriately ensured, such as by redacting the thumbprint if a request for access were submitted and granted. If a signer were unwilling to provide a thumbprint in the notary journal, this author would be suspicious about the signer's identity. I would question the signer about why he or she is unwilling to be thumbprinted. I would ask to review one or more additional ID(s) of the signer, and I would review the additional ID(s). I would note the signer's unwillingness to be thumbprinted in the journal entry and would note the additional ID(s) presented. Then, I would decide whether the signer had established his or her identity with reasonable certainty. If the notarization were refused, that refusal would represent an official act which would need to be journalized, including a statement of the objective reason for doing so. If the notarization were to proceed, I would have taken measures that should assure I had documented my use of reasonable care to identify the signer.

17.9 The notary should record each refusal to perform a document notarization in a separate journal entry.

Since the notary should journalize every official act, that admonition includes refusals to notarize, for such decisions by the notary are made in the course of the notary's official duties. This situation presents one more reason why the notary should complete the journal entry before filling out the notarial certificate. That is, if the reason for refusing to notarize is discovered while completing the journal entry, then the notary will not even move on to filling in the certificate. On the other hand, if the certificate were completed first, before the reason for refusing the notarization was revealed, the risk is that the notarial certificate will have been completed, and the document signer might prematurely and improperly walk off with it.

Of course, the most important part of an entry for a refusal to notarize is the reason for the refusal. In order to refuse to notarize, the notary should have an objective and substantial reason that can be articulated. Perhaps, the document signer had been drinking and was intoxicated, or the signer was ill and heavily medicated and, in either case, the notary was unable to determine the signer was capable of reasonably understanding the nature of the document. Perhaps, an elderly signer was accompanied by a family member who stood to gain from the document to be notarized and who refused to allow the signer to be alone to talk with the notary. In such cases, the notary should refuse to notarize. Fortunately, such cases are very rare. But, when they happen, the notary should note the reason for the refusal in the journal entry, taking as much space as necessary to do so. The columns and lines in printed notary journals should not limit the notary's task of describing and explaining the reason for the refusal to notarize. Since the journal is a public record, and since the journal will be preserved and protected for possible future access, a recorded refusal to notarize may be accessed and may become important information in a future investigation, arbitration, or litigation.

Note: *An Unexpected Benefit of a Refusal to Notarize — and a Caution.* Perhaps surprisingly, one or more refusals to notarize recorded in the journal could prove to be very helpful for the notary in the future. Such a journal record would tend to show the diligence and reasonable care of the notary who had refused to notarize. Clearly, a notary who has refused to notarize would not have cavalierly approved all requests for notarizations. The notary journal, including its refusals to notarize, will constitute highly valuable evidence that could be admitted into a legal proceeding to prove the notary's practice of diligence and habit of prudence. However, a notary should never make up a reason to refuse to notarize. A notary should never refuse to notarize without good cause simply to provide a journal entry for possible future use.

17.10 The notary should proofread the journal entry and make any necessary corrections prior to completion of the notarization ceremony.

Journalize, journalize, journalize. And, proofread, proofread, proofread. Those should be watchwords for all notaries. Preparation of the journal entry is part of a notarization, and it should be treated with the respect it rightfully deserves — including proofreading.

A sizable book could be filled with court decisions about notary cases in which notaries made basic mistakes — omitting required elements from their notarial certificates, or writing incorrect information in their notary certificates. These errors and omissions can lead to refusals to recognize notarizations (such as when county recorders refuse to record real estate documents bearing faulty notarizations), or to legal challenges to the validity of documents bearing faulty notarizations. Such rejections of notarized documents or the suits challenging notarizations could often have been avoided if notaries had maintained detailed journal records and had proofread the journal entries before they finished the respective notarial ceremonies. A proper review and proofreading of the journal entry considers some of the same information contained in the notarial certificate, and if there is an error or omission in the journal, there may be a comparable error or omission in the certificate. The dates should match, the names of the document signer should match, the types of notarization should match, and the kinds of ID documents used to identify the signer should match. This proofreading process also provides the notary with a final chance to compare the signatures on the transactional document and in the notary journal. Furthermore, the proofreading of the journal entry should reveal any errors or omissions in the valuable corollary information recorded in that entry.

The procedure for making a correction to a journal entry during the notarial ceremony is the usual method business and government professionals employ to make written changes on documents. That is, any change by the notary should entail: (a) lining through existing language, (b) writing the replacement information nearby, and (c) initialing and dating in the adjacent margin. When the notary journal is corrected during the notarial ceremony, both the notary and the document signer should initial in the margin. The journal entry should be begun and finalized contemporaneously during the notarial ceremony.

17.11 The notary should, if a material error is later discovered in a completed notarial certificate, not alter the related journal entry, but should prepare an additional journal entry to reflect the new information.

The topic of later discoveries of mistakes in completed notary certificates has not been of much concern because such errors or omissions do not happen very often. Not surprisingly, virtually no one has addressed the follow-up question of what to do about the related journal entry if an error in a notarial certificate is later discovered.

The notary should not attempt to alter or correct the related journal entry. The notarization has been finished. The notary's authority with respect to that completed notarization has expired. The notary should not change the notarial certificate or the related journal entry. See also the discussion of the certificate of notarization in Chapter 7, which includes reference to the *Model Notary Act* provision which differs from this author's recommended practice.

The only time there would be a real concern would be in the case of a material error or omission in the certificate, meaning an error or omission of such substantive consequence that it might affect the notarization's acceptance or validity. To the contrary, discovery of an inconsequential or trivial mistake would not warrant a change or correction in any case. For example, misspelling of a county, parish, state, territory, month, or other common word is not important.

Note: *Difference of Opinion About When Journal May Be Corrected.* If corrections need to be made in the journal entry, the notary should do so prior to completing the notarization, for this author firmly believes it is too late to do so thereafter. Curiously, the *Model Notary Act* of 2010 does not include a provision about correction of the notary journal, except to state that a note should be appended to a journal entry if there is a correction made to the notarial certificate [Section 7-2(e)]. However, this author's opinion is that a notary certificate cannot be corrected, and thus, there should be no accompanying appendix to the journal. Besides, the substance of the original journal entry simply cannot be changed whether by addition or alteration, even if the addition is called an appendix or note. Only a short cross-reference to the date of the new journal entry should be added.

If a material error is later discovered in a notarial certificate, the notary should prepare a new and separate journal entry to explain the discovered error or omission. As pointed out above, a short note merely to cross-reference the date of the new journal entry should be appended to the original journal entry for the notarization. But, the original journal entry should not otherwise be altered.

17.12 The notary should, if a material error is later discovered in a completed journal entry, not alter that entry, but should prepare an additional journal entry to reflect the new information.

Little or no attention has been focused on the subject of errors or omissions later discovered in completed notary journal entries. State and territorial notary statutes do not address the topic, and neither do the *Model Notary Act* of 2010 nor the *Revised Uniform Law on Notarial Acts* of 2010. This author has never heard or read of a later discovery of an error or omission in a journal that has led to any challenge to or dispute about a notarization, or to a complaint or disciplinary action against a notary. The reason is that, although material mistakes are often made in the preparation of journal entries, those mistakes either remain undiscovered or unreported when they are discovered. In the work this author has done consulting on legal cases, I have identified hundreds of mistakes in notary journal entries. Some mistakes I have seen have been minor; some have been quite significant.

The generally accepted view and this author's view are that the notary's authority to make additions or changes to the journal entry ends immediately with the completion of the notarial ceremony, for journal entries are to be made contemporaneously with the notarizations they record. To conclude otherwise opens the door to the possibility of continuing authority of the notary for some unspecified time to alter the official journal entry. Part of the concern is that a mistake discovered in the journal entry may mean there is also a mistake in the notarial certificate — so that there would need to be a correction in both locations. If a mistake is discovered in the notarial certificate and/or journal entry after the notarial ceremony is concluded, the only procedure which is available to effectively "correct" the mistake is to perform a new notarization bearing the new present date and present time. If this procedure is followed, of course, a new journal entry should be completed and a brief notation simply to cross-reference both notarizations should be included in both journal entries (in the entry for the original faulty notarization and in the entry for the new "corrected" notarization). If this process is followed, there is no need to attempt to make changes in the original notary certificate because it will be superseded by the new certificate for the new document notarization. See also the discussion of the certificate of notarization in Chapter 7.

17.13 The notary should keep the journal under the exclusive control of the notary at all times and, when not in use, under lock and key within the exclusive control of the notary.

Unfortunately, there have been many reported instances of loss, theft, misuse, and other mischief regarding notary journals. For instance, employers of notaries, including lawyers, have sometimes "borrowed" their notary-employees' journals and seals as part of schemes to forge notarizations. Careless notaries have sometimes misplaced and lost their journals or have let down their guards and allowed their journals to be stolen. Cavalier notaries have frequently left their journals behind when they have terminated or changed employment, and the journals have been destroyed or lost. None of this should be allowed to happen. And, it is the notary's responsibility to prevent loss, theft, misuse, and other forms of mischief concerning the journal.

The notary journal, both while it is in active use by the notary and after it has become either filled with entries or unused any longer, is a valuable public record deserving of continuous safekeeping. The journal belongs to the notary, regardless of who may have paid for it (and quite often, employers of notaries will have purchased the journal for the notary-employee). As the owner of the journal and as a public official whose services involve the need for journal record-keeping, the notary has the right and the duty to secure and protect the journal at all times.

More specifically, there are a number of reasons to safeguard the journal. First, the journal contains important personal and confidential information about the document signers appearing before the notary. Second, the journal constitutes a public record and, as such, should be protected and preserved. Third, if the journal is not properly secured, it might be misused by thieves or imposters to carry out wrongdoing (such as stalking, identity theft, forgery, and the like). If any of those misdeeds occur or if breaches of privacy or confidentiality occur, the notary could face liability for resulting injuries and damages. See also the discussion of notary liability in Chapter 20.

Protecting the journal at all times means just that. When in use, the journal should be kept in the notary's view and possession. Even when the journal is being signed by the document signer, the notary should not allow the journal outside of her or his immediate presence. The notary should never allow an employer, fellow employee, document signer, or ordinary civilian to handle the journal or to peruse it. If the journal is carried in a bag or briefcase, that carrying case should not leave the view and possession of the notary.

When not in use, the journal should be secured in a locked drawer, storage area, or room for which the notary has possession of the only key or lock combination. If the notary's employer, fellow workers, janitorial workers, or anyone else has access to the locked location of the journal, such a circumstance is unacceptable because another party could access the journal. For example, locking the notary journal in a briefcase to which the notary has the only key may be inadequate if the briefcase is left where other people can handle it, where the briefcase could be pilfered and the briefcase and journal destroyed, or where the briefcase could be stolen and easily broken into, thereby exposing the journal to mischief. If the locked briefcase is better protected, it may meet this security standard.

If the notary journal were to be lost, damaged, destroyed, or stolen, the notary should immediately notify the governmental notary oversight agency. If criminal conduct may have been involved in the destruction, damage, or removal of the journal, the notary should immediately notify police authorities. If the notary is commissioned as a notary public at the time of the loss, damage, destruction, or theft of the journal, the notary should not perform notarizations until a replacement journal has been acquired in which to record further notarizations.

Case Illustration. This author testified as a notary expert in a trial involving a challenge to notarizations, where fraudulent collusion was alleged of the notary and which involved a highly unusual journal situation. The notary had lost her active journal (which still had considerable space left for further entries), so she purchased a new replacement journal and began using it. The notary had not informed the notary oversight agency about the loss of the journal. Then, she found the lost journal, so she had two journals, and she proceeded to use both journals randomly. During the time of the random use of the two journals, she performed the challenged notarizations. This coincidence, coupled with the poor practices of not informing authorities of loss of the first journal and of then unnecessarily using two active journals, caused the notary to appear suspicious and lacking diligence and professionalism.

17.14 The notary should preserve and safeguard the journal for a period of at least 10 years after the date of the last entry, unless directed otherwise by law.

Notaries should be especially aware that if there is ever a challenge to, or complaint about, a particular document notarization and an official agency investigation or lawsuit, all their notary journals — past and present — will be examined by the investigators and lawyers on the case and will be admissible as evidence in the hearings or lawsuit. It will be of great help to notaries to have detailed and accurate journal entries for all of their notarizations and to have entries of the kind suggested here to show the notary has gone above and beyond the bare minimum or the lowest common denominator of simply filling in lines or boxes as they are labeled or captioned on the pages of their journals. This extra effort will pay off by showing prudence and diligence over the entire history of each notary's service.

It will frequently take a long time before a notary journal entry is needed. Almost always, complaints and challenges to notarizations do not surface until many months or even years afterwards, when documents prepared earlier are re-examined as they are needed or relied upon. For instance, wills and powers of attorney are commonly prepared long before they are needed. Real estate documents, affidavits, and contracts are frequently filed away for long periods of time before they are closely examined to answer questions or resolve disputes which have arisen. The statutes of limitations for legal actions in commercial and governmental cases vary somewhat in the states and territories but are typically two, five, or ten years long, and sometimes even longer. Often, there is a discovery rule which extends the running of the statute of limitations, so that it does not even begin to run until the discovery of the problem or mischief causing the dispute or challenge in question. Furthermore, when lawyers and lawsuits are involved, the process itself to resolve a dispute or challenge regarding a notarization can take years.

Notaries should retain and protect their journals for at least 10 years after the date of the last entry in the respective journals, even if the individuals no longer serve as notaries. And better still, the safest practice is to retain and safeguard journals for longer than 10 years — i.e., indefinitely. Notary journals usually do not occupy too much space, so notaries should simply do whatever is necessary to safely store all of their journals. The journals should be shelved or boxed and kept in dry and legible condition. The entries in those journals could save a diligent notary thousands, and perhaps hundreds of thousands, of dollars. Incidentally, in some jurisdictions, when a notary ceases to serve as a notary public, the statutes and/or regulations direct the notary (or someone else if the notary has died) to deliver the notary's journals to a specified governmental agency (usually the notary commissioning official or oversight agency) for storage and safekeeping.

Case Illustrations. The numerous notary cases in which this author has been consulted over the years have always involved monetary values of notarized transactions of at least thousands of dollars, and several of those lawsuits have involved hundreds of thousands of dollars. One case involved millions of dollars of transactions that had been notarized. Almost always, I was consulted years after the notarizations occurred. One of the cases involved the forgery of a document by an imposter and the notarization of the forged signature on that document. My day of testimony in the trial court occurred almost exactly 10 years to the day after the date on which the notarization took place. Yes, 10 years later! Interestingly, the case went on for a few more years, as it went on appeals to the state appellate and supreme courts. Unfortunately, the justice system grinds along too slowly in many cases, so notaries should retain their notary journals for at least 10 years, and preferably longer. Sadly, in this marathon case, the notary journal that had been kept to record the faulty notarization of the imposter's document was discarded and destroyed soon after the notarization because the notary-employee did not properly retain and safeguard the journal. Instead, the negligent notary left the journal behind with the notary employer when the notary went to work elsewhere, and the former employer threw the journal away.

17.15 The notary should understand that the journal is an official public record that is accessible by other parties under limited circumstances.

We live in the age of "transparency," particularly when governmental affairs are involved. There is generally a right of access to official public records.

Notaries are government officers, and their notary journals are, therefore, the records of public officials. Yet, there has been very little written about access to notary journals.

Incidentally, in some jurisdictions, there may be freedom of information laws or public records laws that cover notary journals. If so, the notary oversight agency will certainly inform notaries about such provisions, and notaries should abide by those laws. However, that is not the situation in most states and territories.

Regrettably, the subject of this section and the next two sections, the handling of requests for access to notary journal entries, is a matter not covered at all or not covered in detail in almost any notary statutes or regulations. Nevertheless, a member of the public should have at least a right of limited access to a specified notary journal entry, and there should be a corresponding sound procedure for the notary to follow in receiving, considering, and granting or denying such access. The next two sections of this book propose best practices to fill the statutory gaps.

Without doubt, the notary should adopt a three-step procedure for dealing with requests for access to information in the notary journal, First, the notary should require a request for access to a journal entry to be put into writing. Second, the notary should give thoughtful and prudent consideration to such a request for access. Third, the notary should fully journalize a request for access and the notary's grant or denial of access.

17.16 The notary should understand the confidential and private nature of certain contents of a journal entry and limit access accordingly.

In the absence of applicable law on access to notary journal information, each notary will have to adopt a procedure for dealing with requests for access.

Because some of the information in a journal entry is susceptible to abuse by would-be wrongdoers (such as the full name, address, and/or phone number of the document signer, which could be misused by a stalker or identity thief; or the signature of the document signer, which could be misused by a would-be forger or identity thief), this author would err on the side of caution and require the requester to put the request for access in writing, to identify the particular notarization record being sought, and to state a lawful and satisfactory reason for wanting access. The notary should not allow fishing expeditions for information and should not grant sweeping requests for access to entire journals or large numbers of entries. The requester should have to provide the notary with specific written information identifying the journal entry to be accessed — such as the date of the notarization and the name of the document signer. Of course, the written request should be dated and signed by the requester and should provide the requester's contact information. The notary should verify the requester's identity and contact information through examination of the one or more of the requester's IDs.

The right of access to the type of public record represented by a notary journal should not be absolute and unlimited. If the notary can articulate an objective reason for denial of access (such as a particularly nervous demeanor of the requester, a display of emotional or mental disturbance by the requester, or an expression or indication of violence or hostility of the requester toward the document signer), the notary should deny access. After all, if a request for access is denied by the notary, if the requester feels it is important enough to appeal, and if the requester has no unlawful purpose in mind, the requester can always appeal to the notary commissioning official or oversight agency, or to a court, in order to attempt to obtain access.

If the notary receives a proper written request for access to the journal record for a specified document notarization, and if upon consideration, the notary decides to provide access to the requester, the following procedure should be followed. The notary should not allow the requester to handle the notary journal, and the notary should not allow the requester to see any information other than the single specified entry that has been requested in writing. Indeed, this author is of the opinion that the notary journal itself should be out of sight under lock and key when the requester is present and that the requester should not even be shown the original entry in the journal itself. Instead, the notary should make a photocopy of the requested entry and present that photocopy to the requester. The photocopy should not include any portion of the journal entries which precede or follow the requested entry. To do so, the notary can either cover over the other entries before making the copy of the requested entry or can copy the page on which the requested entry appears and then cut away and shred the other entries.

Note: *Redacting Information in a Disclosed Notary Journal Entry?* Apparently, no notary statute makes any reference to the possibility of the notary redacting information from a notary journal entry before disclosing it to a member of the public who requests access. Notaries sometimes think that if a request for access is doubtful or suspicious, redacting certain information might be the way to cure or dispel the notary's doubt or suspicions. Thus, the notary might redact the signer's full name, address, phone number, email address, signature, and/or thumbprint image. This author would tend not to redact information, although the thumbprint image may be one bit of information that should be redacted. The notary should seek advice and guidance from the notary commissioning official or oversight agency about how to handle the disclosure of a journal entry containing a thumbprint. My view is that if I had doubt or suspicion which I could objectively articulate about the propriety of a request for access, I would deny access altogether. I would not attempt to remove my objections by redacting information from the requested journal entry, for that solution would seem to be like splitting hairs and would create the more difficult decision about what to redact. I would deny the request and advise the requester that my denial could be appealed to the notary commissioning official or oversight agency. Finally, I would be certain to record my decision to deny access, my reasons, and my advice about appeal in the journal entry for the request for access (as discussed immediately below). See also the discussion of signer confidentiality and privacy in Chapter 18.

17.17 The notary should record each request for access to journal information and its disposition in a separate journal entry.

The receipt of a request for access to a notary journal entry (which is a kind of official public record) triggers the granting or denial of such access, which is itself an official act. Hence, the notary should complete a separate entry in the sequential journal each time there is a request for access. Of course, because the notary is diligent and thorough about the procedure for making a request for, and obtaining access to, a notary journal entry, some unwarranted and suspect requests for access will be deterred and prevented.

As previously noted, the procedure adopted by the notary should include: (1) requiring the request to be submitted in writing, dated, and signed by the requester, (2) providing the requester's address and phone number or email address, (3) identifying the date of the notarization to be accessed and the name of the document signer, and (4) providing a reason for the request. The written request should be retained by the notary.

The separate journal entry prepared by the notary should include the requester's name and address, the reason given for the request for access, the date and signer identified by the requester for the requested entry, the method of establishing the requester's identity through IDs, the assessing of the requester's mental competence, and the completion of the other usual elements of a journal entry. The requester should have to sign the journal entry and should be asked to provide a thumbprint in the journal. Certainly, the notary should indicate in the journal entry whether the request was granted or denied, and whether a copy of the accessed entry was provided to the requester. If the request was denied, the reason for the denial should be included in the journal entry. ■

***RELEVANT MODEL NOTARY LAW**

Each notary should read, study, and abide by the notary statute and regulations, if any, of his or her commissioning state or territory.

"'Journal of notarial acts' and 'journal' mean a book to create and preserve a chronological record of notarizations that is maintained by the notary public who performed the same notarizations." *Model Notary Act,* Section 2-6 (2010).

"The Notary shall record every notarial act in a bound journal or other secure recording device and safeguard it as an important public record." *Notary Public Code of Professional Responsibility,* Guiding Principle VIII (1998).

"To exercise extreme care to insure that the notarial seal, stamp and records are kept in a safe place and are not used by any other person ..." *Responsibility Code of Ethics* (1980).

"Maintaining Journal Of Notarial Acts. (a) A notary shall keep, maintain, protect, and provide for lawful inspection a chronological journal of notarial acts that is either: (1) a permanently bound book with numbered pages; or (2) an electronic journal of notarial acts as described in Section 20-2 of this [Act].

(b) A notary shall keep a record of electronic and non-electronic notarial acts in the same journal.

(c) A notary shall maintain only 1 active journal at the same time, except that a backup of each active and inactive electronic journal shall be retained by the notary in accordance with Section 20-2(3) as long as each respective original journal is retained." *Model Notary Act,* Section 7-1 (2010).

"Journal Entries. (a) For every notarial act, the notary shall record in the journal at the time of notarization at least the following: (1) the date and time of day of the notarial act; (2) the type of notarial act; (3) the type, title, or a description of the document or proceeding; (4) the signature, printed name, and address of each principal [document signer]; (5) ... ; (6) the evidence of identity of each principal [document signer] in the form of either: a statement that the person is 'personally known' to the notary; a notation of the type of identification document, its issuing agency, its serial or identification number, and its date of issuance or expiration; ... ; [(7) the thumbprint of each principal [document signer] and witness, or, in the case of an electronic journal , the thumbprint or other recognized biometric identifier, in accordance with Section 20—2(4) of this [Act];] [(8)] the fee, if any, charged for the notarial act; [(9)] the address where the notarization was performed, if not the notary's business address; ...

(b) A notary shall not record a Social Security or credit card number in the journal.

(c) A notary shall record in the journal the circumstances for not performing or completing any requested notarial act.

(d) A notary shall record in the journal the circumstances of any request to inspect or copy an entry in the journal, including the requester's name, address, handwritten signature, [thumbprint or other recognized biometric identifier,] and evidence of identity. The reasons for refusal to allow inspection or copying of a journal entry shall also be recorded.

(e) As required in Section 9-3(4), a notary shall append to the pertinent entry in the journal a notation of the nature and date of the notary's correction of a completed notarial certificate corresponding to the entry." *Model Notary Act,* Section 7.2 (2010).

"Inspection And Copying Of Journal. (a) In the notary's presence, any person may inspect and request a copy of an entry or entries in the notary's official journal during regular business hours, but only if:

(1) the person's identity is personally known to the notary or proven through satisfactory evidence;

(2) the person affixes a signature [and thumbprint or other recognized biometric identifier] in the journal in a separate, dated entry;

(3) the person specifies the month, year, type of document, and name of the principal [document signer] ... for the notarial act or acts sought;

(4) the person is shown or given a requested copy of only the entry or entries specified; and

(5) the other entries on the same journal page are covered to prevent disclosure.

(b) If the notary has a reasonable and explainable belief that a person bears a criminal or harmful intent in requesting information from the notary's journal, the notary may deny access to any entry or entries.

(c) The journal may be examined and copied without restriction by a law enforcement officer in the course of an official investigation, subpoenaed by court order, or surrendered at the direction of the [commissioning official].

(d) Upon complying with a request for copies under Subsection (a), the notary shall charge not more than [dollars] per copy; and if a certified copy is requested, the fee as specified in Section 6-2." *Model Notary Act,* Section 7-3 (2010).

"Security of Journal. (a) A notary shall safeguard the journal and all other notarial records and surrender or destroy them only by rule of law, by court order, or at the direction of the [commissioning official].

(b) When not in use, the journal shall be kept in a secure area under the exclusive control of the notary, and shall not be used by any other notary, nor surrendered to an employer upon termination of employment.

(c) Within 10 days after the journal is discovered to be stolen, lost, destroyed, damaged, or otherwise rendered unusable or unreadable, the notary, after informing the appropriate law enforcement agency in the case of theft or vandalism, shall notify the [commissioning official] by any means providing a tangible receipt, including certified mail and electronic transmission, and also provide a copy or identification number of any pertinent police report." *Model Notary Act,* Section 7-4 (2010).

"Disposal of Journal. (a) Upon resignation, revocation, or expiration of a notary commission, or death of the notary, the journal and notarial records shall be delivered to the [office designated by the commissioning official] in accordance with Sections 12-4(a) or 12-5(3) by any means providing a tangible receipt, including certified mail and electronic transmission, allowing that an electronic journal may be delivered on disk, printed on paper, or transmitted electronically, in accordance with the requirements of the same office.

(b) In the case of an electronic journal and its backup copy whose disks or other physical storage media are not required to be surrendered, no further entries shall be made in the journal and its backup, both of which shall be safeguarded until both shall be erased or expunged after [5] years from the date of the last entry by the notary or the notary's personal representative." *Model Notary Act,* Section 7-5 (2010).

"[Journal. (a) A notary public [other than an individual licensed to practice law in this state] shall maintain a journal in which the notary public chronicles all notarial acts that the notary public performs. The notary public shall retain the journal for 10 years after the performance of the last notarial act chronicled in the journal.

(b) A journal may be created on a tangible medium or in an electronic format. A notary public shall maintain only one journal at a time to chronicle all notarial acts, whether those notarial acts are performed regarding tangible or electronic records. If the journal is maintained on a tangible medium, it must be a permanent, bound register with numbered pages. If the journal is maintained in an electronic format, it must be in a permanent, tamper-evident electronic format complying with the rules of the [commissioning officer or agency].

(c) An entry in a journal must be made contemporaneously with the performance of the notarial act and contain the following information: (1) the date and time of the notarial act; (2) a description of the record, if any, and type of notarial act; (3) the full name and address of each individual for whom the notarial act is performed; (4) if identity is based on personal knowledge, a statement to that effect; (5) if identity of the individual is based on satisfactory evidence, a brief description of the method of identification and the identification credential presented, if any, including the date of issuance and expiration of any identification credential; and (6) the fee, if any, charged by the notary public.

(d) If a notary public's journal is lost or stolen, the notary public promptly shall notify the [commissioning officer or agency] on discovering that the journal is lost or stolen.

(e) On resignation from, or the revocation or suspension of, a notary public's commission, the notary public shall retain the notary public's journal in accordance with subsection (a) and inform the [commissioning officer or agency] where the journal is located.

(f) Instead of retaining a journal as provided in subsections (a) and (e), a current or former notary public may transmit the journal to the [commissioning officer or agency] [the official archivist of this state] or a repository approved by the [commissioning officer or agency].

(g) On the death or adjudication of incompetency of a current or former notary public, the notary public's personal representative or guardian or any other person knowingly in possession of the journal shall transmit it to the [commissioning officer or agency] [the official archivist of this state] or a repository approved by the [commissioning officer or agency].] *Revised Uniform Law on Notarial Acts,* Section 19 (2010).

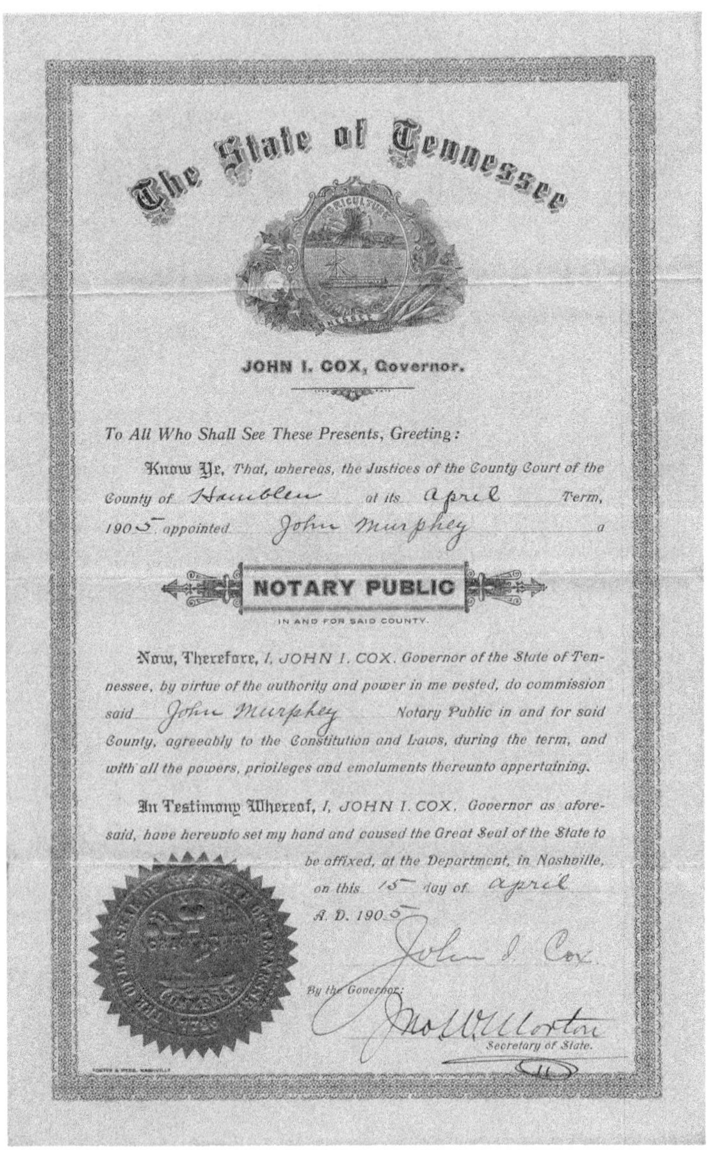

The State of Tennessee

JOHN I. COX, Governor.

To All Who Shall See These Presents, Greeting:

Know Ye, *That, whereas, the Justices of the County Court of the County of* Hamblen *at its* April *Term, 190*5 *appointed* John Murphey *a*

NOTARY PUBLIC

IN AND FOR SAID COUNTY.

Now, Therefore, *I, JOHN I. COX, Governor of the State of Tennessee, by virtue of the authority and power in me vested, do commission said* John Murphey *Notary Public in and for said County, agreeably to the Constitution and Laws, during the term, and with all the powers, privileges and emoluments thereunto appertaining.*

In Testimony Whereof, *I, JOHN I. COX, Governor as aforesaid, have hereunto set my hand and caused the Great Seal of the State to be affixed, at the Department, in Nashville, on this* 15 *day of* April *A. D. 190*5

John I. Cox

By the Governor:

Jno W. Morton
Secretary of State.

1905, official State of Tennessee notary public commission for John Murphey. Notice that the justices of the county court appointed the notary, who was then commissioned by Governor John Cox.

Chapter

18

Document Signer Confidentiality and Privacy

STANDARDS SUMMARY

18.1. The notary should understand the confidential and private nature of document notarizations.

18.2 The notary should not reveal any information that would identify the notarized document or the document signer to unauthorized parties.

18.3 The notary should understand the confidential and private nature of certain personal information about the document signer acquired during a document notarization.

18.4 The notary should maintain the confidentiality and privacy of the personal information about the document signer acquired during a document notarization.

18.5 The notary should not make or retain copies of notarial certificates, transactional instruments, or signer IDs prepared or reviewed during document notarizations.

18.6 The notary should, unless required by law to do otherwise, not record or retain serial numbers of signer IDs reviewed during document notarizations.

STANDARDS EXPLANATIONS

Notaries owe a duty to guard the confidentiality and privacy of information about the individuals and instruments involved in the notarizations they perform. The previous chapter addressed the confidentiality, privacy, and security of the notary journal, so this chapter will not revisit those matters. Instead, this chapter deals with the notary's obligations to refrain from disclosing information learned by the notary about notarized documents and document signers, and to protect the confidential and private information contained in copies of itemized receipts for notary fees, compensation for travel time, and reimbursement of travel expenses. See also the discussion of notary journals in Chapter 17 and the discussion of notary compensation in Chapter 28.

18.1 The notary should understand the confidential and private nature of document notarizations.

The great majority of document notarizations are conducted in private settings, such as in offices, in hospital rooms, in private residences, and the like. Attendance at those document notarizations is typically quite limited, usually to the notary, the document signer, and possibly one or more witnesses or guests. The public is not invited and not allowed to observe. There is a good reason for the degree to which notarizations are protected from greater exposure and transparency — namely, their confidential and private nature, and the desire of document signers not to have their personal and business matters more generally known by others. However, if a document signer wished to have an audience for a notarization, the signer could invite others to attend.

Notaries should appreciate that document signers may not want their personal and financial affairs to be revealed. Notaries should treat everything about document notarizations as confidential and private. Even the fact that a notarization was performed for a specified signer, or that a particular kind of transaction was notarized on a particular date, should be kept confidential and private by the notary. If document signers decide to invite others to their notarizations or to share information about their notarizations, those choices are for signers to make. Furthermore, even if document signers make choices to reveal or disclose information about notarizations to other parties, those actions do not relieve notaries from their obligations to maintain the confidentiality and privacy of information concerning notarizations.

18.2 The notary should not reveal any information that would identify the notarized document or the document signer to unauthorized parties.

During World War II, a well-known security admonition was: "Loose lips sink ships." Loose lips on notaries can also doom the security of notarizations. In a very real sense, all honest and law-abiding people, including notaries, are at war with imposters, identity thieves, stalkers, and other criminals and wrongdoers. Notaries should not engage in casual talk or gossip by telephone, text, email, social media, or any other communication medium about the specifics of their notarial activities, the notarizations they perform, the signers they service, or any other details concerning the official act they perform.

The reason for such a broad prohibition against disclosure is that sometimes bits of information can be pieced together to reveal a larger story. It is sometimes a small world in which we live; coincidences happen; people are curious and nosey; and, gossip and rumors spread. Hypothetically, if a co-worker of the notary or a subsequent customer of the notary had seen and recognized an individual (a known real estate investor) meet with the notary earlier in the day and retire to the notary's private office, and if later the same day the notary were to boast to the co-worker or subsequent customer about having earlier that day notarized a million dollar real estate transaction for the land at 123 Main Street, the pieces of the puzzle of the notarization would have come together. Notaries must not talk to or text unauthorized individuals about their official activities.

Notaries are state or territorial officers and, as such, notaries have the duty to maintain the confidentiality of their official activities. We expect the same protection of confidential matters to be practiced by police officers, judges, court clerks, city inspectors, tax assessors, and other public officials. If notaries violate this prohibition, they could be charged with a disciplinary violation and sanctioned by the commissioning official or notary oversight agency, they could be sued if the unauthorized leak of confidential or private information were to cause financial injury to a party, and they might be charged with the crime of official misconduct or comparable offense. See also the discussion of liability issues for notaries in Chapters 20 and 22.

18.3 The notary should understand the confidential and private nature of certain personal information about the document signer acquired during a document notarization.

A number of the pieces of information learned by the notary in the course of a document notarization constitute sensitive and private information that most people do not want disclosed in this age of identity theft, document fraud, and criminal stalking. Among the important and private bits of information which may be learned by the notary are the document signer's name, address, phone number, and email address.. Obviously, the signer's full correct name is vital to any identity thief or stalker seeking to acquire even more data about a targeted individual. Stalkers need addresses and sometimes phone numbers and email addresses to do their stalking, and other wrongdoers always like as much information as they can get about their potential victims. Further, the document signer may orally volunteer other personal and financial information, such as the reasons why the transaction is being undertaken and details about the contents of the document (perhaps including the goods, realty, or services involved, the price or value of the subject matter of the document, and other information).

Under the peculiar circumstances which so often arise in the real world, any information might be embarrassing to the document signer and helpful to a wrongdoer — even seemingly innocuous matters such as the date or time of the notarization, where the notarization was performed, the length of the notarized document, witnesses or observers who attended the notarial ceremony, and so on. Thus, as suggested earlier in this chapter, everything about a notarization should be treated by the notary as confidential and private. The notary should reveal nothing whatsoever about a notarization performed by the notary to anyone other than the document signer.

There are documented instances in which notaries have been solicited and used as the sources of information that should not have been revealed. If a notary were to improperly reveal, or allow access to, information about a document signer that should have been kept confidential and private and if, as a result, the signer suffered financial and/or personal injuries, the notary could face a claim for legal liability and possibly for punitive damages. See the discussion of notary liability concerns in Chapter 20.

18.4 The notary should maintain the confidentiality and privacy of the personal information about the document signer acquired during a document notarization.

Notaries have properly been described as fiduciaries of the public they serve. As fiduciaries, notaries have the obligation to place the interests of their customers first and foremost, ahead of the interests of other parties, including the notaries themselves. A significant part of the fiduciary responsibility is to protect the signers' confidentiality and privacy interests. Therefore, notaries should never engage in casual conversation in any format about the details of their notarial activities, including talk, text, or email. The notary's obligation of silence about notary-related matters in casual or informal settings is the same responsibility to avoid disclosures of confidential and private information owed by business and government professionals — such as accountants, arbitrators, bankers, clergy, doctors, judges, lawyers, police, teachers, and the like.

Note: *Notary Customer Receipts.* Notaries who charge for their services, and who are compensated for travel time and travel expenses, are obliged to provide itemized receipts to their customers and should retain copies for their own records. Receipts for notarial services and related activities will include confidential and private information about signers and their documents, such as the signer's name and the date of the notarization, possibly the signer's address and other contact information, the type of notarization, and the type of document notarized. Notaries should protect the confidential and private information about signers and documents contained in copies of notary receipts.

Note: *Confidentiality in the Workplace.* A special area of concern for notaries who are employees involves their interactions with their employers and supervisors, who may mistakenly believe their superior positions entitle them to inquire about and learn about all document signers dealt with and all notarizations performed by notary-employees while on duty in the workplace. Employers and supervisors are entitled to inquire and learn about notarizations of company documents and company transactions notarized by their own notary-employees. However, notary-employees should decline to disclose information to employers and supervisors involving noncompany matters. Just because a notarization is performed by a notary-employee while on duty in the workplace does not mean the notarization is business-related and subject to inquiry by the employer and supervisors. See also the discussion of the roles of notaries and their employers in Chapter 24.

Note: *Improper Use of Confidential Information.* Notaries cannot make personal use of confidential or private information relating to the individuals they serve or the instruments they notarize. This duty of notaries not to use protected information for personal gain or to assist the notary's friends or family members must be honored in order to avoid conflicts of interest. See also the discussion of notary ethics in Chapter 19.

On the other hand, there will be limited instances in which notaries will be permitted to reveal some information about notarizations and document signers to authorized parties such as police, prosecutors, and agents of the commissioning official or notary regulator. Thus, notaries may communicate with authorized parties in the course of official investigations about notarizations they have performed and the persons for whom those services were rendered. When the notary discusses or discloses information to investigators, such communications constitute official acts of the notary and should be fully recorded in the notary journal. Document signers themselves may request information about the circumstances of their own notarizations from the notaries who performed them, and notaries should answer those requests.

18.5 The notary should not make or retain copies of notarial certificates, transactional instruments, or signer IDs prepared or reviewed during document notarizations.

Some conscientious notaries, recognizing that the notarial certificates which they execute and which are attached to the notarized transactional documents will be carried away by document signers, have been tempted to create a paper trail to evidence their notarizations by making copies of the completed notarial certificates, of the transactional instruments that are notarized, and/or of the IDs relied upon to identify document signers. However, doing so actually endangers the confidentiality and privacy of signers and should be avoided.

It should be mentioned that notary statutes and regulations do not commonly prohibit notaries from copying and retaining notarial certificates, transactional instruments, and ID documents. Nevertheless, retaining copies of the listed documents risks the security of such copies. Indeed, the more copies that are kept in files in the possession of the notary, the more likely that a notary may carelessly allow access to the copies or that a wrongdoer may gain unauthorized access to the copies.

Moreover, if notaries were to keep such voluminous files of papers gathered in the course of official activities, those papers would become a sort of public record with all of the complicated issues attendant thereto. Those files of so much paper would include a great deal of redundant and superfluous material. Besides, making and storing copies of notarial certificates, notarized transactional instruments, and signer ID documents is unnecessary if notaries maintain and preserve detailed notary journals. The relevant information about each of those documents should be recorded in the notary journal. See the discussion of notary journals in Chapter 17.

18.6 The notary should, unless required by law to do otherwise, not record or retain serial numbers of signer IDs reviewed during document notarizations.

Notaries sometimes too readily accept representations about the identities of document signers, resulting in forgeries and faulty notarizations. Thus, there has been a concern about whether notaries really examine ID documents to be reasonably assured of the true identities of the instrument signers who appear before them for notarizations. The way notary practice had attempted to satisfy this concern in earlier years was to require notaries to record information about ID documents, including serial numbers, in their journals. For many years, this author and other notary instructors advised notaries to note serial numbers of IDs in journal entries for "security" purposes. When the author was in college and law school in the '60s and '70s, student grades were posted on faculty office doors according to the students' Social Security numbers for "confidentiality" purposes.

However, times have changed. Now, notary instructors advise notaries not to record ID serial numbers or to copy and retain IDs, and some state and territorial statutes and regulations direct notaries not to record serial numbers. In these days of widespread identity theft and document fraud, serial numbers of ID documents are particularly valuable to wrongdoers bent on mischief. The reason not to record serial numbers or to copy IDs is the concern that the security of notary journals and other notary files might be breached and the serial numbers accessed by wrongdoers.

Practice Tip: *ID Month and Year of Expiration.* This tip was suggested previously in the chapter about notary journals but is important enough to warrant repeating here. The good news is that there is no need to specifically record serial numbers. Notaries should record in their journal entries the specific type of ID document (for example, a U.S. passport or Florida driver's license) along with its month and year of expiration. That information confirms the notary has examined the ID document. Incidentally, notaries should not record the exact month, day, and year of expiration because, in some jurisdictions, the exact date of expiration is the bearer's birthday, and an individual's birthday is an important personal identifier.

Note: *Statutory Caution.* Although almost no current notary statutes require notaries to record ID serial numbers for instrument signers, there may be a few jurisdictions which still require notaries to write ID serial numbers in notary journals. So, notaries should be sure to know what their respective jurisdictions require in this regard. Hopefully, those few remaining jurisdictions still requiring the recording of ID serial numbers will soon change their laws to remove those now-backward requirements. Although notaries should always carefully protect the security of their notary journals, they should be particularly vigilant in guarding their journals if those records still include ID serial numbers. See also the discussion of notary journals in Chapter 17. ■

***RELEVANT MODEL NOTARY LAW**

Each notary should read, study, and abide by the notary statute and regulations, if any, of her or his state or territory of commissioning.

"The Notary shall respect the privacy of each signer and not divulge or use personal or proprietary information disclosed during execution of a notarial act for other than an official purpose." *Notary Public Code of Professional Responsibility,* Guiding Principle IX (1998).

"To uphold the trust placed in me by the public I serve ...

To not betray the confidence of any individual appearing before me ...

To never divulge the contents of any document nor the facts of execution of that document without prior authority ..." *Responsibility Code of Ethics* (1980).

"Confidentiality. Information required by Section 4-2(7) [[criminal background information about notary applicants]] shall be used by the [commissioning official] and designated [State] employees only for the purpose of performing official duties under this [Act] and shall not be disclosed to any person other than: (1) a government agent acting in an official capacity and duly authorized to obtain such information; (2) a person authorized by court order; and (3) the applicant or the applicant's authorized agent." *Model Notary Act,* Section 4-6 (2010).

"Journal Entries. ... (b) A notary shall not record a Social Security or credit card number in the journal. ..." *Model Notary Act,* Section 7-2 (2010).

"Inspection and Copying of Journal. (a) In the notary's presence, any person may inspect and request a copy of an entry or entries in the notary's official journal during regular business hours, but only if:

(1) the person's identity is personally known to the notary or proven through satisfactory evidence;

(2) the person affixes a signature [and thumbprint or other recognized biometric identifier] in the journal in a separate, dated entry;

(3) the person specifies the month, year, type of document, and name of the principal [[document signer]] ... for the notarial act or acts sought;

(4) the person is shown or given a requested copy of only the entry or entries specified; and

(5) the other entries on the same journal page are covered to prevent disclosure.

(b) If the notary has a reasonable and explainable belief that a person bears a criminal or harmful intent in requesting information from the notary's journal, the notary may deny access to any entry or entries.

(c) The journal may be examined and copied without restriction by a law enforcement officer in the course of an official investigation, [[when]] subpoenaed by court order, or [[when]] surrendered at the direction of the [commissioning official]. ..." *Model Notary Act,* Section 7-3 (2010).

Cover of the book *U.S. Notary Reference Manual* by National Notary Association Vice President and notary expert Charles Faerber, who authored this significant notary resource in numerous editions over many years. He also served as the lead draftsman of the *Notary Public Code of Professional Responsibility* of 1998, the *Model Notary Act* of 2002, the *Model Notary Act* of 2010, and the *Model Electronic Notarization Act* of 2017.

Chapter

19

Notary Ethics and Avoiding Conflicts of Interest

STANDARDS SUMMARY

19.1 The notary should, as a commissioned public officer, understand that during the performance of official functions, the notary is governed by ethical standards.

19.2 The notary should be familiar with the published notary ethics standards.

19.3 The notary should abide by the ethical duty to become, and to remain, informed about notary law and best practices.

19.4 The notary should abide by the ethical duty to follow notary law and best practices in the performance of each document notarization.

19.5 The notary should abide by the ethical duty to act with reasonable care and prudence in the performance of each document notarization.

19.6 The notary should abide by the ethical duty to act with impartiality and honesty in the performance of each document notarization.

19.7 The notary should abide by the ethical duty to refrain from participating in an endorsement, promotion, testimonial, or campaign of any kind.

19.8 The notary should abide by the ethical duty to assess the document signer's mental competence and willingness.

19.9 The notary should abide by the ethical duty to avoid an actual or apparent conflict of interest in the performance of each document notarization.

19.10 The notary should abide by the ethical duty to refrain from notarizing the signature of the notary or notarizing a document in which the notary is named as a party in interest.

19.11 The notary should abide by the ethical duty to refrain from notarizing for any known member of the notary's family in any degree of relationship by blood, marriage, or adoption.

19.12 The notary should abide by the ethical duty to avoid profit or gain from a document notarization, other than the fee assessed for the notarization.

19.13 The notary should abide by the ethical duty to refuse any gift or gratuity in connection with past, present, or future service as a notary.

19.14 The notary should abide by the ethical duty to protect the integrity and corroborate the validity of each document notarization by preparing a notary journal entry for the notarization.

19.15 The notary should abide by the ethical duty to protect the confidentiality and privacy of information about the document signer and the notarized document.

19.16 The notary should abide by the ethical duty to provide sufficient personal assets, bond coverage, and/or liability insurance to adequately protect against notary mistakes and wrongdoing.

STANDARDS EXPLANATIONS

Ethical standards are obligations inherent to the honorable manner of conducting the affairs or functions of an office or profession. Ethical duties are such well-recognized and uncontroversial obligations that virtually all individuals experienced in the field of endeavor will agree with their application. In theory, even if ethical standards have not been gathered together in published form, they would nevertheless apply and govern because they are so generally understood and generally accepted. Although some fields benefit from the existence of a single, published, official ethics code, we have no such single code in the notary field. But, there is no doubt about the fact that notaries are obligated to act pursuant to ethical standards, as has been recognized by a host of national authorities, including the Conference of Commissioners on Uniform State Laws, the American Society of Notaries, the National Notary Association, the Notary Law Institute, and many individual notary experts. Indeed, this author knows of no expert who would disagree.

The notarization field has the good fortune of now having three published sets of ethics standards for notaries. Those three sets of standards include: (1) the 12-point, one-page *Responsibility Code of Ethics* by the American Society of Notaries, published in 1980; (2) the extensive 10-principle, 30-page *Notary Public Code of Professional Responsibility* (with many subsections and a lengthy legal commentary) by the National Notary Association, published in 1998; and (3) this 16-standard chapter. Each of these sets of ethical standards has been developed from several sources, including (a) the state and territorial notary statutes, regulations, and case law; (b) the various model and uniform notary statutes; (c) the body of published books, articles, and papers on notary subjects; and (d) the notarial best practices which have become accepted over time. See the additional references section of this book for the published ethics codes and model notary laws.

The ethical duties listed below include both affirmative responsibilities for notaries to undertake and negative duties requiring restraint by notaries. Several of the ethical standards set out here are really about the subject of disqualifying circumstances — situations in which for ethical reasons notaries should not perform document notarizations. For instance, when a conflict of interest exists, the notary who occupies a conflicted role should not notarize the document in question. More specifically, as an example, the notary should not notarize for a document signer who is the notary's spouse.

19.1 The notary should, as a commissioned public officer, understand that during the performance of official functions, the notary is governed by ethical standards.

Every notary public must appreciate that she or he occupies a special position, different from ordinary people. They have gone through a detailed procedure with the state or territory in order to be commissioned (or in a few jurisdictions, licensed) to perform official notarizations. Notaries should appreciate that some of the documents with which they deal involve important transactions, possibly affecting matters of substantial interest to the document signers and the parties who receive and rely on the notarized instruments, and possibly worth hundreds of thousands or even millions of dollars. And, notaries should realize that they are privy to confidential and private financial and personal information about the document signers contained in ID documents and the instruments to be notarized.

It follows that notaries have to be aware that all of this special position and power comes with special responsibilities — the ethical duties discussed here. Moreover, as the tasks of notaries increase in number and consequence (as notaries take on greater discretion and judgment challenges associated with assessing document signer identification, willingness, and mental competence — in these increasingly difficult times of identity theft, document frauds, and the aging and mental health effects on so many document signers), notaries can expect to face heightened scrutiny in regard to their compliance with ethical standards.

Incidentally, no vocation can rise to the level of a true profession unless its members abide by a generally accepted code of ethics. It is certainly a fact that all of the learned and other business professions are guided by such codes — for accountants, arbitrators, architects, bankers, doctors, engineers, estate planners, judges, lawyers, real estate brokers, psychiatrists, psychologists, and others. If notaries public desire to be promoted to full professional status, they must steadfastly adhere to rigorous ethical standards and must work to formalize a more thorough code of ethical responsibility for notaries.

19.2 The notary should be familiar with the published notary ethics standards.

One of the critical starting points for ethical performance by notaries is for them to read and study the existing published notary ethics codes (cited in the introduction to this chapter), for those standards will make clear that ethical service as a notary involves a wide range of thoughtful and responsible behavior. Notaries should know the statutory law of proper document notarization and should scrupulously adhere to legal requirements. In addition, notaries are ethically obliged to know and follow notarial best practices and should read and study one or more of the publications (like this one) which describe and explain the best practice habits for notaries. The reason for this latter course is that notary statutes do not fully describe the practices necessary to conduct document notarizations (that is, "how" to do the things which comprise notarial best practices).

Importantly, after acquiring and reviewing the notary statutes, ethics codes, and best practice standards, notaries should then keep those resources readily available for reference when performing notarizations. No one can be expected to recall everything about notary ethics, law, and practice (so these resources may need to be consulted to refresh the recollection of the notary), and unforeseen circumstances and unexpected issues sometimes arise in connection with document notarizations (so those unanticipated matters may pose questions which the notary will wish to research and consider).

19.3 The notary should abide by the ethical duty to become, and to remain, informed about notary law and best practices.

Too few jurisdictions mandate education and testing for notary applicants. Nevertheless, notary applicants should take steps to learn about notary ethics, law, and practice. How else can notaries know what their duties are and how to perform those duties? Ethical notaries should undertake this educational process not only at the beginning of their tenure as notaries, but also throughout the time they serve.

No state or territory presently requires notaries to take part in annual continuing notary education. Currently, the closest things to such a mandate are the requirement of continuing notary education every two years in one state and the retesting of notaries upon commission renewals in some jurisdictions, which presumably will require notaries in those states and territories to engage in a review of current notary law and practice in order to pass the re-examinations.

In the true professions, some ethics standards are aspirational in nature, and not subject to strict oversight and enforcement. The ethical mandate to keep current on recent developments and changes in the law, in technological innovations and improvements, and in relevant procedures would fall into this category. Notaries public should be honor-bound to pursue those aspirations. In an ideal world, there could even be some governmental monitoring of the providing of continuing notary education. These goals should be endorsed and adopted by legislatures, commissioning officials, and notary oversight agencies. But until then, notaries should take it upon themselves to become and remain informed.

There are many opportunities for notaries to pursue and achieve this educational aspiration. Many notaries engage in significant continuing notary education by becoming members of notary advocacy and education organizations, attending notary education programs and conferences, authoring notary publications, and presenting notary courses and programs. True professionals take their work seriously, and inherent to their professional status is the desire to achieve continuing education. See also the discussion of notary membership and education organizations in Chapter 29 and of notary continuing education in Chapter 30.

19.4 The notary should abide by the ethical duty to follow notary law and best practices in the performance of each document notarization.

Ethical notaries know notary law, and they obey it. Ethical notaries also know notary best practices (because those notaries realize the notary laws do not cover all issues regarding the performance of document notarizations), and they adhere to those best practices. Ethical notaries do not allow neighbors, friends, or employers to persuade the notaries to take shortcuts or to dissuade notaries from following notary law and best practices. Ethical notaries are diligent and prudent about legal requirements and best practices. Ethical notaries take their duties seriously, and they expect others to take document notarizations seriously as well.

19.5 The notary should abide by the ethical duty to act with reasonable care and prudence in the performance of each document notarization.

The cardinal rule for lawful behavior in general and for sound and proper performance of commercial and governmental tasks in particular is for individuals to act with reasonable care and prudence. In a sense, careful and cautious conduct should be the lowest common denominator of reasonable behavior to be expected and tolerated. Not surprisingly, this duty of reasonable care is also the standard for the performance of notaries.

It is certainly not asking too much of notaries to act carefully and diligently. Neither ordinary people nor notaries public are required to be free from faults or to be perfect. Such a standard would be unrealistic and impossible and would certainly discourage anyone from serving as a notary. Ethical notaries act with reasonable care and prudence, and they are not reckless, careless, or negligent. Ethical notaries strive to perform valid notarizations which will provide heightened security of notarized documents, and ethical notaries will not jeopardize the interests of document signers and those who receive and rely upon notarized documents by performing incomplete or faulty document notarizations. Ethical notaries do the right thing by acting with reasonable care and prudence all of the time while in their public service. See also the discussion of notary liability issues in Chapter 20.

19.6 The notary should abide by the ethical duty to act with impartiality and honesty in the performance of each document notarization.

Ethical conduct by notaries is not simply a matter of notaries performing with basic honesty and integrity. Ethical conduct also requires complete avoidance of any personal financial or other gain by the notaries, unwavering detachment from the personal and financial interests of document signers, and uncompromised diligence in the conduct of all facets of document notarizations. To put it differently, notaries whose official acts are affected or influenced by self-interest are not ethical. Notaries who are biased for or against document signers are not ethical.

Ethical notaries demonstrate exemplary attitudes and behavior in connection with all facets of document notarizations. Notaries must be clear and honest in their advertising and billing. Notaries must be serious about their ethical responsibilities. Indeed, the attitude exhibited by notaries, and the atmosphere thereby created by notaries, establish the ethics settings in which notarial ceremonies are conducted. Hence, even the notary's attitude and temperament can legitimately be considered an ethical factor. It influences the administration of notarizations. When notaries behave ethically, document signers, witnesses, and observers at notarial ceremonies will get the message, will understand it, and will be deterred from misconduct or will be defeated in their attempts at misconduct.

Ethical notaries are always disinterested and honest and will not place their self-interests above those of the document signers they serve. Ethical notaries will not attempt to use information they acquire from notarial service to compete with document signers. Ethical notaries will not attempt to sell information about document signers or belonging to document signers for financial or personal gain.

Unlike the duty to use reasonable care in the performance of notarizations (which standard does not require perfect performance), notaries must perform perfectly when it comes to the obligations of impartiality and honesty. There are no degrees of impartiality or honesty; one is either impartial, or not; one is either honest, or not.

Note: *Notary Impartiality in the Workplace.* A troublesome area of concern for notaries in the workplace is the fundamental need to remain impartial, while at the same time fulfilling their employment responsibilities — especially when notarizing documents to which their employers are parties. Some jurisdictions have enacted statutes which expressly provide that notaries who are directors, officers, or agents of entities may generally notarize for those entities without violating the impartiality obligation. But, three exceptions should nevertheless prohibit a notary-employee who is a director, officer, or agent of the employer from notarizing documents for that employer: (1) when the employee is named in the document; (2) when the employee has drafted, prepared, or reviewed the document on behalf of the employer; and (3) when the employee has a direct financial interest in the document or its underlying transaction (such as a commission, bonus, finder's fee, procurement fee, or other compensation linked directly to the document or its underlying transaction). In those three situations, the notary's obligation as a commissioned public official to be impartial in assuring the propriety of the elements of the notarization conflicts with the notary's interest as a private party in obtaining the notarization of a document in which the notary has an interest. Moreover, the employer and the notary-employee should not wish to jeopardize a notarization by creating even the appearance of impropriety that may taint a notarization and prompt a challenge to it. Thus, the more significant the document to be notarized and the higher the position of the notary in the employment hierarchy, the greater should be the impulse of the notary not to notarize. As has been observed elsewhere in this book, with more than 4,450,000 notaries in the U.S., an independent notary can be found to notarize an employer's document.

19.7 The notary should abide by the ethical duty to refrain from participating in an endorsement, promotion, testimonial, or campaign of any kind.

Notaries bear the ethical responsibility to avoid taking part in endorsements, promotions, testimonials, or campaigns of any kind — with the exception of a genuine charitable cause that is not commercial or political in any way. This duty requires the notary to decline the performance of a document notarization (including the notary title, notary certificate, or notary seal impression) which the notary knows will be used in an endorsement, promotion, testimonial, or campaign.

If the notary were to suspect possible intended misuse of the notarization, notary title, notary certificate, or notary seal impression, the notary should either decline to notarize or inquire directly of the document signer to determine the signer's intentions. If the signer's intention would violate this ethical standard, the notary should refuse to notarize. As always, the notary should prepare a detailed notary journal entry for the notarization (including the inquiry about intended use of the notarization), or for the refusal to notarize. See also the discussion of the notary journal in Chapter 17.

19.8 The notary should abide by the ethical duty to assess the document signer's identity, mental competence, and willingness.

Times have changed dramatically for notaries in the last decade or two. Concerns about identity theft and document fraud have increased sharply. In response, there has been a sustained movement to enlist notaries more directly and more deeply in the fight against identity theft and document fraud by asking notaries to more carefully assess the document signer's identity, mental competence, and willingness for each instrument notarization. These three assessments are now critical to the integrity and security of document notarizations. Consequently, notaries bear the ethical duty to perform these assessments diligently, capably, and thoroughly, and to note the conduct of these assessments in the respective journal entries. See the discussion of signer identification in Chapter 10, of signer mental competence in Chapter 13, and of signer willingness in Chapter 14.

19.9 The notary should abide by the ethical duty to avoid an actual or apparent conflict of interest in the performance of each document notarization.

This standard is stated to emphasize the basic reason for the group of several specific disqualifying settings discussed in the next sections that follow. An alleged conflict of interest is akin to an objection on moral grounds, impugning the integrity of the conflicted notary. It would be dishonest for a notary to serve knowing that there was an actual, or even an apparent, conflict of interest.

At the heart of the post of notary public is the critical need in commerce and government for an independent and unbiased party to witness the signatures on documents in order to help insure the security and integrity of transactions. If a notary is not absolutely impartial and neutral, the notary may be improperly influenced, and the resulting notarization cannot be trusted. Even if there is no actual conflict of interest that can be proven, the mere appearance of a conflict raises questions, diminishes the role of the notary, and should be avoided. At a minimum, an actual or apparent conflict of interest may lay the foundation for a legal challenge to the validity of a notarization, and the legal contest is likely to be protracted and expensive. A notary should not create a setting in which a challenge to the validity of a document notarization is invited due to the notary's conflicted role. Additionally, a legal challenge to a notarization on the basis of an alleged conflict of interest subjects the image of the notary public to expanded examination and possible damage, regardless of the eventual outcome. It is often observed that no one accused of a morals violation ever prevails completely.

The notary should not notarize a document in which the notary has a direct or indirect financial interest (other than the interest in the notary fee). This disqualification includes notarizing a document which is part of a larger transaction in which the notary has a direct or indirect financial interest. Of course, there would be an actual conflict of interest if the notary were to notarize a document in which the notary had a financial interest. The temptation is for the notary to place self-interest (in seeing that the document gets notarized) above the need to assure the notarization proceeds only if the document signer is correctly identified, only if the signer is mentally competent and willing, and only if the notarization procedure is carried out in full and appropriately recorded.

19.10 The notary should abide by the ethical duty to refrain from notarizing the signature of the notary or notarizing a document in which the notary is named as a party in interest.

Notaries should not notarize their own signatures, and notaries should not notarize documents in which they are named as parties in interest in any capacity. These situations would present the worst of all actual conflicts of interest. Most notary statutes prohibit notaries from notarizing for themselves, and the common law has reached the same conclusion. In this author's opinion, a notary should not even notarize a document in which the notary's name appears in any capacity other than notary. It would be comparable to the smell test for food products; if the food smells bad, you do not consume it. It would be unseemly for a notary to notarize a document in which the notary's name and/or signature appears for any reason. The notary should err on the side of caution and reluctance. See also the discussion in Chapter 12 suggesting notaries should not notarize on documents in which they are also named, or on which they have also signed, as witnesses.

19.11 The notary should abide by the ethical duty to refrain from notarizing for any known member of the notary's family in any degree of relationship by blood, marriage, or adoption.

Among the most basic risks of a notary being tempted away from the neutral and impartial position which notaries are required to occupy is the performance by the notary of official acts for fellow family members. Family relationships can be strong bonds, and family members often live in close proximity to one another. Family members may call upon a notary related by blood, marriage, or adoption, thinking they may obtain favored treatment in the notarization process. There is good reason for the old saying: "Blood is thicker than water." Family ties are often the strongest of bonds.

Very few states and territories have enacted any prohibitions against notaries performing document notarizations for their own family members, even against notarizing for their own spouses and significant others. While state and territorial statutes and common law decisions universally hold that notaries have the inherent obligation to be impartial, unfortunately, few state and territorial notary statutes go far enough in expressly prohibiting notaries from performing official acts for family members and significant others. Nevertheless, notaries should steadfastly avoid performing notarizations for any and all known family members and significant others — to avoid even the possible appearance of favoritism.

The *Model Notary Act*, at the end of the chapter, correctly announces a strong stance that disqualifies a notary from performing a notarial act for "a spouse, domestic partner, ancestor, descendant, or sibling" of the notary, including an "in-law, half-, and step-" relative. Of course, a child or parent of the notary by adoption would be included in the disqualification from the group for whom the notary may perform official acts. With more than 4,450,000 notaries in the U.S., there should be no shortage of notaries and no need for a known family member to be providing notarial services to a known family member. What an unseemly picture that would be.

Importantly, the notary and a family member for whom the notary might otherwise perform a document notarization should not wish to open themselves to a challenge to the validity of a notarization based upon a family conflict of interest. Like the first obligation of doctors to their patients, notaries should do no harm to their notary clients. Why risk an attack upon a notarization — especially, why take such an easily avoidable risk?

Note: *A Lesson from Notary History.* This author has always been troubled by an incident from history involving a notary performing an official act for a close family member. It happened in the early 1900s when President Warren Harding unexpectedly died while Vice President Calvin Coolidge was away from Washington, D.C., visiting at the Coolidge family home in Vermont. Calvin's father — a commissioned Vermont notary — was also at the family home when news of the death of Harding was received. The father then administered the presidential oath of office to his son Calvin at the house in Vermont. It has never been clearly determined in the law whether the presidential oath to the successor under such circumstances where the sitting President has died is merely ceremonial (as the successor probably succeeds to the office automatically by constitutional mandate), or an essential substantive step in the elevation of the vice president to the presidency. In either case, I have always been troubled that a notary would undertake to administer an official oath to his own son — especially in such a history-making setting. Interestingly, shortly thereafter when Coolidge arrived back in Washington, a little-known second oath of office was administered to him at the White House by a justice of the U.S. Supreme Court. Was the second oath of office prompted by concern that a father should not administer an official notarial oath to his son? Although not everyone would agree with me, I wish the first oath had not been administered. We need to err on the side of caution in the field of ethics and notarial practice. There is an old adage among lawyers that no one ever truly wins a charge of violation of ethics, for there will be lingering suspicions about the integrity and honesty of the accused whatever the outcome. That same suspicion will likely apply to notaries accused or even suspected of ethics violations.

19.12 The notary should abide by the ethical duty to avoid profit or gain from a document notarization, other than the fee assessed for the notarization.

Numerous professionals in a wide variety of fields also hold notary commissions, partly because notarizations are often sought in those fields — including such fields as law, architecture and engineering, accounting, real estate, health care, banking, stock brokering and investing, insurance, estate planning, and so on. The standard under consideration here is a significant one because it implicates the many settings in which a professional business person — such as a lawyer, immigration specialist, paralegal, real estate broker, financial planner, banker, stockbroker, accountant, health care provider, architect, and so forth — who is also a notary public will prepare, draft, or review a transactional instrument for a client or patient. However, an individual who prepares, drafts, or reviews a transactional instrument and who is also a notary should not notarize that instrument, for such dual service would constitute a conflict of interest. See also the discussion of conflicts of interest when notary-attorneys notarize documents they have prepared, drafted, or reviewed for their legal clients in Chapter 25.

The conflict stems from the opposing positions occupied by the notary (who is required to represent the government and the public as an impartial witness to determine whether the notarization should proceed and whose fee is nominal or zero) and by the document preparer or reviewer (who is an advocate for the document and its notarization and who has a substantial financial interest in the form of the fee for preparing, drafting, or approving the document for notarization). With more than 4,450,000 notaries in the U.S., there is no need to have one individual serve in the conflicted roles of notary and document drafter/preparer/reviewer. The ethical notary should avoid such an actual or apparent conflict.

19.13 The notary should abide by the ethical duty to refuse any gift or gratuity in connection with past, present, or future service as a notary.

The defining characteristics of notaries are their status as public officials and their impartiality. Both characteristics are antithetical to the thought that notaries would accept gifts or gratuities for their official services. Accepting gifts or gratuities would compromise their positions as public officers (as public officials are not allowed to accept gifts or gratuities) and their positions as impartial performers of notarizations (as "gifts" and "gratuities" are antiseptic ways of describing "bribes" for favors and shortcuts). Thus, an ethical notary will not accept a gift or gratuity, no matter how small, offered because of the notary's role as a public official.

19.14 The notary should abide by the ethical duty to protect the integrity and corroborate the validity of each document notarization by preparing a notary journal entry for the notarization.

The responsibility of the ethical notary to prepare and preserve a thorough notary journal entry for each document notarization is so extremely important as to warrant its description in a separate best practice standard. This standard is not about record-keeping simply for the sake of record-keeping. It is set out for the underlying purpose of reinforcing the validity of the notarization by providing a secondary written record to corroborate the notarial certificate and the notarization.

It must be kept in mind that the fundamental obligation of the ethical notary is to create a legally valid document notarization. An important way for the notary to help assure that goal is achieved is to create and preserve backup evidence to verify the notarization was properly performed. Even though the notary statutes of many states and territories do not require notaries to maintain journal records, ethical notaries should prepare and preserve a journal entry for every document notarization to corroborate each one. See also the comprehensive discussion of notary journals in Chapter 17.

19.15 The notary should abide by the ethical duty to protect the confidentiality and privacy of information about the document signer and the notarized document.

A notary who performs document notarizations will hear and/or read confidential and private information about document signers and their documents. Additionally, notaries will create and retain written records regarding those document notarizations in the forms of journal entries and itemized receipts for notary fees and payments received. But, notaries are public servants who are bound by the ethical obligation to protect the interests of their notary clients, including protection of confidential and private information about those clients and their documents. Thus, after notarizations are completed, notaries should not talk about or gossip about particular document signers or about their specific documents. Notaries should secure and safeguard the written records about notarizations to prevent unauthorized access to their contents.

See also the discussion of signer confidentiality and privacy in Chapter 18 and the discussion of notary journals in Chapter 17.

This ethical duty also prohibits the notary from using confidential or private information resulting from a notarization for the personal or financial gain of the notary and the notary's family, friends, or associates. Nor should the notary exploit confidential or private information gleaned from a notarization to compete with the document signer or to advance the interests of the notary. The notary's first and foremost instinct and practice should be to protect the signer's interests.

19.16 The notary should abide by the ethical duty to provide sufficient personal assets, bond coverage, and/or liability insurance to adequately protect against notary mistakes and wrongdoing.

Negligent notary errors and omissions and intentional notary wrongdoing may cause significant financial injuries to document signers and others, such as parties who rely upon notarized documents. When that happens, notaries have full and unlimited personal liability for the damages. Ethical notaries will provide a source of compensation to victims in the event of notarial mistakes and wrongdoing. Indeed, if an individual is unable to assure financial responsibility for such legitimate claims, the individual should not serve as a notary public. In our country, some individuals, such as automobile owners and drivers, doctors, lawyers, and others, are required by law to carry liability or malpractice insurance to assure that they are financially responsible in the event they cause injuries. No state or territory requires its notaries to carry malpractice insurance or even to carry bonds at adequate levels of coverage. Ethical notaries should be financially responsible in the event of a mistake or misconduct.

Notaries or individuals considering becoming notaries should assess the extent of potential liability they might reasonably face as notaries. Then, the notaries or would-be notaries should consider their financial situations to determine whether they have sufficient personal assets to protect against notary mistakes and wrongdoing. The notaries or would-be notaries should either have sufficient assets to pay legitimate claims or should have sufficient assets to purchase adequate notary bonds and liability insurance. See also the discussion of notary liability issues in Chapter 20, and of notary bonds and insurance in Chapter 23. ■

***RELEVANT MODEL NOTARY LAW**

Each notary should read, study, and abide by the notary statute and regulations, if any, of his or her commissioning state or territory.

"The Notary shall, as a government officer and public servant, serve all of the public in an honest, fair and unbiased manner." *Notary Public Code of Professional Responsibility,* Guiding Principle I (1998).

"To uphold the trust placed in me by the public I serve;

To maintain a professional manner suitable to the office I hold;

To treat each individual fairly and equally, with kindness and respect; ...

To not betray the confidence of any individual appearing before me;

To never perform any notarial act in which I am a party in interest or from which I stand to benefit; ...

To not use the office of Notary Public as a means of financial gain, for myself or others, in any other business or profession; ...

To always conduct myself and perform my duties in a manner which will bring credit to myself, my office and the [American Society Of Notaries]." *Responsibility Code of Ethics* (1980).

"The Notary shall not execute a false or incomplete certificate, nor be involved with any document or transaction that the Notary believes is false, deceptive or fraudulent." *Notary Public Code of Professional Responsibility,* Guiding Principle IV (1998).

"The Notary shall give precedence to the rules of law over the dictates or expectations of any person or entity." *Notary Public Code of Professional Responsibility,* Guiding Principle V (1998).

"The Notary shall record every notarial act in a bound journal or other secure recording device and safeguard it as an important public record." *Notary Public Code of Professional Responsibility,* Guiding Principle VIII (1998).

"The Notary shall respect the privacy of each signer and not divulge or use personal or proprietary information disclosed during execution of a notarial act for other than an official purpose." *Notary Public Code of Professional Responsibility,* Guiding Principle IX (1998).

"Refusal To Notarize. (a) A notary shall not refuse to perform a notarial act based on a person's race, advanced age, gender, sexual orientation, religion. national origin, [physical] disability, or status as a non-client or non-customer of the notary's employee." *Model Notary Act,* Section 5-6 (2010).

"The Notary shall act as an impartial witness and not profit or gain from any document or transaction requiring a notarial act, apart from the fee allowed by statute." *Notary Public Code of Professional Responsibility,* Guiding Principle II (1998).

"Disqualifications. (a) A notary is disqualified from performing a notarial act if the notary: (1) is a party to or named in the document that is to be notarized; (2) will receive as a direct or indirect result any commission, fee, advantage, right, title interest, cash, property, or other consideration exceeding in value the fees specified in Section 6-2 of the [Act]; (3) is a spouse, domestic partner, ancestor, descendant, or sibling of the principal [document signer], including in—law, step, and half relatives; or (4) is an attorney who has prepared explained, or recommended to the principal [document signer] the document that is to be notarized. ..." *Model Notary Act,* Section 5-5 (2010).

"Testimonials. A notary shall not use the official notary title or seal to endorse, promote, denounce, or oppose any product, service, contest, candidate, or other offering." *Model Notary Act,* Section 5-11 (2010).

"The Notary shall seek instruction on notarization, and keep current on the laws, practices and requirements of the notarial office." *Notary Public Code of Professional Responsibility,* Guiding Principle X (1998).

"Authority To Refuse To Perform Notarial Act. (a) A notarial officer may refuse to perform a notarial act if the officer is not satisfied that: (1) the individual executing the record is competent or has the capacity to execute the record; or (2) the individual's signature is knowingly and voluntarily made. ..." *Revised Uniform Law on Notarial Acts,* Section 8 (2110).

"[Examination Of Notary Public. ... (b) The [commissioning officer or agency] or an entity approved by the [commissioning officer or agency] shall offer regularly a course of study to applicants who do not hold commissions as notaries public in this state. The course must cover the laws, rules, procedures, and ethics relevant to notarial acts.]" *Revised Uniform Law on Notarial Acts,* Section 22 (2010).

"Prohibited Acts. ... (b) A notary public may not engage in false or deceptive advertising. (c) A notary public, other than an attorney licensed to practice law in this state, may not use the term 'notario' or 'notario publico'. ..." *Revised Uniform Law on Notarial Acts,* Section 25 (2010).

Anderson's

MANUAL

for

NOTARIES PUBLIC

Ninth Edition

2001, cover of the 870-page *Anderson's Manual for Notaries Public*, 9th Edition. It was published by the Anderson Publishing Company.

Chapter

20

The Savvy Notary and Avoiding Liability

STANDARDS SUMMARY

20.1 The notary should be savvy, understand more than just the rules of notary law and best practices, and consider the relevant surrounding circumstances.

20.2 The notary should recognize conditions which may increase the risk of making mistakes in the performance of a document notarization.

20.3 The notary should recognize factors which may increase the risk of heightened financial liability for wrongdoing committed in the performance of a document notarization.

20.4 The notary should understand the values of notarial knowledge, absolute impartiality, reasonable care, and thorough record-keeping in protecting against liability.

20.5 The notary should understand the potential for administrative liability for wrongdoing in the performance of a document notarization.

20.6 The notary should understand the potential for criminal liability for wrongdoing in the performance of a document notarization.

20.7 The notary should understand the potential for civil liability for wrongdoing in the performance of a document notarization.

20.8 The notary should provide sufficient financial resources to cover the costs relating to defense of claims of misconduct and to resulting liabilities.

STANDARDS EXPLANATIONS

Although every notarization is an official act and should be taken seriously by the notary, some notarizations are more important, and perhaps far more important, than others. Thus, this chapter is unconventional for taking that position, and some notary experts may not agree with this author's observations here. In the best of good faith, those other authorities will urge notaries to always be diligent and to treat all notarizations alike, and will, therefore, view much of this chapter to be unnecessary. I respectfully disagree and strongly believe otherwise. In fact, I think this chapter is one of the most valuable in the book.

20.1 The notary should be savvy, understand more than just the rules of notary law and best practices, and consider the relevant surrounding circumstances.

As this book has repeatedly urged, the responsible notary should be thoroughly familiar with the legal requirements and best practice standards for the performance of document notarizations. The responsible notary should obtain and have readily available a copy of those requirements and standards for reference during the performance of notarizations. The responsible notary should stay abreast of developments and changes in notary law and practice. The responsible notary should abide by such requirements and standards at all times when conducting document notarizations. Yet, having done all of that, there is one additional thing every notary should do. The good notary should be grounded; bring common sense and experience along to notarizations; notice the details, but see the big picture; not just hear things, but listen carefully; not take matters for granted, but ask questions; be street-smart.

That fundamental and substantial additional task is to become attuned to all of the relevant circumstances that may affect notarial validity and security. To put it differently, the notary should be savvy, see and understand the big picture of the surrounding notarial context, and either anticipate concerns and avoid them, or respond skillfully to concerns that actually arise and avoid them. The savvy notary has real-life experience and hopefully substantial business experience from which to draw the wisdom to understand rather than merely to superficially see elements in the notarial context. The savvy notary does not leave common sense out of the notarial process, but uses common sense to help detect suspicious circumstances and to stay ahead of them. The savvy notary is appropriately cynical and skeptical. The savvy notary stays calm and thoughtful, does not take shortcuts or hurry the notarial procedure for anyone or any reason, and remains in methodical control of the entire notarial process.

The savvy notary thinks about each step in the notarial procedure and does not allow its aspects to become routine. The savvy notary learns from every notarization performed and is a better notary for the next notarization.

20.2 The notary should recognize conditions which may increase the risk of making mistakes in the performance of a document notarization.

Every document notarization should be conducted with care and prudence. Yet, not all notarial settings are alike. Some should trigger concerns in notaries about opportunities for possible mistakes and other wrongdoing, and notaries should respond accordingly with heightened caution and diligence. For example, if a document signer asks the notary to hurry through a notarization and provides an explanation for the urgency, at least two concerns should appear on the notary's radar. Speedy performance can cause a notary to be less careful, risking errors and omissions. Speedy performance can also cause a notary to be less vigilant in detecting and deterring fraud, risking successful mischief by a wrongdoer. Not only should the notary never hurry a notarization, but also the notary should be suspicious of a signer seeking expedited service and should slow that notarization to help assure nothing improper happens. This author would first suggest to the signer who is in a hurry that she or he postpone the notarization until the signer has more time available because the notarization process cannot be expedited. If the signer were to decline the suggestion to come back on another occasion, I would take more time than ever in performing the notarization to make sure I had exercised reasonable care at every step, had carefully identified the signer (and had asked to examine more than one ID document), had fully recorded the relevant information in my journal, and had proofread every word of the notarial certificate and journal entry.

The notary should beware of any conditions that might reduce the time available for a thorough notarial ceremony, such as a high volume of document notarizations needing to be performed, a document signer presenting multiple documents for notarization at a single time, or the notary's employer, supervisor, or co-worker urging the notary to take shortcuts or to perform a notarization quickly for a valued customer, family member, or friend of the employer, supervisor, or co-worker. The notary should not accede to any request to hurry or take shortcuts to a notarization. A notary should beware of a request to notarize very near the noontime lunch break or near the end of the business day, possibly with the hope that the notary will rush the notarization. The notary should not succumb to any of these temptations to hurry or to take shortcuts.

The notary should trust no one who asks the notary to take shortcuts or who tries to circumvent the full steps to a document notarization. Instead, the notary should perform every document notarization with the utmost diligence and thoroughness. The notary should especially focus on the steps intended to protect against errors and omissions and against imposters and fraud, such as careful identification of the document signer, thorough assessment of the signer's mental competence and willingness, completion of a contemporaneous and detailed notary journal entry, obtaining of the signer's thumbprint in the journal entry (unless prohibited by law), and proofreading of both the notary journal entry and the certificate of notarization prior to the conclusion of each notarization ceremony.

Mistakes can be made in the critically important process of assessing the signer's identity. The notary should always ask to examine one or more IDs of the signer, and the ID document(s) should include a facial photograph, a physical description, and a signature of the signer. The notary should hold the ID in the notary's hands to feel it, look closely at it (both front and reverse sides), and ascertain whether there are any signs of irregularity or tampering with the ID. A mere glance at an ID is not enough. The notary should actually compare each element to the signer and the signer's information in the journal entry. The notary should compare the names and signatures, and the notary should even ask the signer to presently execute additional sample signatures in the journal if the signature on the transactional document and the ID(s) do not match. The notary should compare the appearance of the live signer with the photograph and physical description in the ID and should ask questions of the signer if the appearances do not match. The notary should compare the address provided for the journal entry with the address appearing on the ID(s), and ask questions if the addresses do not match. The notary should ask the signer to provide a thumbprint for the journal entry. See also the discussion of the journal thumbprint in Chapter 17.

Case Illustration. This author has recently been consulted on a legal case involving a notary's misidentification of a document signer. When the document signer appeared for her notarization, the notary asked to see her ID, and she promptly presented a driver's license bearing a photograph. But, the license she presented had been pilfered from her same-sex significant other. The two women looked enough alike that the notary was fooled, and the lady forged the signature of her companion and obtained the notarization. The lesson: People can look a lot alike; and, notaries should pay close attention to the live appearance of document signers when compared to their pictures on their IDs.

Mistakes could also be made by the notary in the assessment of the document signer's mental competence and willingness to execute the document to be notarized. So, the savvy notary should be on the lookout for situations and circumstances which could suggest possible concerns about an individual in respect to those issues. The notary should have a long enough conversation with the signer to be assured of the signer's mental competence and willingness. The notary should ask any witness or guest accompanying the signer to leave the room to allow the notary to speak privately with the signer.

Practice Tip: *Being Direct and Open.* This author has found that most signers are receptive to my conversation and questioning of them when I preface these steps with an open and direct explanation of my purpose. I simply tell the signers that I have the responsibility to assure that document signers are mentally competent and acting willingly, and that is why I want to speak with them and ask them some questions. With that explanation in the open, my questions should not surprise or offend them, and my conversation will last as long as it takes me to decide whether the signer is competent enough and willing to proceed.

Note: *Unnecessary Notarizations.* The savvy notary should also be aware of the many unnecessary notarizations, although there may not be much that can be done about them. Curiously and frequently, business people, laypersons, and lawyers cavalierly add standard form notarial certificates to documents which are not required by law to be notarized. It seems odd, in light of the wide array of possible challenges to the validity of notarizations and the possible liability risks to notaries for faulty performance. However, this propensity can probably be explained by a couple of unfortunate impressions about notarizations. First of all, the people who routinely add notarial certificates are people who will not be performing the notarizations. So, the people creating the need for notarization are not the ones who will face liability for faulty notarial performance. And secondly, the people who routinely add notarial certificates may operate under the misimpression that notarizing "legalizes" the attached instrument. In fact, notarization might have just the opposite result, for the addition of a notarization component adds one more document (the notarial certificate) and one more procedure that may be challenged if any faults can be found.

If the number of unnecessary notarizations were reduced, the number of notary errors and omissions could be reduced as well. Nevertheless, notaries have the responsibility to perform notarizations that are not unlawful. This author mentions the subject at every possible chance in the hope of reducing these unnecessary notarizations.

20.3 The notary should recognize factors which may increase the risk of heightened financial liability for wrongdoing committed in the performance of a document notarization.

Every document notarization should be thoroughly and diligently performed. Not all circumstances surrounding a document notarization are pure and innocent, and not all documents presented for notarization are alike and may not be free of corruption. Some documents are of less consequence and, most assuredly, of less financial value, than others. To illustrate, a three-sentence note granting permission for Susie or Billy to go on the school field trip to the local zoo is not of the same financial magnitude as a 25-page, multimillion dollar contract or transfer of assets. Certain documents should be viewed more seriously than others. Notaries should behave accordingly.

The notary should be on the alert to detect and avoid possible corrupting influences in the notarial process. The notary should not notarize a document to which the notary is a party or in which the notary is named, nor should the notary notarize for any family member, cohabiting companion, lover, or anyone else who is so close to the notary that the notary may not be able to remain impartial and neutral (perhaps an employer, supervisor, or close personal friend). Clearly, the notary should not engage in fraudulent conduct for personal gain, such as by accepting a bribe in connection with the notarization of a document or by allowing another person to falsely use the notary's seal and/or notary journal. See also the discussion of notary ethics and conflicts of interest in Chapter 19.

When the notary notarizes a document under corrupting influences, the notary could be responsible for intentional wrongdoing if the document signer or another party who relied upon the notarized instrument suffered financial injury as a result of the faulty notarization. The notary's liability may be substantially higher than it otherwise would have been due to the intentional nature of the notary's misconduct because the recovery against the notary may include punitive damages (and notary malpractice insurance will not cover intentional wrongdoing).

Although notaries should not read the documents presented for notarization, notaries should look at their titles and page lengths, for that information should even be included in the notary journal entry. If the document is a real estate transfer, a will, a prenuptial agreement, a stock or pension funds transfer, or similar document of financial significance, the notary should be on alert to the heightened potential for financial risk. If the document signer presents multiple financial instruments for notarization, or if the notary is aware that the document signer has been seeking multiple notarizations over a relatively short period of time, these circumstances may signal major financial transactions of major cumulative value.

Other kinds of documents, such as powers of attorney or affidavits for submission in lawsuits, may have more indirect, but still substantial, financial consequences. If signers of these documents are accompanied to the notarial ceremonies by lawyers or other business professionals (such as real estate brokers, financial planners or consultants, accountants, and so forth), it may indicate the documents have financial significance. In addition, the notary may actually know a document signer to be a person of wealth in the community, and such an individual is more likely to present a document of financial magnitude for notarization than other individuals.

The greatest risk that may threaten financial liability for the notary is notarizing for a document signer who is a stranger. A stranger may be an imposter or other wrongdoer attempting to perpetrate a fraud upon the notary and other parties. Correct identification of a stranger through ID documents can be problematic and inexact.

Document signers may be unduly influenced by accompanying parties who are contracting with them or who would benefit from the transaction if the instruments presented for notarization are potentially financially important. The notary should take care to spend a portion of the notarial ceremony in each such case alone and in private with the document signer to assess the signer's true willingness to proceed.

In instances like the ones described in this section, the notary should be on alert, should be thorough and diligent, and should especially be careful to determine the signer's true identity, to assess the signer's mental competence and willingness, to thoroughly record the notarization in a notary journal entry, to request the signer's thumbprint for the journal entry, and to proofread completely both the notary journal entry and notarial certificate prior to the conclusion of the notarial ceremony.

Case Illustration. This author was consulted on a lawsuit involving a series of some 10 notarizations performed by the same bank notary for an elderly signer over about a seven-month period. The quite elderly husband (who suffered from a number of chronic ailments and was being medicated) and his younger wife were known by the notary to be multimillionaires. The notarized documents transferred millions of dollars of assets from the husband to the wife, effectively reversing the couple's prenuptial agreement. But, the notary did not speak privately with the husband at any notarial ceremony although he was accompanied each time by the wife who was receiving assets each time. There were numerous errors in the notarial certificates. And, the notary did not keep a notary journal to record and corroborate any of the notarizations. After the elderly man died, his children from a prior marriage sued the widow, claiming their elderly father had been mentally incompetent and had not acted voluntarily in signing the documents. After years of proceedings, the lawsuit was settled. The notary should have taken these notarizations far more seriously.

20.4 The notary should understand the values of notarial knowledge, absolute impartiality, reasonable care, and thorough record-keeping in protecting against liability.

The four most important things that notaries can and should do consistently to prevent and protect against liability are: (1) to know the notary statute and regulations, if any, and notary best practices, and to remain well informed; (2) to exercise unwavering impartiality at all times in the performance of notarial functions; (3) to act with diligence, prudence, and reasonable care in performing official acts; and, (4) to maintain detailed journal entries for all official acts to demonstrate achievement of the other three practices in this list.

Knowledge is the best defense against potential notary liability. One must know what he or she is supposed to do in order to avoid mistakes and misconduct. Continuing education to review and expand one's knowledge and to stay abreast of changes in law and best practices is part of this process.

The cardinal rule for the notary public is to be trusted and impartial, demonstrating honesty without fail. Notaries should always take the high road among practice choices. Notaries should not tolerate even the appearance of impropriety in what they do. Honesty and impartiality prevent intentional wrongdoing.

Reasonable care for the notary should be the lowest common denominator for acceptable conduct, as the notary should exceed that threshold standard. Due diligence is the higher standard that notaries who are meticulous and prudent should attain. But, even reasonable care stands as the defense against negligence.

Detailed record-keeping in a notary journal provides needed transparency and proves the other attributes of knowledge, honesty, and reasonable care. Detailed journal entries prove the notary knew the notarial requirements and performed them. Detailed journal entries show the notary did what was supposed to be done, has nothing to hide, and has integrity. Detailed journal entries show the habit of the notary over time to care about the duties of a notary and to be thorough and prudent.

Case Illustration. This author observed firsthand the power of the notary journal to impress upon jurors the notarial attributes of knowledge, impartiality, honesty, and reasonable care. I testified in a case where a notary was accused of conspiring with a friend of a terminally ill document signer, falsifying notarizations of three documents to fraudulently obtain the signer's property. The terminally ill signer had granted the friend power of attorney, which, among other things, authorized the friend to sign on behalf of the signer. For the notarizations, the dying signer used a signature stamp to sign the documents being notarized, but the signer asked the friend with power of attorney to place the signer's stamped name in the journal entries, which the friend did, while also signing his own name below the stamped signatures. This journal procedure was highly irregular and improper, but that is how it was done. Thus, in all of the hundreds of journal entries, there were only three entries with two signatures in the "signature" column of the journal pages. Much of my testimony was about the extensive and thorough notary journal entries for hundreds of notarizations performed over several years by the notary. When I testify, I look at the jury so that they can make eye contact with me to better judge my credibility and so that I can see their reactions to my testimony. Near the end of my testimony, I opined to the jury that no notary bent on fraud would have allowed her co-conspirator to co-sign the "signature" column of the journal entries because that irregularity caused those three notarizations to stand out as conspicuously different from all the others. Several jurors smiled or nodded their heads in agreement. The notary won the case with detailed and thorough record-keeping showing her honesty, impartiality, and reasonable care.

Note: *Causation of Financial Injury.* In order for a notary to have liability to the document signer or a third party relying upon a notarized document, there must be financial damage, and the notary's faulty notarization must have been a cause of the financial injury to the signer or the third party. In law, it is called "proximate cause." The faulty notarization does not have to have been the sole cause of the injury; it need only have been a contributing cause or proximate cause of the financial damage to the signer or a third party relying upon or affected by the notarized document.

Note: *Statute of Limitations for Notary Malpractice.* Every legal cause of action must be filed within a statutorily specified period of time, or else the cause of action will be barred or lost due to the expiration of the applicable period of limitations. The time period begins to run from the time the cause of action arises, or if the cause of action is fraudulently concealed or hidden, the limitations period begins to run from the time the cause of action is actually discovered or should have been discovered. Each jurisdiction has enacted statutes of limitation governing specific causes of action, usually including a default provision which applies if no other specific provision applies. Some U.S. jurisdictions have adopted limitations provisions specifically applicable to notary wrongdoing, while in most places, the general limitations provisions on negligence or intentional misconduct apply depending on the particular type of faulty notary performance that has occurred. Many instances of faulty notarizations will not come to light for long periods of time (perhaps years or even a decade or more) because many documents (such as wills, powers of attorney, living wills, health care powers, deeds, and mortgages) are not examined or used by third parties until long after they are notarized. Thus, the potential for a cause of action for notary wrongdoing may last for a very long time.

20.5 The notary should understand the potential for administrative liability for wrongdoing in the performance of a document notarization.

In every jurisdiction, a governmental administrative agency (usually the office of the secretary of state) is statutorily charged with the commissioning and oversight of notaries. Those agencies possess the authority and duty to supervise the performance of notaries, to investigate complaints made against notaries, and, if appropriate, to discipline and sanction notaries for their misconduct.

Each administrative agency has established procedures for disciplinary proceedings against notaries in order to ensure due process of law. At a minimum, those procedures will include notice to notaries of the complaints or concerns directed against them, the right of notaries to be represented by counsel and to respond to the complaints or concerns, an investigative process to obtain the facts and the evidence relevant to prove them, an opportunity for a full hearing on the matter, including a formal process for the taking of various kinds of evidence, the provision of a disinterested hearing officer or administrative law judge to conduct the hearing and to decide the matter, and an appeal process available to those notaries who are found guilty of wrongdoing and against whom some kind of discipline or sanction is imposed.

Incidentally, the notary should self-report to the notary administrative agency material mistakes and wrongdoing discovered by the notary, as well as mistakes and wrongdoing alleged by other parties. Further, the notary should then cooperate fully with the agency's efforts to investigate the situation. Self-reporting and cooperation constitute the honorable course of conduct for the notary and should reduce the agency's efforts to investigate and determine possible discipline. See also the discussion of notary ethics in Chapter 19. Clearly, in connection with self-reporting and possible criminal law implications, there is the co-existing constitutional right to remain silent and not to incriminate oneself. The ethical notary should take the high road, self-report, and face the consequences, which should be mitigated somewhat by the self-reporting.

Notary oversight agencies are authorized to impose administrative discipline and sanctions upon notaries found to have engaged in notarial wrongdoing or official misconduct. Those sanctions may include revocation or suspension of the notary commission, written censure or reprimand, and/or a fine. A record of disciplinary action will become a public record which could have adverse implications for the disciplined notary in the future. Additionally, there may be costs associated with the investigation and disciplinary action that the notary may be required to pay, and the notary may be disqualified from obtaining a notary commission in the future. Administrative agency discipline and sanctions are not the exclusive way by which a notary may face liability for mistakes and wrongdoing. The notary may also face civil law and/or criminal law proceedings prior to, simultaneously with, or after the administrative process.

20.6 The notary should understand the potential for criminal liability for wrongdoing in the performance of a document notarization.

In the U.S., notary and/or criminal statutes include provisions which declare specified notary misconduct to constitute crimes. For instance, violation of the notary statute itself may be a crime — such as the performance by the notary of a notarization when the signer is not present at the notarial ceremony, the predating or postdating by the notary of the notarial certificate, or the failure of the notary to administer the oral oath or affirmation to the signer of a jurat (a verification on oath or affirmation). Some notary statutes include sections which cover non-notaries who participate in or aid offenses, such as impersonation of a notary public, or unauthorized possession or use of a notary seal. Some of the criminal offenses set out in notary statutes require intentional wrongdoing, while other offenses may require only negligent or reckless misconduct (such as occurs in many cases of negligent errors and omissions in the performance of notarizations).

Many criminal statutes contain one or more sections which cover notary misconduct of various types, ranging from negligent or reckless conduct to intentional misconduct. To illustrate, many criminal statutes include a section describing the crime of "official misconduct," or a comparable offense, which, as the title suggests, criminalizes violations of law by public officials, such as notaries public and which may require intentional wrongdoing or the lesser mental state of negligent or reckless misconduct. Again, as noted above, there may be offenses like impersonation of a notary, or unauthorized possession or use of a notary seal, set out in criminal statutes. Of course, notaries may face liability for aiding or abetting other persons to commit notarial offenses.

Criminal offenses and charges are very serious matters, whether they are designated as misdemeanors or felonies. Criminal charges necessitate police and prosecutorial involvement, perhaps including investigations, arrests, detentions in jail, trials, and appeals. The legal evidentiary standard for a conviction of a criminal offense involving notarial misconduct is the same as for every other criminal violation, namely, proof beyond a reasonable doubt — a high standard of proof and the law's highest burden of evidence. The sanctions for a criminal conviction may include a fine, imprisonment, or both.

A criminal offense is a matter which notaries should consider to be especially serious. A conviction for a crime may disqualify a person from obtaining a notary commission, a surety bond, or other professional license in the future. A criminal conviction may be admitted into evidence in an administrative agency proceeding or a civil trial involving the same alleged notarial misconduct and would be damaging to the accused notary's position, if not determinative of an outcome against the notary. Again, as with administrative oversight of notaries, a notary guilty of a criminal violation should consider self-reporting to police or prosecutor's offices — although there is also the constitutional right to remain silent and not to incriminate oneself. As this author recommended above, the ethical notary should self-report. At least the act of self-reporting should help to mitigate the sanctions which may be imposed.

Case Illustration. This author was consulted in a criminal case filed against two notaries and their employer, resulting from the failure of the notaries on two separate occasions to administer the required oral oaths or affirmations to the employer when each of the two notaries performed jurat notarizations for him. The employer was charged with perjury because he had lied in the two documents that were notarized, and the two notaries were charged with official misconduct for failing to administer the oral oaths or affirmations. As the case proceeded, the prosecutor's office granted immunity to the two notaries to get their testimony against the bigger target, their employer. And, as part of the immunity deal, the notaries provided deposition testimony admitting they had not administered the required oaths or affirmations. This situation was very unpleasant, time consuming, and expensive for all three parties. The notaries also had the obligation to report the incidents to the notary oversight agency, which would then have been entitled to sanction them because they admitted their failure to administer the oaths or affirmations.

20.7 The notary should understand the potential for civil liability for wrongdoing in the performance of a document notarization.

Notaries everywhere in the U.S. have full, unlimited, personal liability for any and all financial damages which they cause due to their errors, omissions, or wrongdoing. Included are instances of negligent conduct and intentional misconduct by the notary. Notaries who have caused financial injury to document signers and/or third parties who rely upon or are otherwise affected by faulty notarizations can be pursued by the injured parties for recovery of civil damages (meaning money). This field of law is called tort law, and the process may include the filing of a lawsuit against the notary.

If a notary acts diligently and with reasonable care, but nevertheless makes an error or omission in a notarial act, the notary will not be liable — even for financial injury resulting from the error or omission. Thus, reasonable care is a defense to notary negligence. In other words, notaries are not required to perform perfectly. On the other hand, if a notary acts negligently or commits intentional wrongdoing, the notary may face civil liability for damages. Notaries should keep in mind if they are accused of a mistake or wrongdoing in the civil arena, the burden of proof at a civil trial is the "preponderance of the evidence." That is, the plaintiff (a document signer or a party who relied upon a faulty notarization and was financially injured) would have to present evidence sufficient by a mere preponderance to establish that the notary was negligent or acted with intentional misconduct. It is often said that this evidentiary standard means the plaintiff would need to win the battle of the evidence by a margin of just 51% to the notary's 49%. Thus, the notary should act with reasonable care at all times and should document the notary's diligence by maintaining a thorough notary journal, which will be admissible in evidence to demonstrate the notary's careful performance.

The prospect of possible unlimited accountability for damages should serve as a major deterrent to notarial misconduct. Incidentally, if it can be shown that the notary acted intentionally and injured the plaintiff, the plaintiff may be able to recover punitive damages from the notary as well, and such damages could be substantial. Even a lawsuit can be extremely expensive and time-consuming, for there is the need to pay for the costs of a protracted case, to retain a lawyer, and to pay substantial attorney fees. Thus, even a victory by the notary can come at high emotional and financial costs, not to mention the significant loss of time that would be involved. See also the discussion of notary bonds and insurance in Chapter 23, and of the possible vicarious liability of employers of notaries for notary malpractice in Chapter 24.

20.8 The notary should provide sufficient financial resources to cover the costs relating to defense of claims of misconduct and to resulting liabilities.

The savvy notary will be prepared for potential risks and costs associated with the performance of document notarizations. Because the notary bears unlimited personal liability for financial damages caused due to mistakes and misconduct in performing document notarizations, the personal assets of the notary are at risk in claims against the notary. The notary should keep in mind that the costs of such claims can be significantly higher if lawsuits or administrative proceedings are initiated because the notary will need to hire legal counsel and pay the various expenses which can be triggered (such as the fees for filing documents, depositions, court reporters, appeals, and so on).

An individual should not become a notary public unless and until she or he has sufficient financial resources to protect the public in the event of mistakes or misconduct. Another way to provide the appropriate financial resources to serve as a notary is to obtain a notary bond or notary malpractice insurance in sufficient coverage amounts. Part of the reason to consider a sizable notary liability insurance policy is that the insurance company is required to defend the notary and provide legal assistance commensurate with the amount of a claim. See also the discussion of notary bonds and insurance in Chapter 23. ■

***RELEVANT MODEL NOTARY LAW**

The notary should read, study, and abide by the notary statute and regulations, if any, of her or his state or territory of commissioning.

"To uphold the trust placed in me by the public I serve; ...

To treat each individual fairly and equally, with kindness and respect; ...

To never perform any notarial act in which I am a party in interest or from which I stand to benefit; ...

To never divulge the contents of any document nor the facts of execution of that document without proper authority; ...

To not use the office of Notary Public as a means of financial gain, for myself or others, in any other business or profession;

To exercise extreme care to insure that the notarial seal, stamp and records are kept in a safe place and are not used by any other person ..." *Responsibility Code of Ethics* (1980).

"The Notary shall, as a government officer and public servant, serve all of the public in an honest, fair and unbiased manner." *Notary Public Code of Professional Responsibility,* Guiding Principle I (1998).

"The Notary shall act as an impartial witness and not profit or gain from any document or transaction requiring a notarial act, apart from the fee allowed by statute." *Notary Public Code of Professional Responsibility,* Guiding Principle II (1998).

"The Notary shall not execute a false or incomplete certificate, nor be involved with any document or transaction that is false, deceptive or fraudulent." *Notary Public Code of Professional Responsibility,* Guiding Principle IV (1998).

"The Notary shall give precedence to the rules of law over the dictates or expectations of any person or entity." *Notary Public Code of Professional Responsibility,* Guiding Principle V (1998).

"The Notary shall affix a seal on every notarized document and not allow this universally recognized symbol of office to be used by another or in an endorsement or promotion." *Notary Public Code of Professional Responsibility,* Guiding Principle VII (1998).

"The Notary shall record every notarial act in a bound journal or other secure recording device and safeguard it as an important public record." *Notary Public Code of Professional Responsibility,* Guiding Principle VIII (1998).

"'Official misconduct' means: (1) a notary's performance of any act prohibited, or failure to perform any act or duty mandated, by this [Act] or by any other law in connection with a notarial act; or (2) a notary's performance of an official act or duty in a manner that is negligent, contrary to established norms of sound notarial practice, or against the public interest." *Model Notary Act,* Section 2-12 (2010).

One-of-a-kind, homemade, heavy metal, 1960s–70s, large square notary sign. This sign must have been made for a notary who worked traditional business weekdays and who was available to perform notarizations at home in the evenings and on weekends.

Chapter

21

When Notary Statutes and Regulations Are Silent

STANDARDS SUMMARY

21.1 The notary should understand that many matters relating to document notarizations remain unaddressed or unsettled by notary statutes or regulations.

21.2 The notary should understand how to deal with matters relating to document notarizations that remain unaddressed or unsettled by notary statutes or regulations.

21.3 The notary should, in the absence of statutory or regulatory treatment, understand that a document notarization will be upheld if the notary substantially complies with its legal requirements.

21.4 The notary should, in the absence of statutory or regulatory treatment, prepare a thorough notarial certificate for each document notarization.

21.5 The notary should, in the absence of statutory or regulatory treatment, not attempt to alter or correct a notarial certificate after the notarial ceremony has been completed.

21.6 The notary should, in the absence of statutory or regulatory treatment, understand that the standard of reasonable care applies to the official performance of the notary.

21.7 The notary should, in the absence of statutory or regulatory treatment, acquire a notary seal and affix a seal impression to each notarial certificate.

21.8 The notary should, in the absence of statutory or regulatory treatment, understand and implement procedures to secure and protect the notary seal.

21.9 The notary should, in the absence of statutory or regulatory treatment, understand how to correct an illegible or partial seal impression on a notarial certificate.

21.10 The notary should, in the absence of statutory or regulatory treatment, understand the name and signature requirements for signers for document notarizations.

21.11 The notary should, in the absence of statutory or regulatory treatment, understand the duty to identify the document signer with reasonable certainty, not to guarantee the signer's true identity.

21.12 The notary should, in the absence of statutory or regulatory treatment, identify document signers by reviewing one or more reliable signer IDs.

21.13 The notary should, in the absence of statutory or regulatory treatment, understand the duty to assess the document signer's mental competence and utilize a procedure reasonably calculated to do so.

21.14 The notary should, in the absence of statutory or regulatory treatment, understand the duty to assess the document signer's willingness and utilize a procedure reasonably calculated to do so.

21.15 The notary should, in the absence of statutory or regulatory treatment, understand whether to perform a document notarization for a minor.

21.16 The notary should, in the absence of statutory or regulatory treatment, not perform a document notarization for any known family member of any degree of relationship by blood, marriage, or adoption.

21.17 The notary should, in the absence of statutory or regulatory treatment, not serve as a lay witness and notary for the same document.

21.18 The notary should, in the absence of statutory or regulatory treatment, not serve in the dual roles as drafter, preparer, and/or reviewer of a client's document and as notary for the document notarization.

21.19 The notary should, in the absence of statutory or regulatory treatment, acquire a notary journal and prepare and preserve a detailed journal entry for each document notarization.

21.20 The notary should, in the absence of statutory or regulatory treatment, request the document signer to provide a thumbprint for each notary journal entry.

21.21 The notary should, in the absence of statutory or regulatory treatment, understand the procedure for allowing access to information in the notary journal.

21.22 The notary should, in the absence of statutory or regulatory treatment, not redact information from a journal entry disclosed due to a request for access, except for a signer's thumbprint.

21.23 The notary should, in the absence of statutory or regulatory treatment, understand and implement procedures to preserve and safeguard the notary journal.

21.24 The notary should, in the absence of statutory or regulatory treatment, understand the de facto notary doctrine and its possible effect after the notary commission has expired.

21.25 The notary should, in the absence of statutory or regulatory treatment, understand whether the notary's employer may impose restrictions when the notary is on duty for the employer.

21.26 The notary should, in the absence of statutory or regulatory treatment, understand the notary's employer may have vicarious liability for notary mistakes and wrongdoing.

21.27 The notary should, in the absence of statutory or regulatory treatment, understand the notary cannot avoid liability for wrongdoing because the notary employer ordered the faulty performance.

21.28 The notary should, in the absence of statutory or regulatory treatment, assure financial responsibility for financial injuries caused by notary mistakes and wrongdoing.

21.29 The notary should, in the absence of statutory or regulatory treatment, understand appropriate procedures to be utilized if the notary desires to charge fees for notarial services.

21.30 The notary should, in the absence of statutory or regulatory treatment, not share notarial fees with the notary's employer when the notary is on duty for the employer.

STANDARDS EXPLANATIONS

The subject of this chapter is rarely discussed. Yet, this subject is of fundamental importance for notaries to appreciate. Historically, notary law has been riddled with omissions and ambiguities. Except for coverage of the most general matters about notaries and notarizations, state and territorial statutes and regulations vary widely. Still today, numerous notary practices are not addressed at all by statutes and regulations or are not treated thoroughly enough.

Hence, there are two purposes of this chapter. The first purpose is to emphasize and demonstrate that there are many issues in the notary field which are not fully explained in notary statutes and regulations. We have all heard the old saying: "The devil is in the details." In the context of notary statutes and regulations, the bigger devil can be in the missing details. Indeed, this chapter does not cover all of the missing and ambiguous subjects, for that would not be possible as there are too many such topics.

The second purpose is to provide guidance about some of these missing and ambiguous issues in notary law and practice. To fully address the many missing and ambiguous practices which might be discussed, an entire book of its own would be needed. Thus, numerous topics noted in this chapter and addressed at length in other chapters of this book are cross-referenced to those other locations. The other chapters discuss numerous other matters of consequence that are not addressed at all or not addressed thoroughly by notary statutes or regulations.

21.1 The notary should understand that many matters relating to document notarizations remain unaddressed by notary statutes or regulations.

No notary statute nor regulation can cover every aspect of a subject as complex and important as document notarizations. It is impossible. Statutes are always incomplete and ambiguous. There are numerous reasons for the omissions and uncertainty.

The English language is inherently difficult for defining terms and describing procedures. Legislators are unfamiliar with some of the subjects which they regulate by statutes they adopt and amend. Few legislators have been notaries, and very few seem to appreciate the significance of sound notarization practice in heightening document security and fighting against identity theft and document fraud. The numerous steps involved in document notarizations can be complex and difficult to explain, especially when it comes to describing exactly how to carry out sound and secure notarizations. Notary statutes have tended to remain brief and have not typically been revised or expanded to provide adequate treatment.

The passage of time is the enemy of many statutes and regulations. Statutes and regulations are anchored at a point in time. As time passes, circumstances change, technology advances, people become more sophisticated, and wrongdoers figure out how to more effectively carry out their schemes and frauds. Unless amended and revised, statutes lose their teeth. Some antiquated notary statutes and regulations are now far too brief and ambiguous. The numerous topics discussed below should prove the point.

21.2 The notary should understand how to deal with matters relating to document notarizations that remain unsettled by notary statutes or regulations.

What should a notary do when the applicable statute and regulations, if any, do not cover an issue that confronts the notary? The good news is that there may be other sources of law or best practices to guide the notary.

Notaries should first look to the other important source of law which is called the common law. The common law is the body of law comprised of the published decisions of courts. If courts in the jurisdiction in question, or even in other states or territories, have decided cases on an issue, those common law opinions will provide law on the topic. But, of course, notaries are not expected to be lawyers and to conduct legal research to discover court decisions. If there are relevant court decisions, they will undoubtedly be known by governmental notary oversight agencies, by notary membership and education organizations, and by notary educators and experts. The practices derived from those common law decisions will be published or disseminated in official notary handbooks, notary education courses and conferences, and notary publications and online sites.

If common law cannot be found to govern a notary issue, the other important way to fill gaps in notary statutes and regulations is to consult notary best practice standards. Best practice standards often will address an issue unsettled by the statutory, regulatory, and common law. In the more than 100 years of modern notary practice in this country, most notary issues have been considered and resolved by practicing notaries, notary experts, notary organizations, and notary educators. The official handbook or website of the state or territorial notary oversight agency is the first source to examine for guidance on best practices. Other guidance is commonly published in notary articles, reference books, online materials, and published notary ethics codes. The present book is an example of a publication devoted entirely to compiling notary best practice standards. Also, notary best practice methods are commonly discussed in notary education programs and seminars.

Notary best practice standards are time-tested and thoroughly considered guidelines. Best practice standards are forged from several sources, including statutes and regulations from all around the country, model and uniform notary laws, notary ethics codes, and the writings of notary educators and experts. For example, see the sources cited in this book's additional references and bibliography. A best practice standard is another way of describing reasonable, prudent, and diligent conduct under the particular circumstances. It is the way of doing something that has been thoughtfully considered and endorsed by practitioners and experts in a field of endeavor (like document notarization).

Because notaries are obligated to act with reasonable care, diligence, and prudence, the notary should attempt to find guidance when faced with a matter not covered by notary law. The notary should look at the sources setting out notary best practices. Importantly, the notary should feel comfortable adopting the considered view of other notaries, of notary experts, and of notary organizations.

21.3 The notary should, in the absence of statutory or regulatory treatment, understand that a document notarization will be upheld if the notary substantially complies with its legal requirements.

Must a notarization be perfectly performed to be valid? What happens if a notarial certificate is defective because one element is omitted (let us say, the date is missing)? Are the certificate and the notarization void? What if the month and year are correct, but the day is incorrect? What if the notary seal impression is so smudged that it is illegible in a jurisdiction which requires notaries to obtain and use seals? What if the seal impression is missing altogether? What if the notary's signature does not match the notary's name as it appears on the notary commission and notary seal (the notary's hyphenated surname appears on the commission and seal, but the notary signed using only one of the two hyphenated parts of the name)? What if the notary neglected to sign the certificate at all? Is the certificate and notarization invalid in any of these situations? Notaries are human, and some notaries make accidental errors and omissions.

Notary statutes and regulations do not state that a notarization must be perfectly performed or that the certificate of notarization must be perfectly completed. Notary statutes and regulations do not attempt to sort out all the possible combinations of faulty notarial certificates and faulty notary procedures. Courts have been presented with cases involving particular defects in notarial certificates, and the courts have devised a general rule to handle all such controversies. It is called the substantial compliance doctrine. It means that a notarization will be found valid if the notary has substantially complied with the legal requirements for notary procedures and certificates. A court will weigh the full circumstance of a case, taking into account that some elements of a certificate and notarization are more important than others, and that some faults will be more serious than others. Courts will also examine other evidence about the notarization, including the notary journal entry, if any, and the testimony of witnesses if any can recall relevant facts about the notarization.

Notaries should strive to do their best and to perform perfectly. However, the bottom line is that notaries do not have to perform perfectly. Rather, they are required to substantially comply with the legal requirements. See also the discussion of notary certificates and the substantial compliance doctrine in Chapter 7, Section 7.7.

21.4 The notary should, in the absence of statutory or regulatory treatment, prepare a thorough notarial certificate for each document notarization.

The statutes of two states do not require notaries to prepare and affix notarial certificate language as part of the notarization of documents. Furthermore, many statutes have not been updated to include in their notary certificate formats references to the method of identification of document signers or to the assessments of signer willingness and mental competence. Notaries should prepare and attach a notarial certificate as part of every document notarization, and the certificate should confirm the steps taken to identify document signers and to assess signer willingness and mental competence. See also the discussion of notarial certificates in Chapter 7, Sections 7.1, 7.2, and 7.6.

21.5 The notary should, in the absence of statutory or regulatory treatment, not attempt to alter or correct a notarial certificate after the notarial ceremony has been completed.

The subject of correcting an error or omission in a notarial certificate is almost never covered in notary statutes and regulations. The statutes and regulations do not state that a notary may correct a notarial certificate, but they do not say the notary may not correct a certificate either.

The reason why this topic is not covered in statutes and regulations is fairly obvious — such corrections should not be attempted. The general rule is that the notary's authority over the performance of a notarization ends when the notarial ceremony is concluded. Moreover, if corrections were to be permitted, several difficult issues would have to be resolved — issues that cannot be handled by notaries in the absence of statutory or regulatory guidance.

To illustrate, if correction of a certificate were to be allowed, how long after a notarization could a notarial certificate still be corrected? A week later, a month later, or a year later? Could the notarization of a time-sensitive document be corrected? If a suit had already been filed to challenge the validity of a notarization, could it still be corrected? If the notary's commission has expired or been terminated in the interim, could the notary still make a correction? Who would have authority to seek and obtain a correction — the notary, the document signer, a party named in the notarized document, a third party who received or relied upon the notarized document, or others? If a notary had made an intentional misrepresentation in the notarial certificate, could that intentional falsehood be corrected? If the certificate makes reference to the mental competence assessment and/or willingness assessment of the document signer, could the notary correct one or both of those assessment findings and then cancel the notarization? If copies of the original document and notarial certificate had been made and distributed to third parties, could a correction be made to the notarial certificate, and would the parties in possession of duplicate copies have to be informed of the correction? Would the correction of the notarial certificate have to be noted on the altered original certificate, or would a correct replacement certificate have to be issued? And, the issues would go on and on.

This author's position is contrary to that of the *Model Notary Act*, Section 9-3, as set out at the end of this chapter. A document notarization, including both its certificate and journal entry, may not be altered or corrected after the notarial ceremony is concluded because the notary's authority regarding a particular document notarization ceases when the ceremony is finished. In order to effect the equivalent of a "correction" to a document notarization, a new notarization bearing the correct present date in the certificate and journal entry and the correct present time in the journal entry would have to be performed. Of course, under some circumstances involving time-sensitive instruments, the passage of time may prevent a new notarization from being possible or helpful. See also the discussion of whether completed notarial certificates may be altered or corrected in Chapter 7, Sections 7.11 and 7.12.

21.6 The notary should, in the absence of statutory or regulatory treatment, understand that the standard of reasonable care applies to the official performance of the notary.

Here is a very important point for notaries. Perhaps surprisingly, almost no notary statutes or regulations expressly state that notaries are to exercise reasonable care in the performance of their notarial functions. Thus, notary statutes and regulations do not state that, if notaries exercise reasonable care but nevertheless make mistakes causing financial injuries to other parties, the notaries will avoid liability for their notarial malpractice or negligent errors and omissions. However, numerous court decisions have confirmed that the notary is bound by the same standard as governs other business practitioners, i.e., the duty to act with reasonable care. See also the discussion of avoidance of notarial mistakes and liability in Chapter 20 and the discussion of notary bonds and insurance in Chapter 23.

21.7 The notary should, in the absence of statutory or regulatory treatment, acquire a notary seal and affix a seal impression to each notarial certificate.

A great majority of states and territories require their notaries to obtain and use official notary seals. No U.S. notary statute prohibits its notaries from acquiring and using notary seals. Unfortunately, however, several jurisdictions do not require their notaries to acquire and use seals. No jurisdiction prohibits its notaries from using seal impressions on notarial certificates.

Notaries everywhere should acquire official notary seals and should affix seal impressions for all document notarizations on all notarial certificates. This author agrees with the National Notary Association that the use of an official seal is an ethical responsibility of every notary (see the citation in the "Relevant Model Notary Law" section at the end of this chapter). Affixing of a seal to each notarial certificate increases the reliability and security of a notarization, making more difficult the forgery of a notarial certificate and making more likely the recognition of the notarization across borders in the U.S. and abroad. See the discussion of notary seals in Chapter 8 and the discussion of cross-border recognition of notarizations in Chapter 27.

21.8 The notary should, in the absence of statutory or regulatory treatment, understand and implement procedures to secure and protect the notary seal.

Some notary statutes neglect to satisfactorily provide for the security of notary seals, especially the statutes of those jurisdictions which do not even require notaries to acquire and use seals. As an important symbol of officiality and an important anti-fraud device in the notarization of documents, the notary seal should be secured in the exclusive possession and control of the notary at all times. When the seal is not in use, it should be kept under lock and key within the exclusive control of the notary. See also the discussion of notary seal security in Chapter 8, Sections 8.6, 8.7, and 8.10.

21.9 The notary should, in the absence of statutory or regulatory treatment, understand how to correct an illegible or partial seal impression on a notarial certificate.

The notary's seal impression on the notarial certificate is an important symbol of officiality and an important security feature of a document notarization. Sometimes there will be faults with the notary seal impression stamped by the notary onto the notarial certificate. The seal impression may be smudged or illegible, or only a partial seal impression may have been obtained on the certificate.

Notary statutes and regulations do not address how the notary should correct such faults during the notarial ceremony. The procedure for correcting such difficulties is explained in an earlier chapter. See the discussion of correcting faulty seal impressions in Chapter 8, Sections 8.4 and 8.5.

21.10 The notary should, in the absence of statutory or regulatory treatment, understand the name and signature requirements for signers for document notarizations.

Notary statues and regulations do not address the frequent problems surrounding name and signature inconsistencies for document signers. Statutes and regulations do not guide notaries in determining which form of a document signer's name is to be used when the names on IDs and the instrument to be notarized differ, or when signatures on those instruments either differ from the form of the signer's name selected for the notarization or are illegible. The notary should be prepared to determine the name and signature of the signer to be used for the notarization and to provide guidance to the signer about the form of the name to be signed for notarization purposes. See also the discussion of signer names and signatures in Chapter 11.

21.11 The notary should, in the absence of statutory or regulatory treatment, understand the duty to identify the document signer with reasonable certainty, not to guarantee the signer's true identity.

Notary statutes and regulations do not always explain the notary's duty to identify document signers. Although the statutes and regulations direct the notary to identify the document signer, they do not say the notary must correctly identify the document signer, thereby guaranteeing the accuracy of the identification. The common law is, instead, that notaries are legally required to take steps reasonably calculated to identify signers, without assuring the correctness of the identifications. Thus, if notaries take reasonable steps to identify signers but are deceived by skillful imposters, the notaries will not face legal liability for malpractice. See also the discussion of this legal standard of care for the notary's identification of the signer in Chapter 10, Section 10.3.

21.12 The notary should, in the absence of statutory or regulatory treatment, identify document signers by reviewing one or more reliable signer IDs.

Currently, notary statutes typically allow notaries to identify instrument signers by satisfactory evidence, including identification by personal knowledge of the notary, by a credible witness, or by review of a reliable ID document. The statutes do not generally require notaries to allow use of any of the three methods of identification, but simply describe the three methods that may be used. Notaries are not generally prohibited from using only one of the methods of identification. One state now requires its notaries to identify all signers only by the use of a reliable ID document. This author's opinion is that notaries should identify all document signers exclusively by the use of one or more reliable ID documents. See also the discussion of identification of signers in Chapter 10.

Additionally, some statutes and regulations do not fully describe what constitutes a reliable ID. Certainly, an ID should be government-issued to be reliable. But, other elements may not be clearly described. For instance, is an expired ID reliable? If so, for how long may an ID be expired before it is no longer reliable? If more than one ID is requested by the notary, must each be reliable? Must the second ID also be government-issued? See also the discussion of signer IDs in Chapter 10.

21.13 The notary should, in the absence of statutory or regulatory treatment, understand the duty to assess the document signer's mental competence and utilize a procedure reasonably calculated to do so.

Although several states and territories have adopted statutes or regulations which direct or authorize notaries to assess the mental competence of document signers, most jurisdictions have not yet done so. The statutes and regulations which do so are incomplete. They do not clearly define the mental competence standard and do not set out the steps to be taken to determine signer mental competence or to note or record the procedure. No jurisdiction prohibits its notaries from ascertaining a signer's mental competence.

Hence, the notary should consider the signer's mental capacity, as this consideration is fundamental to the legitimacy and integrity of a document notarization. This author expects that more and more U.S. notaries will be expressly authorized or directed by statutes and regulations to assess signer mental competence. See also the discussion of signer mental competence in Chapter 13.

21.14 The notary should, in the absence of statutory or regulatory treatment, understand the duty to assess the document signer's willingness and utilize a procedure reasonably calculated to do so.

Historically, in regard to acknowledgment notarizations, notaries have been required by notary statutes to assess whether signers are acting willingly. However, as to other types of document notarizations (jurats and signature witnessings), many statutes and regulations do not expressly direct or authorize notaries to assess the voluntariness of signers in executing those notarizations. Of course, no statutes or regulations forbid notaries to consider signer willingness.

Therefore, the notary should assess the willingness of the signer to execute every instrument that is to be notarized, for this factor is fundamental to the integrity and security of document notarizations. See also the discussion of assessing signer willingness in Chapter 14.

21.15 The notary should, in the absence of statutory or regulatory treatment, understand whether to perform a document notarization for a minor.

Notary statutes and regulations do not provide rules for notarizations for minors (persons under the age of majority). Those laws do not prohibit notarizing for minors, nor do laws set age limits below which signers may not obtain notarizations. Thus, notaries should use their judgment and discretion in deciding whether to notarize for a particular minor, taking into account the minor's age and other circumstances.

Under the law of contracts, a minor (being under the age of majority) is not mentally competent to make contracts to which the minor will be bound. Further, minors should be protected from the coercion or undue influence of adults, for a minor who signs a document for notarization must be acting voluntarily. Yet, some minors drive automobiles, attend college, and testify under oath in court cases. So, if a notary is inclined to notarize for a minor, the notary should subject the minor to the same notarial standards required for any adult signer. The process should include the usual assessments of identity, willingness, and mental competence.

This author would recommend for a teenage minor under certain circumstances. An 18- to 19-year-old person is basically a young adult anyway. I would be reluctant to recommend notarizing for a 13- or 14-year-old child. But, if a 15- to 17-year-old young person seemed mentally competent and acted willingly, I would be inclined to recommend notarizing for that minor. For any notarization performed for a minor, the minor's parent or guardian should be present to substantiate the need to notarize for the minor, to serve as a witness, and to sign the notary journal entry. At some point, depending on the nature of the transactional instrument to be notarized, I would recommend asking to speak privately with the minor to confirm the minor's intent to sign the document. I would recommend asking both the minor and the parent or guardian to sign and provide thumbprints in the journal entry. See also the discussion of notarizing for a minor in Chapter 13, Section 13.2.

21.16 The notary should, in the absence of statutory or regulatory treatment, not perform a document notarization for any known family member of any degree of relationship by blood, marriage, or adoption.

Few notary statutes declare that a notary is disqualified from notarizing for family members or even for the notary's spouse or significant other. However, notaries should take the ethical high road and not risk the temptation to show favoritism (and to take shortcuts) for family members, nor even to create the appearance of possible favoritism toward family. The old adage about the thickness of blood is often repeated because of its veracity. Notaries should not notarize for any known family members of any degree of relationship by blood, marriage, or adoption. Nor should a notary notarize for a significant other or domestic partner. See also the discussion of conflicts of interest and family members in Chapter 19, Section 19.11.

21.17 The notary should, in the absence of statutory or regulatory treatment, not serve as a lay witness and notary for the same document.

Notary statutes and regulations generally do not address whether a notary may serve as both a lay witness and notary for the same document. Few, if any, laws prohibit notaries from serving in both roles. However, this author is strongly opposed to notaries occupying these dual roles for the same document. See also the discussion of this topic, which is the subject of Chapter 12.

21.18 The notary should, in the absence of statutory or regulatory treatment, not serve in the dual roles as drafter, preparer, and/or reviewer of a client's document and as notary for the document notarization.

Notary statutes and regulations do not prohibit qualified professionals who draft, prepare, and/or review documents for their clients from also notarizing those same documents. Yet, these dual roles constitute conflicts of interest and should be avoided and forbidden. Just because an activity may be legal does not make it a best practice.

Many professionals in accounting, banking, financial planning, health care, law, real estate, and other fields are also notaries. Those professionals often draft, prepare, and/or review documents for their clients as part of their business activities, and some of the documents will be notarized. Notaries should not notarize the very documents they have drafted, prepared, and/or reviewed for their clients. Those professional have substantial financial interests in obtaining the notarizations of the documents they draft, prepare, and/or review because notarization helps to justify the sizable professional fees they are paid. See also the discussion of conflicts of interest resulting from the drafting, preparing, and/or reviewing by notaries of documents they notarize in Chapter 19, Section 19.12, and the discussion of notary-attorneys who notarize documents they have drafted, prepared, and/or reviewed for their clients in Chapter 25, Section 25.6.

21.19 The notary should, in the absence of statutory or regulatory treatment, acquire a notary journal and prepare and preserve a detailed journal entry for each document notarization.

Unfortunately, more than half of U.S. notary statutes and regulations do not require notaries to maintain and preserve notary journals. Indeed, most statutes and regulations do not even mention the notary journal, but no statute or regulation prohibits notaries from acquiring and using journals. Every notary should obtain a commercially published notary journal, should prepare a journal entry for each official act, and should preserve and safeguard the notary journal.

This author agrees with the National Notary Association that every notary in every U.S. jurisdiction has an ethical responsibility to maintain and preserve a notary journal (see the citation in the "Relevant Model Notary Law" section at the end of this chapter). Maintaining and safeguarding a notary journal is the most important of all of the notary best practices, and the merits of doing so are too numerous to repeat here. Many statutes do not require sufficient details to be included in the journal entry, whereas this author has suggested 13 pieces of information that should always be included. See also the discussion of notary journals in Chapter 17, especially Section 17.7.

21.20 The notary should, in the absence of statutory or regulatory treatment, request the document signer to provide a thumbprint for each notary journal entry.

Fingerprinting and thumbprinting have been used as an effective method of identifying people for more than 100 years. Only two notary statutes require the affixing of document signer thumbprints in notary records. A few jurisdictions have adopted statutes or regulations which prohibit notaries from obtaining document signer thumbprints in notary journals. The rest of the notary statutes and regulations are silent about thumbprinting.

The principal responsibility of the notary is to take steps reasonably calculated to positively identify the document signer. Unless the relevant law prohibits obtaining of thumbprints, notaries should feel comfortable in requesting document signers to provide thumbprints in notary journal entries because it is a proven method by which the notary can positively identify a document signer. Regardless of the name claimed by the signer, if the notary obtains the thumbprint of the signer in the journal entry, the signer has been positively identified. See also the discussion about thumbprinting and identification of document signers in Chapter 10, Section 10.7, and the discussion of thumbprints in the notary journal in Chapter 17, Section 17.8.

If a journal entry is accessed pursuant request, the notary should redact the thumbprint from the entry information that is revealed. See the discussion of that subject in Chapter 17, Section 17.8.

21.21 The notary should, in the absence of statutory or regulatory treatment, understand the procedure for allowing access to information in the notary journal.

Most notary statutes and regulations do not include rules for accessing information in notary journals, especially since the majority do not even require notaries to maintain and preserve such journals. A few jurisdictions may provide some assistance about this topic in their official notary handbooks. But for the most part, notaries will need to rely upon best practice standards for the process of receiving requests to access information in journal entries, of considering what factors should be taken into account in deciding whether and how to disclose information, and of providing appropriate limited access to journal entry information. See also the discussion of access to notary journal information in Chapter 17, Sections 17.8, 17.15, 17.16, and 17.17.

21.22 The notary should, in the absence of statutory or regulatory treatment, not redact information from a journal entry disclosed due to a request for access, except for a signer's thumbprint.

Notary statutes and regulations are silent on the subject of redacting information from notary journal entries when there are requests for access. If a notary receives a request for access to a journal entry and becomes suspicious about the motive of the requesting individual, the notary might think that redacting the confidential or personal information about the document signer (such as the signer's home or business address, the phone number, the email address, or the signer's signature) would make it acceptable to disclose information in the journal entry. Notary law is silent about whether a notary could decide to redact information from a journal entry before disclosing the entry to an individual who requested access. This author has advised against redacting information in the journal. If there is enough concern to warrant redacting information, there is enough concern to deny access altogether. Remember, the requesting party could always appeal the notary's refusal to disclose to the notary commissioning official, the notary oversight agency, or a court.

One exception to the general reluctance to redact information is a signer's journal thumbprint (where not prohibited by law to be collected). The notary should consult the notary commissioning official or oversight agency for guidance about redacting a thumbprint. Unless the notary is officially advised to disclose the thumbprint, this author recommends redacting it. See also the discussion of the notary journal and possible redacting of information in Chapter 17, Sections 17.8 and 17.16.

21.23 The notary should, in the absence of statutory or regulatory treatment, understand and implement procedures to preserve and safeguard the notary journal.

Again, because most notary statutes and regulations do not require notaries to maintain journals in the first place, not surprisingly they say nothing about preserving and protecting notary journals and eventually disposing of journals. Official agency notary handbooks may provide some guidance, but notary best practice standards provide the most extensive and helpful coverage of these topics. See also the discussion of preserving and safeguarding notary journals in Chapter 17, Sections 17.13 and 17.14.

21.24 The notary should, in the absence of statutory or regulatory treatment, understand the de facto notary doctrine and its possible effect after the notary commission has expired.

Every notary statute defines the term and sets the expiration of the notary's commission. The statutes and regulations, however, do not address the effect of a notary continuing to perform notarizations after the commission has expired. Although it does not happen often, there are occasions when notaries do not realize their commissions have expired, and they mistakenly perform one or more notarizations. Are such notarizations valid, or invalid? Common law decisions establish that the general rule is such notarizations are invalid, except under certain circumstances.

It should be noted that all public officials serve for specified terms in office that eventually expire or terminate at some point. There is the possibility that city and county clerks, judges, police officers, and other public officials whose terms in office have expired might continue to act as public officers without genuine authority to do so. While it is not a common occurrence, it happens, just as it sometimes happens with notaries whose commissions have expired and who continue to perform notarizations.

Incidentally, most notaries routinely renew their commissions, so sometimes if the notary has neglected to timely file for the renewal or if there is a delay in the renewal process, there may be a gap between the expiration date of the old commission and the renewal date of the renewed commission. The notary might mistakenly perform notarizations during that gap.

The notary should, however, know the expiration date of the notary's commission and should never perform a document notarization after that date, unless the notary commission has been renewed and that renewal has become effective. Performing a notarization after the commission expiration date constitutes a serious violation of law that could constitute the crime of the ex-notary impersonating a notary and performing an unauthorized act. That impropriety results in the notarial certificate containing a falsehood, namely, that the commission was in effect at the time of the notarization.

Of course, a fake notarization performed by a notary imposter is obviously and absolutely void. So, the general rule is that a notarization performed by a former notary (whose commission has expired) is also invalid. An unauthorized notarization may cause financial damages to the document signer and/or a third party who had relied on the false notarization and for which the ex-notary would be personally liable. And, of course, any notary bond or notary malpractice insurance would also have expired with the notary commission, leaving the ex-notary without a bond or insurance coverage.

In addition, consider that the parties to notarizations — the document signers and the notaries who perform them — have the commission expiration date readily in front of them at the time of the notarization because it appears in the certificate of notarization and/or the notary seal which is affixed to the certificate. All of the parties who process and/or rely upon completed notarizations — such as governmental recorders, court clerks, judges, mortgage processors, loan agents, bankers, health care administrators and practitioners, estate planners, and others — also have it readily in front of them on notarized documents. The expiration date appears in the text of the notary commission itself, which many notaries frame and hang on their walls in full view. Some jurisdictions attempt to help notaries recall their notary commission expiration dates by having the expiration dates fall upon their birthdays or by having all notary commissions expire on the same date. As the notary commission expiration dates approach, individual notaries are bombarded with advertisements for notary renewal and often bond processing services. These advertisements remind the notaries of their commission expiration dates.

However, few parties seem to pay much attention to the date of commission expiration. Making exceptions to invalidating notarizations performed by ex-notaries should garner little support. The adverse effects could have been avoided if notaries, document signers, and third parties who process or rely upon notarizations had exercised more diligence by simply paying attention to the notary commission expiration date.

But the context here can be complicated, since the main responsibility for compliance must rest with the notaries (who are public officials). The law is reluctant to put this responsibility on document signers and third parties (who are not public officials). To do so would require invalidating such faulty notarizations, a result that would penalize document signers or the parties who rely on the notarizations and not the notary (although the notary might also be subject to administrative or criminal sanctions for misconduct).

Therefore, the notary should understand a special doctrine in the law called the de facto public official rule, which may apply to an ex-notary for a brief time after the notary commission has expired, but which does not appear in notary statutes or regulations. It is a common law doctrine, created by court opinions in order to serve justice in a narrow set of cases. In order to allow for the flexibility to do what is fair and just in the small number of unusual cases in which public officials continue to act after the expiration of their terms in office, the common law developed the de facto public official doctrine. Under this well-established doctrine, the law may uphold or validate the otherwise unauthorized acts of public officers whose terms in office have expired, if the facts seem to warrant that result.

For the de facto notary doctrine to be invoked, a couple of requirements about the circumstances must be satisfied. First, the expiration of the notary's term in office must result from the passage of time, not from resignation or from suspension or dismissal due to misconduct of the notary. Second, the parties affected by the actions of the ex-notary cannot actually have known of the expiration of the notary commission. Then, with these two conditions satisfied, the law may find justification for validating the apparently official actions, especially if the ex-notary had not actually been aware of the expiration of the term of office. In other words, the law will not wish to visit upon the unknowing and innocent third parties the faulty, but unintentional, behavior of the former notary.

Of course, the question of whether the unauthorized notarization will be validated is influenced by the full circumstances of each case, especially how much time had elapsed between the commission expiration and the unauthorized notarization, and which party challenges the notarization. To state the obvious, in a contest about the validity of a notarization involving an expired notary commission, either the document signer or third party affected by the notarization will argue the notarization to be invalid, while the other party will argue that it should be upheld. If both parties objected to the notarization, there would be no contest. If the third party was unaware of the expiration of the notary's commission, if that party would be adversely affected by the notarization, and if that party challenges the notarization, there is considerable reason to invalidate the notarization. After all, the notary and the document signer should have noticed the commission's expiration, and it seems unfair to saddle the innocent third party with the faulty notarization under the circumstances. If the document signer was unaware of the commission's expiration and challenges the notarization, the likelihood would be that the notarization should be held valid because the document signer sought out the notary in order to obtain a valid notarization.

21.25 The notary should, in the absence of statutory or regulatory treatment, understand whether the notary's employer may impose restrictions when the notary is on duty for the employer.

Virtually no notary statute or regulation addresses the facets of the relationship between notary-employees and their employers. Yet, most notaries are employees. Therefore, the employment relationship is a significant one for many of the more than 4,450,000 U.S. notaries. This section and others in this chapter will consider some of the notary employment issues.

Can an employer of a notary-employee impose restrictions upon the performance of notarizations by the notary-employee? The statutes and regulations generally do not answer the question. However, a few fundamental guidelines may be applied even without the benefit of statutory or regulatory direction. First, an employer certainly has the authority to prohibit its employees who happen to be notaries from performing notarizations while on duty for the employer. This restriction is permissible because the employer may direct its employees to use company time for the employer's business purposes and to prevent its possible exposure to liability for notary misconduct.

Second, the employer has no authority to restrict or limit its notary-employee when the notary-employee is off duty. Indeed, many U.S. notaries provide notarial services both in their regular employments and at home and elsewhere when they are not engaged in their regular work. Of course, some individuals may work for more than one employer and may perform notarizations while working for one employer but not conduct notarizations when working for another employer.

Third, because the notary-employee is a commissioned public official, the notary employer may not interfere with the manner in which the notary performs notarizations. Even if the notary-employer has asked the employee to become a notary, even if the employer has paid the costs of the commissioning of the notary-employee, and even if the employer holds a notary commission (one notary may not interfere with the manner in which another notary conducts a notarization), the employer may not direct or order its notary-employee to violate notary statutes or best practices. Of course, the notary employer may, and should, encourage and support its notary-employee to obtain notary education and training and to exercise diligence and reasonable care in the performance of all notarizations. See also the discussion of the role of notary employers in Chapter 24.

Note: *Controversy About Notarizing Only for Employer's Customers.* If the employer allows its notary-employees to perform notarizations while on duty for the employer, few, if any, statutes or regulations state whether the employer may restrict notarial services to the employer's customers. In the absence of a statute or regulation addressing this point, there is a difference of opinion. One view is that the employer should be allowed to restrict notarial services performed by its notary-employee to the employer's customers. After all, the employer could prohibit the notary from providing any notarizations while on duty, although the employer may be willing to take the liability risks of allowing notarizations for its customers, but not for strangers. However, this author supports the contrary view. I believe that because the notary is a public servant, the notary employer cannot restrict the provision of notarial services only to the employer's customers. Any and all persons who seek notarizations should be reasonably accommodated and treated equally. Thus, customers of the employer should not be accorded special or preferential treatment — such as paying less notary fees than noncustomers will have to pay. If the employer does not wish to take the risk of its notary-employee notarizing for noncustomers, then the employer has the right to forbid any notarizations from being performed on company time or at the workplace.

21.26 The notary should, in the absence of statutory or regulatory treatment, understand the notary's employer may have vicarious liability for notary mistakes and wrongdoing.

Few notary statutes or regulations impose or even address employer liability for notary misconduct committed by its notary-employee while in the scope of the employment. However, just about everywhere in the U.S., under the common law of agency, employers are likely to share notary malpractice liability with their notary-employees.

Vicarious liability is legal liability of an employer for the mistakes and wrongdoing (possibly including intentional misconduct) of its employee which occur in the scope of the employment. This type of liability has been part of the common law for more than 300 years in order to provide a source of compensation to a party injured by a business enterprise (as most employers have assets or insurance, whereas many employees will have little or no assets or insurance). This liability is entirely derivative. It is a kind of no-fault liability of the employer resulting solely because its employee did something wrong that injured a third party. Thus, the employer need not have done anything wrong to be liable. Liability is simply a risk or cost of doing business.

Employers of notaries face vicarious liability for the errors, omissions, and other possible wrongdoing of their notary-employees. In some jurisdictions, this liability is described, and perhaps somewhat limited, by notary statutes, but most jurisdictions have no statutes on this subject. Nevertheless, the common law will undoubtedly impose vicarious accountability on employers if their notary-employees engage in negligence or possibly other misconduct which injures third parties.

Notaries, as public officials and responsible adults, should be aware of this consequence of what they do. In addition to the usual reasons why a notary-employee should act with reasonable care, diligence, and prudence, the notary-employee should do so in order to protect the notary employer from vicarious liability. See also the discussions of avoidance of notary liability in Chapter 20, of notary bonds and insurance in Chapter 23, and of the role of employers of notaries in Chapter 24.

21.27 The notary should, in the absence of statutory or regulatory treatment, understand the notary cannot avoid liability for wrongdoing because the notary employer ordered the faulty performance.

Notary statutes and regulations generally do not address the subject of an employer directing its notary-employee to engage in wrongdoing. It is not uncommon for employers of notaries to erroneously think they have authority to tell their notary-employees how to perform notarial functions. Unfortunately, notary-employees too often allow employers to direct them in performing notarizations, and, too often, notary employers direct notaries to take improper shortcuts or to otherwise violate notary law and best practices. Notary statutes and regulations do not expressly answer the question whether errant notaries will be relieved from accountability because they obeyed improper orders from their employers. Some notaries believe they should have such a defense. But, they do not. Notaries will have liability under such circumstances, (and so will their employers). Notary-employees should refuse to obey orders to violate notary law and best practices issued by their employers or supervisors.

Notary ethics standards and best practices make clear that a notary-employee has the duty to obey the law rather than directives from any other party, including an employer or supervisor. See also the discussions of avoidance of notary liability in Chapter 20, of notary bonds and insurance in Chapter 23, and of the role of employers of notaries in Chapter 24.

21.28 The notary should, in the absence of statutory or regulatory treatment, assure financial responsibility for financial injuries caused by notary mistakes and wrongdoing.

Although many U.S. jurisdictions statutorily require their notaries to acquire notary bonds, the highest bond amount is currently set at only $25,000 — a level of coverage that may be woefully insufficient. Other jurisdictions have no statutory notary bond requirement. Furthermore, no U.S. jurisdiction requires its notaries to carry any liability or malpractice insurance. Thus, although the law holds notaries fully liable for financial injuries caused by their faulty notarial performance, no state or territory statutorily mandates that its notaries assure adequate financial responsibility for notary mistakes and misconduct. As public officials and responsible adults, notaries should assure that they have a sufficient level of assets, a bond, and/or liability insurance to protect the public against their mistakes and misconduct which cause financial injuries. See also the discussion of notary ethics and financial responsibility in Chapter 19, Section 19.16, and of notary bonds and insurance in Chapter 23.

21.29 The notary should, in the absence of statutory or regulatory treatment, understand appropriate procedures to be utilized if the notary desires to charge fees for notarial services.

Although many U.S. jurisdictions set the maximum fees notaries may charge for various notarial services, many other jurisdictions do not regulate maximum fees. And, few notary statutes or regulations cover the related issues of nondiscriminatory charging of fees, of reasonable fee levels, of satisfactory disclosure of fees, of fee agreements with customers and employers, and of adequate recording of payment of notary fees. Those matters should be considered by notaries and appropriately handled as suggested later in this book. See also the discussion of notary fees and the related issues in Chapter 28.

21.30 The notary should, in the absence of statutory or regulatory treatment, not share notarial fees with the notary's employer when the notary is on duty for the employer.

Almost no statutes address concerns relating to sharing of fees charged for services provided by a notary-employee. Can the employer of the notary-employee retain the fees or at least share them with the notary-employee? In reality, in certain kinds of enterprises (such as copy shops, office supply stores, mailing centers, currency exchanges, check cashing services, and so on) notary services are advertised and provided as one of several business services, and the notary fees are often retained by these enterprises. This arrangement is with the agreement or acquiescence of the notary-employees. But, is it proper?

Note: *Difference of Opinion on Notary Fee Retention and Sharing by Employers.* In the absence of a statute or regulation on the subject, there are two views. Some say that employers should be allowed to retain all or part of the notary fees because the notary service is one of the kinds of services provided by the business, so the business should be entitled to collect or share these fees. The notary-employees know that part of their job for the wages they are paid is to serve as notaries. The contrary view, and the one shared by this author, is that an employer should not assert a right to share in notarial fees for notarizations performed by a notary-employee while on duty, and a notary-employee should resist any employer effort to the contrary. The principal reason is that the notary-employee is the commissioned public official, not the notary employer. A private party should not be collecting the fees for an official government service. Curiously, in the situation in which the notary fees are kept by the employer, the notary still faces the prospect of full personal liability for notarial mistakes and wrongdoing that result in financial injuries. Moreover, an employer should be wary about sharing in notary fees, for such sharing will almost certainly contribute to the notary employer also sharing liability for mistakes and wrongdoing of the notary-employee. See also the discussions of the role of employers of notaries and fee issues in Chapter 24, Section 24.6, and of notary fees in Chapter 28. ■

***RELEVANT MODEL NOTARY LAW**

Each notary should read, study, and abide by the notary statute and regulations, if any, of his or her commissioning state or territory.

"To uphold the trust placed in me by the public I serve;

To maintain a professional manner suitable to the office I hold ...

To always be satisfied that the individual appearing before me understands the contents of the document to be executed or oath to be administered before proceeding;

To always satisfy myself as to the identity of the individual appearing before me in my capacity as Notary Public;

To not betray the confidence of any individual appearing before me;

To never perform any notarial act in which I am a party in interest or from which I stand to benefit;

To never divulge the contents of any document nor the facts of execution of that document without proper authority;

To keep informed of the law regarding the duties and powers of the office of Notary Public in my jurisdiction and not compromise that law;

To not use the office of Notary Public as a means of financial gain, for myself or others, in any other business or profession;

To exercise extreme care to insure that the notarial seal. stamp and records are kept in a safe place and are not used by any other person;

To always conduct myself and perform my duties in a manner which will bring credit to myself, my office and the [American] Society [of Notaries]." *Responsibility Code of Ethics* (1980).

"The Notary shall, as a government officer and public servant, serve all of the public in an honest, fair and unbiased manner." *Notary Public Code of Professional Responsibility,* Guiding Principle I (1998).

"The Notary shall act as an impartial witness and not profit or gain from any document or transaction requiring a notarial act, apart from the fee allowed by statute." *Notary Public Code of Professional Responsibility,* Guiding Principle II (1998).

"The Notary shall give precedence to the rules of law over the dictates or expectations of any person or entity." *Notary Public Code of Professional Responsibility,* Guiding Principle V (1998).

"The Notary shall affix a seal on every notarized document and not allow this universally recognized symbol of office to be used by another or in an endorsement or promotion." *Notary Public Code of Professional Responsibility,* Guiding Principle VII (1998).

"The Notary shall record every notarial act in a bound journal or other secure recording device and safeguard it as an important public record." *Notary Public Code of Professional Responsibility,* Guiding Principle VIII (1998).

"The Notary shall respect the privacy of each signer and not divulge or use personal or proprietary information disclosed during execution of a notarial act for other than an official purpose." *Notary Public Code of Professional Responsibility,* Guiding Principle IX (1998).

"Purposes. This [Act] shall be construed and applied to advance its underlying purposes, which are: (1) to promote, serve, and protect the public interest;

(2) to simplify, clarify, and modernize the law governing notaries;

(3) to foster ethical conduct among notaries;

(4) to enhance cross-border recognition of notarial acts ..." *Model Notary Act,* Section 1-2 (2010).

"Bond. (a) A notary commission shall not [become effective / be issued] until an oath of office and [25,000] dollar bond have been filed with the [designated office]. ..." *Model Notary Act,* Section 3-3 (2010).

"Disqualifications. (a) A notary is disqualified from performing a notarial act if the notary: (1) is a party to or named in the document that is to be notarized;

(2) will receive as a direct or indirect result any commission, fee, advantage, right, title, interest, cash, property, or other consideration exceeding in value the fees specified in Section 6-2 of this [Act];

(3) is a spouse, domestic partner, ancestor, descendant, or sibling of the principal, including in-law, step, and half relatives; or

(4) is an attorney, who has prepared, explained, or recommended to the principal the document that is to be notarized. ..." *Model Notary Act,* Section 5-5 (2010).

"Maintaining Journal of Notarial Acts. (a) A notary shall keep, maintain, protect, and provide for lawful inspection a chronological journal of notarial acts that is either: (1) a permanently bound book with numbered pages; or (2) an electronic journal of notarial acts as described in Section 20-2 of this [Act]. ..." *Model Notary Act,* Section 7-1 (2010).

"Journal Entries. (a) For every notarial act, the notary shall record in the journal at the time of notarization at least the following: ... [(7) the thumbprint of each principal [signer] and witness, or, in the case of an electronic journal, the thumbprint or other recognized biometric identifier, in accordance with Section 20-2(4) of this [Act] ..." *Model Notary Act,* Section 7-2 (2010).

"Inspection and Copying of Journal. ... (b) If the notary has a reasonable and explainable belief that a person bears a criminal or harmful intent in requesting information from the notary's journal, the notary may deny access to any entry or entries. ..." *Model Notary Act,* Section 7-3 (2010).

"Official Seal. (a) In notarizing a paper document, a notary public shall affix an official seal on the notarial certificate at the time the notarial act is performed. ..." *Model Notary Act,* Section 8-2 (2010).

"Correcting Notarial Certificates. A notary public may correct an error or omission made by that notary in a notarial certificate if: (1) the original certificate and document are returned to the notary;

(2) the notary verifies the error by reference to the pertinent journal entry, the document itself, or to other determinative written evidence;

(3) the notary legibly corrects the certificate and initials and dates the correction in ink, or replaces the original certificate with a correct certificate; and

(4) the notary appends to the pertinent journal entry a notation regarding the nature and date of the correction." *Model Notary Act,* Section 9-3 (2010).

"Liability of Notary, Surety, and Employer. (a) A notary is liable to any person for all damages proximately caused that person by the notary's negligence, intentional violation of law, or official misconduct in relation to a notarization.

(b) A surety for a notary's bond is liable to any person for damages proximately caused that person by the notary's negligence, intentional violation of law or official misconduct in relation to a notarization during the bond term, but this liability may not exceed the dollar amount of the bond or of any remaining bond funds that have not been disbursed to other claimants. Regardless of the number of claimants against the bond or the number of notarial acts cited in the claims, a surety's aggregate liability shall not exceed the dollar amount of the bond.

(c) An employer of a notary is liable to any person for all damages proximately caused that person by the notary's negligence, intentional violation of law, or official misconduct in performing a notarization during the course of employment, if the employer directed, expected, encouraged, approved, or tolerated the notary's negligence, violation of law, or official misconduct either in the particular transaction or, impliedly, by the employer's previous action in at least one similar transaction involving any notary employed by the employer.

(d) An employer of a notary is liable to the notary for all damages recovered from the notary as a result of any violation of law by the notary that was coerced by threat of the employer, if the threat, such as of demotion or dismissal, was made in reference to the particular notarization or, impliedly, by the employer's previous action in at least one similar transaction involving any notary employed by the employer. In addition, the employer is liable to the notary for damages caused the notary by demotion, dismissal, or other action resulting from the notary's refusal to engage in a violation of law or official misconduct. ..." *Model Notary Act,* Section 13-1 (2010).

"Authority To Refuse To Perform Notarial Act. (a) A notarial officer may refuse to perform a notarial act if the officer is not satisfied that: (1) the individual executing the record is competent or has the capacity to execute the record; or (2) the individual's signature is knowingly and voluntarily made. ..." *Revised Uniform Law on Notarial Acts,* Section 8 (2010).

"Official stamp. The official stamp of a notary public must: (1) include the notary public's name, jurisdiction, [commission expiration date,] and other information required by the [commissioning officer or agency]; and

(2) be capable of being copied together with the record to which it is affixed or attached or with which it is logically associated." *Revised Uniform Law on Notarial Acts,* Section 17 (2010).

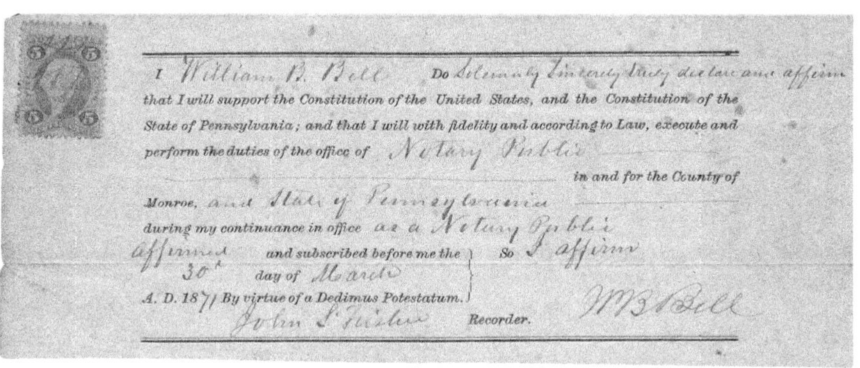

I William B. Bell Do Solemnly Sincerely truly declare and affirm that I will support the Constitution of the United States, and the Constitution of the State of Pennsylvania; and that I will with fidelity and according to Law, execute and perform the duties of the office of Notary Public in and for the County of Monroe, and State of Pennsylvania during my continuance in office as a Notary Public

affirmed and subscribed before me the 30th day of March A. D. 1871 By virtue of a Dedimus Potestatum.

So I affirm

John S. Fisher Recorder.

W B Bell

Rare, 1871, Pennsylvania paper oath of office form for the post of notary public executed by William Bell, who handwrote that he did "solemnly sincerely truly declare and affirm" he would execute his duties with fidelity according to the law. Customarily, a newly appointed notary is required to file an oath of office in the county where the notary resides and to pay a filing fee — in this instance, evidenced by the 5-cent stamp appearing in the margin of the form.

Chapter

22

Notary Discipline and Commission Expiration and Renewal

STANDARDS SUMMARY

22.1 The notary should understand the disciplinary authority and process of the state or territorial notary oversight agency.

22.2 The notary should understand the disciplinary sanctions which may be imposed for notarial misconduct and their consequences.

22.3 The notary should self-report material mistakes and misconduct to the commissioning official or notary oversight agency and temporarily cease notarial functions until approved.

22.4 The notary should report the material mistakes and misconduct of other notaries to the commissioning official or notary oversight agency.

22.5 The notary should report any material change in status to the commissioning official or notary oversight agency and temporarily cease notarial functions until approved.

22.6 The notary should be aware of the commission expiration date and record the commission expiration date on each notarial certificate.

22.7 The notary should, after the expiration of the notary commission, not perform notarizations or other notarial functions, except in connection with the maintenance and accessing of the notary journal.

22.8 The notary should, if intending to renew the notary commission, timely apply for renewal in order to avoid a lapse in the notary commission.

22.9 The notary should, prior to completion of each notarial ceremony, proofread the notary commission expiration date in the notarial certificate.

STANDARDS EXPLANATIONS

This chapter is about the operation of the office of the state or territorial commissioning official or notary oversight agency and the interaction of the notary with that office. Most often, that agency is the office of the secretary of state, but in some places it may be the office of the governor, the office of the lieutenant governor, or another agency. The notary should be generally familiar with the agency in order to obtain assistance and information when needed by the notary and in order to deal appropriately with the agency if there should be concerns or complaints directed to the notary about possible material mistakes or misconduct. With a notary population of more than 4,450,000 individuals, there will be notaries who will need assistance, will have questions, and will have committed serious mistakes and misconduct.

22.1 The notary should understand the disciplinary authority and process of the state or territorial notary oversight agency.

Every state and territory has a governmental agency charged with the responsibility to commission notaries and oversee their functioning, including the authority to investigate alleged notary misconduct and to discipline wayward notaries. The jurisdictions vary somewhat in their notary disciplinary systems, but their fundamental features are fairly similar. The process for considering complaints against notaries includes an investigative process and, if it is determined there are grounds to go forward, a hearing conducted before a hearing officer or administrative law judge. The hearing provides the opportunity for the notary to participate, to be represented by counsel, to present evidence and question witnesses, and to appeal an adverse finding. The agency has the authority to impose sanctions against notaries, as more fully described in the next section.

22.2 The notary should understand the disciplinary sanctions which may be imposed for notarial misconduct and their consequences.

If in the course of the disciplinary process, notaries are found to have committed misconduct, the oversight agency has authority to impose a range of sanctions. Those sanctions typically include a formal reprimand, prescribed notary education or re-education, suspension or revocation of the notary commission, payment of the costs of the disciplinary procedure, and/or a fine. Suspension or termination of the notary commission is a most serious matter. The notary whose commission is suspended must immediately cease to perform notarizations and await reinstatement of the commission. If the commission has been terminated, the individual named in the commission is no longer a notary and must immediately cease to perform notarizations.

Further, if the commission has been suspended or terminated, the reason or reasons for the action may well involve serious misconduct, possibly including violations of civil and criminal law and the potential for liabilities in those venues. Typically, notary misconduct must have been fairly serious in order to result in such a consequence as suspension or termination of the notary commission. Usually, it involves material negligence, recklessness, or intentional wrongdoing. Although simple, unintentional errors or omissions should not be committed by notaries, those faults do not ordinarily result in substantial notary sanctions.

However, every adverse finding against a notary is serious because it creates a public record which the notary will have to disclose if the notary holds or seeks other public or professional positions, commissions, or licenses. Thus, for example, if a notary is disciplined and is also a licensed attorney, the notary-attorney is required to inform the bar licensing agency about the notary discipline. If the notary violation is serious and shows dishonesty and unprofessional conduct by the notary-attorney, the individual's law license could be in jeopardy. The same scenario could play out if the disciplined notary is also licensed as a stockbroker, certified public accountant, doctor, real estate broker, or other business professional.

Additionally, a record of discipline as a notary public may prevent the individual sanctioned from obtaining a bond in the future as a notary or otherwise. Because the record of notary discipline is a matter of public record, the notary misconduct may become known in other contexts as well. Thus, the notary should recognize the serious risks involved if he or she engages in notarial wrongdoing.

22.3 The notary should self-report material mistakes and misconduct to the commissioning official or notary oversight agency and temporarily cease notarial functions until approved.

As a business professional and public official, the notary public has the ethical responsibility to self-report misconduct of consequence (negligent material errors or omissions and any intentional misconduct). This self-reporting should be promptly directed in writing to the commissioning official or notary oversight agency, and if criminal conduct may be involved, to the police agency with jurisdiction in the geographic area where the notary misconduct occurred. In conjunction with self-reporting, the notary should immediately cease serving as a notary public and await action from the notary agency. Of course, notary misconduct is a ground for possible notary discipline, and self-reporting should serve as a mitigating circumstance if the agency determines the notary engaged in misconduct that warrants some kind of disciplinary sanction. See also the discussion of notary ethics in Chapter 19.

22.4 The notary should report the material mistakes and misconduct of other notaries to the commissioning official or notary oversight agency.

There are a number of reasons why notaries should report the material mistakes and misconduct of fellow notaries, besides the fact that such reporting is simply the right thing to do. First, people in the same fields of service are the ones most likely and most able to detect the misconduct of their fellow service providers. So too with notaries and fellow notaries who violate notary law. Second, notaries, as a group, benefit if neglectful and wrongdoing notaries are identified, appropriately sanctioned, and rehabilitated. All notaries should recognize this prospect. Third, as public officials and business professionals, notaries have an ethical responsibility to report notary misconduct whenever and wherever it is detected. See also the discussion of notary ethics in Chapter 19.

22.5 The notary should report any material change in status to the commissioning official or notary oversight agency and temporarily cease notarial functions until approved.

Under some notary statutes, certain specified changes in the notary's circumstances — such as a change of address, a change of name, a conviction for a felony, or payment on a claim reducing the mandatory notary bond amount — will cause the automatic suspension or termination of the notary commission. Regardless of whether there are statutory provisions about changed circumstances, the notary, as a business professional and public official, has an ethical responsibility to keep his or her official record current and accurate. Thus, the notary should self-report any important changes in his or her circumstances to the governmental notary oversight agency so that it may consider the changes for possible administrative action. The notary whose commission is suspended or terminated and the notary who self-reports changed circumstances should immediately cease to perform notarial functions and await reinstatement or approval from the oversight agency before again undertaking official notarial functioning. If the notary is unsure whether the changed circumstance are such that the notary should not perform notarizations, the notary can inquire with the agency before performing further notarizations.

22.6 The notary should be aware of the commission expiration date and record the commission expiration date on each notarial certificate.

Notary commissions are issued for exact time periods. A notary is authorized to perform notarial acts only during the prescribed time she or he is commissioned. Immediately upon the expiration of the commission, the notary's authority to perform notarizations ceases. Yet, sometimes a notary will not recall or notice the date the commission expires and will innocently continue to perform notarizations. Rarely, a notary may knowingly continue to perform notarial acts after the commission has expired.

Serious consequences for the notary as well as document signers and third parties can result if a notary continues to perform document notarizations without lawful authority. Notarizing without authority constitutes violations of both civil and criminal law, for which the notary could be sued by private individuals who suffer financial injuries and/or be sanctioned by the government. The notary could also be disciplined by the governmental notary oversight agency. As a general rule, notarizations performed after the notary's commission has expired are invalid, so the underlying business and government documents and transactions may be invalidated as well (although there is one exception under the De Facto Notary Doctrine, discussed in the next section).

The notary should always know the notary's commission expiration date. That bit of information tells the individual named in the commission during what period of time she or he holds the post of notary public and, thereby, is authorized to perform notarizations. The notary commission expiration date is well publicized for the notary. That date appears on the commission document itself (which many notaries frame and hang on their home or office walls), and the commission expiration date usually appears as part of the text of the notary seal. In some jurisdictions, the commission expiration date coincides with the birthdate of the notary, which should help to remind the notary of the expiration. It is the responsibility of the notary to be aware of the expiration date and to cease performing notarizations when the commission expires (if the commission has not been renewed to provide for an uninterrupted continuation of commissioning). Generally, neither the commissioning official nor the notary oversight agency takes steps to advise the notary of the commission expiration and to cease notarial functioning.

The notary should record the notary commission expiration date in the notarial certificate for each document notarization. After all, the notarial certificate certifies the facts supporting the notarization, and a key fact is the authority of the notary to perform the notarization (as shown by the commission expiration date). In the notarial certificate, the commission expiration date could either be recorded by the notary as part of the notary seal impression affixed to the certificate, or if the expiration date is not part of the notary seal, then the notary should write, print, or type the commission expiration date onto the certificate.

22.7 The notary should, after the expiration of the notary commission, not perform notarizations or other notarial functions, except in connection with the maintenance and accessing of the notary journal.

When the notary commission expires, the individual named in that commission immediately ceases to be a notary and loses the authority to perform notarizations. However, even after the notary commission expires, there are a couple of lingering responsibilities of the former notary. The former notary has the duty to properly dispose of the notary seal and protect the notary journal. This duty arises in part from the concern to prevent the seal and journal from falling into the hands of a wrongdoer who might misuse those tools to commit fraud.

Some jurisdictions have statutes which direct the former notary to secure and/or safely dispose of the seal and to preserve and protect the notary journal (perhaps by transmitting the journal to the commissioning official or notary oversight agency or by retaining and safeguarding the journal). Unfortunately, many jurisdictions' notary statutes do not address these matters. In the absence of express statutory rules, the former notary should deface, disable, and destroy the seal so that it cannot be misused to perform falsified notarizations. And, the former notary should preserve and safeguard the notary journal, which raises the other lingering area of responsibility for the former notary — namely, to consider and fulfill requests for access to information contained in the notary journal. See also the discussion of notary seals in Chapter 8 and the discussion of notary journals in Chapter 17.

Note: *De Facto Notary Doctrine.* Government officials, whose authority to act has expired without their realizing it, sometimes will continue to act as government officers, and the law will sometimes uphold what they have done because it seems like the fair thing to do. Similarly, if a notary accidentally and unintentionally performs a document notarization after the notary commission has expired, and if there is a challenge to the validity of the notarization, sometimes under the common law De Facto Notary Doctrine, the notarization will be upheld. The reason for this unusual result is basic fairness and justice. A court will assess the impact on the innocent parties — the innocent document signer and any innocent third party relying on the notarization, who were apparently unaware of the expiration of the notary commission. If the equities seem to favor upholding the notarization, the court will do so. See also the discussion of the De Facto Notary Doctrine in Chapter 21.

22.8 The notary should, if intending to renew the notary commission, timely apply for renewal in order to avoid a lapse in the notary commission.

Some notaries decide not to renew their commissions (and then change their minds) or procrastinate in renewing them. As a result, their commissions expire, and those individuals lose both their status as notaries and their authority to perform notarizations. Depending upon the length of the lapse in the commission and the jurisdiction in which the lapse occurs, a notary who has not timely renewed the notary commission may be able to "renew" the commission, or instead may be required to apply as a new notary applicant (possibly with the need to retake notary education programs and to be re-examined).

In the meantime, during the period of the commission's lapse, the former notary has no authority to perform notarizations. Therefore, the responsible former notary should not perform notarizations during the time of the lapse. Indeed, if the individual with a lapsed notary commission were to perform notarizations, there would be serious violations of the civil and criminal law — such as impersonation of a notary, unlawful use of a notary seal, and so forth. The "notarizations" performed during the lapse would be invalid, and the notary could face civil liability for damages if a document signer or other party suffered financial injury as a result of an invalid notarization. See also the discussion of notary liability issues in Chapter 20.

22.9 The notary should, prior to completion of each notarial ceremony, proofread the notary commission expiration date in the notarial certificate.

Before a document notarization ceremony is completed, the notary should re-examine the commission expiration date set out in the notarial certificate. By doing so before each notarization is finished, the notary will either confirm the authority to perform the notarization or discover the commission has expired in sufficient time to discontinue and void the not yet complete notarization. If the commission expiration date was incorrectly recorded on the certificate, the mistake should be corrected. ■

***RELEVANT MODEL NOTARY LAW**

Each notary should read, study, and abide by the notary statute and regulations, if any, of her or his commissioning state or territory.

"The Notary shall not execute a false or incomplete certificate, nor be involved with any document or transaction that is false, deceptive or fraudulent." *Notary Public Code of Professional Responsibility,* Guiding Principle IV (1998).

"Jurisdiction And Term. A person commissioned as a notary may perform notarial acts in any part of this [State] for a term of [4] years, unless the commission is earlier revoked under Section 13-3 or resigned under Section 12-3." *Model Notary Act,* Section 12-3 (2010).

"Bond. ... (c) If a notary bond has been exhausted by claims paid out by the surety, the [commissioning official] shall suspend the notary's commission until: (1) a new bond is obtained by the notary; and (2) the notary's fitness to serve the remainder of the commission term is determined by the [commissioning official]." *Model Notary Act,* Section 3-3 (2010).

"Commissioning Documents. Upon issuing a notary commission, the [commissioning official] shall provide to the notary: (1) a commission document stating the commission serial number and starting and ending dates ..." *Model Notary Act,* Section 3-4 (2010).

"Recommissioning. A current or former notary applying for a new notary commission shall submit a new completed application and comply anew with all of the provisions of Chapters 3 and 4." *Model Notary Act,* Section 3-5 (2010).

"Image Of Official Seal. (a) Near the notary's official signature on each paper notarial certificate, the notary shall affix a sharp, legible, permanent, and photographically reproducible image of the official seal that shall include the following elements: ... (3) the words 'Notary Public' and '[State] of [name of jurisdiction]' and 'My commission expires (commission expiration date)' ..." *Model Notary Act,* Section 8-3 (2010).

"Commission As Notary Public ... (d) ... A notary public may perform notarial acts in this state only during the period that a valid assurance [bond] is on file with the [commissioning officer or agency].

[(e)] On compliance with this section, the [commissioning officer or agency] shall issue a commission as a notary public to an applicant [for a term of [ ] years]. ..." *Revised Uniform Law on Notarial Acts,* Section 21 (2010).

"Grounds To Deny, Refuse To Renew, Revoke, Suspend, Or Condition Commission Of Notary Public. (a) The [commissioning officer or agency] may deny, reuse to renew, revoke, suspend, or impose a condition on a commission as notary public for any act or omission that demonstrates the individual lacks the honesty, integrity, competence, or reliability to act as a notary public, including: (1) failure to comply with this [act]; (2) a fraudulent, dishonest, or deceitful misstatement or omission in the application for a commission as a notary public submitted to the [commissioning officer or agency]; (3) a conviction of the applicant or notary public of any felony or a crime involving fraud, dishonesty, or deceit; (4) a finding against, or admission of liability by, the applicant or notary public in any legal proceeding or disciplinary action based on the applicant's or notary's fraud, dishonesty, or deceit; (5) failure by the notary public to discharge any duty required of a notary public, whether by this [act], rules of the [commissioning officer or agency], or any federal or state law; (6) use of false or misleading advertising or representation by the notary public representing that the notary has a duty, right, or privilege that the notary does not have; (7) violation by the notary public of a rule of the [commissioning officer or agency] regarding a notary public; [or] (8) denial, refusal to renew, revocation, suspension, or conditioning of a notary public commission in another state[;or] [(9) failure of the notary public to maintain an assurance [bond] as provided in section 21(d) ...

(c) The authority of the [commissioning officer or agency] to deny, refuse to renew, suspend, revoke, or impose conditions on a commission as a notary public does not prevent a person from seeking and obtaining other criminal or civil remedies provided by law." *Revised Uniform Law on Notarial Acts,* Section 23 (2010).

AD. BOUDOUSQUIE,
NOTARY PUBLIC.
CITIZENS' BANK
OF LOUISIANA.

New Orleans, May 22nd 1858

To R. B. Hubbard

Please to take Notice, That a Note drawn by the New Orleans Jackson & Great Northern Railroad Co to the order of, and endorsed by Wm. S. Charles Treasurer

for the sum of $ 500.00.
dated January 19th 1858
payable Four months after date
was this day **Protested,** by me for non payment (the same having been first legally demanded and refused) and the Holders look to you for payment as Endorser thereof.

I am,
your obedient Servant,

A. Boudousquie
NOTARY PUBLIC.

1858, notarial protest of a bank note on a paper form, bearing an early notary stamp for AD. Boudousquie, of Citizens' Bank of Louisiana. Notice that the old notary stamp did not include a serial or commission number or a commission expiration date.

Chapter

23

Notary Bonds and Liability Insurance

STANDARDS SUMMARY

23.1 The notary should understand the advantages and disadvantages of notary bonds.

23.2 The notary should acquire a bond, if required by law, and maintain the bond in good standing during the term of the notary commission.

23.3 The notary should understand the advantages and disadvantages of notary liability insurance.

23.4 The notary should acquire liability insurance in an amount sufficient to protect against negligent notarial performance.

23.5 The notary should promptly report notary mistakes or misconduct to notary bond and insurance companies.

23.6 The notary should cooperate with any investigation of alleged notarial mistakes or misconduct undertaken by bond and insurance companies.

STANDARDS EXPLANATIONS

Since at least the 1800s, many states and territories have required their notaries to be bonded. Today, more U.S. jurisdictions than not require notary bonds. In addition, in modern times, notary liability insurance, or what is called errors and omissions (E&O) insurance, is available for purchase by notaries everywhere in the U.S.

Since a notary is a governmental officer and public servant, the notary has an ethical responsibility to the public to assure adequate financial responsibility to compensate for injuries and liabilities caused by the notary. While the notary's personal assets are available and at risk to pay for financial damages caused by the notary, most notaries do not have enough personal assets to adequately provide a fund for recovery of damages by injured parties. Most notaries should not wish to put their own assets at risk. Thus, notaries should consider whether to obtain notary bonds and/or notary malpractice insurance. See also the discussions of notary ethics in Chapter 19 and of notary liability issues in Chapter 20.

23.1 The notary should understand the advantages and disadvantages of notary bonds.

Many states and territories require their notaries to obtain notary bonds in modest amounts as a condition of being granted notary commissions, while some jurisdictions do not require notary bonding at all. Presently, the coverage limits of the required notary bonds range from just $500 to $25,000, with most jurisdictions setting their required bond amounts between $5,000 and $15,000. Of course, notaries everywhere can voluntarily purchase notary bonds at coverage limits of their choice.

A notary bond is issued by a surety company to cover breaches in the performance of the official acts of a notary. The notary pays a premium to a surety company to purchase the bond for the term of the notary commission. A notary bond will cover both intentional wrongdoing and negligent errors and omissions that result in financial injury to document signers or third parties with interests in notarized instruments. In contrast, liability insurance covers only negligent acts and omissions of the notary. Liability insurance does not cover intentional wrongdoing. Thus, for example, notary fraud and theft by the notary would be covered by a notary bond, but not by notary liability insurance.

The principal purpose of a notary bond is to protect both document signers and third parties affected by notarized documents in the event the signers or third parties suffer financial injuries as the result of a faulty notarization performed by a notary covered by the bond. Importantly, the injured party can recover damages in an amount not to exceed the face value of the bond, usually an amount between $5,000 and $15,000. If the surety company pays on a claim filed against the notary's bond, the notary is required to reimburse the surety company to the extent it has paid. To illustrate, if a claimant receives $10,000 from a surety company due to a claim against a notary bonded by the surety, the notary must repay the $10,000 to the surety company. Thus, a notary bond does not operate like liability insurance, which does not require the covered notary to repay an amount paid by the insurance company on a claim against the covered notary.

In a couple of ways, notary bonds benefit notaries who are covered by the bonds. First, notary bonds assist the image of notaries. When a notary is "bonded," the notary benefits from the general view that individuals who are bonded are more diligent and trustworthy. And certainly, the public image is due in part to the general knowledge that some amount of financial accountability is guaranteed by the notary bond, although the general public is not well-informed about the face value of notary bonds. Second, in cases involving small claims for damages, payment of the claims under notary bonds may be sufficient to conclude the cases, without the need for protracted and expensive litigations. To emphasize the important point already made, if the surety company settles a small claim against the bonded notary, the notary will have to repay the bond company. Thus, bonds are intended to protect third parties up to the coverage limits of the bonds, but not really to protect notaries.

It must be emphasized that the small coverage limits for required notary bonds is woefully inadequate in many cases. After all, many faulty notarizations result in claims for more than $5,000 to $15,000. This fact is the main reason so many jurisdictions do not require notary bonding. This author has been consulted as a notary expert on numerous cases involving claims for $100,000 or more.

When a notary bond is purchased, it covers claims against the performance of the notary for the term of the notary commission, up to the cumulative maximum amount of the bond. For instance, if a notary has a $15,000 bond and the surety company pays $10,000 on a claim against the notary, only $5,000 in coverage remains. After the surety company pays on claims, the notary is required to repay those amounts. Depending on the jurisdiction, if at any time during the term of the notary commission, the bond coverage amount has been reduced below the statutorily mandated level or has been exhausted and not repaid, the bond may be canceled and the notary commission suspended or terminated. If that were to happen, and if the notary wished to continue as a notary public, the notary would have to obtain a new bond, seek reinstatement, or reapply for a new notary commission.

If a claim is filed against a notary for conduct that occurred during the time covered by the bond, the surety company will investigate the circumstances to determine whether it appears there are grounds to believe the notary had acted improperly. The notary is contractually obligated to cooperate with the bond company in its investigation. The surety or bond company defends the bond, not the notary. When the surety company concludes that a claim is without merit, it is supposed to defend against the claim. But, because of the low bond limits that are involved, the bond companies will typically pay on claims that have merit because the cost of defending the bond would far exceed paying the bond limit and being relieved of its bond obligation. Besides, the bond company has an incentive to settle claims efficiently because the bond company enjoys the right of reimbursement from the bonded notary.

Notaries should self-report any errors and omissions and other misconduct they commit to both their surety companies and state or territorial commissioning officials or notary oversight agencies. Some jurisdictions require claims against notary bonds to be reported by the bond companies to the state or territorial agency which issues notary commissions and oversees the performance of notaries. Those claims will be reviewed by the agency to determine whether to discipline the notary for misconduct or to reinstate, renew, or recommission an individual as a notary public.

23.2 The notary should acquire a bond, if required by law, and maintain the bond in good standing during the term of the notary commission.

Notaries have full and unlimited personal liability for notarial mistakes and misconduct that cause financial injuries to document signers and other parties. In addition, if the notary engages in intentional wrongdoing, the notary may have liability for punitive damages to punish the knowing misconduct.

Notaries must follow the law requiring the purchase of notary bonds in many jurisdictions. In fact, notaries will not be granted a commission unless they have acquired the statutorily mandated bond. Thereafter, as explained in the section above, notaries must keep their bonds in good standing by repaying amounts paid out by surety companies to claimants.

In the other states and territories, the purchase of bonds by notaries is optional. In those bond-optional jurisdictions, in the opinion of this author, notary bonds should be purchased to protect third parties against intentional wrongdoing (such as fraud and theft by a notary) and to protect third parties against unintentional errors and omissions (negligence by a notary). Since a notary will know whether she or he would ever commit intentional misconduct, an honorable notary may reasonably decide not to purchase a notary bond at all because it would never be needed to compensate for intentional wrongdoing. But, every notary should strongly consider having liability insurance.

Practice Tip: *Employer's Possible Interest in a Notary Bond.* In many situations, the notary employer may feel the need to obtain a bond for its notary-employee (with the agreement of the notary-employee) in order to provide some level of protection for the business, especially if the notary-employee were to engage in intentional wrongdoing. Even though the employer may pay the premium for the bond, the bond will be obtained in the name of the notary-employee. Again, if the surety company were to pay on a claim against the notary for intentional misconduct, there would be an obligation on the notary-employee to reimburse the surety for the amount it paid on the claim, although the employer and notary could agree between themselves that the employer would be responsible for all or part of the amount of the reimbursement. In deciding the coverage limit for such a notary bond to be obtained at the behest of the notary employer, several factors should be considered, such as: the length of time the notary-employee has been employed with the notary employer, how well the notary employer knows the notary-employee, the length of time the employee has been a notary, whether there have been any incidents of deceit or dishonesty by the employee, the employee's criminal history, the types of transactional instruments that will be notarized by the notary-employee, the monetary values for those instruments, the volume of notarizations to be performed by the notary-employee, and whether the signers of those instruments will be known to the notary-employee and/or the notary employer (or will be strangers to the notary and the employer). At the present time, the author would suggest purchasing a notary bond in the amount of at least $100,000. There are numerous surety companies, so the notary-employee and the notary employers should obtain more than one quote for the bond premium in order to compare costs.

23.3 The notary should understand the advantages and disadvantages of notary liability insurance.

Notary liability insurance, notary malpractice insurance, or errors and omissions (E&O) insurance covers notaries for their negligence in the performance of notarizations. Unlike a notary bond, notary liability insurance does not cover intentional wrongdoing, such as the knowing failure to perform steps of the notarization process, fraud, misrepresentation, theft, and official misconduct resulting from intentional misconduct. And, unlike a payment made under a notary bond, an insurance payment made to a claimant does not have to be repaid by the notary.

Notary liability insurance will cover financial injuries resulting from faulty notarizations and notarial activity up to the policy limit. The insurance company will have the obligation to provide legal assistance for the covered notary to defend against negligence claims and/or to settle such claims. Importantly, the insurance company will weigh the cost of defending against a claim in its consideration of whether, and for how much, to settle a claim.

Practice Tip: *Informing the Notary Employer About Liability Coverage.* Notaries would be well-advised to inform notary employers about liability issues and insurance coverage, which can and should protect both the notary and the employer in the event of liability claims for notary mistakes. The notary has full, unlimited, personal liability for mistakes and misconduct which cause financial injury to a document signer, a party receiving or relying on a notarized document, or other party (such as the victim of an imposter who obtains a notarization in the victim's name). If an employer encourages or requires an employee to become a notary to service the employer or the employer's customers, the notary should request the employer to purchase appropriate liability insurance coverage for the protection of both the notary and the employer. In many cases, under the law of agency, the employer of a notary faces the same full, unlimited liability as the notary, so appropriate insurance coverage for both the notary and employer should be considered.

Note: *Insurance for the Notary's Employer.* Liability insurance for a notary public will cover only the conduct of the notary, not the conduct and the liability of the notary employer. Notary employers can separately be held liable for negligence relating to notarizations performed by their notary-employees — either directly for negligent instruction or supervision of those notaries or indirectly through vicarious liability under notary statutes or the common law of agency. Thus, notary employers may wish to purchase liability insurance to cover their businesses for such possible negligence liability, and notary employers should strongly consider purchasing notary malpractice insurance for their notary-employees. Alternatively, there are E&O group policies available for employers that cover the employer and all of its notaries. If the notary employer pays for liability insurance for its notary-employees, this step will promote employee morale and goodwill. After all, many (if not most) employees would not become notaries but for the wishes of their employers. Many employees would not be inclined to accept the risk of unlimited personal liability to become company notaries. Additionally, since notary employers will quite often face vicarious liability for the mistakes and misconduct of their notary-employees anyway, there will frequently be a kind of joint liability for which the employer would be accountable, so employers would be well-advised to bring the risks together under one policy with one insurance company that could then attempt to settle claims efficiently and cost-effectively.

Practice Tip: *Using the Same Company for the Bond and Insurance.* Notaries and their employers should consider purchasing a bond and insurance from the same surety or insurance company. An important advantage would be that, if a claim were made against the notary bond which the insurance would also cover, the surety or insurance company will put the insurance in front of the bond. This approach would prevent a payment of a claim under the bond which would have to be reimbursed and which, in some jurisdictions, would result in suspension of the notary commission.

It should be observed that liability insurance (as with notary bond coverage) entitles the insured notary to be defended by the insurance company against claims of notary malpractice and to have the insurance company pay for any legitimate or successful claims. However, notary insurance companies can decide to settle claims and, thereby, avoid the substantial costs of defending against those claims. Thus, there is an incentive, especially on smaller malpractice policies, for the insurance companies to settle. Paying a claim may simply constitute a lower business cost for the insurance company than paying more to defend against the claim.

Incidentally, many businesses, including law firms, commonly carry umbrella insurance coverage to protect against negligence liability caused by their agents and employees. These umbrella policies should be carefully reviewed to determine whether the conduct of notary-employees is covered. Indeed, some umbrella policies contain express exclusions for notarial activity or notarial misconduct.

Case Illustration: *Small Bond and Small Insurance Policy.* This author testified as an expert witness in a lawsuit in which the notary and the notary's employer were both sued as the result of the notarization of a forged, real estate document. The plaintiff, whose signature had been forged, was suing for more than $100,000. The notary had the state-mandated notary bond of $5,000 and a $25,000 liability insurance policy. The case ended up lasting for several years, and included a trial and appeals to the state's appellate and supreme courts. Not surprisingly, within the first few months of the case, the bond company paid to the plaintiff its $5,000 cap on its notary bond, and the insurance company paid to the plaintiff its $25,000 on its notary malpractice policy. Hence, both the bond company and the insurance company settled with the plaintiff, minimized their costs, and did not have to participate in years of protracted and expensive litigation.

23.4 The notary should acquire notary liability insurance in an amount sufficient to protect against negligent notarial performance .

As noted above, notaries have full and unlimited personal liability for their negligent notarial errors and omissions which cause injuries to document signers or other parties. This personal liability means that any and all of the notaries' personal assets are at risk, including houses, cars, bank accounts, salaries, and so on. Such expansive risk should stand as strong incentive for notaries to consider acquiring malpractice insurance, because anyone may make an accidental error or omission.

No state or territory requires its notaries to obtain notary liability insurance. Rather, such insurance is optional and readily available through private insurance companies. Indeed, the cost of the premiums for most notary malpractice insurance is quite affordable.

Some notaries will not feel the need to purchase liability insurance, for a variety of reasons. Some notaries will trust in their knowledge of notary practice and their diligence and/or will perform so few notarizations that coverage will seem unnecessary. Some notaries will not perform any high-risk or high-value notarizations (such as notarizations of pricey financial instruments for strangers or notarizations of estate planning documents or property transfer documents for terminally ill individuals). Some notaries will not really need liability insurance.

In deciding whether to obtain liability insurance, notaries should take into consideration the other parties who may be affected financially by their negligence, namely, their customers, parties who rely upon notarized instruments, and employers of notaries. Notary liability insurance will protect not only the notary but also the signers of documents and the members of the public who rely upon notarized documents. Notary liability insurance may even benefit notary employers who are drawn into disputes about faulty notarial practice by providing a source of compensation to injured parties (rather than having injured parties sue to recover against notary employers).

Notaries should carefully consider how much liability insurance coverage to purchase, based upon numerous factors. The types and values of transactional instruments the notaries commonly notarize, the frequency with which the notaries perform notarizations for strangers, the volume of document notarizations the notaries perform, the value of the assets of the notaries that are exposed to liability for notarial mistakes, and the cost of the premiums for such insurance are some of the most important factors. Currently, the maximum coverage under most notary liability policies is $100,000. Data indicate that the typical payout on notary insurance claims is about $15,000, and many notaries purchase $25,000 E&O policies. Significantly, this author has, over the years, been retained to consult on a number of notary cases involving claims for hundreds of thousands, and even millions, of dollars. Hence, many notaries should certainly consider acquiring liability coverage of $100,000.

23.5 The notary should promptly report notary mistakes or misconduct to notary bond and insurance companies.

When material or serious notarial mistakes and misconduct occur, such faults should be immediately self-reported to the appropriate authorities, including the notary's bond and/or insurance company. This standard does not mean that every trivial error or omission should be disclosed, but certainly all mistakes or misconduct of consequence should be reported, such as any fault which might invalidate a notarization and any misconduct which tends to show evidence of deceit or dishonesty on the part of the notary. Likewise, wrongdoing on the part of the notary employer that may invalidate a notarization or that suggests dishonest or unlawful conduct should be disclosed by the notary.

Business and governmental professionals have a duty to self-report mistakes and misconduct. This responsibility to place self-interest and self-preservation secondary to the higher interest of notary customers and clients is an ethical duty. Moreover, as public officials, notaries owe fiduciary duties to the public they serve, including the obligation to disclose their own mistakes and misconduct. Notaries should honor this ethical responsibility to do the right thing.

If any material notarial errors, omissions, and/or misconduct are caused by the notary, the notary should, promptly upon the discovery of such faults, report them to the parties to the notarized instrument, to the commissioning official or notary oversight agency for the relevant jurisdiction, and to the surety company and liability insurance company which issued the notary bond and insurance. Obviously, the sooner the reporting occurs, the more likely that resulting financial injuries can be avoided or minimized. If a notary is named as a party to a lawsuit, the notary should immediately notify the notary's bond and insurance companies, and the commissioning official or notary oversight agency. Additionally, if alleged criminal conduct is involved, such misconduct should be self-reported to the appropriate law enforcement agency or agencies.

23.6 The notary should cooperate with any investigation of alleged notarial mistakes or misconduct undertaken by bond and insurance companies.

Regardless of who reports alleged notary misconduct and who files a complaint against the notary, the notary is contractually required by the terms of the bond or insurance contract, to cooperate fully with the investigation undertaken by the surety bond and insurance companies, by the commissioning official or notary oversight agency, and by law enforcement agencies that may also become involved. Business professionals bear the heavy responsibility to put aside their self-interest in avoiding detection and avoiding official findings of fault for misconduct. Professionals must cooperate fully and fairly in any and all investigations of wrongdoing. Notaries, as commissioned public officials, have this duty as well. ■

***RELEVANT MODEL NOTARY LAW**

Each notary should read, study, and abide by the notary statute and regulations, if any, of his or her state or territory of commissioning.

"Official Misconduct. 'Official misconduct' means: (1) a notary's performance of any act prohibited, or failure to perform any act or duty mandated, by this [Act] or by any other law in connection with a notarial act; or (2) a notary's performance of an official act or duty in a manner that is negligent, contrary to established norms of sound notarial practice, or against the public interest." *Model Notary Act,* Section 2-12 (2010).

"Liability Of Notary, Surety, And Employer. (a) A notary is liable to any person for all damages proximately caused that person by the notary's negligence, intentional violation of law, or official misconduct in relation to a notarization.

(b) A surety for a notary's bond is liable to any person for damages proximately caused that person by the notary's negligence, intentional violation of law, or official misconduct in relation to a notarization during the bond term, but this liability may not exceed the dollar amount of the bond or of any remaining bond funds that have not been disbursed to other claimants. Regardless of the number of claimants against the bond or the number of notarial acts cited in the claims, a surety's aggregate liability shall not exceed the dollar amount of the bond.

(c) An employer of a notary is liable to any person for all damages proximately caused that person by the notary's negligence, intentional violation of law, or official misconduct in performing a notarization during the course of employment, if the employer directed, expected, encouraged, approved, or tolerated the notary's negligence, violation of law, or official misconduct either in the particular transaction or, impliedly, by the employer's previous action in at least one similar transaction involving any notary employed by the employer. ..." *Model Notary Act,* Section 13-1 (2010).

"Criminal Sanctions. (a) In performing a notarial act, a notary is guilty of a [class of offense], punishable upon conviction by a fine not exceeding [dollars] or imprisonment for not more than [term of imprisonment], or both, for knowingly: (1) failing to require the presence of a principal at the time of the notarial act; (2) failing to identify a principal through personal knowledge or satisfactory evidence; or (3) executing a false notarial certificate under Subsection 5-8(a).

(b) A notary who knowingly performs or fails to perform any other act prohibited or mandated respectively by this [Act] may be guilty of a [class of offense], punishable upon conviction by a fine not exceeding [dollars] or imprisonment for not more than [term of imprisonment], or both." *Model Notary Act,* Section 13-6 (2010).

"Additional Remedies And Sanctions Not Precluded. The remedies and sanctions of this chapter do not preclude other remedies and sanctions provided by law." *Model Notary Act,* Section 13-7 (2010).

"Bond. (a) A notary commission shall not [become effective /be issued] until an oath of office and [25,000] dollar bond have been filed with the [designated office]. The bond shall be executed by a licensed surety, for a term of [4] years, commencing on the commission's effective date and terminating on its expiration date, with payment of bond funds to any person conditioned upon the notary's misconduct as defined in Section 2-12.

(b) The surety for a notary bond shall report all claims against the bond to the [commissioning official].

(c) If a notary bond has been exhausted by claims paid out by the suety, the [commissioning official] shall suspend the notary's commission until: (1) a new bond is obtained by the notary; and (2) the notary's fitness to serve the remainder of the commission term is determined by the [commissioning official]." *Model Notary Act,* Section 3-3 (2010).

"Commission As Notary Public; Qualifications; No Immunity Or Benefit. ... (d) [Not more than [30] days after] [Before] issuance of a commission as a notary public, the [notary public][applicant for a commission] shall submit to the [commissioning officer or agency] an assurance in the form of a surety bond or its functional equivalent in the amount of $[____]. The assurance must be issued by a surety or other entity licensed or authorized to do business in this state. The assurance must cover acts performed during the term of the notary public's commission and must be in the form prescribed by the [commissioning officer or agency]. If a notary public violates law with respect to notaries public in this state, the surety or issuing entity is liable under the assurance. The surety or issuing entity shall give [30]-days notice to the [commissioning officer or agency] before canceling the assurance. The surety or issuing entity shall notify the [commissioning officer or agency] not less than [30] days after making a payment to a claimant under the assurance. A notary public may perform notarial acts in this state only during the period that a valid assurance is on file with the [commissioning officer or agency[.] ...

[(f)] A commission to act as a notary public authorizes the notary public to perform notarial acts. The commission does not provide the notary public any immunity or benefit conferred by law of this state on public officials or employees." *Revised Uniform Law on Notarial Acts,* Section 21 (2010).

Vintage 1920s era, black and white magazine photograph with caption stating: "John Calvin Coolidge, Notary Public. The bible on the table is the one used by President Coolidge on taking the oath of office." The caption refers to the event when Vermont notary John Coolidge administered the presidential oath of office to his son, Vice President Calvin Coolidge, at the Coolidge's Vermont family home, upon the sudden death of President Warren Harding.

Chapter

24

Proper Roles of Notary-Employees and Their Employers

STANDARDS SUMMARY

24.1 The notary-employee should, when necessary, assist the employer to understand and accept its proper role in their unique relationship.

24.2 The notary-employee should understand the limited role which the employer has in the supervision and control of the notary-employee in the performance of official notarial functions.

24.3 The notary-employee should not allow the employer to direct or influence the notary-employee to violate notary law or notary best practices in the performance of official notarial functions.

24.4 The notary-employee should not allow the employer to possess, use, alter, discard, or destroy the notary-employee's official notary seal, journal, or other records under any circumstances.

24.5 The notary-employee should restrict access to the notary journal and should require the employer to access the notary journal in the same manner as any other party.

24.6 The notary-employee should, unless the law provides otherwise, not permit the employer to determine whether the notary-employee will charge notarial fees, the amount of the fees, or whether to share fees with the employer.

24.7 The notary-employee should understand that the employer may have vicarious liability for the misconduct of the notary-employee in the performance of official notarial functions.

24.8 The notary-employee should request the employer to pay for a notary bond for the notary-employee and liability insurance for the notary-employee and the employer.

24.9 The notary-employee should request the employer to provide notary education and to purchase a membership in at least one notary association for the notary-employee.

STANDARDS EXPLANATIONS

When a notary is also an employee, a genuinely unique employment relationship exists. Many employers and notaries do not fully understand it. Yet, the proper roles of the employer (whom we will assume is not a notary) and the notary-employee are quite important to the correct performance of document notarizations. If the relationship is mishandled, if a faulty notarization results, and if some party is injured financially as a result, both the notary-employee and the employer may face substantial liability risks. So, the employer and notary-employee relationship is serious business, and it should be taken seriously and should be well-understood by both of them.

Most notary-employees serve as notaries because their employers have asked them to become notaries or because it is customary for notaries to be available in certain business settings. Very often, employers want and need notaries working in their businesses — such as in accounting, estate planning, banking, real estate, health care, law firms, and elsewhere. Frequently, employers will urge or require employees to become notaries; employers will pay for the commissioning fees of their new notaries; and, employers will purchase the notary seals, notary bonds, and other materials for their notary-employees. However, regardless of why and how a notary becomes associated with the business, if the employer allows notary-employees to perform document notarizations at the workplace while employees are on duty, there will be numerous implications for both parties. Incidentally, even volunteer notaries may be regarded in the eyes of the law as notary-employees when they serve as notaries at nursing homes, hospitals, jails and prisons, homeless shelters, colleges and universities, and elsewhere, and those institutions may be regarded as notary employers. For the reasons to be discussed throughout this chapter, this section necessarily includes best practice standards for both notary-employees and notary employers.

This chapter is not about those notaries who do not perform notarial services during their work shifts or in conjunction with their work duties.

As mentioned, the employment relationship introduces a number of issues into notarial practice. It presents the possibility that the employers may attempt to influence the performance of notary-employees. It raises the issue of what notary-employees should do to foster the proper relationship with their employers. It also presents the responsibilities that are imposed upon employers and whether notary employers can be held liable for the errors and wrongdoing of their notary-employees. In turn, it poses the issue of the relevance of notary bonds and liability insurance.

24.1 The notary-employee should, when necessary, assist the employer to understand and accept its proper role in their unique relationship.

If businesses do not want to take on the concerns associated with providing notary services at the workplace, including the associated liability risks, those businesses can prohibit employees from performing notarizations at the workplace and while on duty wherever they are. Employers are not required to provide notary services to customers and are not required to permit employees who happen to be notaries to conduct notarial functions while at work.

If employers of notary-employees decide to provide or allow notarial services to be provided at work, those employers should certainly appreciate from the very beginning that there will be resulting implications for them. Hence, when employers make the decision to have one or more notaries on staff to provide notarial services, those employers accept the responsibility to understand their proper role regarding their notary-employees and notarial activities. When employers do not live up to that responsibility, notary-employees should assist their employers in understanding their respective roles, for it is in the best interests of both parties for the proper roles to be respected.

Each notary-employee confronted by this challenge will have to decide how to most effectively educate the employer on the subject. But, whether the notary-employee's strategy is more circumspect and delicate, or direct and firm, the subject should be addressed. And, the sooner the better, before serious conflict surfaces, or worse, serious damage is done to a high-value notarization. When the assistance of the notary-employee is needed to educate the employer regarding its proper role, the employer should welcome the clarification.

24.2 The notary-employee should understand the limited role which the employer has in the supervision and control of the notary-employee in the performance of official notarial functions.

Both notaries public who work as employees and their employers have the responsibility to become informed about their respective rights and duties arising out of the dual positions each occupies. That is, the notary is simultaneously an ordinary employee and a notary public (a government officer), and the employer simultaneously has an ordinary employee and a notary public (a government official) working within its organization. This situation is unique in that, during business hours, while on business premises, the employee may be called upon to perform the public service of document notarization, without the usual supervision and control exercised by the employer.

There may be a temptation for employers to think that, just as they have authority to manage and control the customary business activities of their employees, employers can supervise and direct their notary-employees in regard to the performance of official notarizations. Such broad thinking is not only incorrect but also dangerous. Of course, employers can be generally involved in the supervision and control of notary-employees in order to foster correct notary practices in compliance with the law and established notarial standards. For instance, the employer might insist on its notary-employee attending a notary education program, on its notary-employee taking more time to assure that document notarizations are thoroughly performed, or on its notary-employee maintaining a notary journal to record document notarizations (in a state where the law does not require notaries to do so). However, employers cannot supervise and control notary-employees in the specific manner in which they conduct document notarizations for the purpose of evading, violating, or taking shortcuts to notary law and sound notarial practices.

This unique circumstance means that, while employers have their usual powers over the notary-employees when they perform their customary duties as employees (for instance, the authority to supervise and control the details of the ordinary work of employees and the authority to fire employees), employers have only limited authority over notary-employees when they are serving as public officials performing notarial functions. To put it differently, because notary-employees are the commissioned public officials (not the employers), employers have no real authority to direct their notary-employees while they are conducting notarial functions. Employers can suggest and urge notary-employees to be careful, cautious, prudent, and thorough and to abide by notary law and standards, but, ultimately, the notary-employees are the public officers who will decide how to perform the details of document notarizations.

***Note:** Who Paid the Commissioning Costs Is Irrelevant.* Even if the employer has paid for the notary's application fee, for the notary's seal and journal, for the notary bond and/or liability insurance, and for other incidental costs of being a notary, the employer does not acquire any additional power simply because of the payment of those costs. To repeat the key point, it is the notary-employee who is the public officer (not the employer) who serves as the commissioned official.

***Note:** When the Employer or Supervisor Is Also a Notary.* Let us say the notary-employee's company owner or supervisor is also a notary public. Does this fact change the circumstances described previously in this section? Can a boss or supervisor who happens to be a notary direct and order exactly how the notary-employee performs a notarization? No, and No. The individual notary who performs a particular notarization is the one and only party officially and legally authorized to conduct it. A boss or supervisor who is a notary can provide advice and guidance about notarial practice, but a notarization is performed and certified only by the notary who seals and signs the certificate of notarization. If the boss or supervisor who is a notary wishes to control a notarization completely, then the boss or supervisor should perform the notarization.

24.3 The notary-employee should not allow the employer to direct or influence the notary-employee to violate notary law or notary best practices in the performance of official notarial functions.

It is the ethical and legal duty of the notary-employee to abide strictly by notary law and sound notarial practices and, thus, to resist any efforts exerted by the employer to the contrary. It will be no defense for an errant notary to contend that the employer told the notary to perform a notarization incorrectly.

While most employers are honorable and adequately informed so that they will not attempt to persuade their notary-employees to engage in any wrongdoing in the performance of document notarizations, this ideal situation does not always exist. One of the most difficult challenges in the workplace arises when the employer attempts to influence, or worse, directs the notary-employee to violate notary law or sound notary practice in the performance of notarizations. Employers will sometimes suggest that notary-employees take shortcuts to save time or avoid perceived inconvenience to customers. Or, employers who do not appreciate the legal requirements for document notarizations will urge the omission or disregard of some of those requirements. Notary-employees cannot permit such unlawful practices just because employers are ill-informed or misinformed.

The obvious problem for the notary-employee is the perceived risk of losing his or her job, or at least the perceived risk of creating a hostile work environment, if the employer's attempt to influence or direct misconduct is rebuffed. Certainly, the employer has the power to terminate the employment, or at a minimum, the employment relationship may be impaired when the notary-employee refuses to engage in notarial misconduct at the behest of the employer. How can the notary-employee most tactfully refuse the employer's attempt to get the notary-employee to violate notary law or notary standards? There are a number of ways to handle this serious problem if it should arise — and education is part of each answer.

First, hopefully the notary-employee will have laid the groundwork for dealing with this situation early in the notarial relationship with the employer. That is, in the beginning, right after the company employee first became a notary, or if the employee had been a notary who was hired into the company and asked to continue as a notary, the notary-employee will have discussed with the employer or supervisors the role of the notary-employee, including the importance of notarizations, the notary's obligation to follow the law, and the legal liabilities (both civil and criminal) faced by both the notary-employee and the employer (and possibly supervisors) if notary law and notary practice standards are not followed. In other words, the notary-employee should educate the employer about notary basics before there is time for the employer to direct or suggest anything improper. Incidentally, it is never too late to have this "Notary 101" session with the employer or supervisors (although, the sooner the better).

Second, if the employer, nevertheless, directs or suggests improper conduct to be undertaken by the notary-employee, the notary-employee should immediately discontinue any notarization that may be in progress and ask to speak privately with the employer or superior. Then, the notary-employee can privately remind the employer or superior of the basic notary principles previously discussed, especially the obligation of the notary to follow the law, rather than the dictates of the employer. The notary-employee should explain the proper procedure for performing the notarization, as opposed to the method directed or suggested by the employer, along with an explanation of the reason(s) why the proper procedure is required, and of the liability risks (both civil and criminal) to the notary and the employer if the improper method is adopted. Lastly, the notary should also note that if the improper method were employed, the validity of the notarization and the underlying transaction would be jeopardized. That outcome would hurt the customer or company agent for whom the notarization was performed. Having this conversation in private allows the notary-employee to tactfully counter the erroneous suggestion or direction of the employer or superior, free from the embarrassment which a public airing would involve.

Third, if the employer is suggesting misconduct in order to accommodate or "help" a client, such as a client who cannot attend the notarization ceremony, a client who does not have proper identification, or a client who is simply in a hurry, the notary-employee should remind the employer that people regularly change their minds (called "signer remorse"). If the client later decides the transaction was not a good idea after all and wants to challenge the notarization, the client can reveal the faulty aspects of the notarization. Then, there will be a conflict with a business customer. Furthermore, the notary-employee and the notary employer will have to either confess to the faults or else perjure themselves — thereby compounding their offenses.

Fourth, if the employer or superior has not yet been persuaded to accept the notary-employee's position about the impropriety of the employer's suggestion or direction as to the manner of performing the notarization, the notary-employee should be prepared to provide written evidence in support of the notary-employee's point of view. The notary-employee should have a number of key notary references available at the workplace, including a copy of the state or territorial notary statute, a copy of the *Notary Public Code of Professional Responsibility*, a copy of the official state or territorial notary handbook or manual (published in hard copy or online by the commissioning official or notary oversight agency), a copy of the *Model Notary Act* of 2010, and a copy of this book. Then, written evidence should be readily available to address virtually any matter involved in the performance of a notarization. Indeed, with these notarial sources on hand, there should usually be more than one source of information to support the notary-employee's correct point of view. Reasonable employers and supervisors should be amenable to being educated when they see information in published form.

Fifth, the notary-employee (who, of course, maintains a detailed notary journal) should remind the employer that the faulty document notarization will be recorded in writing in the notarial certificate and in the official notary journal (which is an official public record that can be accessed by the governmental notary oversight agency, police, prosecutors, and lawyers represented injured parties). The notary-employee cannot falsify those written records without violating civil and criminal laws, and if the certificate or journal entry is falsified at the direction of the employer, then the employer will face possible civil and criminal liability as well.

Sixth, if, however, the errant employer or supervisor has not been convinced by the steps enumerated above, the notary-employee must have the gumption to stand up for the correct notarial procedure and insist on doing the notarization properly, or not doing it at all. As a result, the notary-employee may risk termination of employment or other employment sanctions but the notary's role as a responsible public official must prevail whatever the cost in the workplace. If the notary-employee is unlawfully terminated or sanctioned, there may a legal remedy available to be pursued against the employer for the retaliatory firing or for a workplace financial injury. In addition, if the employer then managed to obtain the falsified notarization from another notary, the notary-employee can inform authorities to investigate that faulty notarization, and both the employer and the business customer will become involved in the controversy. They will have to confess to their misconduct or else perjure themselves. Will it be worth the risks to the employer and its goodwill?

Of course, none of these steps should really be necessary in the real world of business and notarization. Employers should prefer their notary-employees to be thorough and prudent in performing every notarization, including and especially for favored clientele, because such notarial practices will best serve their clients and customers in the long run (by better assuring the integrity and validity of notarizations). Indeed, employers should actually inform their clientele that their notarization services are meticulous and thorough, and they should boast of such notarial practices as a means of furthering business goodwill.

Note: *Employer's Direct Liability.* An employer that interferes in the notarial functioning of its notary-employee should be aware of the increased risk of liability which will result from such involvement. Direct liability results because the employer did something wrong. To illustrate, if the employer tells the notary-employee to do something that turns out to be wrong, and the notary-employee does what the employee was told to do (that was wrong), causing financial injury to the document signer or a party relying on the invalid notarization, the notary-employee is liable for doing the wrong thing, and the employer is liable for telling the employee to do the wrong thing.

24.4 The notary-employee should not allow the employer to possess, use, alter, discard, or destroy the notary-employee's official notary seal, journal, or other records under any circumstances.

The ultimate responsibility for safeguarding the notary seal, journal, and other notary records (such as itemized receipts for notary fees) rests entirely with the notary-employee. The obligation in this regard is so important that the notary-employee should resist any efforts to the contrary. If the employer or its staff request access to one or more notary journal entries or other records, the notary-employee should insist upon compliance with the detailed and protective steps required of third parties who seek such access. See also the discussion of notary journals in Chapter 17.

The notary-employee should protect the notary seal, journal, and any other notary records, keeping them under lock and key under the exclusive control of the notary-employee when not being used. Moreover, the notary-employee should not allow anyone else in the workplace (not employers, supervisors, fellow workers, or customers) to possess or even to handle the notary seal, journal, or other records. These items are official tools of the notary office, which could be misused to forge or falsify notarizations, and the journal and other records may contain confidential and private information about document signers. So, the notary should protect the security of the seal, journal, and other records at all times.

If the notary-employee leaves the employment for any reason during the term of the notary's active commission, the commission of the notary-employee remains in full force and effect until the commission expires, is resigned, or is revoked by the commissioning official or notary oversight agency. Similarly, the notary seal, journal, and other notary records remain the property of the notary for use after the employment has ended and while the notary is still commissioned. Thus, the notary should not abandon these items when the notary leaves the employment, and the notary should not surrender these items to the employer or its staff. See also the discussion of notary seals in Chapter 8, of notary journals in Chapter 17, and of notary fee records in Chapter 28.

Too many employers erroneously think that if they have paid the costs for their notary-employees' seals and journals, the employers either own these tools or at least have the right to possess them. Nevertheless, the notary seal, journal, and any other paper records created by the notary are the property solely of the notary, and the employer (including supervisory personnel) should not possess or even handle the notary seal, journal, or other records.

If the notary seal, journal, or other notary records were to be abandoned by the notary-employee at the employer's place of business, the employer should immediately secure the seal and journal and other records, inform the commissioning official or notary oversight agency, and should arrange to transmit these items to the agency. The death of a commissioned notary-employee presents a logistic issue about the seal and journal. Some state statutes have a provision describing who should act and what should be done about the seal and journal, and those statutes should be followed. But, if there is no statute that provides otherwise, the employer should not alter, use, copy, discard, or destroy the seal and journal of a deceased notary-employee. The seal and journal might be evidence in any pending claim against the notary-employee or in any future claim. The employer should immediately secure the seal, journal, and other records, inform the commissioning official or oversight agency of the death of the notary-employee, and ask that agency for instructions for the transmission of the seal, journal, and records to the agency.

Case Illustration. This author testified in a trial about a notary-employee who had kept a journal for the notarizations which were performed for customers at the employer's place of business. The notary-employee changed employment and left the notary journal behind at the first employer's company, but the abandoned journal was discarded by a supervisor at the company and was destroyed. Not surprisingly, years later at the trial, the notary could not recall any of the details about the notarization that was being challenged.

24.5 The notary-employee should restrict access to the notary journal and should require the employer to access to the notary journal in the same manner as any other party.

Notaries have an ethical and legal responsibility to safeguard the notary journal and to limit access to it at all times, regardless of whether the notaries' employers may have paid for the journals and regardless of whether the journals may be housed on the employers' premises.

Access to the contents of the notary journal can sometimes become a matter of contention between the notary-employee and the employer, especially when the employer has paid for the notary journal and when the employer is uninformed about the ownership, possession, and control of the journal. On the one hand, the notary journal, being the official record book of a government officer, is a public record which can, therefore, be accessed. On the other hand, the notary journal contains important confidential and private personal and financial information about document signers — possibly numbering into the hundreds of such signers. Thus, only limited access to the notary journal should be permitted by the notary-employee to anyone, including the notary employer. See also the discussion of notary journals in Chapter 17 and of signer confidentiality and privacy concerns in Chapter 18.

The notary journal belongs exclusively to the notary, should never leave the control of the notary, and should never be in the possession of any other person such as the employer (except perhaps in the possession of agents of the commissioning official or notary oversight agency or of law enforcement officials pursuant to court order or subpoena). A notary-employee should allow limited access by the notary employer to a specified notary journal entry under restricted precautions in the same manner as the notary would permit access by any other party. These limitations are discussed in Chapter 17 dealing with the subject of notary journals.

The employer should appreciate that the notary journal will contain confidential and private financial and personal information about document signers, that the journal belongs to the notary-employee, that the journal should remain in the exclusive possession and control of the notary-employee, that access to the notary journal should be restricted, and that the employer should be entitled to no greater access to the journal than any other party is permitted. In other words, the employer should truly respect the notary-employee's superior position in regard to notarial functions, even in the notary employer's own place of business.

24.6 The notary-employee should, unless the law provides otherwise, not permit the employer to determine whether the notary-employee will charge notarial fees, the amount of the fees, or whether to share fees with the employer.

Some businesses customarily provide notarial services to their customers (such as banks, law firms, hospitals, nursing homes, and others), and, typically, there is no charge for those notarial services. The notary-employee has agreed not to charge for notarizations as part of the employment agreement — and, hopefully, in the notary-employee's salary there is compensation in part for the notary service along with liability insurance coverage paid for by the employer. Such an arrangement is proper because the notary-employee has agreed not to charge for notary services. If the notary-employee were to insist on charging notary fees to customers, the employer could simply direct the notary not to perform notarizations at the workplace, and if the employer desired to provide free notary services to customers, the employer could undoubtedly find another notary-employee willing not to charge notary fees.

Unless the relevant notary statute provides otherwise, because the notary is the commissioned official who performs document notarizations, it is the notary who possesses the authority to make all decisions about notarial fees — including whether to charge fees, how much to charge, and whether to share collected fees with the employer. Of course, the notary employer and notary-employee can and should discuss these issues, and they should reach a mutual understanding and agreement about fees. But, the notary-employee has the final word. Incidentally, in some jurisdictions, the notary law will allow government agencies to charge and retain fees for notarizations performed by their notary-employees.

The notary-employee may have to educate the employer on these issues, reminding the employer that the notary-employee is the public official (not the employer), that the notary-employee is required to report fees collected as income for tax purposes, and that the notary-employee has unlimited liability for notary malpractice. Furthermore, the employer should realize that it may not have liability for the notary's errors and omissions, although the collecting of fees by the employer will almost certainly cause the employer to share in legal liability for notarial malpractice. If the employer does not wish its customers to pay fees for notarial services, but if the notary-employee wants to assess notarial fees, perhaps the employer and notary-employee can reach an agreement for compensation to the notary-employee or for an increase in the wage or salary of the notary-employee to compensate for the performance of the notarial services and the heightened risk of personal financial liability. See also the discussion of notary liability issues in Chapter 20 and of notary fees in Chapter 28.

If it is decided that customers will be charged notary fees to be retained by the employer or shared by the employer, the employer should be aware of the implications of such a decision. First, the employer will have a responsibility to inform customers of such fees through signage and/or print materials. Second, employers will have the responsibility to account for such fees and to report the fees as income for tax purposes. Third, as previously noted, the collection of fees for notary services by the employer will almost certainly cause the employer to have vicarious legal liability for notary malpractice. In some large-scale and high-volume businesses (such as office supply stores, copying and shipping businesses, and currency exchanges), the fees to be collected for notarial services would be substantial, and employers may want to retain or share in those fees. If so, employers should reach accords with their notary-employees about fees, and employers should consider obtaining appropriate insurance protection. See also the discussion of notary bonds and liability insurance in Chapter 23 and of notary fees in Chapter 28.

24.7 The notary-employee should understand that the employer may have vicarious liability for the misconduct of the notary-employee in the performance of official notarial functions.

Under the statutory or common law of every U.S. jurisdiction, it is possible and often likely that employers will have unlimited legal liability for notary misconduct committed by their notary-employees under agency principles (called vicarious liability). This result is so serious that it ought to persuade employers (a) to support notary education and continuing education for their notary-employees, and (b) to acquire sizable liability insurance coverage for notarial malpractice. Employers should understand all of that and should act on it by supporting notary education for notary-employees and obtaining liability insurance coverage for notary-employees and the employers.

Under the law of negligence and agency law, ordinary employers are usually liable for injuries, including financial damages, caused by their employees when the employees are acting within the scope of their employment (that is, when the employees are on duty and doing their jobs). It is simply one of the risks of doing business that has been accepted as part of our commercial law. The same is true for the employers of notaries.

Under the law of agency, the notary-employee is an agent of the employer (even though the employer cannot control the details of the performance of its notary-employee). Furthermore, under the law of agency in most jurisdictions, the liability faced by the employer is no-fault vicarious liability for the negligence of its notary-employee. That means, even if the notary employer has acted reasonably and has done nothing wrong, and if the notary-employee simply makes an error or omission in performing a notarization, both the notary-employee and the employer are legally liable for any financial injury caused by the faulty notarization. It is merely the way commercial law protects parties injured by the negligence of the employees of businesses.

That information is presented to underscore an important reason why employers may wish to exercise some degree of supervision and direction over notary-employees, because if the notary-employee makes a mistake and someone is injured by the faulty notarization, the employer will likely pay the price for that mistake. But, employers should knowingly and willingly face the reality that their notary-employees possess the ultimate authority to determine exactly how notarizations will be performed.

The hiring practices of many employers have contributed considerably to the view that they should be held legally responsible for the misconduct of their notary-employees. Many notary-employees become notaries in the first place only because employers have requested or required them to be notaries to service the company's notarial needs and/or the notarial needs of customers. Employers will often pay some or all of the costs for employees to become notaries — including notary application fees and bond premiums, and the costs of notary seals and journals. And, importantly, employers frequently will advertise to their customers the availability of notarial services as part of the business operation. Holding the employer legally liable appears to be, at least in part, a result of a kind of risk-reward analysis. That is, if employers are going to enjoy the reward of having notary-employees on staff to provide notarial services to customers and to facilitate business, then employers should bear the risk that their notary-employees will make mistakes and cause financial injuries.

24.8 The notary-employee should request the employer to pay for a notary bond for the notary-employee and liability insurance for the notary-employee and the employer.

A notary bond along with notary liability insurance is essential in protecting the public, the notary-employer, and the notary-employee in situations in which the notary-employee will be notarizing documents with some frequency, especially if such documents involve substantial monetary values and are signed by individuals not personally known to the employer and/or notary-employee. A notary bond and liability insurance protect against somewhat different notary faults, which is why the notary employer and notary-employee would be well-advised to consider acquiring both. Since the employer is presumably the entity desirous of the notary services of the notary-employee, since the employer is presumably in a much better financial position to pay for a notary bond and insurance, and since the notary-employee and employer face possible unlimited liability for notary errors and omissions, the notary-employee should certainly urge the employer to pay the costs of adequate bond and insurance coverage. See also the discussion of liability issues in Chapter 20 and of bonds and insurance in Chapter 23.

It is the coverage of intentional misconduct by a bond which is important to protect the public because liability insurance does not cover intentional misconduct. Thus, there should be a substantial bond to cover the notary-employee in the event the notary-employee were to commit intentional wrongdoing. Notary malpractice insurance, or errors and omissions insurance, covers negligent performance of notarizations and should also have substantial liability limits. The employer should wish the public, including its customers, to be adequately protected against possible negligence and intentional wrongdoing by its notary-employee and should be willing — as a cost of doing business — to consider the purchase of a notary bond and malpractice insurance in substantial amounts to cover its notary-employee and itself.

It may be that the business of the notary employer will have an umbrella liability insurance policy and that the umbrella policy will either already cover notary malpractice of the notary-employee or such coverage could be added to the umbrella policy. Importantly, an umbrella business policy that covers notary malpractice should also cover the direct negligence of the notary employer in improperly instructing and supervising the notary-employee. If the employer has an umbrella policy in place, the employer should check with the insurer to determine whether notary malpractice is covered.

24.9 The notary-employee should request the employer to provide notary education and to purchase a membership in at least one notary association for the notary-employee.

Education or knowledge is the best insurance against notary liability for the notary-employee and employer, and the best assurance that notarizations performed for customers of the employer will be properly performed with resulting goodwill generated for the employer. Thus, it is in the interests of both the notary-employee and employer for the notary-employee to be as capable and knowledgeable as possible about notary law and best practices. As the far greater interests reside with the employer in terms of company goodwill and financial risk, and as the employer is in the much better financial position, the notary-employee should request assistance and support from the employer to educate the notary-employee. And, the employer would be well-advised to support its notary-employee. See also the discussion of continuing notary education in Chapter 30.

The costs to the employer for the benefits of notary education of the notary-employee are small in comparison to the risks avoided and the benefits attained.

For example, there are the modest costs of notary education classes and membership in one or more notary membership and education organizations. There might also be the need for time off for the notary-employee from the employment to attend notary education and notary conferences, perhaps with pay, since the time involved is for business-related activities. There might also be the cost of travel to and from notary education programs and notary conferences. The employer should be delighted to have a notary-employee who is interested and concerned about being well-prepared to render notarial services. The costs associated with the support of the notary-employee will be deductible business expenses that the notary employer should be willing to bear.

Honorable and law-abiding business people should want all of their employees to know and obey the law, as well as to know and follow sound business practices. Moreover, those reasonable and capable business people should recognize the goodwill value to their businesses to be gained by faithful compliance with legal requirements and sound practices. Providing an important public service is beneficial as well. After all, a notary is first and foremost a public official and public servant. Hence, the provision of proper notarial services for document notarizations should satisfy all of those business and public-spirited purposes. Savvy business people will recognize the notary-related expenses noted to represent a sound investment in the integrity and security of their companies. ■

***RELEVANT MODEL NOTARY LAW**

Each notary should read, study, and abide by the notary statute and regulations, if any, of her or his commissioning state or territory.

"The Notary shall, as a government officer and public servant, serve all of the public in an honest, fair and unbiased manner." *Notary Public Code of Professional Responsibility,* Guiding Principle I (1998).

"The Notary shall give precedence to the rules of law over the dictates or expectations of any person or entity." *Notary Public Code of Professional Responsibility,* Guiding Principle V (1998).

"To uphold the trust placed in me by the public I serve; ...

To treat each individual fairly and equally, with kindness and respect; ...

To keep informed of the law regarding the duties and powers of the office of Notary Public in my jurisdiction and not compromise that law ..." *Responsibility Code of Ethics* (1980).

"Purposes. This [Act] shall be construed and applied to advance its underlying purposes, which are: (1) to promote, serve, and protect the public interest; ... (3) to foster ethical conduct among notaries; ..." *Model Notary Act,* Section 1-2 (2010).

"Refusal to Notarize. (a) A notary shall not refuse to perform a notarial act based on a person's race, advanced age, gender, sexual orientation, religion, national origin, disability, or status as a non-client or non-customer of the notary's employer. ..." *Model Notary Act,* Section 5-6 (2010).

"Fees of Employee Notary, (a) An employer may prohibit an employee who is a notary from charging for notarial acts performed on the employer's time, but shall not condition imposition of a fee on attributes of the principal [[document signer]] as described in Section 5-6(a).

(b) A private employer shall not require an employee who is a notary to surrender or share fees charged for any notarial acts.

(c) A governmental employer who has absorbed an employee's costs in becoming or operating as a notary shall require any fees for notarial acts performed on the employer's time either to be waived or surrendered to the employer to support public programs." *Model Notary Act,* Section 6-4 (2010).

"Liability of Notary, Surety, and Employer, (a) A notary is liable to any person for all damages proximately caused that person by the notary's negligence, intentional violation of law, or official misconduct in relation to a notarization.

(b) A surety for a notary's bond is liable to any person for damages proximately caused that person by the notary's negligence, intentional violation of law, or official misconduct in relation to a notarization during the bond term, but this liability may not exceed the dollar amount of the bond or of any remaining bond funds that have not been disbursed to other claimants. Regardless of the number of claimants against the bond or the number of notarial acts cited in the claims, a surety's aggregate liability shall not exceed the dollar amount of the bond.

(c) An employer of a notary is liable to any person for all damages proximately caused that person by the notary's negligence, intentional violation of law, or official misconduct in performing a notarization during the course of employment, if the employer directed, expected, encouraged, approved, or tolerated the notary's negligence, violation of law, or official misconduct either in the particular transaction or, impliedly, by the employer's previous action in at least one similar transaction involving any notary employed by the employer.

(d) An employer of a notary is liable to the notary for all damages recovered from the notary as a result of any violation of law by the notary that was coerced by threat of the employer, if the threat, such as of demotion or dismissal, was made in reference to the particular notarization or, impliedly, by the employer's previous action in at least one similar transaction involving any notary employed by the employer. In addition, the employer is liable to the notary for damages caused the notary by demotion, dismissal, or other action resulting from the notary's refusal to engage in a violation of law or official misconduct. ..." *Model Notary Act,* Section 13-1 (2010).

"Impersonation. Any person not a notary who knowingly acts as or otherwise impersonates a notary is guilty of a [class of offense], punishable upon conviction by a fine not exceeding [dollars] or imprisonment for not more than [term of imprisonment], or both." *Model Notary Act,* Section 14-1 (2010).

"Wrongful Possession. Any person who knowingly obtains, conceals, defaces, or destroys the seal, journal, or official records of a notary is guilty of a [class of offense], punishable upon conviction by a fine not exceeding [dollars] or imprisonment for not more than [term of imprisonment], or both." *Model Notary Act,* Section 14-2 (2010).

"Improper Influence. Any person who knowingly solicits, coerces, or in any way influences a notary to commit official misconduct is guilty of a [class of offense] , punishable upon conviction by a fine not exceeding [dollars] or imprisonment for not more than [term of imprisonment], or both." *Model Notary Act,* Section 14-3 (2010).

Wonderful, scarce, 1950s–60s, burwood composite 3-D sign, identifying the Western Surety Company as the bond provider for the notary. The sign also shows the company's signature covered wagon logo, along with the language "One of America's oldest bonding companies ... since 1900."

Chapter

25

Attorneys, Notary-Attorneys and Conflicts of Interest

STANDARDS SUMMARY

25.1 The notary who is not an attorney and who is employed or supervised by an attorney should assist the attorney to understand the significance of proper notarial functioning and notary best practices.

25.2 The notary-attorney and the attorney who employs or supervises a notary should understand the significance of proper performance of notarizations.

25.3 The notary-attorney and the attorney who employs or supervises a notary should understand the substantial legal and ethical risks associated with violations of notary law and sound notarial practice.

25.4 The notary-attorney and the attorney who employs or supervises a notary should insist upon strict compliance with notary law and sound notarial practice.

25.5 The notary-attorney and the attorney who employs or supervises a notary should not direct or influence a notary to violate notary law or sound notarial practice.

25.6 The notary-attorney should not serve in the dual role as attorney and notary for a document drafted, prepared, or reviewed on behalf of a legal client.

25.7 The notary-attorney and the attorney who employs or supervises a notary should complete, or direct the completion of, a notary journal entry for each document notarization.

25.8 The notary-attorney and the attorney who employs or supervises a notary should self-report notarial misconduct committed by the attorney and by a notary employed or supervised by the attorney.

25.9 The notary-attorney and the attorney who employs or supervises a notary should report notarial misconduct committed by other attorneys and notaries.

25.10 The notary-attorney and the attorney who employs or supervises a notary should assure that an adequate notary bond and insurance are acquired.

STANDARDS EXPLANATIONS

This chapter is included because it is so desperately needed. Due to the close relationship between law and document notarization, most lawyers are either notaries or employ or supervise notaries. Unfortunately, non-notary lawyers, lawyers as notaries, and lawyers as employers and supervisors of staff notaries are among the worst offenders of notary law and sound notarial practice. So, attorneys as a group need the benefits of this chapter more than any other set of professionals.

Notary-attorneys acting as dual agents, notarizing documents they have drafted, prepared, or reviewed for their own clients, have committed many kinds of notarial violations. Those notary-attorneys have falsified the dates of documents and have notarized the falsified documents with falsified dates of notarizations. Notary-attorneys have falsified the contents of documents and have notarized the falsified documents. Notary-attorneys have forged the signatures of absent clients or directed law firm staff to forge the signatures and then notarized the forged signatures.

In addition, non-notary attorneys have impersonated notaries by pilfering notary seals and forging notarizations for documents of their own clients. Non-notary attorneys have committed numerous other types of notary-related violations in order to accomplish notarizations for their own clients. Those non-notary attorneys have falsified the dates of client documents and obtained notarizations of those documents. Non-notary attorneys who supervise notaries have directed subordinate non-notary staff members to forge signatures of clients on documents so that actual notaries could then notarize for the absent clients. Attorneys have directed their staff notaries to falsify the dates on notarizations, to notarize signatures of absent document signers, and to forge signatures of absent clients and then to notarize those falsified signatures. These types of violations have been recorded in hundreds of published court decisions in attorney disciplinary proceedings in which attorneys have been sanctioned for their violations of notary law and lawyer ethics standards.

This last point is significant, because every violation of notary law results in one or more violations of the lawyer ethics code. The knowing notarial misconduct of attorneys is evidence of dishonesty and deceit, and undoubtedly constitutes the crime of official misconduct or conspiracy to commit official misconduct. Criminal conduct by a lawyer is an especially damning ethics infraction. Significantly, most notarizations of documents performed by lawyers and their staff notaries are likely to be submitted to opposing parties and their lawyers and/or filed for governmental recording or filed in court as part of litigations. The knowing submission and filing of fraudulent documents is a serious ethics violation, for it involves committing a fraud upon other parties, a government agency, and/or a court. Many times, the attorneys take additional steps to conceal their misconduct, such as by destroying evidence or coercing witnesses to their offenses, which shows further evidence of deceit and dishonesty. These unlawful notarial actions jeopardize the interests of attorneys' clients, which is a most fundamental lawyer ethics infraction. Often, there is evidence of a pattern of multiple notary violations by attorneys over extended periods of time, which suggests significant disregard of the law and lawyer ethics. The attorneys' actions in directing and involving subordinate staff members and clients in their schemes of notarial wrongdoing is despicable and highly unethical. Lawyers have an ethical responsibility to self-report misconduct, and rarely do attorneys ever come forward to reveal their notarial wrongdoing — until they are otherwise discovered and charged with their offenses. Thus, the notary violations committed by attorneys are always compounded and exacerbated by accompanying lawyer ethics breaches — often implicating several lawyer ethics violations. Finally, there would be a number of corresponding violations of notary ethics as well. See also the discussion of notary ethics in Chapter 19.

Believe it or not, the compounding of attorney violations stemming from notarial misconduct does not end here, for notary-attorneys and attorneys regularly make matters worse in defending their own disciplinary cases and in misguided efforts to mitigate the circumstances. In those proceedings, notary-attorneys and attorneys have often argued that (a) notarization is unimportant or that their transgressions were merely technical violations, (b) everyone else violates notary procedures too, (c) the misconduct was undertaken with the approval of their clients, (d) the misconduct was undertaken for the benefit or protection of their clients, and (e) no one was harmed by the infractions. The disdain for notarization and notary law is exposed by these "defenses" or "mitigation." Lawyer discipline officials and judges have frequently expressed their shock and disapproval of these contentions.

Not surprisingly, many lawyers have received substantial sanctions for their notarial and ethics violations, including many who have appropriately been suspended or disbarred. Unfortunately, attorney notarial violations that are discovered represent an extremely small fraction of the attorney notarial wrongdoing which goes undetected. Nevertheless, attorneys who engage in notarial wrongdoing should be concerned because so often there still exists evidence, and there have been witnesses to their misdeeds (clients, paralegals and other law firm staff members, fellow attorneys). If the forgeries or falsifications by attorneys are discovered or if the witnesses decide to come forward to report the misdeeds, the attorneys will be in jeopardy. There is no statute of limitations to protect one's reputation from disclosure of the magnitude of the violations of law and ethics described above.

25.1 The notary who is not an attorney and who is employed or supervised by an attorney should assist the attorney to understand the significance of proper notarial functioning and notary best practices.

Attorneys are not educated about notary law and practice in law school or in the bar review course, and they are not tested on notary law on the bar examination. Many jurisdictions have adopted little or no mandatory notary education or testing for applicants for notary commissions. Thus, attorneys in general and notary-attorneys in particular, have little knowledge about notary law and sound practices, unless they have consciously studied the subject or gained correct knowledge about notaries and notarizations through experience. Realizing this deficiency, many attorneys will be receptive to assistance from commissioned notaries about the importance of proper notarization of documents and about notary best practices.

Moreover, notaries who are employed or supervised by attorneys will be familiar with the personalities of those attorneys and should be in the position to know the type of approach that will be most likely to succeed in getting the attention of their employers and supervisors. These notaries should also recognize that it is in their best interests to succeed in helping attorneys to respect the notarization process and to promote (or at least to tolerate) notary best practices.

Because non-notary attorneys are unlikely to read this book, the author has included this section to help notaries avoid the difficulties associated with improper influences and directives from supervisors who do not appreciate the importance of sound notarizations. This best practice should empower notaries to help themselves, help their attorney employers and supervisors, help clients of those attorneys, help the legal profession, and help the general public.

25.2 The notary-attorney and the attorney who employs or supervises a notary should understand the significance of proper performance of notarizations.

Attorneys, perhaps more than any other group, should recognize the importance of notaries public and notarizations to commercial and governmental functioning. Notaries are government officers created by statute and commissioned by the state or territory. Notaries in many jurisdictions must be bonded. Notarizations are also created and governed by statute, and document notarizations are mandated for many kinds of transactions, such as some real estate documents which are filed with county recorders, certain litigation documents which are filed in courts, and certain estate and personal planning documents such as some powers of attorney and wills. In addition, countless other documents are either required by law to be notarized or notarized by agreement or arrangement of private parties.

More than 4,450,000 U.S. notaries perform many millions of document notarizations each week. It has been correctly observed time and time again that the affairs of business and government would grind to a halt if notaries were to go on strike. Furthermore, if notaries were generally to carelessly perform their functions and if, as a result, document notarizations could no longer be trusted to be proper and valid, uncertainty and chaos would grip the commercial, financial, and government systems. Lawyers, as some of the principal users and guardians of these systems, should be keenly aware of the fundamental and essential need for competent and diligent notaries and for accurate and trustworthy document notarizations.

25.3 The notary-attorney and the attorney who employs or supervises a notary should understand the substantial legal and ethical risks associated with violations of notary law and sound notarial practice.

As pointed out in the introduction to this section, when an attorney is involved in notarial misconduct, the serious consequences for the attorney are that there will have been violations of notary law and lawyer ethics. The violations go hand in hand, often with several violations triggered by an initial act of notarial misconduct. As noted, what begins as a single offense is quickly compounded.

Hypothetical Example. Here is a common, realistic, and unfortunate hypothetical situation. An attorney contacts a client to obtain the client's signature and notarization for an affidavit, but the client is unavailable to appear for the notarization by the deadline on which it is needed. So, the attorney asks the client's permission to prepare the affidavit and sign the client's name without the client being present, and the client agrees. If a notary-attorney notarizes an affidavit for a lawsuit for the client who is not present for the notarial ceremony, the result is far more than the one violation of notarizing for the absent signer.

(1) There is the violation for notarizing for the absent signer.

(2) There is the notarial violation for forgery of the client's signature.

(3) There is the notarial violation for falsely certifying in the certificate of notarization that the jurat or affidavit notarization was verified under oath or affirmation, which could not have been accomplished with the signer absent.

(4) There is the lawyer ethics violation for dishonesty and deceit for intentionally engaging in the three notary violations.

(5) Since the affidavit is for a lawsuit, when it is filed with the court and opposing parties, it is untruthful and invalid, and that falsification is a fraud perpetrated upon the court and opposing counsel and parties.

(6) There is the lawyer ethics violation for placing the client's case at risk.

(7) There is the lawyer ethics violation for involving the client in the series of falsifications and violations.

(8) The notary-attorney's intentional failure to abide by notary law in regard to the absent signer and the failure to administer the required oath or affirmation are official misconduct, which constitutes a crime.

(9) There is the failure of the attorney to self-report the violations to the notary oversight agency and the lawyer discipline agency, which is further deceit by the attorney and which is yet another ethics violation.

When attorneys engage in notary misconduct, they risk their law licenses, and if they are notaries, the lawyers also risk their notary commissions. If the notary misconduct has been undertaken in misguided efforts on behalf of law clients, the attorneys will have jeopardized the interests of their clients. If the notarial wrongdoing constitutes official misconduct or violation of a similar criminal provision, the attorneys may be prosecuted and convicted of crimes, and they could face imprisonment, fines, or both. These matters are very serious and should be taken seriously by notary-attorneys and attorneys.

25.4 The notary-attorney and the attorney who employs or supervises a notary should insist upon strict compliance with notary law and sound notarial practice.

For a host of unfortunate reasons, lawyers (who should know better) regularly engage in notarial misconduct. Sometimes, greed takes over and lawyers stretch themselves too thinly. So, they take shortcuts in an unhealthy attempt to have more time to squeeze in more billable hours, including shortcuts in notarial procedures. Sometimes, lawyers will allow individual notarial abuses to snowball into more and more violations.

However, diligent lawyers will recognize that the far better attitude is to rigorously comply with notary law and best practices, including to prepare a detailed notary journal entry for each document notarization. This approach will protect everyone with an interest in a notarization — the document signer client, the notary, and the attorney for the client. Lawyers should also realize that, if they either involve their clients in notarial wrongdoing or simply falsify notarizations for clients without telling the clients, those clients may at some point in the future change their minds and disavow the documents which were falsely notarized. This turn of events will result in the clients turning on their lawyers and will result in the lawyers and former clients becoming adversaries.

25.5 The notary-attorney and the attorney who employs or supervises a notary should not direct or influence a notary to violate notary law or sound notarial practice.

Lawyers have legal and ethical responsibility for subordinates whom they employ or supervise, including notaries. Of course, lawyers should want these notaries to perform properly, and, most certainly, lawyers should not wish to direct or influence their subordinate notaries to violate notary law and best practices. One reason lawyers should never involve subordinates in misconduct is that doing so constitutes an attorney ethics violation. Moreover, people who are pressured by their employers or supervisors into engaging in misconduct may have a change of heart and roll over on the boss or supervisor at some time in the future, especially if the wrongdoing is discovered and the subordinates are at risk of financial liability and/or disciplinary sanctions.

For the record, it should be emphasized that a notary, as a commissioned public official, should not allow an employer or supervisor to pressure or coerce the notary to violate notary law or best practices. It is the notary's duty to stand up against the pressure and to follow the law. However, in the real world, especially when the employer or supervisor is a lawyer, notary subordinates often fall prey to directives or pressure from their superiors. The law is clear that it will be no defense for a notary that he or she was ordered or pressured to violate notary law.

25.6 The notary-attorney should not serve in the dual role as attorney and notary for a document drafted, prepared, or reviewed on behalf of a legal client.

Nearly every published court disciplinary case in which notary-attorneys were found guilty of notarial misconduct involved notary-attorneys who notarized documents which they had drafted, prepared, and/or reviewed for their own clients. Obviously, the temptation to commit fraud is too great for many attorneys who take advantage of dual roles in serving their clients. There is a conflict of competing interests for the notary-attorneys. The interests as private attorneys to advocate for their clients overwhelms the interests of the public official role of impartial notaries obliged to perform thorough and meticulous notarizations. Why do notary-attorneys insist on serving in the dual capacities for their clients when there are more than 4,450,000 notaries? It seems suspicious that an attorney would have the instinct and mindset to serve in the dual roles. The answer for many attorneys has been so that they can lie and cheat and take advantage of the notary position.

When a notary-attorney serves in the dual roles for a document drafted, prepared, or reviewed for the client, a conflict of interest arises. In the role of lawyer, the attorney represents the private client, with a vested interest for a substantial legal fee to validate the document, while in the role of notary, for little or no fee, the notary represents the government, with the obligation to serve as an impartial witness. How can the attorney be an interested advocate for the legal client but claim to be an impartial notary in dealings for the same client? The fact is many notary-attorneys acting as dual agents have engaged in wrongdoing designed for the purpose of benefiting their clients through violations of notary law. Indeed, virtually none of those hundreds of published attorney discipline opinions about notarial violations were perpetrated in cases where notary-attorneys were notarizing for nonclients.

The imbalance between the respective fees in the dual roles is telling and troubling. The lawyer will likely have been paid hundreds or thousands of dollars for the representation regarding the document to be notarized, or the lawyer will have a contingent interest of possibly tens of thousands or hundreds of thousands of dollars in the outcome of the case about which the document to be notarized is a part. Moreover, the attorney needs and wants to have the document notarized if the substantial fee for drafting, preparing, and/or reviewing the document is to be justified. On the other extreme, the notarial fee for service as an impartial judge of the worthiness of the document to be notarized and for the performance of a meticulous notarial procedure is trivial by comparison. So, the David versus Goliath imbalance is obvious. The attorney role trumps the notary role.

Curiously, if a challenge to the validity of a notarization performed by a notary-attorney for her or his own client on a document drafted, prepared, and/or reviewed by the notary-attorney were to be asserted in a lawsuit, the lawyer would have to be a witness. Then, there are two dual roles: notary-attorney and attorney-witness. No attorney should place herself or himself in the position to possibly be attorney and witness in the same matter, especially in instances in which the attorney knows she or he has engaged in notarial misconduct. To the contrary, an attorney should want the client to be best served and protected, and that ideal is achieved by having an independent and diligent notary perform the client's document notarization.

Incidentally, attorneys are not being singled out here. No business professional who is qualified and assists in the drafting, preparation, or review of a document should perform the notarization of that document. Thus, accountants, bankers, financial planners, health care professionals, paralegals, real estate brokers, stockbrokers, and the like, who are also notaries, should not serve in the dual roles on a document drafted, prepared, or reviewed for a client. There would be a disqualifying conflict of interest.

Note: *Special Statutory Exemptions.* In a few states, legislators (many of whom are lawyers) have enacted laws granting attorneys the express authority to serve as notaries for their own clients on documents the attorneys have drafted, prepared, or reviewed. And, why were such laws granting special treatment to lawyers thought by legislators to be necessary? Because without such laws, the lawyers might well be considered to be engaging in conflicts of interest. Indeed, the California statute's comparable provision is entitled: "Conflicts of Interest: Exception" — because the provision expressly excepts California lawyers from engaging in what otherwise might well be conflicts of interest by serving in the dual notary-attorney role for their own clients. That title proves the point of this section. Attorneys in the states with these express statutory provisions should, nevertheless, not take advantage of them and should not serve in the dual roles for a client.

25.7 The notary-attorney and the attorney who employs or supervises a notary should complete, or direct the completion of, a notary journal entry for each document notarization.

Journalizing a document notarization is critically important to the corroboration of the authenticity and integrity of the notarization. Unfortunately, as noted earlier, many notary-attorneys and law firm notaries have a poor record when it comes to notarial performance. On behalf of their clients obtaining notarizations, lawyers should understand the value of journal entries to the validity of notarizations and should enthusiastically support detailed journalizing. See also the discussion of notary journals in Chapter 17.

Lawyers sometimes cannot make up their minds. They tell their clients to keep thorough records, to document everything, and to "get it in writing." Yet, when it comes to the keeping of a detailed notary journal entry for each document notarization, most bar organizations and many of their attorney members urge that lawyers should be exempt from mandatory notary journal provisions and should not maintain notary journals. Attorneys justify their misguided contention with a number of concerns. Journalizing takes too much time. Journals are unnecessary because the lawyers keep copies of the notarized documents. Lawyers are different than every other business professional and should be the only profession exempt from mandatory journal laws. Journalizing is inconvenient. Journalizing violates the attorney-client privilege. And so on.

Of course, doing a thing carefully, thoroughly, and correctly is usually inconvenient and more time-consuming than doing it quickly and carelessly. Time and inconvenience are the prices we pay for prudent business practices. Copies of notarized documents, including the notarial certificates, are insufficient records on which lawyers should rely because the copies do not corroborate the authenticity of the notarization. Almost all faulty notarizations appear proper on the face of their notarial certificates. One cannot tell from the face of the notary certificate if the date of the certificate is correct, if the document signer really appeared at the time of the notarization, if the document signer was properly identified, if the document signer pre-signed or post-signed the transactional instrument, if the signer's mental capacity was assessed, if the signer's willingness to sign was assessed, or if the document signer was really administered an oath or affirmation for a jurat. A detailed notary journal entry will corroborate each of those points of concern.

Note: *The Attorney-Client Privilege Mirage.* Violation of the attorney-client privilege sounds impressive, but that argument against journalizing is unconvincing in substance. First, there is no information of consequence to the attorney-client privilege in a notary journal entry (what could it be — the client's name or address, the document type or notarization type, the date or the number of pages in the document?). Second, the only reason for the alleged attorney-client violation is because the attorney is personally performing the notarization or having the notarization performed in-house. But, the lawyer should not be serving as both the lawyer and the notary on a document drafted, prepared, or reviewed for the client by the attorney. As has already been pointed out, with more than 4,450,000 notaries available, there should be no reason an attorney could not have an independent notary perform the notarization and prepare a corresponding notary journal entry. Third, if the journalizing of a notarization were truly an issue for the attorney-client privilege, then the attorney should simply have the client waive the privilege as to the journal entry, in order to gain the benefit that journalizing provides. Fourth, the trade-off for lawyers and their law firm notaries should be considered, and the balancing of interests should be considered. If there is a challenge to a notarization, then the notary who performed it (the notary-attorney for the client) can be required to appear as a witness and to be questioned about the notarization procedure and its validity. Should an attorney be willing to expose client information to such a process simply because the attorney wanted to serve the dual role of notary-attorney to control the document notarization? Apparently, the client information is highly valued by attorneys regarding the attorney-client privilege but not so important as to protect it from disclosure by the notary-attorney upon a challenge to the notarization's validity. Many attorneys appear to be taking inconsistent positions.

25.8 The notary-attorney and the attorney who employs or supervises a notary should self-report notarial misconduct committed by the attorney and by a notary employed or supervised by the attorney.

As members of the bar and officers of the courts where they are licensed to practice, attorneys have the professional responsibility to self-report their misconduct, including their neglect of matters, their material mistakes, and their intentional wrongdoing. This obligation against self-interest is taken very seriously in the legal professional by courts and disciplinary agencies. One reason for the concern is that the other side of the coin is so often knowing concealment of violations. Thus, lawyers have the duty to report their own notarial misconduct, as well as the misconduct of staff notaries — such as paralegals, law clerks, and secretaries who are notaries — because lawyers have responsibility for the performance of legal staff under their supervision and control.

For attorneys, the self-reporting obligation involves disclosing notary misconduct to at least two agencies — the attorney disciplinary agency (possibly a court) and the notary commissioning official or notary oversight agency. Furthermore, if the notarial misconduct were to involve a violation of the criminal law, there would be an obligation to disclose the misconduct to the police.

25.9 The notary-attorney and the attorney who employs or supervises a notary should report notarial misconduct committed by other attorneys and notaries.

Under professional ethics codes for attorneys, licensed attorneys are supposed to report the misconduct of other attorneys. When the misconduct to be reported involves notarial wrongdoing by a notary-attorney or an attorney, the reporting should be made to at least two agencies — the relevant court or lawyer disciplinary agency and the governmental notary oversight agency. In either case, if the notarial misconduct constitutes a crime, the report of wrongdoing should also be made to the police and/or the prosecutor's office.

25.10 The notary-attorney and the attorney who employs or supervises a notary should assure that an adequate notary bond and insurance are acquired.

A practicing attorney who is also a practicing notary, and a law firm with one or more notaries on staff, should review their bond and insurance coverage to be assured that notarial misconduct is adequately covered. To the surprise of some attorneys, their legal malpractice insurance may, but may not, cover notary malpractice. Some legal malpractice insurance expressly excludes coverage of notary practice. Moreover, liability insurance will not cover intentional wrongdoing, such as fraud and theft, although bond coverage does include intentional misconduct. So, lawyers and their notaries should beware, consider both bond and liability insurance, and obtain sufficient liability coverage. ■

***RELEVANT MODEL NOTARY LAW**

Each notary should read, study, and abide by the notary statute and regulations, if any, of his or her commissioning state and territory.

"To never perform any notarial act in which I am a party in interest or from which I stand to benefit; ...

To not use the office of Notary Public as a means of financial gain, for myself or others, in any other business or profession ..." *Responsibility Code of Ethics* (1980).

"The Notary shall act as an impartial witness and not profit or gain from any document or transaction requiring a notarial act, apart from the [notary] fee allowed by statute." *Notary Public Code of Professional Responsibility,* Guiding Principle II (1998).

"The Notary shall give precedence to the rules of law over the dictates or expectations of any person or entity." *Notary Public Code of Professional Responsibility,* Guiding Principle V (1998).

"Disqualifications. (a) A notary is disqualified from performing a notarial act if the notary: ... (2) will receive as a direct or indirect result any commission, fee, advantage, right, title, interest, cash, property, or other consideration exceeding in value the fees specified in Section 6-2 of this [Act]; ... (4) is an attorney who has prepared, explained, or recommended to the principal [document signer] the document that is to be notarized. ..." *Model Notary Act,* Section 5-5 (2010).

1978, cover of the 192-page *Notary Public Practices & Glossary* by National Notary Association founder Raymond C. Rothman. It was published by the National Notary Association.

Chapter

26

Avoiding the Notary's Unauthorized Practice of Law

STANDARDS SUMMARY

26.1 The notary who is not an attorney should understand that the unauthorized practice of law constitutes a serious violation of law.

26.2 The notary who is not an attorney should not claim to be an attorney nor create the appearance that she or he is an attorney.

26.3 The notary who is not an attorney should not use the designation *"notario"* or *"notario publico"* or any non-English translation of "notary" or "notary public."

26.4 The notary who is not an attorney should not advise, counsel, or represent a notary client in such a way as to engage in the unauthorized practice of law.

26.5 The notary who is neither an attorney nor a professional in a law-related field should not draft or prepare the instrument to be notarized.

26.6 The notary who is neither an attorney nor a professional in a law-related field should not advise or consult the signer about the document to be notarized.

26.7 The notary who is neither an attorney nor a professional in a law-related field should not read or review the document to be notarized.

26.8 The notary who is not an attorney, but who is a professional in a law-related field, should be especially careful to avoid engaging in the unauthorized practice of law.

26.9 The notary who is not an attorney should be authorized to advise the notary client in the selection of the type of document notarization to be performed.

STANDARDS EXPLANATIONS

For a host of reasons, the "unauthorized practice of law" is a scary subject in the minds of most non-attorney notaries. The phrase is mentioned time and time again in notary publications and at notary conferences, and seems always to be referenced in menacing ways for notaries. Many notaries do not understand the concept well enough, so there is a degree of fear of the unknown and the unfamiliar. Moreover, since lawyers are the primary guardians against the unauthorized practice of law and since notaries often feel intimidated and threatened by lawyers, the unauthorized practice of law presents them with two foes at the same time.

Some of the non-attorney notaries who may be most vulnerable to the temptation to engage in the unauthorized practice of law are likely to be notaries serving as professionals in law-related fields, such as paralegals, real estate brokers, bankers, financial planners, accountants, signing agents, mortgage lenders, and the like. Nevertheless, although the unauthorized practice of law should be avoided by non-attorney notaries, neither the concept nor its enforcement should continue to unduly concern notaries — at least, not after review of this chapter.

26.1 The notary who is not an attorney should understand that the unauthorized practice of law constitutes a serious violation of law.

Individuals who are not licensed attorneys, including the great majority of U.S. notaries, must avoid the unauthorized practice of law (UPL). Statutes, governmental agency regulations, court rules, and court decisions throughout the U.S. declare that the UPL is prohibited and unlawful. Civil and criminal sanctions may be leveled against violators, and notaries who violate this prohibition can also lose their notary commissions. It is the unauthorized provision of legal services itself that determines whether there has been UPL, not whether there was compensation for the unauthorized practice. Certainly, though, substantial payment or compensation of some kind may be a relevant consideration on the issue of possible UPL.

The principal reason to avoid the UPL is the protection of the public against individuals who are not qualified to render legal services. Such individuals would include both outright charlatans who simply desire to profit from their deception, as well as persons who, for a variety of reasons, want to play amateur lawyers. On the other hand, individuals who are licensed to practice law have spent years of legal study, have almost always had to pass an extensive written bar examination, and have usually acquired substantial professional malpractice liability insurance. These steps have been taken to protect the public by providing them with qualified and competent lawyers and by providing them with a source of recovery if legal malpractice should happen to occur.

Regardless of how much experience and knowledge in business and law-related matters non-attorneys may have acquired, unless they are licensed as attorneys at law, they may not engage in the practice of law. It will be no defense for a non-attorney charged with the UPL to assert that she or he was correct in their advice or counsel. She or he will be guilty as charged and may suffer the consequences. Although the exact definition of unauthorized practice of law is illusive, it has not deterred the legal profession, governmental agencies, and the courts from roundly declaring the UPL to be prohibited and from acting against parties thought to be engaging in the UPL to stem its abuse and spread.

The UPL could take one or more of several forms, as will be discussed below. And, the UPL could be committed orally, in writing, in advertising, in private communications, in online postings, in news accounts, in filings with courts or government agencies, and in any combination of these methods.

26.2 The notary who is not an attorney should not claim to be an attorney nor create the appearance that she or he is an attorney.

The definition of the UPL is not exact. Certainly, non-lawyers may not claim to be lawyers or hold themselves out as licensed attorneys, counselors, or lawyers, and they may not use any of the common designations permitted for lawyers, such as "Esquire," "Esq.," "Juris Doctor," "JD" or "LLB." Notaries who are paralegals should be particularly cautious not to misrepresent themselves or to mislead clients by using these designations.

As will be addressed more fully in the next section, notaries who are not also attorneys may not use the terms *"notario," "notario publico,"* or any other non-English translation of the words "notary" or "notary public." We have already reviewed these prohibitions in regard to notary advertising (in Chapter 3). The reason for these restrictions is to avoid confusion for people who are familiar with notary practice in so many other countries of the world, where virtually all notaries are also lawyers. Non-attorney notaries who are paralegals and who work with individuals filing papers in immigration matters should be particularly cautious to avoid creating the impression they are attorneys.

Practice Tip: *From the Author's Legal Experience.* As a lawyer and law school professor, I represented numerous clients pro bono, including one who was a tenants' rights advocate, who had been charged with the unauthorized practice of law, and who had to appear to defend himself before a panel of commissioners of the state Supreme Court. The case was complicated, but we succeeded in convincing all seven commissioners that my client had not engaged in the unauthorized practice of law. One of the most persuasive facts in his favor was that he had the foresight to expressly advise his clients that he was not an attorney. He posted a sign in his office which read: "I am not an attorney. I cannot provide legal advice." He recorded a statement on his automated voice message system which announced as part of his greeting that he was not an attorney and could not provide legal advice. And, he orally reminded each client with whom he met that he was not an attorney. While taking all of those steps should not be necessary, posting a sign is a very good idea, for a couple of reasons. First, it is tangible, and in writing, and could be produced as evidence if needed. Second, such a sign almost certainly will discourage some clients from asking legal questions in the first place. Incidentally, the making of such disclaimers does not automatically protect against charges of the UPL if the individual in question then proceeds to dispense legal advice and legal services. Remember the old saying: "Actions speak louder than words."

26.3 The notary who is not an attorney should not use the designation *"notario"* or *"notario publico"* or any non-English translation of "notary" or "notary public."

As already noted, non-attorney notaries must avoid advertising their notarial services in such a way as to create the appearance that they are also lawyers or that they are also qualified to provide legal advice and counsel. Claiming to be a lawyer, or creating the appearance that one is a lawyer, constitutes the UPL. Unfortunately, many immigrants and visitors to the U.S., and even our fellow citizens from Puerto Rico, have been taken advantage of by unscrupulous notaries engaging in the UPL. Of particular concern has been the abuse by notaries of individuals seeking assistance with immigration matters.

This topic is so important that it is set out separately here for emphasis, even though it has been mentioned previously. Many persons, especially people familiar with practices in other parts of the world, and even people familiar with the legal system of Puerto Rico, may mistakenly think that all U.S. notaries are lawyers because so many of the rest of the world's notaries are also, in fact, lawyers, including many of the solicitors in the United Kingdom and the *"notario publico"* of Puerto Rico and the Hispanic countries. Additionally, since the notaries of the world so often notarize legal instruments, many people think that notaries are familiar enough with the law to provide legal advice and assistance. Thus, notaries should not use the term *"notario,"* the phrase *"notario publico,"* or any non-English translation of "notary" or "notary public" in any form of communication, oral or written. These restrictions cover all kinds of business communications, including advertising, business cards, invoices, letterheads, stationery, and signage — with no exceptions.

26.4 The notary who is not an attorney should not advise, counsel, or represent a notary client in such a way as to engage in the unauthorized practice of law.

Among the most well-known activities of lawyers is the representation of clients in courts, before governmental administrative agencies, and in negotiations of all kinds. Thus, non-lawyers may not represent parties in courts, administrative agencies, arbitrations, tribunals, or any other settings, regardless of whether the non-lawyers are paid for their representation. Non-lawyers may not consult or advise clients about legal matters, or in regard to the filing of documents in government agencies, courts, arbitrations, or other official public or private settings. For example, a notary who is not an attorney should not represent or assist a notary client at a hearing for a variance before a city zoning board. A notary who is not an attorney should not represent or assist a notary client with the filing of papers in a proceeding before a justice of the peace.

> ***Practice Tip:*** *Stay at the Office or at Home.* Notaries should not accompany notary clients to hearings or even to government offices, for notaries who remain at their own homes or places of business will be less likely to become involved too deeply in legal matters beyond their knowledge and authority. Notaries should not file instruments for notary clients with government agencies or courts, or even deliver instruments for notary clients to private parties or private institutions. The handling of notarized instruments after notarizations have been completed is beyond the typical duties of notaries and suggests greater involvement than impartial notaries should possess.

The prohibition against the unauthorized practice of law is particularly important for notaries because so many notaries regularly deal with legal documents (such as affidavits, contracts, corporate documents, deeds, liens, mortgages, powers of attorney, wills, and so on). The substantial experience gained by some notaries may tempt them to offer advice and counsel with the best of intentions and without any compensation. But, there is no excuse for crossing the line between proper notarial practice and the UPL.

Because the UPL cannot be defined with precision, the line between the lawful performance of notarial services and the UPL is not perfectly clear. Non-attorney notaries should be cautious to avoid even approaching the line by not advising, counseling, or representing notary clients about legal matters. Further, as a non-attorney notary gets closer and closer to that hypothetical line, the pathway tends to become a slippery slope downward to violation of the law.

Avoiding the unauthorized practice of law should be simple for the informed and thoughtful notary. When a notary has any doubt whatsoever about whether she or he may be edging close to the unauthorized practice of law, the cautious notary should not proceed any further. The notary should tell the party seeking the notarization and further assistance or advice that the notary is not a licensed attorney, and should suggest that the party seek the advice of a licensed attorney. If the party seeking the notarization wishes to proceed with the notarization, the notary will have to determine whether to perform the notarization based upon the applicable notary statute and the other best practice standards set out in this book.

26.5 The notary who is neither an attorney nor a professional in a law-related field should not draft or prepare the instrument to be notarized.

The cardinal rule for a notary public is to serve the public as an impartial governmental witness to a document signing. A notary cannot be a disinterested and unbiased public official if he or she has drafted or prepared the instrument to be notarized, or has advised or consulted about the document to be notarized, for a private party. A notary in such circumstances would not only violate the prohibition against the UPL, but also would violate the admonition to avoid actual and apparent conflicts of interest.

The restriction set out by this practice standard is the simplest of the guides for avoiding the UPL. Non-attorney notaries who are not professionals in law-related fields should not draft or prepare legal documents, or assist in the preparation or drafting of such a document. Every instrument that is important enough to be notarized is a legal document, and every instrument which is notarized has legal consequences. In light of the somewhat uncertain definition of the UPL, notaries public should be careful not to encroach, nor even to appear to encroach, upon those areas of conduct limited to licensed attorneys. The notary's sole responsibility is to notarize, or to decline to notarize, the instrument in question. The notary's only need to draft or prepare any writing occurs at the time of the notarization and is strictly limited to completion of both the notary journal entry for the notarization and the notary's certificate of notarization. The notary should not draft or write anything anywhere else on the instrument being notarized at any time.

Certainly, non-attorney notaries who are professionals in other fields of business, may be qualified and authorized to consult, draft, and/or prepare documents for their business clients — including professionals in accounting, architecture, banking, engineering, pension planning, real estate, stocks and bonds, and so on. However, if notaries have legitimately participated in consulting, drafting and/

or preparing their clients' documents in their professional capacities in such areas, then the notaries should not perform notarizations on those documents. Similarly, notary-attorneys who consult about, draft, or prepare documents for their legal clients should not perform notarizations on those documents. There would otherwise be both an apparent and an actual conflict of interest for such notary-attorneys. See the discussion of notary ethics and conflicts of interest in Chapter 19, and the discussion of attorneys and conflicted notarial practices in Chapter 25. With more than 4,450,000 notaries in the U.S., there is absolutely no legitimate reason for any notary to have been involved in the notarization of an instrument which the notary prepared or drafted.

26.6 The notary who is neither an attorney nor a professional in a law-related field should not advise or consult the signer about the document to be notarized.

This practice standard is less certain than the preceding restriction against preparing or drafting an instrument. Obviously, what constitutes advising or consulting about an instrument is less clear than what is involved in preparing or drafting a document. Nevertheless, advising and consulting about a document important enough to be notarized is the province of lawyers or non-attorney professionals in specialty fields.

In the typical notarial setting, the notary enters the picture late in a document's life, as it is already fully drafted, finalized, and ready for its notarization. Moreover, the notary typically spends only minutes in performing the notarial ceremony, which does not allow much time for the notary to engage in advising and consulting about the instrument to be notarized — that would constitute the unauthorized practice of law. Then too, there is the small notary fee, if any, which is hardly appropriate compensation for legal advice or consultation (although compensation is not required as part of the UPL).

In any event, the notary could conceivably offer brief advice and consultation of a legal nature about an instrument to be notarized. Doing so would almost always result from questions posed by the document signer. So, notaries should resist the temptation to answer such inquiries about the application, coverage, wisdom, advantages, disadvantages, or legality of the instruments to be notarized. Notaries should abide by the suggestions offered earlier in this chapter, as well as those set out below.

Practice Tip: *Recording Steps Taken to Avoid UPL.* There are some concrete steps the notary should take to protect against claims of UPL. The notary could post a sign informing notary clients that the notary is not an attorney and cannot provide legal advice or assistance. Such a disclaimer could also be published on the notary's fee schedule and on the front or back of the notary's business card. In the notary journal, the notary should record the start and end times of the notarial ceremony, which should document a very brief period during which it would be unlikely much legal advice could be provided. The journal should also record either that no fee was charged or the amount of the fee charged to the notarial client, which amount will be a quite modest sum at most — much less than would be expected for one dispensing valuable legal advice or service. If the notary client were to ask any question seeking legal advice, the notary should note such query in the journal entry along with the notary's response declining to answer and reminding the client that the notary is not an attorney.

26.7 The notary who is neither an attorney nor a professional in a law-related field should not read or review the document to be notarized.

This practice standard is important for a couple of reasons. First, notaries are not document police. Hence, notaries should not be reading, reviewing, or closely perusing the documents they notarize. The only matters which notaries need to know about the instruments to be notarized are: (a) the type of document, its number of pages, and its date (for notation in the notary journal), (b) whether there are blank spaces in the instrument which should be filled or marked out (with "not applicable" or "NA" or "X"), and (c) if the signer is accompanied to the notarial ceremony by someone else, whether that person has an interest in the instrument (so that the notary may wish to exclude the person from all or part of the notarial ceremony).

Second, if notaries have not read the documents to be notarized, it is much more difficult for them to be able to discuss or consult about the instruments with signers. Thus, notaries will not be in the position to answer questions about the application, coverage, wisdom, or legality of the instruments. Of course, notaries should never volunteer comments or suggestions about the instruments to be notarized or the circumstances of the signers.

Practice Tip: *Ask Questions, Do Not Answer Questions.* Although notaries could be questioned generally about legal matters relating to the signers and their transactions, notaries should steadfastly refuse to do so. Remember, notaries are in control of notarial ceremonies. Generally, notaries should ask questions of the signers, not answer questions. If a notary has neither read the instrument to be notarized nor answered questions from the signer, the chance that the notary would engage in the UPL is almost nonexistent.

26.8 The notary who is not an attorney, but who is a professional in a law-related field, should be especially careful to avoid engaging in the unauthorized practice of law.

Because so many non-attorney notaries are professionals in law-related fields (such as real estate brokers, accountants, signing agents, paralegals, immigration assistants, mental health professionals, stockbrokers, bankers, insurance agents, financial planners, medical professionals, civil engineers, and the like), those notaries have acquired considerable legal knowledge and are particularly at risk of crossing the gray line which separates their lawful professional services from the unlawful UPL. Those professionals will often participate in the advising and consulting about, and preparing of, documents in their fields of professional activity for their clients.

A number of court cases have held that such notary-professionals have engaged in the UPL. In those reported legal cases, the notary-professionals notarized the documents which they had prepared for their clients, and this dual practice contributed to the case against the notary-professionals. It is undoubtedly true that non-attorney professionals who are also notaries possess so much law-related knowledge they have been tempted to go too far and stray into the forbidden field of the practice of law. At a minimum, the dual service causes the notary to be more involved than she or he otherwise would have been.

Moreover, this author, many other experts, and the *Notary Public Code of Professional Responsibility* hold the view that it constitutes a conflict of interest for a notary to notarize a document prepared by the notary while also acting as a professional in a law-related field. Because the private-document preparer has a direct interest in validating the document, such a professional cannot serve as an impartial notary. Even if it is claimed that such a dual role by a non-attorney professional serving as a notary does not amount to an actual conflict of interest, it certainly creates the appearance of a conflict. See Chapter 19 about conflicts of interest.

At a minimum, non-attorney professionals in the fields mentioned above should not notarize the documents which they have consulted about, drafted, or prepared for their clients. This restraint will help avoid actual or apparent conflicts of interest and diminish the risk that such individuals will commit the UPL. In addition, this restraint will demonstrate that they recognize the ethical issue of conflicts of interest and that they are concerned enough to avoid it. This posture may assist the professionals if they are faced with defending claims of UPL, too.

See the previous Practice Tip entitled "Recording Steps Taken to Avoid UPL."

26.9 The notary who is not an attorney should be authorized to advise the notary client in the selection of the type of document notarization to be performed.

Note: *This Is a Controversial Practice Standard.* The issue here is one that has been debated for decades within the notarial community, and capable authorities are lined up on both sides of the issue. Importantly, some notary regulations and official notary guides direct notaries not to select the form of notarial certificate to be used for a notarization. The National Notary Association concurs in that view.

The question is, when a document does not contain a notarial certificate or the document signer is unsure what type of notarization should be performed, is the notary qualified and authorized to advise the notary client in the selection of the kind of notarization to be performed, along with the corresponding notarial wording? Interestingly, no state or territorial notary statutes expressly address this question, and no reported court opinions do either. At least one state regulation permits the notary to provide the signer with sample notarial certificates from which the signer may then choose.

The majority of authorities take the view that notaries should not advise clients of the type of notarization that should be performed and should not select the notarial wording for the certificate of notarization. Those experts, many of whom are my respected colleagues in the notarial community, conclude that the notary has no authority to do so and, further, that a notary who does so engages in the UPL.

This author disagrees. If notaries public are notary professionals, they must be trusted with the most basic of all judgments — the type of document notarization that is appropriate. After all, notaries are entrusted with the important and often challenging judgments about the true identity of the document signer, the mental competence of the document signer, and the voluntariness of the signer's execution of the document. We also entrust the notary with the responsibilities to perform the critical paperwork correctly, to maintain and preserve the notary journal as a public record, and to protect the confidentiality and privacy of information about the signer. Importantly, in connection with the selection of the type of notarization to be performed, the notary should only advise the notary client, explaining the differences between the various document notarizations, and should allow the client to make the final choice about the form of notarization to be conducted. There are only three types of document notarizations from which to choose, and the three are different enough that every notary should be able to explain their differences. In my opinion, an acceptable alternative is for the notary to have a set of samples of the three forms of notarial certificates, to present the three samples to a client, and to ask the client to select the form to be executed. Notaries had better be qualified and authorized to address this matter with signers and to then allow the signers to select the form of notarization, or else notaries are not entitled to walk upright. ■

***RELEVANT MODEL NOTARY LAW**

Each notary should read, study, and abide by the notary statute and regulations, if any, of her or his commissioning state or territory.

"To uphold the trust placed in me by the public I serve; ...

To never perform any notarial act in which I am a party in interest or from which I stand to benefit; ...

To not use the office of Notary Public as a means of financial gain, for myself or others, in any other business or profession ..." *Responsibility Code of Ethics* (1980).

"The Notary shall, as a government officer and public servant, serve all of the public in an honest, fair and unbiased manner." *Notary Public Code of Professional Responsibility,* Guiding Principle I (1998).

"The Notary shall act as an impartial witness and not profit or gain from any document or transaction requiring a notarial act, apart from the fee allowed by statute." *Notary Public Code of Professional Responsibility,* Guiding Principle II (1998).

"The Notary shall act as a ministerial officer and not provide unauthorized advice or services." *Notary Public Code of Professional Responsibility,* Guiding Principle VI, Guiding Principle VI (1998).

"Unauthorized Practice of Law. (a) A non-attorney notary shall not assist another person in drafting, completing, selecting, or understanding a document or transaction requiring a notarial act.

(b) If notarial certificate wording is not provided or indicated for a document, a non-attorney notary shall not determine the type of notarial act or certificate to be used." *Model Notary Act,* Section 5-12 (2010).

"Permissible Advice. Section 5-12 does not preclude a notary who is duly qualified, trained, licensed, or experienced in a particular industry or professional field from selecting, drafting, completing, or advising on a document or certificate related to a matter within that industry or field." *Model Notary Act,* Section 5-13 (2010).

"Misrepresentation And Improper Advertising. (a) A notary shall not claim to have powers, qualifications, rights, or privileges that the office of notary does not provide, including the power to counsel on immigration issues.

(b) A non-attorney notary who advertises notarial services in a language other than English shall include in the advertisement, notice, letterhead, or sign the following, prominently displayed in the same language: (1) the statement: 'I am not an attorney and have no authority to give advice on immigration or other legal matters'; and (2) the fees for notarial acts specified in Section 6-2(a).

(c) A notary may not use the term 'notario publico' or any equivalent non-English term in any business card, advertisement, notice, or sign." *Model Notary Act,* Section 5-14 (2010).

"Prohibited Acts. (a) A commission as a notary public does not authorize an individual to: (1) assist persons in drafting legal records, give legal advice, or otherwise practice law; (2) act as an immigration consultant or an expert on immigration matters; (3) represent a person in a judicial or administrative proceeding relating to immigration to the United States, United States citizenship, or related matters; or (4) receive compensation for performing any of the activities listed in this subsection.

(b) A notary public may not engage in false or deceptive advertising.

(c) A notary public, other than an attorney licensed to practice law in this state, may not use the term 'notario' or 'notario publico'.

(d) A notary public, other than an attorney licensed to practice law in this state, may not advertise or represent that the notary public may assist persons in drafting legal records, give legal advice, or otherwise practice law. If a notary public who is not an attorney licensed to practice law in this state in any manner advertises or represents that the notary public offers notarial services, whether orally or in a record, including broadcast media, print media, and the Internet, the notary public shall include the following statement or an alternative statement authorized or required by the [commissioning officer or agency], in the advertisement or representation, prominently and in each language used in the advertisement or representation: "I am not an attorney licensed to practice law in this state. I am not allowed to draft legal records, give advice on legal matters, including immigration, or charge a few for those activities." If the form of advertisement or representation is not broadcast media, print media, or the Internet and does not permit inclusion of the statement required by this subsection because of size, it must be displayed prominently or provided at the place of performance of the notarial act before the notarial act is performed. ..." *Revised Uniform Law on Notarial Acts,* Section 25 (2010).

Early 1910s–20s, black and white photograph reproduction, showing a storefront window advertising "John Best — Notary, Real Estate, and Insurance."

Chapter

27

Interstate and International Recognition of Notarial Acts

STANDARDS SUMMARY

27.1 The notary should understand that notarized documents may cross borders and need to be recognized in other U.S. and foreign jurisdictions.

27.2 The notary should understand that U.S. states and territories have adopted statutes which expressly recognize lawful notarizations performed in sister states and territories.

27.3 The notary should understand that a lawful U.S. notarization must be recognized in a sister state or territory under the U.S. Constitution's "Full Faith and Credit Clause."

27.4 The notary should understand that the law of the place of notarization will govern whether the notarization is lawful and entitled to recognition in another U.S. jurisdiction.

27.5 The notary should understand that whether a U.S. notarization will be recognized in a foreign country is a matter of discretionary judgment exercised by the recipient country.

27.6 The notary should be especially careful in completing the notarial certificate, including affixing the notary seal impression, to foster possible cross-border recognition of a notarized document.

27.7 The notary should be especially careful in completing an official notary journal entry to foster possible cross-border recognition of a notarized document.

STANDARDS EXPLANATIONS

Historically, an important feature of notarizations was to have those notarizations recognized and approved from country to country between commercial trading partners, and in America between the colonies and between the colonies and trading partners in Europe. Now, in our increasingly mobile and global village, many notarized U.S. instruments cross state, territorial, and international borders and are presented for acceptance or recognition. Accordingly, there are basic steps and precautions that should be taken as part of sound notarial practice to help facilitate the interstate and international recognition of U.S. notarizations.

U.S. states and territories have enacted statutes that, under certain conditions, recognize the notarizations of sister states and territories and of foreign countries. But, of course, whether foreign countries will recognize U.S. notarizations is a different matter that is left largely to the discretion of those countries.

27.1 The notary should understand that notarized documents may cross borders and need to be recognized in other U.S. and foreign jurisdictions.

In this modern age of interstate and international commerce, thoughtful and responsible notaries should be well-aware of the possibility that their document notarizations will travel too. Furthermore, notaries should always be conscious of and vigilant about their obligations to conduct notarizations so notarizations will be approved not only in the jurisdictions where they are performed but also in other locations. This consciousness is simply part of life in the global village.

Notaries must be mindful that cross-border recognition of document notarizations is not a matter of certainty, either within the U.S. or in foreign jurisdictions. Especially in the international arena, the question of whether cross-border approval of document notarizations in a foreign land should be granted is somewhat unsure, and it is a matter of considerable discretion, as will be explained below.

Case Illustration: *A Personal Example.* This author, in my non-notary capacity, recently experienced a personal example of an international notarization transfer. I had taken my vintage 1948 travel trailer, which was titled in Florida, to my summer house in Maine. From Maine, I decided to place the rare camper for sale online. To my surprise, the buyer was from Spain. The camper and its paperwork, including the Florida title with its title transfer that I signed and had notarized in Maine, were transported by ship from Maine to Spain. Of course, this process included international customs examinations of the paperwork and the trailer at both the ports of departure and arrival. Who would have thought that an old RV, accompanied by its notarized title transfer, would be sent thousands of miles across both land and sea? Thankfully, everything went smoothly, and the notarized title was recognized in Spain. It is a small world in which we live.

27.2 The notary should understand that the U.S. states and territories have adopted statutes which expressly recognize lawful notarizations performed in sister states and territories.

In the U.S., document notarizations are fundamentally alike everywhere. Hence, the basic types of notarial acts on paper documents (acknowledgments, jurats, and signature witnessings) are defined almost identically, and those notarial acts are conducted in virtually the same manner. Also, the qualifications and jurisdictional authority of notaries are comparable throughout the U.S. These similarities favor the interstate recognition of notarial acts, which is the desired result in both governmental and commercial settings. The reliability of instruments, including the assurance of interstate recognition, is the goal individuals wish to achieve when they present documents for notarizations. Interstate recognition of notarizations also helps the economy significantly by encouraging commerce between the states and territories.

Beginning in the 1800s, statutes were adopted to expressly recognize the notarizations of other U.S. jurisdictions, and, at present, every state and territory has enacted such laws which recognize notarizations performed elsewhere in the U.S. As will be addressed separately below, the one prerequisite is that the notarization must be lawful in the place where it is performed if it is to be accorded recognition under the notarization-recognition statute of a sister state or territory.

However, state and territorial statutes may be amended to change their effects. Thus, a state or territorial notary recognition statute could be amended to limit or restrict its application. Could a state or territory, for instance, amend its notarization-recognition statute to prohibit recognition of a remote or webcam notarization lawfully performed in a sister state or territory? Although such a prohibition might be enacted under state or territorial law, it may run afoul of the U.S. Constitution (and would be unconstitutional in the opinion of this author) — as will be discussed in the next section.

27.3 The notary should understand that a lawful U.S. notarization must be recognized in a sister state or territory under the U.S. Constitution's "Full Faith and Credit Clause."

The U.S. Constitution, Article IV, Section 1, contains the "Full Faith and Credit Clause" which provides, as would be expected in a multistate or multiterritory federal system, that sister states and territories not only must respect the authority of one another to make decisions to govern themselves but also must respect those decisions throughout the nation. The clause provides: "Full Faith and Credit shall be given in each State to the public acts, records, and judicial proceedings of every other State." Thus, such official matters are constitutionally required to be recognized elsewhere in the federal system, provided those matters are legal in the states and territories where they originate.

Although the U.S. Supreme Court has never decided the issue of whether the Full Faith and Credit Clause applies to notarial acts, this author is firmly of the view that notarizations are entitled to the Constitution's full faith and credit recognition. Some judges and other notary experts have reached the same conclusion, and no authorities are known to disagree with that conclusion. Notarizations in particular must be among the official acts and records that are covered under the clause. Notaries are state and territorial officials (not mere city or county officers). Millions of notarized documents cross borders within the U.S. each year, promoting governmental and business activity and facilitating interstate commerce. The states and territories have demonstrated their concurrence about the importance of such notarizations and the need to recognize notarizations cross-border by enacting statutes that expressly endorse such recognition. A key purpose of the Full Faith and Credit Clause was its goal of preserving and fostering harmony among the states and territories. Its purpose is served if notarizations are within its coverage.

One might ask whether this constitutional issue is important in light of the fact that the states and territories have already provided for cross-border recognition in their statutes. It is important. State and territorial statutes may be written so as to create exceptions or limitations to application of their notarization recognition provisions. In other words, a state or territory could adopt an anti-recognition law. So, for example, a state or territory could draft a law which provides that the state or territory will not recognize a notarization performed remotely or by webcam, even though such remote or webcam notarization was legal in the state or territory where it was conducted. If the Full Faith and Credit Clause applies to notarizations, the anti-recognition statute just described would be unconstitutional, null, and void. The importance, therefore, is this — the U.S. Constitution trumps a statutory anti-recognition provision.

Because the cross-border recognition of notarial acts is not discretionary among the states and territories but, instead, is constitutionally mandated, one prerequisite is especially significant. That is, as noted earlier, a notarization must be lawful in the jurisdiction where performed if it is to be entitled to full faith and credit recognition in other U.S. states and territories. This prerequisite of legality of the notarial procedure makes the role of notaries particularly important to the Constitutional recognition of sister-state and sister-territorial notarizations and means notaries must be diligent in how they perform notarizations.

27.4 The notary should understand that the law of the place of notarization will govern whether a notarization is lawful and entitled to recognition in another U.S. jurisdiction.

When a notarization is performed in one U.S. state or territory and the notarized document is taken to another U.S. state or territory, the notarization must be given effect in the second state or territory if the notarization is lawful. So, the question is, does the law of the place of performance or the law of the place of recognition govern whether the notarization was legally performed?

The answer in U.S. law is clear. The law of the place of the performance of the notarization determines if the notarization was properly and legally performed for the purpose of cross-border U.S. recognition. This approach is the reasonable and appropriate standard, for notaries should only be required to know and abide by the law of their own commissioning states and territories and cannot be expected to know or predict where else their notarizations will be transmitted. In other terms, if the notarization is legal where it is performed, it is legal and valid everywhere in the U.S. Consequently, the notary must be particularly diligent and thorough in complying with the law of the notary's commissioning jurisdiction, in order to assist the cross-border approval of notarizations.

27.5 The notary should understand that whether a U.S. notarization will be recognized in a foreign country is a matter of discretionary judgment exercised by the recipient country.

International recognition of U.S. notarizations is less certain, for a number of reasons to be addressed here. Yet, just as with interstate recognition of U.S. notarizations, international recognition is expected by document signers and is good for international commerce.

Internationally, the official certificate and seal of a notary public are recognized around the world, making the notary a kind of international public officer. However, in the international arena, the issue of recognition of notarial acts is much more complicated than in regard to interstate recognition, and there is greater uncertainty about the recognition by foreign countries of notarizations performed by U.S. notaries. Interestingly, the U.S. will almost always recognize notarizations performed in other countries (and performed by the English notaries and civil law notaries who practice there) because those foreign notaries are virtually always highly qualified professionals and are usually lawyers as well. Further, those notarizations certainly satisfy the key elements required of our U.S. notarizations (particularly, reliable identification of the document signers and the established competence and willingness of those signers).

Less often, other countries will recognize U.S. notarizations. Other countries tend to accord less respect to U.S. notaries and their notarial acts. U.S. notaries are not usually as well-qualified as foreign notaries, and the function of U.S. notaries is less substantive and more ministerial than what foreign notaries do. In addition, U.S. notarizations appear far different in format and length, being very brief by contrast to the substantial length and depth of foreign notarizations (which tend to be more like reports or opinion letters in support of the transactions involved). Indeed, in the civil law nations, civil law notaries serve as counsel for the situation, meaning that they determine and document the legitimacy of the transaction — a role unknown to U.S. notaries. Foreign notaries resemble document police; U.S. notaries do not. Nevertheless, as recognition by foreign countries is within the discretion of foreign agents and officials, in many instances, U.S. notarizations will be recognized. It just depends on the full circumstances.

When it comes to the possible recognition of a U.S. notarization in a foreign country, the process for making the decision is much different than it is for possible sister-state or sister-territorial approval of a US notarization. Again, the starting point will almost certainly be to confirm that the U.S. notarization was proper under the relevant U.S. law. In the transnational arena, each nation and, in turn, the agencies or entities within those individual nations will exercise their discretion in deciding whether the U.S. notarization should be approved. Proper U.S. notarizations are sometimes rejected in other countries.

27.6 The notary should be especially careful in completing the notarial certificate, including affixing the notary seal impression, to foster possible cross-border recognition of a notarized document.

The cardinal rule of recognition of a document notarization is that a notarization must be valid in the jurisdiction where it was performed before it will even be entitled to consideration for approval in another jurisdiction. This fundamental rule is the law everywhere in the U.S. and foreign countries.

A notarization is the performance of the notarial ceremony and its recordation in the notarial certificate. After the notarial ceremony is finished, the remaining tangible evidence of its completion is the certificate of notarization (along with a journal entry, discussed in the next section). The certificate is the key element which will affect whether a document notarization performed in one U.S. jurisdiction will be accorded recognition in another U.S. jurisdiction, or in another country. In turn, the most important part of the certificate in relation to the recognition question is undoubtedly the presence of a clear and legible notary seal impression, for the notary seal is the symbol of officiality around the world. Even if the notary statute of the notary's commissioning jurisdiction does not require the notary to affix a seal, no statute anywhere prohibits a notary from affixing seals to notarial certificates, and the notary should affix a seal impression as part of every document notarization. Just as curb appeal helps to sell houses, certificate appearance helps notarization acceptance. The more complete and thorough the appearance of the certificate, the better its likelihood of cross-border recognition. Of course, the notary should diligently complete all of the elements of the notarial certificate — including the venue, the present date, the name of the document signer, the type of notarial act performed, the means of identifying the document signer, the name of the notary, the notary seal impression, and the notary commission expiration date (if it is not a part of the seal impression).

Notaries should always remember, as they conduct notarizations, to focus upon the certificate. If notaries have thoroughly and accurately completed the notarial certificate, the notarization should be recognized in other U.S.

jurisdictions and foreign countries. The notary should thoroughly and accurately conduct the notarial ceremony and record it thoroughly and accurately in the certificate of notarization, for the certificate is the written record of the notarization. See also the discussion of the notary certificate in Chapter 7 and of the notary seal in Chapter 8.

27.7 The notary should be especially careful in completing an official notary journal entry to foster possible cross-border recognition of a notarized document.

The notary journal is an invaluable part of the document notarization process in large part because the journal entries serve as contemporaneous and secure written records to corroborate and verify the authenticity of document notarizations. Since the official notarial certificate is a public record and contains the detailed information that confirms the performance of the document notarization, and since that certificate often is removed from the possession of the notary and taken by the document signer, the certificate may be subject to possible post-notarization tampering or forgery. The journal entry in the exclusive possession of the notary constitutes a most reliable and worthwhile supplemental official public record of the notarization.

As pointed out previously, not all U.S. jurisdictions require their notaries to prepare and preserve notary journal entries, but no U.S. jurisdiction prohibits notaries from keeping journal records. One of the several valuable reasons why every notary should prepare a journal entry for every notarization and securely preserve such records is to assist with cross-border recognition of notarizations.

If a document notarization were to be challenged at the time it is received in another U.S. jurisdiction or in a foreign country, the notary journal entry for the notarization should be considered on the question of validity of the notarization and its entitlement to cross-border recognition. The evidentiary significance of the journal record is in keeping with the cardinal rule noted above — that only a notarization valid in the place where it was conducted will be entitled to consideration for recognition in another U.S. or foreign jurisdiction. And, of course, if the issue of the validity of the document notarization and its entitlement to cross-border recognition is not resolved from examination of the certificate of notarization and the relevant notary journal entry, the notary may be questioned about the notarization. The notary journal entry would assist the notary's recollection of the circumstances relating to the specific notarial act and, thus, support cross-border recognition. See also the discussion of the notary journal in Chapter 17. ■

***RELEVANT MODEL NOTARY LAW**

Each notary should read, study, and abide by the notary statute and regulations, if any, of his or her commissioning state or territory.

"Purposes. This [Act] shall be construed and applied to advance its underlying purposes, which are: (1) to promote, serve, and protect the public interest; ...

(4) to enhance cross-border recognition of notarial acts ..." *Model Notary Act,* Section 1-2 (2010).

"The Notary shall affix a seal on every notarized document and not allow this universally recognized symbol of office to be used by another or in an endorsement or promotion." *Notary Public Code of Professional Responsibility,* Guiding Principle VII (1998).

"Recognition Of Notarial Acts. Notarial Acts By Officers Of Other United States Jurisdictions. (a) A notarial act has the same effect under the law of this [State] as if performed by a notarial officer of the [State] if performed in another state, commonwealth, territory, district, or possession of the United States by any of the following persons: (1) a notary public of that jurisdiction; (2) a judge, clerk, or deputy clerk of a court of that jurisdiction; or (3) any other person authorized by the law of that jurisdiction to perform notarial acts.

(b) The official signature, title, and, if required by law, seal of a person whose authority to perform notarial acts is recognized by Subparagraph (a) are prima facie evidence that the signature and seal are genuine and that the person holds the indicated title, and, except in the case of Subparagraph (a)(3), conclusively establishes the authority of a holder of that title to perform a notarial act." *Model Notary Act,* Section 11-2 (2010).

"Recognition Of Notarial Acts. Notarial Acts By Foreign Officers. (a) A notarial act has the same effect under the law of this [State] as if performed by a notarial officer of this [State] if performed within the jurisdiction and under authority of a foreign nation or its constituent units or a multi-national or international organization by any of the following persons: (1) a notary public or other notarial officer; (2) a judge, clerk, or deputy clerk of a court of record; or (3) any other person authorized by the law of that jurisdiction to perform notarial acts.

(b) The official seal or stamp of a person whose authority to perform notarial acts is recognized by Subsection (a) are prima facie evidence that the signature is genuine, that the person holds the indicated title, and, except in the case of Subsection (a)(3), conclusively establishes the authority of a holder of that title to perform a notarial act.

(c) The authority of an officer to perform notarial acts is conclusively established if the title of the office and indication of authority to perform notarial acts appears either in a digest of foreign law or a list customarily used as a source for that information.

(d) An Apostille in the form prescribed by Section 10-3 conclusively establishes that the signature and seal of the notarial officer referenced in the Apostille are genuine and that the person holds the indicated office.

(e) A certificate of a foreign service or consular officer of the United States stationed in the nation under whose jurisdiction the notarial act was performed, or a certificate of a foreign service or consular officer of that nation stationed in the United States, conclusively establishes any matter relating to the authenticity or validity of the notarial act referenced in the certificate." *Model Notary Act,* Section 11-4 (2010).

"Notarial Act In Another State. (a) A notarial act performed in another state has the same effect under the law of this state as if performed by a notarial officer of this state, if the act performed in that state is performed by: (1) a notary public of that state; (2) a judge, clerk, or deputy clerk of a court of that state; or (3) any other individual authorized by the law of that state to perform the notarial act.

(b) The signature and title of an individual performing a notarial act in another state are prima facie evidence that the signature is genuine and that the individual holds the designated title.

(c) The signature and title of a notarial officer described in subsection (a)(1) or (2) conclusively establish the authority of the officer to perform the notarial act." *Revised Uniform Law on Notarial Acts,* Section 11 (2010).

"Notarial Act Under Authority Of Federally Recognized Indian Tribe. (a) A notarial act performed under the authority of a federally recognized Indian tribe has the same effect as if performed by a notarial officer of this state, if the act performed in the jurisdiction of the tribe is performed by: (1) a notary public of the tribe; (2) a judge, clerk, or deputy clerk of a court of the tribe; and (3) any other individual authorized by the law of the tribe to perform the notarial act.

(b) The signature and title of an individual performing a notarial under authority of and in the jurisdiction of a federally recognized Indian tribe are prima facie evidence that the signature is genuine and that the individual holds the designated title.

(c) The signature and title of a notarial officer described in subsection (a)(1) or (2) conclusively establish the authority of the officer to perform the notarial act." *Revised Uniform Law on Notarial Acts,* Section 12 (2010).

"Notarial Act Under Federal Authority. (a) A notarial act performed under federal law has the same effect under the law of this state as if performed by a notarial officer of this state, if the act performed under federal law is performed by: (1) a judge, clerk, or deputy clerk of a court; (2) an individual in military service or performing duties under the authority of military service who is authorized to perform notarial acts under federal law; (3) an individual designated a notarizing officer by the United States Department of State for performing notarial acts overseas; or (4) any other individual authorized by federal law to perform the notarial act.

(b) The signature and title of an individual acting under federal authority and performing a notarial act are prima facie evidence that the signature is genuine and that the individual holds the designated title.

(c) The signature and title of an officer described in subsection (a)(1), (2), or (3) conclusively establish the authority of the officer to perform the notarial act." *Revised Uniform Law on Notarial Acts,* Section 13 (2010).

"Foreign Notarial Act. (a) In this section, 'foreign state' means a government other than the United States, a state, or a federally recognized Indian tribe.

(b) If a notarial act is performed under the authority and in the jurisdiction of a foreign state or constituent unit of the foreign state or is performed under the authority of a multinational or international governmental organization, the act has the same effect under the law of this state as if performed by a notarial officer of this state.

(c) If the title of office and indication of authority to perform notarial acts in a foreign state appears in a digest of foreign law or in a list customarily used as a source for that information, the authority of an officer with that title to perform notarial acts is conclusively presumed.

(d) The signature and official stamp of an individual holding an office described in subsection (c) are prima facie evidence that the signature is genuine and the individual holds the designated title.

(e) An apostille in the form prescribed by the Hague Convention of October 5, 1961, and issued by a foreign state party to the Convention conclusively establishes that the signature of the notarial officer is genuine and that the officer holds the indicated office.

(f) A consular authentication issued by an individual designated by the United States Department of State as a notarizing officer for performing notarial acts overseas and attached to the record with respect to which the notarial act is performed conclusively establishes that the signature of the notarial officer is genuine and that the officer holds the indicated office." *Revised Uniform Law on Notarial Acts,* Section 14 (2010).

S-29

Commonwealth of Massachusetts

Suffolk, ss. $ 44. Boston, MAY 7 - 1921 192

To Creston National Bank, Creston, Ia.

A Bill of Exchange, drawn by W. A. Dollarhide

on Charles Clements

for the sum of Forty-four and no/100 Dollars,

dated April 28, 1921

payable At sight

to the order of Land Credit Bank

endorsed by you, is protested for non-acceptance; acceptance having been duly demanded at office of the drawee.

and refused. The holder requires of you payment thereof with interest, cost and damages.

Done at the request of the First National Bank of Boston.

L. P. Everett Notary Public

70 Federal Street, Boston, Mass.

Please Notify the Other Parties

1921, standard form, Commonwealth of Massachusetts notarial protest of a bill of exchange, prepared and signed by notary public L.P. Everett. The protest of bank, marine, and other commercial instruments by notaries was an important part of their duties from the early days in America until about the mid-1900s. The performance of such protests has been almost entirely abandoned by notaries and has been deleted from most notary statutes, although some laws still make reference to the authority of notaries to perform protests.

Chapter

28

Notary Fees and Travel Costs

STANDARDS SUMMARY

28.1 The notary should understand the notary's unique role as the only public official permitted to bill for official services and to personally retain the fees collected.

28.2 The notary should understand that there is no obligation to charge fees to notarial clients.

28.3 The notary should, if fees are to be charged and unless provided otherwise by law, not share those fees with notary employers.

28.4 The notary should charge no more than the statutory maximum or reasonable levels and should charge such fees uniformly to clients.

28.5 The notary should, if fees are to be charged, create a written fee schedule and conspicuously post or publish that schedule to inform prospective clients prior to the rendition of services.

28.6 The notary should, if fees are to be charged, orally inform prospective clients of the fees prior to the rendition of services and obtain agreement from clients to pay such fees.

28.7 The notary should, if compensation for travel costs is to be assessed, inform prospective clients prior to the rendition of services and obtain agreement to pay such costs.

28.8 The notary should, if paid for fees and travel costs, provide an itemized receipt to each client and retain a copy for the notary's purposes.

28.9 The notary should note in the journal entry that no fee was assessed or note the amount of any payment for fees and travel costs.

28.10 The notary should, prior to the completion of the notarial ceremony, proofread the itemized receipt and the journal entry notation of fees and costs and make any necessary corrections.

STANDARDS EXPLANATIONS

Notaries occupy peculiar positions in the world of government and commerce. Although notaries are public servants, notaries are not typically salaried separately as notaries, unlike other public servants such as police officers, judges, and county recorders who are salaried for their roles as public officers. Although notaries are public officials, most notaries are privately employed. Although many notaries public do not collect fees for their official services, notaries are entitled to charge and collect fees for their notarizations. Of course, if notaries do actually charge fees for notarial services, such fees constitute income that must be reported and upon which taxes must be paid for income tax purposes.

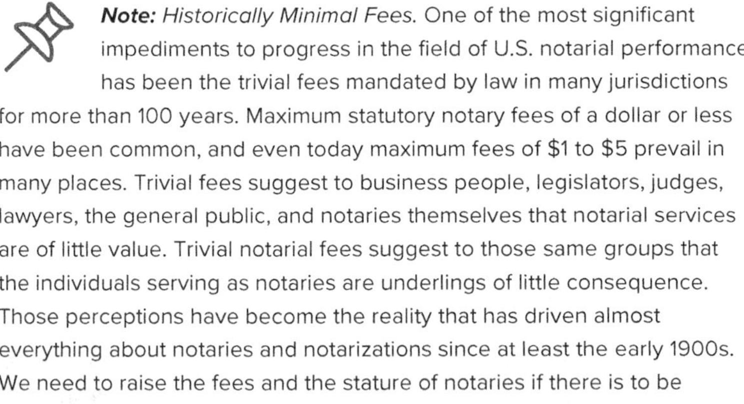

Note: *Historically Minimal Fees.* One of the most significant impediments to progress in the field of U.S. notarial performance has been the trivial fees mandated by law in many jurisdictions for more than 100 years. Maximum statutory notary fees of a dollar or less have been common, and even today maximum fees of $1 to $5 prevail in many places. Trivial fees suggest to business people, legislators, judges, lawyers, the general public, and notaries themselves that notarial services are of little value. Trivial notarial fees suggest to those same groups that the individuals serving as notaries are underlings of little consequence. Those perceptions have become the reality that has driven almost everything about notaries and notarizations since at least the early 1900s. We need to raise the fees and the stature of notaries if there is to be significant progress on the path to professionalism for notaries.

An astounding irony about the minimal fees charged by notaries is that notaries face unlimited personal liability for the faulty performance of the notarial services for which the fees are so paltry. Notary fees have remained minimal even though, in recent decades, notaries have taken on greater and greater liability risks as the monetary values of the instruments and transactions requiring notarizations have continuously risen and as the challenges faced by notaries have risen along with the heightened incidence of identity theft and document frauds. To illustrate, over the last 20 years, this author has been retained as expert consultant and/or expert witness on several notary cases that have involved claims for hundreds of thousands, and sometimes millions, of dollars.

28.1 The notary should understand the notary's unique role as the only public official permitted to bill for official services and to personally retain the fees collected.

In earlier times, some justices of the peace were allowed to retain part or all of the fines they assessed against individuals appearing before them as the compensation for the services rendered. But, that practice ended many decades ago. Today, the one and only public official who is allowed to charge fees and to personally retain those fees is the notary public.

A number of factors undoubtedly contribute to this special situation in regard to the collecting and retention of fees for official services. First and foremost, there is the fact that such a large number of notaries is needed to perform the many millions of notarizations completed each year. There are more than 4,450,000 U.S. notaries. Moreover, almost all notaries work only part-time as notaries, while holding other full-time positions as business owners or as employees in either the public or private sector. Next, in light of the fact that notarial activities are largely ministerial in nature, there is little concern that the retention of the modest notary fees will create actual or apparent conflicts of interest. And, unfortunately, there is such indifference about notaries in general that few people even understand how the notary system functions or have concerns about the fees notaries charge.

28.2 The notary should understand that there is no obligation to charge fees to notarial clients.

No state or territory requires notaries to assess and collect fees for official services. Notaries are public servants, and they may prefer to render their services without charge. This is permitted. There are many persons of limited means for whom the provision of notarial services without charge would be appreciated. Furthermore, there are active duty military personnel, clergy, the elderly, emergency responders, fellow notaries, hospital patients, nurses, school teachers, veterans, and others deserving of free notarial services to be provided by notaries who are able and willing to do so. For instance, this author has never charged anyone or accepted compensation for any notarizations I have performed. Such charitable efforts by notaries should be allowed and encouraged.

Of course, notaries as public servants should not unlawfully discriminate in charging fees. Notaries should not discriminate against individuals on the basis of advanced age, disability, gender, health status, marital status, national origin, noncustomer status, race, religion, or sexual orientation by charging fees to them while not charging fees to other people or by charging higher fees to them than to other people.

28.3 The notary should, if fees are to be charged and unless provided otherwise by law, not share those fees with notary employers.

Note: *Statutory Coverage of This Issue.* There tends to be some confusion among notary-employees and their employers about whether employers may retain the fees paid for notary service provided by their notary-employees while at the workplace or while on duty for the employers. The vast majority of notary statutes and regulations are silent on this issue. If there is a notary statute which permits notary employers to take, or to share in, the fees paid for notarial services provided by their notary employees, then the employers may do so. Sometimes, government employers are authorized to assess and collect notary fees. That is, governmental agencies sometimes employ notary-employees in part to assist in the government functions by performing occasional notarizations for which notary fees are paid by members of the public and are retained by the agencies.

Note: *Some Disagreement About This Issue.* In the absence of statutory or regulatory coverage of the issue of employers retaining or sharing notary fees, there is some controversy about whether employers by agreement with their notary-employees may retain or share fees. This author's opinion is that, in the absence of statutory or regulatory authority, notary-employees themselves are the only ones who are entitled to assess, collect, and retain notary fees. Because it is the employee who is the notary (rather than the employer), any fee that is paid for notarial services belongs solely to the notary, the employee. However,

> in reality, some private employers do receive the fees or share the fees for notarial services performed by their notary-employees while the notary-employees are in the course of their employment. Although improper, this result may happen because the employer requested the employee to become a notary to serve the employer's customers, paid the expenses for the notary to apply and become a notary, advertised the availability of notarial services, or had control of the workplace and employees and, therefore, had a right to collect fees generated by the notary-employee. Yet, these reasons are insufficient to justify the employer's receipt of the fees for notary services. The fact the situation is often mishandled does not change the correct answer. Notaries should not have to share their fees with their employers, unless the law expressly authorizes the practice.

Parenthetically, employers should carefully consider whether they really want to accept the heightened risk of legal liability for possible notary malpractice as the result of receiving minimal notary fees. Employers of notary-employees may face liability for the wrongdoing of their notary-employees under the law of agency. If the employer (principal) receives compensation for the actions of its employee (agent/notary), this financial benefit will almost certainly create the employer's responsibility under agency law (called vicarious liability) for damages caused to a third party by the notary's wrongdoing. See also the discussion of the employer-employee relationship when the employee is a notary in Chapter 24.

28.4 The notary should charge no more than the statutory maximum or reasonable levels and should charge such fees uniformly to clients.

As public officials and public servants, notaries have the responsibility not to overcharge for their official services. Some jurisdictions have enacted statutes which set maximum limits on the fees that can be charged for specific notarial acts, and notaries may not charge in excess of those maximum amounts. Notaries, of course, may charge less than the maximum amounts or no fees at all.

In several other jurisdictions, there are no such laws establishing maximum notary fees. This does not give notaries carte blanche to assess any level of fees. In those jurisdictions, notaries are bound by the duty to charge not more than reasonable fees for their services. Obviously, what constitutes a reasonable fee for specific notarial acts is somewhat uncertain, although some guidance can be provided from the maximum fee statutes in other jurisdictions.

Certainly, notaries should not attempt to take advantage of the absence of statutory maximum fee schedules to unlawfully or improperly discriminate against individuals or groups by charging some people more, or less, for the same notarial acts. If notary fees are assessed, all clients should be charged the same fees for the same services — unless fees are sometimes waived for legitimate, charitable reasons.

28.5 The notary should, if fees are to be charged, create a written fee schedule and conspicuously post or publish that schedule to inform prospective clients prior to the rendition of services.

Even though notary fees tend to be quite modest, notaries should be careful to clearly display the sums involved and to clearly record the payments. The notary who charges fees for services is engaged in business and should conduct such affairs as a business professional would be expected to operate.

If a notary intends to charge for official services, the notary should create an itemized fee schedule for the types of notarial services offered. That fee schedule should then be published in plain and clear language and numerals, and displayed in a conspicuous way so that prospective clients will likely be informed of the fees before obtaining notarizations. To satisfy the conspicuousness standard, the notary should post a sign bearing the fee schedule and print the fee schedule on a page or brochure to give to individual prospective clients.

When the notary posts a sign with the fee schedule, a number of features about the sign should be considered. Both the sign and fee schedule should be large enough to be readily seen and read. Perhaps, depending on the circumstances, more than one color and one type of font could be used, and more than one sign could be posted. Of course, the notary fee sign or signs should not be placed in locations where they cannot be easily seen or are psychologically concealed among other signs.

When the notary fee schedule is produced on handout materials, some of the same kinds of issues should be considered. The print size of the piece needs to be large enough to be easily read. It could include more than one color and different fonts. And, the handout itself should be large enough to be easily read. The handout should be devoted exclusively to notary fees and should not include unrelated material, such as advertising, which might detract from its message.

28.6 The notary should, if fees are to be charged, orally inform prospective clients of the fees prior to the rendition of services and obtain agreement from clients to pay such fees.

When a prospective client approaches the notary for service, the notary should orally ask whether the client has read and understands the fee schedule. The notary should inquire about the type of notarial service being sought and should orally inform the client of the total cost for such service. The notary and client should agree upon the total fee so that there will be no surprise or dispute later about the cost of the notarial service. After all, regardless of the posted or printed fee schedule, clients will not necessarily have paid sufficient attention to it. This additional step of providing information orally should insure that clients are fully aware of the costs of notarizations prior to contracting for the services. This businesslike practice is the only fair and legitimate way to proceed.

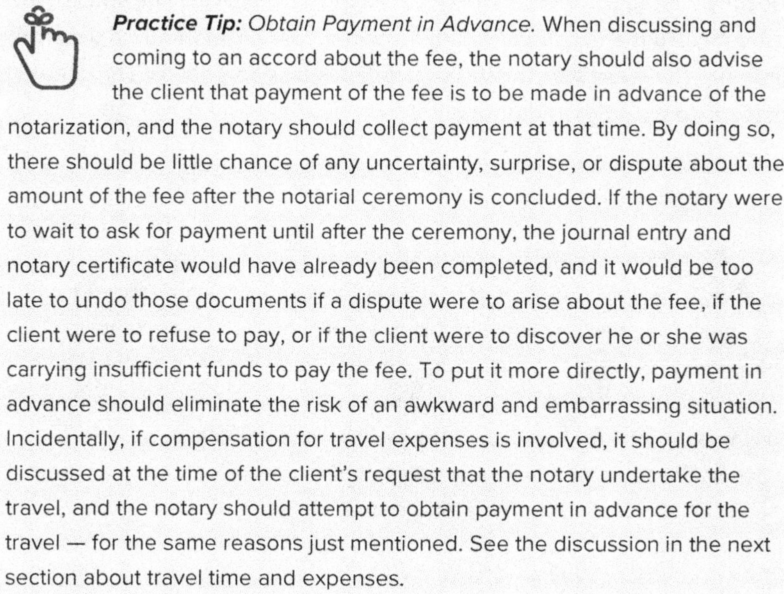

Practice Tip: *Obtain Payment in Advance.* When discussing and coming to an accord about the fee, the notary should also advise the client that payment of the fee is to be made in advance of the notarization, and the notary should collect payment at that time. By doing so, there should be little chance of any uncertainty, surprise, or dispute about the amount of the fee after the notarial ceremony is concluded. If the notary were to wait to ask for payment until after the ceremony, the journal entry and notary certificate would have already been completed, and it would be too late to undo those documents if a dispute were to arise about the fee, if the client were to refuse to pay, or if the client were to discover he or she was carrying insufficient funds to pay the fee. To put it more directly, payment in advance should eliminate the risk of an awkward and embarrassing situation. Incidentally, if compensation for travel expenses is involved, it should be discussed at the time of the client's request that the notary undertake the travel, and the notary should attempt to obtain payment in advance for the travel — for the same reasons just mentioned. See the discussion in the next section about travel time and expenses.

28.7 The notary should, if compensation for travel costs is to be assessed, inform prospective clients prior to the rendition of services and obtain agreement to pay such costs.

Ordinarily, notary clients will come to notaries at their places of employment or business, or perhaps to notaries' residences, so that notaries will not have to travel to customers to perform notarizations. Nor will there typically be the need for travel costs to be incurred, for which notarial clients should have to compensate and reimburse notaries. However, notaries may be asked by clients to travel to perform notarizations, and, in such cases, notaries are not required to accommodate such requests. It will be up to the notary whether to agree to travel.

If notaries decide to travel to perform notarizations, they should be permitted to charge reasonable compensation for their time spent for that travel. Additionally, if notaries incur costs associated with travel (such as the cost of gasoline, or subway or taxicab fare), notaries should be entitled to reimbursement for those costs. Importantly, if notaries are asked to travel to perform notarizations, and if they charge for their travel time and costs, they should inform clients in advance about travel time and costs. Further, before the notarization is performed, the notary should determine or estimate the sums for travel time and expenses and obtain the client's agreement to pay those amounts.

Note: *Do Maximum Fee Statutes Bar Payment for Travel? No.* Notaries sometimes mistakenly believe that a statutory maximum fee schedule prohibits a notary from charging for travel time and expenses. The maximum fee schedule applies to the official act of the notarization itself (such as an acknowledgment, a jurat, or a signature witnessing). The fee schedule does not apply to non-notarial activities. Hence, driving an automobile or using a taxi to travel to a notary customer is not an official act of a notary. This distinction is one reason why the notary should be certain to itemize the customer's receipt and journal entry for the fee payment — separating the notarization itself, travel time, and travel expenses.

Practice Tip: *Written Agreement and Payment in Advance of Travel.* If possible, notaries should record the agreement about compensation for travel time and expenses in writing in advance of the travel. This writing could be an email, a text message, or a standard letter. Even a voice message recording would suffice. Additionally, the notary should obtain payment or a deposit toward payment in advance of travel. The reason to do so is to protect the notary should the notarization not proceed after the notary has already traveled to the site of the planned notarization. The notary would have already expended travel time and incurred travel costs, but the notary might not be compensated and reimbursed.

28.8 The notary should, if paid for fees and travel costs, provide an itemized receipt to each client and should retain a copy for the notary's purposes.

It is customary for clients to be provided with receipts when they pay for purchases and services. Indeed, receipts constitute important records for tax and other purposes. The same practice should prevail in the notarial field. Additionally, the notary should retain a copy of the receipt for the notary's own purposes.

The notary should provide a written receipt to each client, itemizing each separate fee that is assessed. The receipt should identify the type and number of notarizations of each kind that are performed. Parenthetically, it should be noted that some clients will seek multiple notarizations of different documents or may request multiple notarizations of the same document — in order to obtain multiple "originals" of the notarized instrument. In addition, there may be charges for time and travel costs and for incidental services, such as photocopy charges, all of which should be separately itemized.

Because fees collected by notaries for their official services constitute income for tax purposes, notaries are required by law to report such income. Hence, notaries should create contemporaneous and detailed records to document their proceeds from the performance of official notarial acts, and they should maintain and secure those records. Retaining copies of the itemized client receipts is the most effective and efficient method by which the notary can do this. Also, the itemized receipts protect the notary against any false claims of overcharging. See also the practice standard set out immediately below about noting the itemized fees in the notary journal entry.

28.9 The notary should note in the journal entry that no fee was assessed or note the amount of any payment for fees and travel costs.

The main purpose of the notary journal is to provide a written record to document every official notarial act so that notaries and clients do not have to rely upon notarial certificates and their recollections of what transpired at document notarizations. One of the parts of an official notarial act is the collection of a fee, if any, which is charged to the client, and the fee should be noted in the journal entry. In fact, many notary journals now include a column or area specifically designated for the recording of the notary fee. If no fee is charged, that fact should be indicated in the journal entry. If a fee is charged for a single notarial act, the amount should be identified. And, if fees are charged for multiple items (such as multiple notarizations, oaths or affirmations, copies, travel time, and travel expense reimbursement), those payments should be itemized in the journal entry. If more space is needed to itemize fees or payments, the notary should use additional columns or sections or additional lines in the journal.

The journal entries containing reference to the amounts of any notary fees that are charged and collected can also serve to document income for tax purposes, thus corroborating the fee receipts and their copies. This portion of the journal entry would also become helpful if there were an allegation against the notary for overcharging clients. It just makes sense to have a complete summary of the official notarial act, including the notary fee, if any, recorded in a single place — the journal entry.

28.10 The notary should, prior to completion of the notarial ceremony, proofread the itemized receipt and the journal entry notation of fees and costs and make any necessary corrections.

Notaries are human, and humans sometimes lose concentration and make mistakes that go undetected and uncorrected, unless the notaries proofread their documents. If notaries charge fees, notaries should proofread the itemized receipts which they prepare for their clients and themselves. Regardless of whether fees are assessed, notaries should also proofread the fee portion of the journal entry to see that it correctly identifies no fee charged or the itemized fee that was assessed. This proofing should be accomplished before the notarial ceremony is concluded in order to allow the notary to make any needed corrections. ■

***RELEVANT MODEL NOTARY LAW**

Each notary should read, study, and abide by the notary statute and regulations, if any, of her or his commissioning state or territory.

"To uphold the trust placed in me by the public I serve; ...

To treat each individual fairly and equally, with kindness and respect; ...

To not use the office of Notary Public as a means of financial gain, for myself or others, in any other business or profession ..." *Responsibility Code of Ethics* (1980).

"The Notary shall, as a government officer and public servant, serve all of the public in an honest, fair and unbiased manner." *Notary Public Code of Professional Responsibility,* Guiding Principle I (1998).

"The Notary shall act as an impartial witness and not profit or gain from any document or transaction requiring a notarial act, apart from the fee allowed by statute." *Notary Public Code of Professional Responsibility,* Guiding Principle II (1998).

"The Notary shall record every notarial act in a bound journal or other secure recording device and safeguard it as an important public record." *Notary Public Code of Professional Responsibility,* Guiding Principle VIII (1998).

"Imposition And Waiver Of Fees. (a) For performing a notarial act, a notary may charge the maximum fee specified in Section 6-2, charge less than the maximum fee, or waive the fee.

(b) A notary shall not discriminatorily condition the fee for a notarial act on the attributes of the principal [document signer] ... , though a notary may waive or reduce fees for humanitarian or charitable reasons." *Model Notary Act,* Section 6-1 (2010).

"Fees For Notarial Acts. (a) The maximum fees that may be charged by a notary for notarial acts are: (1) for an acknowledgment, [dollars] per signature; (2) for an oath or affirmation without a signature, [dollars] per person; (3) for a jurat, [dollars] per signature; (4) for signature witnessing, [dollars] per signature; ...

(b) A notary may charge a travel fee when traveling to perform a notarial act if: (1) the notary and the person requesting the notarial act agree upon the travel fee in advance of the travel; and (2) the notary explains to the person requesting the notarial act that the travel fee is both separate from the notarial fee prescribed in Subsection (a) and neither specified nor mandated by law." *Model Notary Act,* Section 6-2 (2010).

"Payment Prior To Act. (a) A notary may require payment of any fees specified in Section 6-2 prior to performance of a notarial act.

(b) Any fees paid to a notary prior to performance of a notarial act are non-refundable if: (1) the act was completed; or (2) in the case of travel fees paid in compliance with Subsection 6-2(b), the act was not completed after the notary traveled to meet the principal [document signer] because it was prohibited under Section 5-2, or because the notary knew or had a reasonable belief that the notarial act or the associated transaction was unlawful." *Model Notary Act,* Section 6-3 (2010).

"Fees Of Employee Notary. (a) An employer may prohibit an employee who is a notary from charging for notarial acts performed on the employer's time, but shall not condition imposition of a fee on attributes of the principal [document signer] as described in Section 5-6(a).

(b) A private employer shall not require an employee who is a notary to surrender or share fees charged for any notarial acts.

(c) A governmental employer who has absorbed an employee's costs in becoming or operating as a notary shall require any fees for notarial acts performed on the employer's time either to be waived or surrendered to the employer to support public programs." *Model Notary Act,* Section 6-4 (2010).

"Notice Of Fees. Notaries who charge for their notarial services shall conspicuously display in their places of business, or present to each principal [document signer] outside their places of business, an English-language schedule of fees for notarial acts, as specified in Section 6-2(a). No part of any notarial fee schedule shall be printed in smaller than 10-point type." *Model Notary Act,* Section 6-5 (2010).

"Journal. ... (c) An entry in a journal must be made contemporaneously with performance of the notarial act and contain the following information: ... (6) the fee, if any, charged by the notary public. ..." *Revised Uniform Law on Notarial Acts,* Section 19 (2010).

Vintage 1960s–70s, metal embosser stamp, which reads "Notary Public — Virginia Smith — Cook County, Ill." In earlier times, almost all notary seals were embosser stamps that, under pressure, affixed raised text onto either a blank seal which would be glued or pasted to a notarial certificate, or directly onto the notarial certificate. Ink-stamp seals have virtually fully replaced the embosser stamps because ink seals can be more readily photocopied.

Chapter

29

Notary Membership Organizations

STANDARDS SUMMARY

29.1 The notary should understand the substantial benefits provided by notary membership, education, and advocacy organizations.

29.2 The notary should join, and actively participate in, one or more notary membership, education, and advocacy organizations.

STANDARDS EXPLANATIONS

There are numerous privately operated notary membership, education, and advocacy organizations at the state, territorial, and national levels. Individuals may join one or more of these organizations for only a modest annual fee. At the state or territorial level, there are several notary groups, for instance, with one of the better-known organizations being the Pennsylvania Association of Notaries. This author has been a member of a number of national groups, including the American Society of Notaries, the Notary Law Institute, and the National Notary Association. And, I proudly continue my association with, and support of, these national organizations.

29.1 The notary should understand the substantial benefits provided by notary membership, education, and advocacy organizations.

Each of the various notary membership, education, and advocacy organizations engages in a variety of worthwhile activities. Virtually all of the notary groups provide notary education services, such as live classes and online programs, notary conferences or meetings, and paper or online publications. The publications are important and include a range of aids, such as newsletters, magazines, and books, to assist notaries with basic information and with keeping current.

Some notary membership organizations advocate in support of notaries and on behalf of notaries. The notary groups are undoubtedly the most well-positioned and effective advocates for changes such as progressive and improved notary statutes and regulations and such as better support and conditions for practicing notaries. Indeed, among the most significant developments fostering better laws governing notaries and the performance of notarizations have been the model laws drafted and published by the National Notary Association, including the *Model Notary Act* of 1984, the *Notary Public Code of Professional Responsibility* of 1998, the *Model Notary Act* of 2002, the *Model Notary Act* of 2010, and the *Model Electronic Notarization Act* of 2017.

Of course, not all notary organizations are alike. Some notary businesses have adopted names which sound like membership groups, but which are purely for-profit businesses focused on selling services connected with the processing of notary commission applications and renewal applications, the provision of notary education as part of that application process, and the sale of notary supplies, notary bonds, and notary errors and omissions insurance. These companies provide important services, and notary applicants and notaries should do their homework before selecting an entity to provide those services. In addition, notary applicants and notaries should do their homework before choosing a notary membership, education, and advocacy organization to join.

29.2 The notary should join, and actively participate in, one or more notary membership, education, and advocacy organizations.

All notaries should take their positions as commissioned public officials seriously and should strive to improve themselves and their profession. All notaries should want the public they serve to be even better served by their fellow notaries. And, all notaries should desire better compensation for their services and better working conditions (such as improved and progressive notary laws and greater respect from customers and notary employers). One of the marks of a true professional is the recognition of the obligation of self-improvement. If notaries are to move in the direction of greater professionalism in their ranks, they must work individually to improve themselves and work collectively to improve the quality of their performance.

One way to promote these goals is for each notary to take part in the advocacy and education activities of one or more of the notary membership and education organizations. A notary might volunteer to help write an article in an organization's newsletter. A notary might offer to become a speaker at a notary conference or to teach a notary education class. A notary might agree to become a mentor for new notaries under the supervision of a notary organization. At a minimum, each notary should regularly read the publications of a notary organization and regularly attend continuing notary education sessions offered by a notary organization. See the discussion of continuing notary education in Chapter 30.

In other words, it is not enough for a notary to simply pay the fee or dues to join a notary group, to do nothing more than that, and then to think or claim to have promoted the individual notary's qualifications or the notary profession as a whole. If a notary does not want to do more, that individual should not be a public servant and should not be a notary. ■

***RELEVANT MODEL NOTARY LAW**

Each notary should read, study, and abide by the notary statute and regulations, if any, of his or her commissioning state or territory.

"To keep informed of the law regarding the duties and powers of the office of Notary Public in my jurisdiction and not compromise that law ..." *Responsibility Code of Ethics* (1980).

"The Notary shall seek instruction on notarization, and keep current on the laws, practices and requirements of the notarial office." *Notary Public Code of Professional Responsibility,* Guiding Principle X (1998).

Vintage embosser notary stamp, c. 1983.

Chapter

30

Notary Continuing Education

STANDARDS SUMMARY

30.1 The notary should understand that, with the passage of time, there will be changes affecting the notary's duties.

30.2 The notary should undertake continuing education on a regular basis, at least annually.

30.3 The notary should, at the time of commission renewal, engage in continuing education, regardless of whether required by law.

STANDARDS EXPLANATIONS

One of the characteristics that defines a field of endeavor as a profession is the obligation of its members to engage in continuing education. Thus, every one of the established learned professions — accounting, architecture, banking, law, medicine, and others — have created extensive voluntary continuing education programs, and sometimes mandatory continuing education. However, few jurisdictions require continuing notary education (mostly upon renewal of the multiyear notary commission). Mandatory annual notary continuing education needs to be adopted by all U.S. jurisdictions.

In the notary field, while there are many opportunities for voluntary continuing education, not nearly enough notaries avail themselves of those opportunities. And, until the state and territorial governments see fit to impose statutory or regulatory provisions for mandatory annual notary continuing education, notaries public cannot achieve the heightened status as true business professionals.

30.1 The notary should understand that, with the passage of time, there will be changes affecting the notary's duties.

Continuing education is an old and popular concept in the learned professions and so many other callings — with airline pilots, automobile mechanics, cosmetologists, firefighters, insurance agents, law enforcement officers, nurses, and on. Just about every kind of endeavor changes and advances enough to warrant instruction of its practitioners on a continuing basis. Notary practice cannot possibly be immune from the need for continuing education. Indeed, notarization is a vital field which has flourished in size and which is ever changing, especially in the current era of heightened concerns about identity theft and document security and increasing responsibilities for notaries.

Like everything else in the world that is affected by technology, that is governmentally regulated, and that is targeted by criminals, with the passage of time, the field of notarial practice is impacted and changes in various respects. New statutes may be adopted, or existing laws may be amended or repealed. Perhaps, technological advancements may affect notarizations. Possibly, new or different standards of notarial performance may be developed. Sometimes, new practices evolve, or old practices must be modified or abandoned.

Moreover, with the mere passage of time, practitioners often forget some of what they have learned. Skills and procedures used only infrequently by practitioners may not remain as well honed as they should be. Notaries should recognize the need for lifelong learning and for refreshing their knowledge about notarial practice. Continuing notarial education is the only way for notaries to remain well-informed and current about their functions.

Practice Tip: *Avoiding Complacency.* Importantly, complacency and indifference are real dangers for many notaries, for many of them either serve so infrequently that they don't seem to care, or they serve so often that their functions become routine and rote. However, every notarization should be taken seriously and should be performed diligently. In hindsight, nearly every challenged notarization that results in bond and insurance claims, criminal investigations, and legal proceedings seemed routine when it was performed. This unfortunate reality demands that notaries take advantage of continuing education, if for no other reason than to revisit and refresh fundamental skills and strategies for sound notarizations.

30.2 The notary should undertake continuing education on a regular basis, at least annually.

In a field as important and complex as document notarization, no one can anticipate every possible situation that may develop, and no one can know everything about the subject. Everyone, including this author, needs continuing education. Indeed, one reason this author serves so often as an instructor of notary continuing education sessions is that I learn from those programs every time I teach a class. I learn from my notary students — from their stories, concerns, and questions.

Continuing notary education classes are variously offered by government agencies, by notary membership organizations, and by private providers. In-person classroom courses, self-study materials, and online courses are available. Therefore, there are plenty of chances for diligent notaries to obtain accurate information and quality instruction in notary law, ethics, and practice.

In some of the learned professions, practitioners are required to undertake several hours of continuing education each and every year of their professional service. In the legal profession, lawyers in many states are even required as part of their licensure process to participate in continuing education, specifically in legal ethics every year, and there is a very active continuing education program available for state and federal judges. It is certainly not asking too much of notaries to participate in some kind of continuing education at least annually. No one can be too prepared to serve in the important and trusted position as a notary public.

Practice Tip: *Involving the Employer.* Notaries who serve in their places of work and, especially, if serving at the request of their employers, should consider using the need for continuing education as a way to inform their employers about the quality of notarial services. Perhaps, employers could even be encouraged to support continuing education by granting notary-employees paid time at the workplace for online continuing notary education or away from the job site for attendance at live notary education programs. Better yet, employers or supervisors could take a notary course themselves along with their notary-employees.

30.3 The notary should, at the time of commission renewal, engage in continuing education, regardless of whether required by law.

Few jurisdictions require their notaries who renew their commissions to undergo continuing notarial education as a prerequisite to the issuance of their new commissions. Yet, the occasion of commission renewal is a critical time when continuing education should be required or should be undertaken, even if not required.

After all, most notary commissions are issued for terms of four years in duration. Some commissions last even longer. That is a long period of time during which most notaries under the present system will have received no continuing education. If notaries renew their commissions without any additional notary education or training, it may well result in their practicing for another four-year term without continuing education — an astounding total of eight years during which notary practitioners will have received no new formal education about their duties and functions. Tragically, many notaries obtain renewal commissions several times over the period of their careers. They may serve for 20 to 30 years, or longer, without continuing notary education.

Of course, jurisdictions that adopt testing of notaries as a requirement prior to issuance of commission renewals, effectively require a kind of continuing education in order for notaries to be fully prepared to take and pass such renewal examinations. Nevertheless, the better approach would be for states and territories to adopt both a continuing education and a mandatory testing requirement.

As already mentioned, this author has been teaching notary continuing education programs every year for some 25 years across many states, and I can say without hesitation that I have learned and improved my skills as a notary with every continuing education session I have taught — for I have learned from my notary students. And, since I have had the opportunity to teach thousands of notaries, I have observed many of their reactions when they have heard something new or have realized there is another view of how to do something. It can be an inspiring experience, and I am confident that every notary has room to grow and improve. ■

***RELEVANT MODEL NOTARY LAW**

Each notary should read, study, and abide by the notary statute and regulations, if any, of her or his commissioning state or territory.

"To keep informed of the law regarding the duties and powers of the office of Notary Public in my jurisdiction and not compromise that law ..." *Responsibility Code of Ethics* (1980).

"The Notary shall seek instruction on notarization, and keep current on the laws, practices, and requirements of the notarial office." *Notary Public Code of Professional Responsibility,* Guiding Principle X (1998).

"Qualifications. ... (b) A person qualified for a notary commission shall: ... (5) pass a course of instruction requiring a written examination under Section 4-3 ..." *Model Notary Act,* Section 3-1 (2010).

"Recommissioning. A current or former notary applying for a new notary commission shall submit a new completed application and comply anew with all of the provisions of Chapters 3 and 4." *Model Notary Act,* Section 3-5 (2010).

"Course and Examination. (a) Every applicant for a notary commission shall take, within the 3 months preceding application, a course of instruction of at least 4 hours approved by the [commissioning official], and pass a written examination of this course.

(b) The content of the course and the basis for the written examination shall be notarial laws, procedures, and ethics." *Model Notary Act,* Section 4-3 (2010).

"[Examination Of Notary Public. (a) An applicant for a commission as a notary public who does not hold a commission in this state must pass an examination administered by the [commissioning officer or agency] or an entity approved by the [commissioning officer or agency]. The examination must be based on the course of study described in subsection (b).

(b) The [commissioning officer or agency] shall offer regularly a course of study to applicants who do not hold commissions as notaries public in this state. The course must cover the laws, rules, procedures, and ethics relevant to notarial acts.]." *Revised Uniform Law on Notarial Acts,* Section 22 (2010).

Additional References

For additional information on the topics in this book, there are several resources that will be excellent references for you. An online search of the following publications will allow you to view the resources in their entirety:

Responsibility Code of Ethics of the American Society of Notaries (1980) by American Society of Notaries
https://www.asnnotary.org/?form=about

Notary Public Code of Professional Responsibility (1998) by National Notary Association
https://www.nationalnotary.org/file%20library/nna/reference-library/notary_code.pdf

Revised Uniform Law On Notarial Acts (2010) by Uniform Laws Commission
http://www.uniformlaws.org/shared/docs/notarial_acts/rulona_final_10.pdf

Model Notary Act (2010) by National Notary Association
https://www.nationalnotary.org/file%20library/nna/reference-library/2010_model_notary_act.pdf

Model Electronic Notarization Act (2017) by National Notary Association
https://www.nationalnotary.org/file%20library/nna/reference-library/model-enotarization-act.pdf

Bibliography

A

A. Carlisle & Co. *The Notary's Manual* (5th Ed. 1916).

Aguirre, Armando. "Border Crossings: Using One, Sometimes Two Commissions, Notaries Operate Across State Lines," The National Notary, March 2005, p. 34.

Aguirre, Armando. "States Set Bar Low for Notary Applicants," The National Notary, July 2001, p. 16.

Ahlers, Glen-Peter. "The Impact of Technology on the Notary Process," 31 John Marshall Law Review 911–926 (1998).

Ahlers, Glen-Peter. "Notaries Public: A Pathfinder," 32 John Marshall Law Review 1065–1121 (1999). An extensive research tool summarizing information resources, including 50+ pages and 240+ footnotes.

American Society of Notaries. "Apostilles: Authenticating Documents for Use in Foreign Countries," American Notary, April–June 1997, p. 7.

American Society of Notaries. *Responsibility Code of Ethics of the American Society of Notaries* (1980), reprinted in 32 John Marshall Law Review 1195 (1999). A one-page, 12-point ethics code.

American Society of Notaries. "Should Record Books Be Required?" American Notary, July–August 1997, p. 4.

Anderson, John & Michael Closen. "Document Authentication in Electronic Commerce: The Misleading Notary Public Analog for the Digital Signature Certification Authority," 17 John Marshall Journal of Computer & Information Law 833 (1999).

Anderson, John & Michael Closen. "A Proposed Code of Ethics for Employers and Customers of Notaries: A Companion to the Notary Public Code of Professional Responsibility," 32 John Marshall Law Review 887–934 (1999).

Anderson Publishing. *Anderson's Manual for Notaries Public* (9th Ed. 2001).

Anthony, Phil. *California Notaries' Law Primer and Business Guide* (1963).

Athanasopoulos-Arvanitakis, Dina & Marilynn Dye. "A Proposed Code of Professional Responsibility for Certification Authorities," 17 John Marshall Journal of Computer & Information Law 1003 (1999).

B

Baker, Stewart & Theodore Barassi. "The International Notarial Practitioner," International Law News (American Bar Association), Fall 1995, p. 1.

Barich, Nevin. "Creating a Paper Trail: The Journal as Evidence," The National Notary, July 2003, p. 31.

Barich, Nevin. "Good Journal Keeping," The National Notary, May 2004, p. 33.

Barich, Nevin. "So Now You're a Notary," The National Notary, January 2005, p. 38.

Barich, Nevin. "The World Has Changed for Notaries and the NNA, but Our Duty Is More Important Than Ever," The National Notary, January 2007, p. 26.

Berton, Lee. "It's a Proud Calling, but the Notary's Lot Is Full of Indignities," The Wall Street Journal, June 15, 1993, p. A1.

Birenbaum, Marc. "Enforcing the Law," The National Notary, September 1997, p. 10. Discusses violations that notaries commit.

Birenbaum, Marc. "Protecting Your Invaluable Journal," The National Notary, November 1997, p. 12.

Brooke, Richard. *A Treatise on the Office and Practice of a Notary of England* (5th Ed. 1890). A leading reference source on English notaries, published in numerous editions, and still published.

Brooks, C.W., R.M. Hemholz & P.G. Stein. *Notaries Public in England Since the Reformation* (1991).

Browne, Phillip. "eClosings Are Coming, Embrace the Change," The National Notary, August 2017, p. 20.

Browne, Phillip. "Fifty Years of Leadership, Professionalism and Trust: The National Notary Association," The National Notary, November 2006, p. 16.

Bruno, Klint. "To Notarize, or Not to Notarize ... Is Not a Question of Judging Competence or Willingness of Document Signers," 31 John Marshall Law Review 1013–1043 (1998).

Bryson, W. Hamilton. "Notary Public in England Since the Reformation," 38 American Journal of Legal History 89–90 (1994).

Burke, D. Barlow & Jefferson Fox. "The Notaire in North America: A Short Study of the Adaptation of a Civil Law Institution," 50 Tulane Law Review 318 (1976).

C

Chen, Tung-Pi. "The Chinese Notariat: An Overlooked Cornerstone of the Legal System of the People's Republic of China," 35 International and Comparative Law Quarterly 63 (1986).

Clarke, Carole & Peter Kovach. "Disqualifying Interests for Notaries Public," 32 John Marshall Law Review 965–984 (1999).

Closen, Michael. "Caution About Notarizing After Commissions Expire," Notary Bulletin, April 2001, p. 1.

Closen, Michael. "The Dangers of On-Line Sales of Notary Seals," The Notary, March–April 2001, p. 5.

Closen, Michael. "The De Facto Notary Doctrine and How to Avoid Tardy Notarizations," The Notary, May–June 2001, p. 4.

Closen, Michael. "'Do No Harm' First Rule for Oaths," Notary Bulletin, February 2005, p. 7.

Closen, Michael. "Ethics Code Key to Professionalism," Notary Bulletin, February 2007, p. 7.

Closen, Michael. "Experts Can Help Win Lawsuits," Notary Bulletin, August 2006, p. 7.

Closen, Michael. "Lawyers Worst Violators of Law, Part I," Notary Bulletin, December 2007, p. 7.

Closen, Michael. "Lawyers Worst Violators of Law, Part II," Notary Bulletin, February 2008, p. 7.

Closen, Michael. "The Lost Art of Administering Oral Notarial Oaths," American Notary, Second Quarter 2001, p. 6.

Closen, Michael. "Model Laws Encourage Uniformity," Notary Bulletin, June 2007, p. 7.

Closen, Michael. "Must Notaries Be Perfect? The Truth Is, Courts Sometimes Forgive Errors," Notary Bulletin, April 2004, p. 7.

Closen, Michael. "The NNA as 'Amicus Curiae,'" Notary Bulletin, October 2006, p. 7.

Closen, Michael. "Notaries and Literacy Requirements," American Notary, 4th Quarter 2001, p. 4.

Closen, Michael. "Notaries and Literacy Requirements," The Notary, January–February 2002, p. 4.

Closen, Michael. "The Notary's Interstate Reach," Notary Bulletin, October 2004, p. 7.

Closen, Michael. "Oath Is Not Just Empty Ceremony," Notary Bulletin, February 2005, p. 7.

Closen, Michael. "The Public Official Role of the Notary," 31 John Marshall Law Review 651–702 (1998). An extensive 50+ page article with 270+ footnotes.

Closen, Michael. "Reform the Potential Attorney-Notary Conflict," National Law Journal, July 6, 1998, p. A24.

Closen, Michael. "Seniors Can Present Challenges," Notary Bulletin, June 2004, p. 7.

Closen, Michael. "10 Steps to Sound Risk Management for Companies with Notaries," The National Notary, November 2001, p. 25.

Closen, Michael. "Thumbprints on Documents Would End Identity Theft," Miami Herald, December 6, 2004 (2004 WL 99610131).

Closen, Michael. "To Swear, or Not to Swear, Document Signers: The Default of Notaries Public and a Proposal to Abolish Oral Notarial Oaths," 50 Buffalo Law Review 613–701 (2002).

Closen, Michael. "Why Notaries Get Little Respect," National Law Journal, October 9, 1995, p. A23.

Closen, Michael, Glen-Peter Ahlers, Robert Jarvis, Malcolm Morris & Nancy Spyke. *Notary Law & Practice: Cases & Materials* (National Notary Association, 1997). A 630-page legal casebook on notary law, ethics, and practice.

Closen, Michael & Klint Bruno. "Notaries Public and Document Signer Comprehension: A Dangerous Mirage in the Desert of Notarial Law and Practice," 44 South Dakota Law Review 494–551 (1999).

Closen, Michael & Klint Bruno. "To Judge, or Not to Judge, Competence and Willingness," American Notary, 1st Quarter 1998, p. 4.

Closen, Michael & G. Grant Dixon. "Notaries Public from the Time of the Roman Empire to the United States Today, and Tomorrow," 68 North Dakota Law Review 873 (1992).

Closen, Michael & Charles Faerber. "The Case that There Is a Common Law Duty of Notaries Public to Create and Preserve Detailed Journal Records of Their Official Acts," 42 John Marshall Law Review 231–461 (2009). A 230-page history and discussion of the notary journal with 943 footnotes.

Closen, Michael, Dem Hopkins & Trevor Orsinger. "Notarial Records and Preservation of the Expectation of Privacy," 35 University Of San Francisco Law Review 159–253 (2001).

Closen, Michael & Thomas Mulcahy. "Conflicts of Interest in Document Authentication by Attorney-Notaries in Illinois," 87 Illinois Bar Journal, June 1999, p. 320.

Closen, Michael & Trevor Orsinger. "Family Ties That Bind and Disqualify: Toward the Elimination of Family-Based Conflicts of Interest in the Provision of Notarial Services," 36 Valparaiso Law Review 505–627 (2002).

Closen, Michael & Trevor Orsinger. "Is Blood Thicker Than ... Professional Responsibility?" The National Notary, July 2001, p. 25.

Closen, Michael & Trevor Orsinger. "Me, Myself, And I: Why Notaries Must Not Notarize for Themselves," American Notary, 3rd Quarter 2001, p. 1.

Closen, Michael & Trevor Orsinger. "Potential Identity Crisis," Chicago Daily Law Bulletin, September 19, 2000, p. 6. About possible unauthorized access to notary journals.

Closen, Michael & Trevor Orsinger. "Protecting the Privacy of Notary Public Records," Wisconsin Lawyer, April 2002, p. 26.

Closen, Michael & Michael Osty. "Illinois' Million-Dollar Notary Bond Deception," Chicago Daily Law Bulletin, May 2, 1995, p. 6.

Closen, Michael & Michael Osty. "The Illinois Notary Bond Deception," Illinois Politics, March 1995 p. 13.

Closen, Michael & R. Jason Richards. "Cyberbusiness Needs Supernotaries." National Law Journal, August 25, 1997, p. A19.

Closen, Michael & R. Jason Richards. "Notaries Public — Lost in Cyberspace, or Key Business Professionals of the Future?" 15 John Marshall Journal of Computer & Information Law 703 (1997).

Closen, Michael & Christopher Shannon. "The 10 Commandments of Notarial Practice for Lawyers," American Notary, 3rd Quarter 1999, p. 1. Reprinted in Florida Bar News, June 1, 1999, p. 32.

Cole, Nathan. "The Naval Officer Notary Public," Judge Advocate General Journal, November–December 1959, p. 14.

Craig, Joseph. "Notaries Discover Prison Is a Different World," The National Notary, July 2004, p. 26. About notarizing for prisoners.

D

Duncan, Laura. "Notaries Take Law Schools to Task for Violations," Chicago Daily Law Bulletin, November 16, 1994, p. 1.

E

Elliot, Karla. "The Notary Seal — The Last Vestige of Notaries Past," 31 John Marshall Law Review 903–910 (1998).

Elliot, Karla. "Notary's Misconduct Is the Employer's Liability, Too!" The National Notary, May–June 1996, p. 6.

Elliot, Karla. "The Unlicensed Practice of Law," American Notary, July–September 1997, p. 1.

F

Faerber, Charles. "Being There: The Importance of Physical Presence to the Notary," 31 John Marshall Law Review 749–776 (1998). About the need for document signers to personally appear at notarizations.

Faerber, Charles. "John Henderson, Hearing Examiner, Pennsylvania Department of State," The National Notary, May 2004, p. 28.

Faerber, Charles. "Law Text a Landmark," The National Notary, July 1997, p. 8.

Faerber, Charles. "The Model Notary Act," The National Notary, November 2002, p. 12.

Faeber, Charles. "States Take Steps to Raise Notary Public Fees," Notary Bulletin, April 2002, p. 15.

Faerber, Charles. *2012–2013 U.S. Notary Reference Manual* (National Notary Association, 11th Ed. 2011). An extensive biannual resource for every U.S. jurisdiction, by the country's leading authority on notarization.

Fischer, Douglas. "Being There: The Dangers of Nonappearance," The National Notary, July 1995, p. 12.

Fischer, Douglas. "Cancel a Notarization?" The National Notary, September 1995, pp. 12–13.

Fischer, Douglas. "Guardians of the Gate: Investigators Maintain Integrity of Notary Office," The National Notary, January 1995, p. 16.

Fischer, Douglas. "The Seal: Symbol of Security," The National Notary, November 1995, p. 10.

Fischer, Douglas. "Where Can I Notarize?" The National Notary, July 1997, p. 10.

Fisher, Lisa. "American Society of Notaries: History of a Legacy," 31 John Marshall Law Review 1001–1006 (1998).

G

Gibeaut, John. "Sign on the Dotted Screen: ABA Takes Lead in Developing Guidelines for Electronic Document Verification," 83 ABA Journal 100 (May 1997).

Gnoffo, Vincent. "Notary Law and Practice for the 21st Century: Suggested Modifications for the Model Notary Act," 30 John Marshall Law Review 1063 (1997).

Gnoffo, Vincent. "Requiring a Thumbprint for Notarized Transactions: The Battle Against Document Fraud," 31 John Marshall Law Review 803–818 (1998).

Gottshalk, J. Michael. "The Negligent Notary Public-Employee: Is His Employer Liable?" 48 Nebraska Law Review 503 (1969).

Greene, Lawrence. *Law of Notaries Public* (2nd Revised Ed. 1967).

H

Haberkorn, Gerald & Julie Wulf. "The Legal Standard of Care for Notaries and Their Employers," 31 John Marshall Law Review 735–748 (1998).

Hamilton, Phillip. "The International Notary Public," 65 Law Institute Journal 746 (1991).

Hamm, Lori. "Preventing Elder Financial Exploitation: The Role Notaries Should Play," The National Notary, December 2014, p. 14.

Harvey, William. "The United States and The Hague Convention Abolishing the Requirement of Legalization of Foreign Public Documents," 11 Harvard International Law Journal 476–489 (1970).

Henderson, John. "Accused Notaries Are Allowed Their 'Day in Court,'" Notary Bulletin, February 1997, p. 5.

Henderson, John & Peter Kovach. "Administrative Agency Oversight of Notarial Practice," 31 John Marshall Law School 857–878 (1998).

Howland, Richard. "The Notary and Family Law," American Notary, July–August 1996, p. 6.

Humphrey, Richard. *The American Notary Manual* (4th Ed. 1948). An outstanding early treatise on notary law and practice.

I

Israelson, Consuelo. "The Power of the Written Word," The National Notary, July 2001, p. 38.

Israelson, Consuelo. "Working Together to Avoid Document Rejection," The National Notary, July 2000, p. 16.

J

John, Edward & Frederick Campbell. *John's American Notary and Commissioner of Deeds Manual* (6th Ed. 1951).

K

Koehler, Robert. *Notarial Practice in the State of Florida* (2010).

L

Larner, Robin. "Notaries Public," 58 American Jurisprudence 2d, 519–567 (1989).

Leich, Marian. "The Hague Convention Abolishing the Requirement of Legalization for Foreign Public Documents," 76 American Journal of International Law 182 (1982).

Levine, Jason. "Notary Law and Practice: An Annotated Bibliography," 31 John Marshall Law Review 1007–1012 (1998).

Lewis, Michael. "Backdating: Temptation Runs Amok," The National Notary, May 2007, p. 40.

M

Madge, B. Edward. "Staying Ahead of Identity Theft: On the Front Line in the War on Fraud," The National Notary, July 2004, p. 9.

Malavet, Pedro. "Counsel for the Situation: The Latin Notary, a Historical and Comparative Model," 19 Hastings International & Comparative Law Review 389 (1996).

Malavet, Pedro. "The Foreign Notarial Legal Services Monopoly: Why Should We Care?" 31 John Marshall Law Review 945–970 (1998).

Margadant, Guillermo. "The Mexican Notariate," 6 California Western Law Review 281 (1970).

Marroquin, Art. "Victims of Notario Deception," The National Notary, September 2003, p. 28.

Meier, Carl. *Anderson's Manual for Notaries Public* (1940).

Merwick, Donna. *Death of a Notary: Conquest & Change in Colonial New York* (1999).

Mink, Michael. "The Paper Chase: ID Fraud Threats Are Close to Home," The National Notary, May 2007, p. 48.

Mink, Michael. "The Uniform Notary Act Changed the Landscape," The National Notary, January 2008, p. 24.

Mink, Michael. "When Personal Beliefs Collide with Notary Impartiality," The National Notary, July 2006, p. 24.

Morris, Malcolm. Comments, National Notary Association, *Model Electronic Notarization Act* (2017). Dean Morris served as reporter and wrote the extensive official comments.

Morris, Malcolm. Comments, National Notary Association, *Model Notary Act* (2002). Professor Morris served as reporter and wrote the extensive official comments.

Morris, Malcolm. Comments, National Notary Association, *Model Notary Act* (2010). Professor Morris served as reporter and wrote the extensive official comments.

Morris, Malcolm. Comments, National Notary Association, *Notary Public Code of Professional Responsibility* (1998). Professor Morris served as reporter and wrote the extensive official comments.

Morris, Malcolm. "Nomadic Notaries," 32 John Marshall Law Review 985–1002 (1999).

N

National Conference of Commissioners on Uniform State Laws. *Revised Uniform Law on Notarial Acts* (2010).

National Conference of Commissioners on Uniform State Laws. *Uniform Acknowledgment Act* (1939, with 1960 amendments).

National Conference of Commissioners on Uniform State Laws. *Uniform Acknowledgments Act* (1892).

National Conference of Commissioners on Uniform State Laws. *Uniform Foreign Acknowledgments Act* (1914).

National Conference of Commissioners on Uniform State Laws. *Uniform Law on Notarial Acts.* (1982).

National Conference of Commissioners on Uniform State laws. *Uniform Recognition of Acknowledgments Act* (1968).

National Notary Association. "Achievement Award '98: Michael L. Closen," The National Notary, May 1998, p. 15.

National Notary Association. "Administering Oaths, Affirmations and Jurats," The National Notary, March 1999, p. 22.

National Notary Association. "Apostilles: Jet-Age Authentication," The National Notary, July 1996, p. 10.

National Notary Association. "Are You an 'Average' Notary?" Notary Bulletin, February 1996, p. 14.

National Notary Association. "Body Language: A Silent Advantage," The National Notary, November 2009, p. 19.

National Notary Association. "Case Law Book Is Introduced at the NNA Conference," The National Notary, September 1997, p. 25.

National Notary Association. "Commuting Notaries," The National Notary, January 2011, p. 9.

National Notary Association. "Correcting Mistakes," The National Notary, March 2003, p. 39. About correcting mistakes in notarial certificates.

National Notary Association. "Creating a Paper Trail: The Journal as Evidence," The National Notary, July 2003, p. 30.

National Notary Association. "The Crisis of Responsibility," The National Notary, May 1995, p. 1.

National Notary Association. "Do Aid Those in Need with Your Service," Notary Bulletin, August 1995, p. 11.

National Notary Association. "Do Be Helpful but Not Too Specific," Notary Bulletin, February 1995, p. 11.

National Notary Association. "Do Try for Consistency in Levying Any Fees," Notary Bulletin, August 1995, p. 11.

National Notary Association. "Do Use Care When Charging a Fee," Notary Bulletin, October 1996, p. 15.

National Notary Association. "Don't Certify Falsehood Regarding a Date," Notary Bulletin, June 1995, p. 11.

National Notary Association. "Don't Drop Everything," The National Notary, March 1997, p. 21.

National Notary Association. "Don't Notarize if Signer Is Not Competent," Notary Bulletin, April 1995, p. 11.

National Notary Association. "Embracing the Disabled Signer," The National Notary, January 1996, p. 7.

National Notary Association. *The Enduring Benefits of Interstate Recognition of Notarial Act Laws* (2017). A position statement.

National Notary Association. "ENJOA (Electronic Notary Journal of Official Acts): Into the Future of Notarization," The National Notary, July 2003, p. 18.

National Notary Association. "The 50 Most Influential People in Notarization in the Last 50 Years," The National Notary, May 2007, p. 32.

National Notary Association. "5 Sound Practices that Steer You Clear of Lawsuits, Costly Errors," The National Notary, August 2015, p. 18.

National Notary Association. "Four Case Studies in Notary Liability," The National Notary, December 2016, p. 15.

National Notary Association. "Four Keys to Keeping Your Notary Journal," The National Notary, January 2007, p. 45.

National Notary Association. "How to Determine if an ID Card Is Acceptable," The National Notary, August 2017, p. 26.

National Notary Association. "Imposter Impersonates Notaries and Former Pro Baseball Player," Notary Bulletin, October 2004, p. 8.

National Notary Association. "Incomplete Documents," The National Notary, January 1995, p. 18.

National Notary Association. *Integrity in the Global Community* (August 1998). A report.

National Notary Association. "Journal Entry Is First," The National Notary, March 2003, p. 39.

National Notary Association. "A Journal Thumbprint: The Ultimate ID," The National Notary, May 1996, p. 9.

National Notary Association. *Model Electronic Notarization Act* (2017).

National Notary Association. *Model Notary Act* (1984).

National Notary Association. *Model Notary Act* (2002).

National Notary Association. *Model Notary Act* (2010).

National Notary Association. "More States OK Webcam Notarization," The National Notary, August 2017, p. 8.

National Notary Association. "The National Notary Association Official 2017 Notary Census," The National Notary, August 2017, p. 10. Reporting a U.S. notary population of 4,462,573.

National Notary Association. "The NNA 2002 Notary Census," The National Notary, May 2002, p. 13.

National Notary Association. "NNA Study Shows ID Standards Deficient in Majority of States" Notary Bulletin, February 2003, p. 5.

National Notary Association. "No Multiple Journals," The National Notary, July 1997, p. 8.

National Notary Association. "Notaries and Their Employers: Doing What's Right," The National Notary, July 2001, p. 21.

National Notary Association. "Notaries Have Responsibility to Correct Their Certificates," Notary Bulletin, April 2002, p. 6.

National Notary Association. "Notaries Public in American History," Notary Bulletin, April 1997, p. 3.

National Notary Association. "Notaries Then and Now: How the Notary Role Has Evolved Since the 18th Century," The National Notary, February 2015, p. 17.

National Notary Association. "Notarizing for Juveniles," The National Notary, November 2006, p. 34.

National Notary Association. "Notarizing Documents: What You Can and Cannot Do," The National Notary, January 2008, p. 43.

National Notary Association. *Notary Public Code of Professional Responsibility* (1998), reprinted in 32 John Marshall Law Review 1123–1194 (1999).

National Notary Association. *Pilot Anti-Fraud Program: Why the Los Angeles County Program to Reduce Real Estate Fraud Is Working and Should Be Expanded Statewide* (1995). A report and analysis.

National Notary Association. "Quadriplegic Can't Retain Commission," Notary Bulletin, April 1993, p. 1.

National Notary Association. "Reasonable Care: Being a Prudent Notary Ensures Professionalism and Lessens Your Liability," The National Notary, May 2006, p. 32.

National Notary Association. "Safety Spelled J-O-U-R-N-A-L," The National Notary, November 1996, p. 16.

National Notary Association. "Seal Use in Fraud Case," Notary Bulletin, October 2004, p. 3.

National Notary Association. "Simple Rules for Dates," The National Notary, July 2004, p. 47.

National Notary Association. "The State of Notary Fees," The National Notary, October 2016, p. 10.

National Notary Association. "Staying Ahead of Identity Theft, Combating Terrorism One Notarization at a Time," The National Notary, May 2006, p. 15.

National Notary Association. *Taking Personal Responsibility* (August 1999). A report.

National Notary Association. "There's No Substitute for Personal Appearance," The National Notary, May 2011, p. 12.

National Notary Association. "They Made Me Do It," The National Notary, March 2003, p. 37. About an attorney-notary misconduct case.

National Notary Association. "Thumbprinting: 'The Notary's Best Anti-Fraud Weapon' Now," Notary Bulletin, June 1995, p. 1.

National Notary Association. *Twelve Steps to a Flawless Notarization* (2nd Ed. 1996).

National Notary Association. "When Notaries Turn Bad," The National Notary, March 2007, p. 42.

National Notary Association. "When Personal Appearance Really Counts," The National Notary, May 1998, p. 36.

National Notary Association. "Woman Sentenced to Prison for Forgeries," Notary Bulletin, June 2004, p. 7.

Navarrete, Jennifer. "West Feliciana Parish's Unique Heritage and History," The National Notary, July 2003, p. 32.

Notary Law Institute. "Ask Your Signers Probative Questions," The Notary, March–April 2003, p. 5.

Notary Law Institute. "Handing Your Notary Journal to the Government for Safe Keeping: It May Not Be as Safe as You Think," The Notary, September–October 1997, p. 4.

Notary Law Institute. "Requiring Ink Thumbprints in Notary Journals Misses the Mark," The Notary, November–December 1996, p. 5.

Notary Law Institute. "The Truth About Your Legal Authority: Selecting Notarial Certificates," The Notary, September–October 1997, pp. 1–2.

Notary Law Institute. "Witness Signatures and Notarizations," The Notary, July–August 1997, pp. 1–2.

Nugent, Meg. "Little-Known, Oft-Needed Notaries Fall Short of Seal of Approval," Star-Ledger, Newark, NJ, February 25, 1995, p. B1.

O

O'Connor, E.R. *The Irish Notary* (1987).

Osty, Michael. "Notary Bonds and Insurance: Increasing the Protection for Consumers and Notaries," 31 John Marshall Law Review 839–856 (1998).

P

Perovich, John. Annotation, "Liability of Notary Public or His Bond for Negligence in Performance of Duties," 44 American Law Reports 3d 55 (1973).

Piombino, Alfred. *Notary Public Handbook: Principles, Practices & Cases* (Nat'l Ed. 1996).

Proffatt, John. *A Treatise on the Law Relating to the Office and Duties of Notaries Public* (1887).

R

Ray, Stacia. "Interstate Documents: What Certificate Wording Should You Use?" The National Notary, July 2006, p. 28.

Reiniger, Timothy. "'eApostille' Program Promises a Secure Future," The National Notary, May 2007, p. 23.

Reiniger, Timothy. "Leading the Way to a Digital Future," The National Notary, March 2008, p. 23.

Reiniger, Timothy. "NNA Advocacy, Partnerships Build a Promising Future for Notaries," The National Notary, November 2006, p. 24.

Reiniger, Timothy. "State of the (National Notary) Association: Laying a Foundation for the Future," The National Notary, March 2007, p. 24.

Rex, Benjamin & J.H. McMillan. *The Notaries' Manual* (5th Ed. 1900).

Reyerson, Kathryn & Debra Salata. *Medieval Notaries and Their Acts: The 1327–1328 Register of Jean Holanie* (2004).

Richards, R. Jason. "Disabilities in Notary Law and Practice," 32 John Marshall Law Review 1033–1064 (1999).

Richards, R. Jason. "Stop! ... Go Directly to Jail, Do Not Pass Go, and Do Not Ask for a Notary," 31 John Marshall Law Review 879–902 (1998). About the problems associated with providing notarial services to prisoners.

Ross, Ronni. "The American Notary Celebrating a 350-Year Heritage," The National Notary, November 1989, p. 11.

Rothman, Raymond. *Notary Public Practices & Glossary* (National Notary Association, 1978).

Rush, Barbara. "Notaries Public: Duties and Liabilities," 52 Oklahoma Bar Journal 969 (1981).

Russell, Bernard. *Office and Practice of a Notary of Canada* (1916).

S

Scott, Kenneth & Kenn Stryker-Rodda (Eds.). *The Register of Salmon Lachaire, Notary Public of New Amsterdam 1661–1662* (1978).

Seth, John. "Notaries in the American Colonies," 32 John Marshall Law Review 863–886 (1999). The only law review article ever to present a substantial history of the colonial American notary.

Sherry, Keith. "Old Treaties Never Die, They Just Lose Their Teeth: Authentication Needs of a Global Community Demand Retirement of The Hague Public Documents Convention," 31 John Marshall Law Review 1045–1084 (1998).

Skinner, Joseph. *A Handbook for Notaries Public and Commissioners of Deeds* (3rd Ed. 1963).

Slind-Flor, Victoria. "Legal Locksmiths Moving into Cyberspace as Notaries: The Need to Authenticate Electronic Documents Is a New Frontier for Attorneys," National Law Journal, December 18, 1995, p. A1.

Snyder, William. *The Notaries' and Commissioners' Manual* (1912).

Spyke, Nancy. "Promoting the Intermediate Benefits of Strict Notary Regulation," 31 John Marshall Law Review 819–838 (1998). Argues for heightened statutory oversight for notaries and their employers.

Spyke, Nancy. "Taking Note of Notary Employees: Employer Liability for Notary Employee Misconduct," 50 Maine Law Review 23 (1998).

Swinney, Ian. "The Notary Public and the Apostille," 37 Journal of the Law Society of Scotland 141 (1992).

T

Thaw, Deborah. "The Feminization of the Office of Notary Public: From Femme Covert to Notaire Covert," 31 John Marshall Law School 703–734 (1998).

Thaw, Deborah. "Journal Thumbprinting Is the Notary Public's Strongest Weapon Against Fraud," Notary Bulletin, August 1995, p. 3.

Thun, David. "Attorneys & Notaries: Building a Working Relationship," The National Notary, November 1999, p. 12.

Thun, David. "A Brave New World: International Notaries," The National Notary, November 2007, p. 34.

Thun, David. "Don't Take Identity at Face Value," The National Notary, May 2007, p. 31.

Thun, David. "Educating Yourself as a Notary," The National Notary, September 2001, p. 12.

Thun, David. "The Emergence of the Notary Signing Agent," The National Notary, July 2002, p. 12.

Thun, David. "Finding Government and Notary Resources on the Internet," The National Notary, May 2003, p. 32.

Thun, David. "Here's What's Keeping You Awake at Night," The National Notary, April 2016, p. 10. About notary anxieties.

Thun, David. "The Importance of Personal Appearance," The National Notary, January 2007, p. 22.

Thun, David. "Journal Records & Privacy: The Notary's Responsibility," The National Notary, March 2000, p. 14.

Thun, David. "The National Notary Association Official 2017 Notary Census," The National Notary, August 2017, p. 10. Arriving at a U.S. notary population of 4,462,573.

Thun, David. "No Laughing Matter," The National Notary, September 2000, p. 10. About notary bonds and liability insurance.

Thun, David. "On the Clear Path to Professionalism," The National Notary, May 2005, p. 18.

Thun, David. "Security in Paper or Electronic Transactions," The National Notary, May 2006, p. 18.

Thun, David. "Steps You Can Take to Prevent Being Sued," The National Notary, October 2015, p. 15.

Thun, David. "Targeting Identification in the Post-9/11 Era," The National Notary, September 2004, p. 16.

Thun, David. "10 Steps to Minimize Your Liability," The National Notary, August 2016, p. 20.

Thun, David. "Training, Good Journal Entries Help Stop Fraud — But More Is Needed," Notary Bulletin, October 2007, p. 13.

Thun, David. "Why Notaries Are 'Easy Targets' for Lawsuits," The National Notary, September 2010, p. 21.

Tinnes, Christy. "Digital Signatures Come to South Carolina: The Proposed Digital Signature Act of 1997," 48 South Carolina Law Review 427 (1997).

Tobin, Thomas. "The Execution 'Under Oath' of US Litigation Documents: Must Signatures Be Authenticated?" 31 John Marshall Law Review 927–944 (1998).

Tsuchiya, Shinichi. *A Comparative Study of the System and Function of the Notary Public in Japan and the United States* (1996). A National Notary Association report.

V

Valera, Milton. "America's Notaries: Ever Faithful and True," The Wall Street Journal, July 26, 1993, p. 3.

Valera, Milton. "The National Notary Association: A Historical Profile," 31 John Marshall Law Review 971–1000 (1998).

Valera, Milton. "New Technology and a Global Economy Demand that American Notaries Better Prepare for the Future: Upgrading the Current Common Law System May Mean Establishing a New Class of Cyber Professional," 32 John Marshall Law Review 935–964 (1999).

Valera, Milton. "Respecting the Past, Embracing the Future," The National Notary, July 2003, p. 20.

Van Alstyne, Peter. *Notary Law, Procedures & Ethics* (1998).

Van Alstyne, Peter. *Notary Public Encyclopedia* (2001). A comprehensive 468-page reference source authored by one of the nation's leading legal authorities on notary ethics, law, and practice.

Van Alstyne, Peter. "The Notary's Duty of Care for Identifying Document Signers," 32 John Marshall Law Review 1003–1032 (1999).

Van Alstyne, Peter. "The Notary's Duty to Meticulously Maintain a Notary Journal," 31 John Marshall Law Review 777–802 (1998).

W

Wigmore, John. "Notaries Who Undermine Our Property System," 22 Illinois Law Review 748 (1928).

Willer, Michele. "Using Journal Signatures to Help Prevent Fraud," The National Notary, March 1998, p. 23.

Y

Young, Christopher. "Signed, Sealed, Delivered ... Disbarred? Notarial Misconduct by Attorneys," 31 John Marshall Law Review 1085–1110 (1998).

Index

Alphabetical listing of topics with chapter (i.e., 1) and/or section (i.e., 2.2) references.

A

B

C

D

E

F

G

H

I

J

L

M

N

O

P

Q

R

S

T

U

V

W